# Charisma and Compassion

# Charisma and Compassion

*Cheng Yen and the Buddhist
Tzu Chi Movement*

C. Julia Huang

Harvard University Press

Cambridge, Massachusetts

London, England

2009

*Library of Congress Cataloging-in-Publication Data*
Huang, C. Julia, 1967–
Charisma and Compassion : Cheng Yen and the Buddhist Tzu Chi
movement / C. Julia Huang.
p.   cm.
Includes bibliographical references.
ISBN 978-0-674-03133-3 (alk. paper)
1. Buddhism–Charities.   2. Buddhism–Taiwan.   3. Buddhism–Social aspects–
Taiwan.   4. Fo jiao ci ji ci shan shi ye ji jin hui.   I. Title.   II. Title: Cheng Yen
and the Buddhist Tzu Chi movement.
BQ649.T32H83   2009
294.3'65–dc22           2008012636

*For my mom, Lee Pi-hwa, who inspires me,*
*and my dad, Huang Ching-ling, who nurtures me*
獻給我的父母：黃清霖與李碧華

# Contents

# Note on Romanization

This book uses the pinyin system of romanization for all Mandarin Chinese words, except the following: (1) place names that have well-known romanizations (such as "Taipei" instead of "Taibei"), (2) personal names that are known in their original spelling (for example, "Chiang Kai-shek" and "Chiang Ching-kuo"), (3) names of authors who have published in English (for example, "Chang Kwang-Chi" instead of "Zhang Guangzhi"), and (4) personal names in the preferred form of the individual. I decided to use "Tzu Chi" instead of *"Ciji"* and "Cheng Yen" instead of *"Zhengyan"* because the two names are now known internationally and on the World Wide Web in their original spelling according to the Wade-Giles system, and in response to a request by the new generation of the group's English-speaking followers.

Where the words were spoken in the *Minnan* (also called Hoklo or Taiwanese) in the ethnographic, romanization in both Minnan and in Mandarin are provided. Romanization of Taiwanese terms is according to Robert L. Cheng and Zheng-Xie Shujuan ([1977] 1994).

# Charisma and Compassion

**Map 1** Taiwan and the Basic Region

# Introduction

According to legend, in the quiet of a late spring day in the 1960s, thirty housewives on Taiwan's eastern shore knelt at the feet of a young Buddhist nun and tearfully asked her not to leave them. The nun listened attentively, and considered what she had been asked. Moments later, she granted the women's wish and agreed to stay under one condition: that they devote themselves to the charitable mission that she and her five monastic disciples had been endeavoring to establish. This exchange marked the creation of the Buddhist Compassion Relief Tzu Chi Merit Society *(Fojiao Ciji Gongdehui)*, a lay Buddhist movement under monastic leadership whose goal was to defray medical costs for the poor. Every day, each of the housewives donated NT$0.50 (New Taiwan dollar, currently equal to about US$0.025) from their grocery money and persuaded their friends and families to do the same. The nuns made and sold handicrafts, the proceeds of which supported the monastic order and added to the relief funds. The charity funds collected during the first year came to less than US$30 per month.

Tzu Chi *(Ciji)*, as the organization popularly became known, survived its initial hardships, growing slowly in its first decade and then rapidly across the island during the late 1980s—a period when Taiwan's economy was becoming wealthier and its polity more democratic. Three decades after it was founded, Tzu Chi had become the largest formal association in Taiwan with a growing transnational association among overseas Chinese. By 2000, it claimed five million members worldwide (Ma 2000), with branches in more than thirty countries. In Taiwan today, Tzu Chi runs four state-of-the-art hospitals, each with nine hundred beds; a television channel; and a secular four-year university with a standard medical school. The organization controls more than NT$12 billion (approximately US$342 million) in

1

funds (Himalaya Foundation 2002: 28);[1] US$300 million was raised in 1999 (*Business Week* 2000: 72). During the past decade, Tzu Chi has delivered relief to more than thirty countries around the world. Such accomplishments have won international honors for its leader, the Buddhist nun named Dharma Master Cheng Yen *(Zhengyan)*, which include the 1991 Philippine Magsaysay Award (the so-called Asian Nobel Peace Prize) and a 1993 nomination for the Nobel Peace Prize.[2]

The legend of this nun and her tearful followers has grown into the miracle of the "Mother Teresa of Asia" (Ching 1995) and her Tzu Chi humanitarian "kingdom." In becoming a successful modern organization, Tzu Chi's religious charismatic elements have not waned; rather, the Venerable Cheng Yen projects herself as both a powerful chief executive officer (CEO) and a magnificent living bodhisattva. Indeed, she has been compared to *Guanyin* ("Perceiver of Sounds"), the Chinese name for Avalokiteśvara, the Bodhisattva of Compassion (Yü 2001: 1), whose thousand eyes and thousand hands see and help those in distress—with the eyes and hands transformed into and embodied by Cheng Yen's thousands of devotees.[3] Under her leadership, the army of Tzu Chi devotees impressively fulfilled its mission: huge funds were raised, enormous institutions established, monthly care and welfare checks for four thousand needy families delivered, garbage sorted for recycling, more than three and a half million trees saved, disaster victims promptly rescued, and government bureaucracy outrun. The same disciplined Tzu Chi devotees also prostrated themselves at the Venerable Cheng Yen's feet, submitted their contributions with trembling hands, and delivered tearful testimonials of their volunteer experiences with life and death. Indeed, anyone who encountered Tzu Chi in the 1990s could not escape the contrast between its institutional secular appearance and its devotees' religious, emotional expression—both powerfully focused on one individual. In the glitter of the Venerable Cheng Yen's charisma, Tzu Chi devotees experienced dramatic emotions and joined together to address causes effectively. I argue that the brilliant success of the Tzu Chi movement lies in the way emotion and discipline are harnessed, that is to say, dialectically ordered in a religious charismatic movement: they transform and structure each other.

This book is an ethnography of a charismatic cult writ large, as a living reality among many Taiwanese women and men, as well as many Chinese-speaking people around the world. It depicts how a Taiwanese charismatic religious movement became rationalized as a modern organization, while still retaining its devotees' personal relationship with their leader. By focusing on the Tzu Chi movement as a multifaceted process, this book considers how and why charismatic commitment can be retained in the interplay between personal emotion and organizational expansion on local, national, and global levels. It attempts to address "why others should give up [everything] . . . in service to charismatic leaders and their causes"—a question that "American social science has great difficulty understanding" (Lindholm 2002: 357), and it also delineates *how* this was possible on a global stage.

## Considering Charisma

The term "charisma," originally drawn from the vocabulary of early Christianity, literally means "gift of grace" (Weber [1968] 1978: 216). The German sociologist Max Weber (1864–1920), whose influence on Anglophone anthropology has recently been delineated (Keyes 2002), was the first to develop a theory of charisma and also a theory of one of its significant consequences: charismatic authority. As Weber defines it:

> "[C]harisma" shall be understood to refer to an extraordinary quality of a person, regardless of whether this quality is actual, alleged, or presumed. "Charismatic authority," hence, shall refer to a rule over men, whether predominantly external or predominantly internal, to which the governed submit because of their belief in the extraordinary quality of the specific person. (Weber [1946] 1958: 295)

Weber's statement, along with his subsequent elaboration on the nature and the short-lived fate of charisma as being irrational, generated half a century of prolific literature that included cross-disciplinary criticisms, revisions, and clarifications of his theory (for example, Eisenstadt [1968] 1974; Geertz 1983; Greenfeld 1985; Shils 1965; Willner 1984; and Worsley 1968). The body of literature, which argues both for and against Weber, attests to the charisma of the concept of charisma. Most of the discussions, however, revolve around Weber's conceptualization of charisma as personal appeal that is recognized by followers, based upon emotional (and hence transient) commitments, and its antistructural nature (as opposed to legal-rational and traditional types of authority or domination). Three overlapping issues in the discussion are particularly relevant to the subject of this book.

The first of these issues concerns value and change. It has been generally accepted that charisma can be a source of unconventional and creative power, a reservoir of possibilities of change (Comaroff 1994: 305–311;

Keyes 2002). But to what extent does the quality to inspire change consist "primarily" or even solely of personal attributes (and, are the processes completely psychological), and is personal charisma incompatible with established institutions (for example, Geertz 1983; Shils 1965)?[4] How could Cheng Yen's exquisite magnetism persist within her gigantic organization?

The second issue concerns culture. Drawing on his insights into Theravada Buddhism, Tambiah (1984: 321–334) convincingly lays out how Weber's theory of charisma is "plagued by . . . dualities and . . . antithetical propositions"—for example, the emissary prophet of the occult religions as opposed to the exemplary prophet of the oriental—and therefore fails to address the source of charisma, especially the Buddhist conception of *bhiksu* and its emphasis on rule and discipline.[5] Cases in point are Tzu Chi's monastic order from the outset, as well as its more recent mandatory precepts for the lay followers.

The third issue shifts the concern from critiquing the dichotomies to asking the question of how charisma works in a comparative context. For example, Willner (1984) refocuses charisma on the personal, and argues that political charisma should be treated as a catalyst in the respective contexts: all of the political charismatic leaders she cites, including Sukarno and Gandhi, were assimilated to the "dominant myths" of the society and culture, capable of performing "extraordinary or heroic feats," and of projecting themselves as possessing "an uncanny or a powerful aura" and an "outstanding rhetorical ability" (1984: 61).

Building on the recognition of the personal and comparative approach, Lindholm ([1990] 1993) argues that the desire for charisma is part of human nature: to pursue an extraordinary experience by following a magnetic character who is born with the quality to manifest it in such a way that ordinary people can partake in it "here and now." His model of emotion for charisma requires "a collective milieu of heightened emotion and suggestibility often precipitated by a crisis of cultural and personal identity," and within this milieu, the "performance of the leader reflects and amplifies the desires of the followers, and stimulates a self-obliterating fusion in a charismatic union" ([1990] 1993: 216).

Csordas (1997: 139–140) offers a different perspective by pointing out that the varieties of "locus" of charisma can be summarized as "*among* participants of a religious movement," and proposes to recast the question by viewing charisma as "rhetoric . . . a particular mode of interpersonal efficacy: not a quality but a collective, performative, intersubjective self process." In his award-winning article, Csordas shows his model of synthesizing phenomenology and practice—the two seemingly opposed embodiment approaches—in an analysis of the Charismatic healings.

Each of the recent theories offers new approaches to charisma. Interestingly, while these approaches differ, they share a common concern in simultaneously differentiating and combining the uncanny experience and phenomenological embodiment on the one hand, and the interpretive structure and agency on the other. In other words, I would argue that considering charisma implies a new ethnographic approach that allows emotion into the theory of practice, and enables nonverbal corporeality to be taken as seriously as cultural construction and symbolic interpretation.

Tzu Chi is an interesting example of charisma because of its female leadership and its Mahayana Buddhist tradition. More important, Tzu Chi seems to be an anomalous case in that it transcends or bypasses the series of dualities that characterize previously theorized models of charisma. The processes of synthesizing personal appeal and organizational success—as well as other dualities in considering charisma—are patently visible in Tzu Chi,[6] yet it synthesizes these dualities into a shapeless bureaucracy with centripetal and centrifugal rites of renewal, formalized collective corporeality, and Protestant Buddhism.

The deep emotional attachment of Tzu Chi followers to their charismatic leader has not hindered the organization's embrace of modern managerial techniques. On the contrary, Tzu Chi's success derives both from a unique synthesis of its followers' unswerving devotion to the mission of its leader and from a systematic adaptation of modern organizational techniques. To the observer, this multibillion-dollar enterprise appears to be an orthodox bureaucracy. Nonetheless, upon closer scrutiny, the organization of this social movement follows a different model: there are no clear lines of authority, demarcated departmental divisions, task specializations, or refined divisions of labor. Furthermore, the charismatic authority of Cheng Yen remained pervasive throughout Tzu Chi's domestic and international development in the 1990s. With the vehicle of Taiwanese Buddhism, hundreds of thousands of Tzu Chi followers set themselves in motion to embody a nun's tale in a human typography of the global power of personality.

## Taiwan or Global?

Tzu Chi is everywhere in "late-capitalist" Taiwan. Chiang Kai-shek International Airport appears to be a "hyperspace" (Jameson 1991: 44), filled with signs of wealth and politically correct messages that are manifested through, respectively, commercials for skin-care products and weight-loss programs, and those positing the attractions of Aboriginal ethnicity. Travelers who navigate through the enthusiastic salespersons of the twenty-four-hour duty-free shops and ease their way through the immigration process feel a moment of relaxation at the baggage claim area upon realizing that the carts are free of charge. Among the commercials printed on the carts is Tzu Chi's fund-raising advertisement for the tsunami cause, "Great Love Entering South Asia." It features volunteers wearing uniforms of blue polo shirts and white pants, their arms full of relief goods.

The same Tzu Chi tsunami relief commercials can be seen, along with buses that display ads for Motorola and Benetton, when entering the "global city" of Taipei (Adrian 2003: 33; Lee 2007; Sassen 2001). Devotees and outsiders tune in to Tzu Chi television for its prime-time Taiwanese soap opera and indulge themselves in the narratives of ordinary people who find their identities through Tzu Chi. In a few corners of busy shopping districts in the expensive and fashionable eastern Taipei City, one finds conspicuous spots full of meticulously sorted piles of recyclable trash, proudly crowned with a plain green sign of Chinese characters that read, "*Ciji ziyuan huishou zhan*" (Tzu Chi recycling post). Above all, it would be relatively difficult to find a local who does not know about Tzu Chi.

In 2003, I was invited to speak on religion and globalization at a round-table on "Religion in a Pluralist Society," organized by a religion department at a national university in Taipei. Not surprising for any conference on religion in contemporary Taiwan (see Chapter 6), four out of the six panelists evoked Tzu Chi as an example. During the open discussion, a young female student raised the question about Tzu Chi's globality: "I recently participated in an exhibit of nongovernmental organizations affiliated with the United Nations. Tzu Chi was there, too. But they still talked in such inappropriate *(bu deti)* terms as *da'ai* (universal love) and *gan'en* (thanksgiving). Can someone teach them how to talk at an international event?"

The above vignettes illustrate some nuances in conceptualizing the global aspects of a grassroots religious group from a tiny island of about 13,900 square miles, smaller than the state of Connecticut and bigger than Maryland, or smaller than the Netherlands and bigger than Belgium. Indeed, Tzu Chi is interesting because it is simultaneously an intrinsically Taiwanese phenomenon and a cultural deterritorialization that does not conform to the primary imagination of missionary work, and from a place not commonly considered a powerhouse of global culture.

In some ways, Tzu Chi's ability to adapt to a world in motion resonates with, albeit remotely and reversely, Taiwan's colonial past as an island of, in Eric Wolf's (1982) term, "people without history" in the older version of globalization. Archaeologists trace the Taiwan Aborigine[7]—whose descendants played a key role in one of the two events that triggered Cheng Yen to found Tzu Chi—back to 4500 B.C., putting Taiwan as a probable homeland of the Proto-Austronesians before they spread into insular Southeast Asia and the Pacific (Chang and Goodenough 1996; Li 1997). Within six decades in the seventeenth century, Taiwan changed hands three times: from the Dutch (1624–1661) to the Zheng (1661–1683) and to the Qing.[8] From the late seventeenth century to the mid-twentieth century, Taiwan changed hands another three times: from the Qing (1683–1894) to the Japanese (1895–1945) and to the Nationalist or Kuomintang (KMT).[9]

In some ways, Tzu Chi's rise from Han Taiwanese grassroots to a prominent phenomenon harkens back to a century of breaking through the cocooned Taiwanese cultural identity. The twentieth century saw Taiwan's political transformation from colonialism to authoritarianism, and to full (presidential) electoral democracy. Tzu Chi as a cultural repertoire of grassroots is an apolitical and nonoppositional narrative of the formation of Taiwanese identity that emerged from under Japanese colonization,[10] was compelled underground by the retrocession to the Nationalist regime after the end of World War II in 1945—culminating in the February 28 incident in 1947—and survived the ensuing repression after Chiang Kai-shek retreated with the Nationalists to Taiwan in 1949.[11] Under the KMT authoritarian regime, the ethnic politics between the Taiwanese and the Mainlanders—namely, the post-1945 Chinese immigrants—persisted through the Opposition Movement *(dangwai yundong)* of the 1970s and the forming of the first opposition party, the Democratic Progressive Party (DPP), in 1986, the same year that Tzu Chi opened its first general hospital.

In 1987, Chiang Ching-kuo *(Jiang Jingguo)*, the heir and successor of Chiang Kai-shek, ended the forty years of martial law. Taiwan entered rapid democratization and held its first presidential election in 1996. In 2000, the DPP was elected to the presidency, and Taiwan formally entered its multiparty polity. Concomitant to the political transformation is a pronounced Taiwanese consciousness and cultural nationalism (Hsiau 2000) and an avalanche of protests from different social sectors (Hsu and Sung 1989), including voices from the long-marginalized Aborigine (Hsieh 1987: 1994).

The brief history of Tzu Chi from grassroots to nationwide and world-wide reflects a cultural repertoire that is drawn from the freeing of Taiwan's civil society and the surfacing of Taiwanese identity over forty years of political transformation. Tzu Chi came into being during the late 1960s, when Taiwan's associative life and economic development shifted from bleakness to limited openness, began its first nationwide mobilization during the period of political transformation and economic "miracle" (from 1979 to the 1980s), and precipitated major and rapid growth while Taiwan underwent economic restructuring and rapid sociopolitical transformation (for example, Lee 2004). The particular timing of Tzu Chi's meteoric growth suggests, on the one hand, a peaceful and compassionate response to the boiling unrest; and, on the other, as Weller (1999) argues, that Buddhist universalism provides a moral refuge and solution to the dominant market value brought about by global capitalism. Indeed, there are several ways that this example of Taiwanese Buddhism engages global and transnational issues.

A growing number of studies in anthropology, sociology, political science, and international relations have begun to address the relation between religion and globalization (for example, Beckford 2000; Beyer 1994; Hefner 1993; Robertson 1987). The conventional "world religions" are now reintroduced as "global religions" (Jurgensmeyer 2003), and the new expansion of Buddhism also receives comparative studies in light of the "era of globalization" and suggests a practice of missionary work different from that of Christianity (Learman 2005a). At the same time, the growth of border-crossing religious movements has received increasing attention and led to new perspectives on religion and globalization. For example, religion can characterize globalization, as one of its "faces" posited by Berger (1997, 2002) and examined by Srinivas (2002) in the case of the Sai Baba movement from India. Vasquez (2003: 158) further argues that the worldwide growth of evangelical Christianity and the multiple levels of its expansion—from personal renewal to global network—show that it is "not merely an example of how religious practices and institutions adapt creatively to globalization but rather is, in fact, a key conduit for globalizing processes usually associated with modernity."

The worldwide growth of Tzu Chi, especially in the last decade, is itself a statement that religion and globalization are not incompatible. Indeed, in tracking charisma on a global stage, one gains access to the cultural dimensions of globalization through the lens of religion. For one thing, Tzu Chi's global career—which moved from the East to the West, and from such an "out-of-the-way" place (Tsing 1993) on the global edge as Taiwan (Weller 2000)—seems to present an exception to the discourse of cultural imperialism and global cultural homogenization prediction (Inda and Rosaldo 2002; Tomlinson 1999). At the same time—as the local/global duality has been well examined (for example, Watson 1997)—ideas and terms such as democracy, civil society, and feminism that originated in the West traveled in the global arena and landed in different cultures while creating their own idiosyncratic local forms and contents, constituting "ideoscapes" as summed up by Appadurai (1996). The public positioning of Tzu Chi from a grassroots local do-gooder forty years ago to a non-governmental organization (NGO) that is recognized by the United Nations in 2004 tells a genealogy of NGOness as well as of civil society negotiated between cultural practice and global discourse. Moreover, Tzu Chi's rapid growth and outreach abroad happened when Taiwan experienced intensive political and economic change, a coincidence that suggests Tzu Chi's development is itself a part of the larger structural change undergone by Taiwan. Together with other equally globalizing Buddhist movements from Taiwan, Buddha's Light Mountain (*Foguangshan*) and Dharma Drum Mountain (*Fagushan*), the Buddhist revival in the last two decades suggests that religion can be a cultural conduit for Taiwan under globalization no less visible than such domains as consumption (Adrian 2003) and nation-statehood (Wang 2000).[12]

An increasing number of studies, mostly conducted in non-Western societies, have examined religion *in* and *of* transnationalism—broadly understood as processes that straddle two or more nation-states (for example, Basch, Glick Schiller, and Szanton Blanc 1994; Kearney 1995: 548). The results have been inspiring in terms of both the cross-cultural comparative perspectives they contribute and the variety of approaches they use.[13] In fact, studies of the overseas Chinese began with research on religions.[14] These contributions pioneer the comparative issue of the "ethnicization of religion" (van der Veer 1995: 8–11), and the issue of whether religion may provide an "additional cement to bind a diasporic consciousness" or constitute a diaspora in and for itself: the religion of the displaced members of an ethnic group may give a name to and be a unifying symbol for a diaspora as long as it manifests the adherents' propensity for a homeland—to create one or return to it (Vertovec 2000).

The transnational aspect of Tzu Chi is a topic that combines two recent and prominent sociocultural phenomena—Chinese Buddhist revivals and

Taiwanese transnationalism. The 1987 repeal of martial law in Taiwan and, more important, the 1989 adoption of a revised law on the organizations of civic groups have resulted in a rapid expansion of formal Buddhist groups (Jiang 1997) and "a new phase of increased Buddhist pluralization" (Jones 1999: 180). Post–martial law Buddhist revivals can be measured by the rapid growth of large-scale, well-endowed modern organizations, the proliferation of welfare institutions, and, more important, internationalization in terms of increased overseas Chinese participation and established linkage across national borders. For example, Tzu Chi as well as Buddha's Light Mountain and Dharma Drum Mountain gained importance at home and abroad precisely when Taiwanese were leaving home.

The same period of significant Buddhist revivals saw an intensified Taiwanese transnationalism. From 1990 to 1996, the number of emigrants from Taiwan increased by more than four times, from 25,500 to 119,100 (Wang 1999: 214). The phenomenon is not merely a surge of migration. Rather, it is one facet of an ongoing process in which Taiwanese become increasingly mobile. Not only do migrants shuttle back and forth—a practice called "two-legged existence" among those whose lives straddle Taiwan and one or more countries (Tseng 1995)[15]—but also those who stay behind frequently fly abroad. The total number of outbound travelers who are Republic of China nationals shot up from half a million in 1980 to more than one million in 1987, and then grew rapidly to more than seven million by 2000.[16]

The combination of the scale of Tzu Chi's modern Buddhist organization and its high-profile overseas Taiwanese and female constituency is unique in the context of overseas Chinese. In some ways, Tzu Chi can be viewed as the latest example of the "redemptive societies" that thrived in and out of China in conjunction with the multiple Manchurian, Japanese, and Nationalist regimes (Duara 1997) or the "Salvationist" religious associations among the Chinese in Singapore in the 1950s (Freedman and Topley 1961). Like these movements, Tzu Chi has high-profile female followers and leadership and a Buddhist-inspired focus on social welfare. Yet, Tzu Chi differs from its predecessors: first, because it is comprised primarily of Taiwanese migrants; second, because of intensified globalization during the twentieth century; third, because of the political transformation of Taiwan; and fourth, because of its clear Buddhist identity.

Drawing from my multisited ethnography (Marcus 1995), this book attempts to delineate how the historically diverse strains of Buddhism blended, if not "creolized" (Hannerz 1996), in Tzu Chi, and to describe the structure of mission and missionary practices through which Tzu Chi engages its global vision and transnational expansion (Chapters 7 and 8). In addition, it seeks to tease out the moral career of Tzu Chi's cosmopolitan identity—a genealogy that addresses the cultural issues involved in a now widely accepted global term, NGO.

## The Three Bodies of Charisma

This book endeavors to address, at least in some speculative ways, the issues and the questions encountered while considering and tracking charisma, by proposing a three-body model for analyzing charisma that is drawn from my fieldwork with Tzu Chi.[17] In the Tzu Chi context, the body is a representation and an existential foundation of the culture. Consider the "three bodies" in this religious charismatic movement: First is *the leader's body,* the personal appeal of the female charismatic leader, which performs from the outset and throughout, and is glorified especially in the processes of routinization, and which the devotees perceive, interpret, and wish to merge with (in Lindholm's ([1990] 1993: 74-89) sense of selfless merger with) or find one's identity within, charisma. Second is *the follower's body,* which is the medium of charismatic ecstasy in Weber's (Weber [1946] 1958: 278, [1968 ]1978: 401-2) sense, the object to be disciplined in Foucault's (1979) sense, and the source of experience that renders the intersubjective self in Csordas's (1990; 1997: 133-153) conceptualization of charisma. Third is *the collective body* or *the musical body,* which is transformed and transmogrified from an inchoate and formless emotional *communitas* to a choreographed and formalized interpretive community.

With regard to social life, the three-body model is part and parcel of the three geographical levels—local, national, and global. As long as the personal appeal of the magnetic leader works face-to-face as well as by means of media; as long as her followers are mobile—whether toward or from the charismatic center, in or out of their "homeland"—and, above all, as long as the collectivity invoked and maintained by charisma can cross over the borders between nation-states, then the three bodies are to exist within, acknowledge, and transcend the three levels of the local, national, and global. In so doing, the three bodies of charisma may serve as a comment on the assumed dichotomies of local, global, and perhaps even center-periphery models for our understanding of the world in motion.

The three-body model is fleshed out in the main body of the book. The leader's body, in its phenomenological sense, is depicted in Chapter 1, which delineates how the leader's body is perceived by the followers. The ethnography of "emotional traffic" between the followers and their feelings for, as well as perception and interpretation of the leader's body tells why the personality of a frail nun matters in embodying—in stark contrast to—her mission. The phenomenology of the leader-follower draws further personal accounts of devotees in Taiwan (Chapter 5) and overseas (Chapter 8). The leader's body continues to unravel organizationally and geographically in the chapters that follow. Chapter 2 lays out how the leader's personality inhabits and shapes a gigantic bureaucracy into an organization that is simultaneously shapeless in terms of the intradepartmental links, yet centralized through one authority. Chapter 3 maps out the centrifugal and centripetal mechanism of Cheng Yen's charisma in motion across Taiwan. Chapter 4 presents the collective or the musical body that synthesizes the leader's and the followers' bodies. Continuing on the mechanism of charisma in motion is the leader's body in an iconographic sense. The power of a charismatic figure is unbound in levels of typography: Taiwan's public sphere, as described in Chapter 6; on a global stage, in Chapter 7; and spurring toward the locality of one of its global expansions, Malaysia, in Chapter 8.

## Positioning the Ethnographer: Some Methodological Matters

To recapture the "ethnoscape" of a global charismatic community (Appadurai 1991), the ethnographic research for this book renders multiple sites (Marcus 1995). The major part of the fieldwork for this book was conducted in Taiwan from November 1997 to June 1999. I stayed in three places during this period: Dalin Township and Jiayi City in southwestern Taiwan from November 1997 to June 1998, and in June 1999; Hualian, on the eastern coast, between July and September 1998, and in May 1999; and the remaining time in the capital city of Taipei. I lived in the Tzu Chi Abode and sometimes in the hospital during my stay in Hualian, where I talked mainly to Tzu Chi nuns, staff members, and a variety of followers and event onlookers, and held a few interviews with local non–Tzu Chi followers, including an environmental group. Some preliminary data collection began in 1993 in New York and Taiwan. I participated in the New York Tzu Chi branch and interviewed core members there between 1993 and 1994; conducted field research at the Boston branch among active members, participating in their formal and informal activities between 1996 and 1997, and following up in 1999. I made a brief visit to the Japan branch in December 1997 and to the two Malaysia branches in April 1999, spent a summer interviewing core members in the Singapore and Malacca branches in 2004, and an additional month in Malacca in January 2006.

Throughout my research, I am constantly reminded of what Cunningham (2000) called an "ethnographic conundrum." Tzu Chi talks as much about globalization as we do; it masters multimedia better than most of us. The group has a penchant for numbers and statistics as well as cosmopolitanism and globe-trotting. As a result, the ethnography present in my book has been tenaciously "historical" and "local" by default. As an anthropologist, I take pleasure and hence pride in this default limitation of my ethnography, since it shows that we no longer "confine" our informants to the local. Moreover, it demonstrates how the subject of our study, charisma, could make a change in the object of our discipline, that is, culture. The following pages are about how and why a Taiwanese Buddhist nun could make a difference in the lives of women and men in Taiwan and around the world.

# — 1 —

# From Filial Daughter to
# Embodied Bodhisattva

In 1997, at the beginning of the year-end convocation of volunteers at Tzu Chi's Taipei branch, a young emcee in staff uniform asked the full house of hundreds of mainly middle-aged women: "Why do you volunteer for Tzu Chi?" There was a brief silence, then slowly an answer was sounded by diffident yet distinct female voices from different corners of the auditorium: "[Because we] love the supreme person *(ai shangren)*." Blushing, the emcee smiled and, in the tone of a schoolteacher, replied: "Oh. Of course, we all love the supreme person. But we volunteer for Tzu Chi because we are *shanxin dashi* (benevolent persons). We are here because of *da'ai* (great love, universal love)."

The emcee's answer was correct, but the audience's was truer. Sitting at the rear, lower level of the two-thousand-square-foot hall, I was no less astonished than the emcee by the audience's answer. Since 1993, I had conducted interviews and researched the literature to find an answer to one simple question: Why do people join and become committed to Tzu Chi? Four years later, in this unrehearsed event, Tzu Chi followers collectively gave their answer, which was uttered shyly but unanimously: "Because we love the supreme person."

## Introduction

The Venerable Cheng Yen is the founder and head of Tzu Chi. Although she teaches classic Buddhist scriptures, her own *fa* (dharma) is considered paramount by the entire movement. Her portrait is seen in every Tzu Chi branch and in every piece of Tzu Chi literature. Followers display her portrait in their living rooms at home, behind the sales counters of their small

15

shops, above the glove compartments in their cars, and inside their wallets, and every devotee wears a prayer-bead bracelet with her photo inserted in one of the beads. Two-thirds of Tzu Chi's huge literature consists of Cheng Yen's sermons, and the rest includes reflections on and applications of her teaching. No followers interviewed failed to describe Cheng Yen's influence on them; in fact, many joined the movement because of her immediate personal appeal, which often provoked inexplicable floods of tears (as discussed in Chapter 4). Whether they attribute their commitment to Cheng Yen's personal appeal or her teaching, Tzu Chi devotees are followers of Cheng Yen. Oftentimes, they summed up: "I am just so grateful to be her follower. It is my *fubao* (merit reward) from several past lives." The press in Taiwan uses "Cheng Yen" as synonymous with "Tzu Chi."

Cheng Yen is therefore the key to an understanding of Tzu Chi. This chapter is an analysis of her personal appeal or charisma, which, as defined by Weber ([1968] 1978: 1133), refers to "a personal quality which turns whoever possesses it into an impressive personality." Based on Weber's definition and contemporary theories of charisma, this quality, as it exists in reality, has three aspects: first, charisma in its pure form refers to personal

Portrait of the Venerable Cheng Yen Displayed on the Dashboard of a Follower's Car

magnetism (Greenfeld 1985; Lindholm [1990] 1993); second, this magnetism "appears only in interactions with others who lack it" (Lindholm [1990] 1993: 7); and third, such interactions turn the relationship into an asymmetrical power relation through a certain "tutelage," that is, the personal magnetic quality is considered by those who lack it as "extraordinary and its holder is treated as endowed with supernatural, superhuman, or at least specifically exceptional powers or qualities . . . regarded as of divine origin or as exemplary, and on the basis of them the individual concerned is treated as a 'leader'" (Weber [1968] 1978: 241). In other words, charisma refers to inborn personal magnetism that arises in interaction and may serve as the basis of leadership when it is regarded as a manifestation of power that is embedded in a broader symbolic framework, such as divinity.

This chapter consists of three parts: (1) Cheng Yen's personal transformation as described in her hagiography; (2) how her "innate" magnetism appeared in interactions with followers, or, put differently, how her devotees expressed their attraction to her personal appeal; and (3) the management of Cheng Yen's charisma as the source of authority that directed the mechanisms of the spectacular Tzu Chi organization in the 1990s.

## The Legend

Cheng Yen's legend is important not only because it tells the origin of Tzu Chi but also because it provided a mediated appeal to those who did not have personal contact with the movement. The first wave of national press coverage of Tzu Chi in the early 1980s centered on Cheng Yen's acclaimed goal of building a general hospital in Hualian, as well as on her legend. In addition to the press, a small free pamphlet that featured Cheng Yen's legend was widely distributed in Taiwan and came to be in great demand.[1] Many followers who came to the movement after its peak were initially intrigued by Cheng Yen's legend. And many who encountered the movement through other means became devoted to the group and decided to stay after they learned more about Cheng Yen's legend.

According to Tzu Chi publications, press reports, and some supplementary accounts and clarification from her disciples and followers, Cheng Yen's legend generally includes three parts: (1) her family background and transformation from a filial daughter to a resolute nun with a mission, (2) her creation of Tzu Chi, and (3) her campaign for the organization's first hospital. None of the sources elaborate on her childhood. (More recent versions, namely those that came out in the 1990s, only update the introduction to Tzu Chi's various humanitarian programs after the completion of the first hospital.)

## Wealthy Family Background and Filial Piety

Cheng Yen was born in west central Taiwan on May 14, 1937, in Qingshui Zhen (town), Taizhong Xian (county). She was the third daughter of the Wang family and was named *Jinyun* upon birth.[2] At eleven months, she was adopted by her biological father's younger brother. Wang Jinyun became the first child of her new parents; her mother gave birth to four children after her adoption. In all interviews and Tzu Chi publications, Cheng Yen refers to her adoptive parents as her only parents.[3]

Before she left home to become a nun, Wang Jinyun was already a distinguished teenage girl. Her family was relatively wealthy in Fengyuan, the largest city of Taizhong County. After the end of World War II and Japanese colonialism in 1945, her father's business expanded from one Taiwanese opera theatre to seven cinemas across Taizhong County. While Taiwan was still struggling to survive the postwar economy, Wang Jinyun's parents were already leading an affluent life; they had a private chauffeur (for a rickshaw) and could afford to give her a diamond platinum necklace as a gift (Chen [1983] 1998: 14, 17). However, this wealthy family background did not make Wang Jinyun a girl of leisure. As the eldest child of a mercantile family, after graduating from elementary school and until the age of twenty, she was a capable young businesswoman who helped with both the family business and household chores (Chen [1983] 1998: 5).

When she was a teen, Wang Jinyun was already a natural beauty, as described by her mother in a published interview: "[Jinyun] never used any makeup. She wore her hair long and straight. She wasn't trying to attract attention, but when she walked by, men and women, old and young, all turned their heads" (Ching 1995: 160).

Nevertheless, Wang Jinyun did not follow the usual course of a wealthy, desirable girl. "Her attitude [was] a protective wall keeping her admirers at bay" (Ching 1995: 160). One day, a handsome young Japanese man brought his proposal to the family. Her father consulted her—unusual in Taiwan at the time, when most parents decided their children's marriages. Wang Jinyun declined immediately, and she would hear nothing more about marriage. In the same interview, her mother wondered whether Wang Jinyun's disillusionment with romantic love and her refusal to marry at such an early age were a result of her witnessing people's suffering during the bombings of World War II, or an extraordinary perception of life that was determined long ago in a past life (160).

Perhaps more important was Wang Jinyun's reputation for filial piety.[4] Indeed, the first miracle in her life was closely linked to—or a result of—her exemplary conduct in that regard. Tzu Chi literature describes how, to help her mother overcome a serious stomach illness, fifteen-year-old Wang Jinyun prayed to the only deity she knew of in childhood, Guanyin, the most popular goddess in Chinese societies (Chen [1983] 1998: 5–6; Faun 1991: 3–4; Pen 1992: 243). Wang Jinyun vowed to Guanyin that she would give up twelve years of her life and become a vegetarian in exchange for her mother's good health.[5] In a dream that recurred to Wang Jinyun for three consecutive nights, Guanyin granted her wish by delivering medicine to her mother. Slowly, yet miraculously, her mother's illness waned, without the surgery that was still life-threatening at that time. Wang Jinyun kept her word and became a vegetarian. Tzu Chi literature stresses that her change of diet was not yet a practice of Buddhist dharma but an act solely of filial piety (Chen [1983] 1998: 6; Pen 1992: 243).

## Personal Transformation and the Journey to Becoming a Great Nun

In 1960, five years after the Guanyin miracle, Jinyun's father had a stroke and passed away the next day. Although his death resulted from a doctor's malpractice, Jinyun blamed herself because she had moved him while he was unconscious. This trauma left her nearly insensible for several days. She was unable to cry during the first week of mourning, and day after day she asked repeatedly, "Where is my father?" This so worried her family and friends that they referred her to a shaman and a few local Buddhist temples for an antidote.

The loss of her father changed Jinyun, and then Buddhism provided a path for her rebirth from the family tragedy. She first became close to local Buddhist nuns and began to think in accordance with Buddhist teachings; however, she did not follow a Buddhist priest or join a monastic order. The local nuns gave her inspiration, yet she reached critical enlightenment through her own reflections.

Still bereaved and depressed, she thought about leaving home (chujia) to become a nun, but was held back by her family responsibilities. One day, she asked a nun at a local temple, the Venerable Xiudao of *Ciyun Si* (Compassionate Cloud Temple), what kind of woman lives in the greatest bliss *(xingfu).*[6] "The woman who can lift the grocery basket," the nun replied. "But I carry grocery baskets every day," Jinyun responded. "Why don't I feel bliss?" She pondered the question while she resumed her routine of family business and chores, until she suddenly thought it through:

> Did the Venerable mean that the woman who can lift the grocery basket is one who has control over the money in her purse? But would this mean bliss? A woman shouldn't just have the right to control her purse, to live for one *jiating* (family, household); she should be, *like a man,* capable of responsibility to society! If some day I can *chujia* (leave home) to promote this compassion for all humans . . . I'd like to extend everyone's *aijia* ('love for family') to love for society, for all living things . . . isn't this bliss? (Chen [1983]1998: 9; emphasis mine)

In this way, Wang Jinyun saw Buddhism as the path toward a universal vocation—one that allows women to contribute to society, and that "cannot be achieved inside the *'jia'* (family, home, or household)" (Chen [1983] 1998: 10). She transformed her mourning for her father into the pursuit of a universal identity that could transcend finite love and a woman's traditional roles.

Despite her mother's objections, she was determined to enter a refuge in Buddhist priesthood. Her subsequent yearlong tearful struggle between her family ties and her religious pursuits began a few months after her father's death. In the fall of 1960, she took a northbound train to Taipei, where she was taken in at a Buddhist temple, *Jingxiu Yuan,* in Xizhi of Taipei County, to which she had been referred by the nun of Ciyun Si. However, her mother tracked her down after three days and brought her back home. A year after that first futile attempt, at the age of twenty-four, Wang Jinyun was on her way home from grocery shopping one day when she stopped to help the Buddhist nuns of a local temple who were harvesting in the field. With the Venerable Xiudao's encouragement, she suddenly decided to drop everything and run away with the nun.

Hastily, the two randomly boarded a train that happened to be southbound. In this way, Wang Jinyun embarked on her journey of wandering around the island with the goal of "leaving home" (becoming a nun). The train took them to Gaoxiong City in southern Taiwan, where they "followed the flow of karma," and transferred to a cross-island bus. When they arrived in Taidong in southeastern Taiwan, they encountered a family friend, who became suspicious. To prevent this friend from reporting her whereabouts back to her mother, Wang Jinyun and Xiudao boarded another train at random, which took them to the Luye Village in the remote mountains of the eastern coast. The two stayed there and studied in a semiabandoned temple, sang sutras for local people, and lived off the land by foraging for produce and wild vegetables, while enduring the hardships of cold and hunger in winter.[7]

The difficulties of her legendary journey were also accompanied by adventures. One day, Wang Jinyun and her companions went deep into the mountain in search of a mysterious "superman."[8] Hand in hand, they crossed a stream, and trekked the whole day on foot through the jungle. However, there was no mysterious superman: only two ordinary herbal dealers who camped in the mountain. Nevertheless, this event added a shamanistic flavor to her legend of personal transformation.

But adventure was not enough to sever her family ties—the critical obstacle to her transformation. Wang Jinyun's whereabouts were revealed to her mother through the Ciyun Si of her hometown.[9] Her mother immediately sought her out to persuade her to come home, and threatened to follow her if she refused. Determined, Wang Jinyun vowed to stay or die. Emotionally, solemnly, she returned the precious diamond necklace to her mother, keeping her coat and watch as necessities, and formally said farewell to her family ties.[10] Her heartbroken mother cried all the way home; this was the last time she attempted to take Wang Jinyun back with her.

The severing of her family ties marked the critical transition from lay identity into priesthood. Wang Jinyun and the Venerable Xiudao continued to travel and study Buddhism among different temples in Taidong and Hualian in eastern Taiwan.[11] During this period, two significant events occurred: First, they met Mr. *Xü Congmin*—a learned and virtuous lay Buddhist who played a significant role in Wang Jinyun's transformation to Cheng Yen, initially through his support and later by becoming her lay teacher of ordination. The other event was the linkage to (by preaching the sutra of) *Dizang* Bodhisattva—Bodhisattva Kṣitigarbha, who was determined to refrain from attaining nirvana until all souls had been saved from the suffering of hell. This linkage to Dizang preludes the theme of Cheng Yen's humanitarian mission. The two events converged when Mr. Xü introduced Wang Jinyun and Xiudao to a new small temple he sponsored in Xiulin *Xiang* (township), the *Puming Si* (the Universal Light Temple), wherein the main deity was Dizang Bodhisattva. Puming Si is located two hundred meters from the Tzu Chi Still Thoughts Abode ( jingsi jingshe), and at the time of her formal ordination, would become Cheng Yen's meditation location.

Although Puming Si had just been completed on the day of her arrival, Wang Jinyun had a sense of déjà vu, and then realized that this was the temple in which Guanyin had delivered medicine for her mother in her dream eight years ago. Now she was sure that she had finally arrived at her destination. This was in 1962, one year after she had stepped onto the first southbound train. The Venerable Xiudao, who had accompanied Wang Jinyun throughout the journey, was too ill to go on, and suggested that she take Mr. Xü as her teacher in order to continue her pursuit of priesthood. Mr. Xü gave Jinyun a Buddhist name, Xiucan.[12] She then shaved her own head and "revealed the Buddhist priestly appearance" (xian chujia xiang).

Taking refuge with a layperson and studying sutras (Buddhist scriptures) alone without formal ordination, according to Li (1996: 37), resembles the tradition of Taiwanese indigenous lay Buddhism, zhaijiao ("vegetarian sect"), the most prevalent form of Buddhist practice in Taiwan until the Japanese colonization (1895–1945). Despite her physical transformation, Wang Jinyun, now Xiucan, was not yet ordained as a Buddhist nun (biqiuni, and bhiksuni in Sanskrit). The next year, in 1963, she left for Taipei for the ordination ceremony at the Arriving Relief Temple (Linji si), but was unable to register because she had no Buddhist priest tonsure master (tidushi) for ordination. Disappointed, she went to the Wisdom Day Lecture Hall (Huiri jiangtang) to purchase Buddhist sutras, where she encountered the most revered abbot Yinshun (1906–2005). Xiucan seized her chance and asked Yinshun to take her as his student. Although it was known that Yinshun no longer accepted new students, he surprisingly granted her wish. He told her: "Now you have already 'left home' and become a nun, you must do everything for Buddhism and for all living things (wei fojiao, wei zhongsheng)" (Chen [1983] 1998: 23). He named her Cheng Yen (Zhengyan) and gave her a brief ritual of taking a refuge. It was one hour before the closing for ordination registration. Cheng Yen made it back to Arriving Relief Temple in time and then completed the formal thirty-two days of precepts required for bhiksunis. Cheng Yen became the fifth disciple of the Venerable Yinshun, one of the most important figures in contemporary Mahayana Buddhism and the major advocate of reformist humanitarian tradition in Chinese Buddhism.

At this point, the lay identity of the filial daughter, Wang Jinyun, had been subsumed by the priestly identity of the Venerable Cheng Yen. However, she had yet to become a priestly virtuoso; to reach this level requires another period of transformation through one's own personal power until proof of the new status is manifested through a miracle.

After her ordination, from the fifth month of the lunar calendar to the end of 1963, Cheng Yen lived in solitude in the small straw hut (a little smaller than Thoreau's famous cottage in Massachusetts) built by Mr. Xü behind the Puming Si for her postordination meditation. She endured hardships, refused to accept offerings, and meditated daily on the Lotus Sutra with discipline: one word, one prostration. Each day she ate only one meal, slept only two hours, got up at one o'clock in the morning to chant sutras, and offered worship to the Buddha by burning spots on her arms (*ranbei gongfuo*). Such austere meditation led to a miracle by the end of the year: local people reported witnessing mysterious beams of light shining over her small hut every morning at one o'clock. Cheng Yen was not aware that her meditation had brought about this miracle and she was surprised when a policeman called on her to witness it from outside.[13]

The miracle attracted people from afar, but fueled local hostility. Endless visitors trampled the village farms, and the miraculous light led local people to associate Cheng Yen's already conspicuous solitary meditation with "the demonic" (*yaomo*). Worse still, some "heterodox Buddhists" of Puming Si's management board accused Cheng Yen of bringing misfortune to their geomancy (*fengshui*) (Chen [1983] 1998: 26). However, amid rising hostility, two additional miracles or coincident events followed that reinforced her orthodox identity: First, her hut was blown toward the south by a typhoon, but by the time her followers came to repair it, an unusual southern wind had moved it back to its original location. One follower sighed: "Even *tian* ('the sky' or nature) supported you. Why can't people?" The second event occurred when Cheng Yen finally decided to leave: Local people who came to destroy the mysterious hut were stopped by a powerful gust of wind. One of the workers who was involved had a car accident the next day, and the others called off the demolition.

Cheng Yen was not destined for local temple politics. She resumed her journey and traveled among different temples in eastern and northern Taiwan.[14] By the autumn of 1964, she already had a handful of monastic disciples and was invited to return and stay in the original small hut behind Puming Si.

## Leadership and the Creation of Tzu Chi

Although the Tzu Chi literature (Chen [1983] 1998: 27) indicates that Cheng Yen and her companions were "meditating together" (*jieban xiuxing*) rather than forming a hierarchy, Cheng Yen's return to Puming Si marked the nascence of her monastic order in the sense that she set the rules for the group. In keeping with her vow to "re-establish the dignity of Buddhist *sangha* (monastics)" by leading an autonomous life (an idea inspired earlier by the Venerable Xiudao's reflection on the dependent monastic life in Taiwan as opposed to independent monastic life in Japan), Cheng Yen set out three principles: (1) no sutra chanting service for a fee (*bu gan jingcan*); (2) no dharma ritual service for a fee (*bu zuo fahui*); and (3) no alms receiving (*bu huayuan*) (27). Instead, her followers made a living by subcontracting to produce handicrafts for factories, such as sewing paper bags and making baby shoes, in order to abide by the Chan (Zen) master Baizhang's motto of "no toil, no meal" (*yiribuzuo, yiribushi*). This practice of economic independence was in sharp contrast to the primary livelihood of Buddhist monastics in Taiwan, and inevitably provoked subtle hostility from their fellow monastic communities;[15] but Cheng Yen persisted in the practice. Yet the full impact of her reformism on the Buddhist community—and the larger society—was yet to come.

Two events in 1966 induced Cheng Yen to found Tzu Chi. One day, when she visited the father of a disciple at the clinic, she saw a pool of blood in the hallway and inquired about it. She was told that an Aboriginal woman had suffered a miscarriage. The woman's family had walked for eight hours carrying her to the hospital, but she did not receive treatment because, according to Tzu Chi literature, she could not afford the NT$8,000 deposit (about US$200) (Chen [1983] 1998: 28).[16] Upon hearing that the unfortunate woman had died (Faun 1991: 10), Cheng Yen was shocked and nearly fainted: "How could humans be so cruel to each other?" she asked herself (Chen [1983] 1998: 28).

The second event occurred when three Catholic missionary nuns in Hualian learned about a Buddhist nun (Cheng Yen) from some local Aboriginal girls who had carried water for her on the mountain. The nuns decided to meet with Cheng Yen and tried to convert her to Christianity, but she convinced them instead that Buddha's compassion was as great as the universal love of the Lord God (*tianzhu*). The nuns then asked Cheng Yen why Buddhists, with their concept of universal love, concentrated only on improving themselves and did not build schools or hospitals as the Christians did. "We rarely see Buddhists doing what benefits society," the Catholic nuns observed. Cheng Yen met the question with her usual quick thinking: "We Buddhists accumulate covert merit points *(jiyinde)*. The anonymous contributions you see are from Buddhists." "Then you Buddhists are powerful," the Catholic nuns remarked.[17]

The tragedy of the Aboriginal woman made Cheng Yen realize the importance of medical funds, and the Catholic nuns' remarks led her to consider mobilizing the "anonymous" Buddhists. She began to ponder practical solutions and awaited the chance to achieve her plans.

In the second month of the lunar calendar in 1966, the Venerable Yinshun assigned Cheng Yen and her disciples the task of assuming his lectureship at a temple in Jiayi, a city in southwestern Taiwan.[18] Fearing that they would lose their beloved master, Cheng Yen's local lay followers tearfully begged her to remain in Hualian. Observing this group of housewives as they implored her to stay, Cheng Yen suddenly realized the collective power of the laity (Ching 1995). She agreed to stay under one condition: they must help her realize her idea of a humanitarian mission to defray medical costs for the poor. She first proposed that baby shoes be made for sale by both the lay and monastic members (according to various Tzu Chi sources, there were five or six monastic disciples at that time).[19] Second, she demanded that each lay follower contribute NT$0.50 (then about US$0.025) each morning, and place it in a bamboo container before the daily grocery shopping. In one month, this practice of daily donation, "fifty cents to save one human life," spread widely by word of mouth. In 1966, on the twenty-fourth day of the third lunar month,[20] the Buddhist Persevering Compassion Relief Merit Society *(Fojiao kenan ciji gongdehui)* was formally born.

With the increasing prominence of Tzu Chi, more and more people wanted to become Cheng Yen's disciples and followers. The Tzu Chi literature (Chen [1983] 1998: 31) reasons that, although she had vowed to practice three principles upon being ordained—(1) never to become a "dharma master" *(fashi)*, (2) never to become a temple principal *(zhuchi)*, and (3) never to take any disciples or lay followers—Cheng Yen "had to" make an exception in accepting those followers who agreed to be devotees of the Tzu Chi mission. This combined sense of mission and personal magnetism formally sounded the overture to Cheng Yen's influential charismatic leadership. The legend itself is absorbing; it states that many of Cheng Yen's present charismatic characteristics existed long before her Tzu Chi leadership: for example, her great beauty, her competence, her early disillusionment with romantic love, the moral foundation of her filial piety, her sensitivity toward tragedies and suffering, and her reformist ideas.

The legend also tells of her transformation—from a filial daughter into a great nun and, eventually, a charismatic leader—which had four major stages: It began with her personal contact with the divine power, when, in answer to her prayers, Guanyin performed the miracle of restoring her mother's health. The second stage began with her father's death and continued through her journey in search of priesthood. Many significant people appeared during this stage, and her adventures and hardships in remote mountains demonstrated her discipline and commitment to the pursuit of a "new," autonomous Buddhist priesthood. Cheng Yen's déjà vu experience at the Dizang Bodhisattva temple demonstrated her personal contact with another divine power, culminating in her accidental encounter with the most revered reformist abbot Yinshun. The fact that she did not have an ordination teacher until then demonstrated her predetermined linkage to a reformist Buddhist tradition. As she acquired her new identity as a Buddhist nun, she entered the third stage: solitary meditation until she could perform a miracle through her own power, the production of a mysterious light above her hut. Cheng Yen's contact with divine power and her ability to perform a miracle attested to her "superhuman" and "extraordinary" qualities. The fourth and final stage of her transformation, in which she embarked on her path toward charismatic leadership with a mission, occurred at the moment when her lay followers' petition made her realize both the collective power of the laity and her strength to guide them. This mutual recognition of her charisma propelled the creation of the Tzu Chi movement.

Cheng Yen's relationship with her family changed in parallel with her transformation. From the start, her family's affluence gave her a sophisticated upbringing. Devotees said that their uniforms were well designed by Cheng Yen, who had developed good taste in her teen years when she always wore custom-made outfits with matching handbags and shoes. At the same time, her background put her on an equal footing with her wealthy followers. These origins contradicted the common stereotype of a "poor" Buddhist priest in Chinese societies. Until recently, people often believed that only poor families would leave their daughters in a monastery. Buddhist priesthood had a connotation of begging for a living. In contrast, Cheng Yen grew up in affluence and transcended her material privilege by pursuing Buddhist priesthood.

Perhaps more important than wealth was the interweaving of Cheng Yen's family ties (especially to her mother) with her religious pursuits (especially that of the Buddhist priesthood). Her identity as a filial daughter and as a devout nun remained joined throughout her transformation, even after she became a leader. Her first contact with the divinity (the Guanyin miracle) resulted from her sacrifice for her mother. Her father's death alienated her from traditional female roles and caused her to seek a more universal identity in Buddhist priesthood, yet she could achieve this only by severing family ties. Cheng Yen's perception of the Dizang Bodhisattva temple as her final destination brought her full circle. She had not vowed to become a nun in exchange for her mother's health when she prayed to Guanyin, but when she arrived at the temple where, in her dream, Guanyin had delivered medicine for her mother, Cheng Yen knew that her sacrifice and contact with the divinity had laid the foundation for her later identity in the Buddhist priesthood.

The connection between her relationship with her mother and her religious pursuits did not end there, but was instead transformed. By the time Cheng Yen attained her leadership, her mother had become a primary supporter of her religious mission. It was her mother who purchased the first piece of land for Cheng Yen to build the Still Thoughts Abode, now the Tzu Chi monastery and headquarters. According to the Venerable Dexin, when Cheng Yen's mother saw her daughter living in the straw hut, she felt enormous grief and sighed: "Even a daughter marrying would be given a dowry from her family. So when a daughter leaves home to become a nun, she should have a gift from her family as well." Her mother thus became a devout Tzu Chi commissioner and an active representative of Cheng Yen at many Tzu Chi events. I even saw Tzu Chi devotees fall on their knees when offering donations to Cheng Yen's mother at a fund-raising bazaar in Jiayi in 1998.

The transforming and transformed relation between family identity and religious pursuit is significant in two ways: First, Cheng Yen's religious pursuit runs counter to the traditional Confucian role of women in the family and resonates with the stories of many goddesses in Chinese religion (for example, *Miaoshan*, an incarnated Guanyin; *Linshui Furen;* and *Mazu;* see Huang and Weller 1998: 381–382). Though each founding myth differs in detail, Cheng Yen shared with these goddesses a resistance to marriage (and, hence, to the obligation of producing descendants for the patrilineal family) and a higher loyalty to the universal salvation of all living things. At the same time, religious pursuit did not involve total opposition to traditional values. All of the goddesses eventually performed lifesaving acts for the men in their families, and the death of Cheng Yen's father compelled her to approach Buddhism. These acts show that family ties, and gratitude to one's family, can be sustained without fulfilling the obligation of marriage and continuation of descent lines. The foci on parents in the stories of Cheng Yen and Miaoshan (who eventually saved her father's life with her bodily sacrifice and divine power) emphasize that filial respect and emotion, at least from the perspectives of these two female figures, can be reconciled with religious pursuits and expressed in spite of the patrilineal ideology.[21]

Cheng Yen's story differs from those of the goddesses in its emphasis on her strong ties to her mother—a second significant point of the family-religion theme in Cheng Yen's transformation. That connection drew much attention from female Tzu Chi followers, who were the great majority from the beginning. While they generally downplayed Cheng Yen's running away from home against her mother's wishes, they showed their empathy with the tension and emotions of Cheng Yen's filial links. For example, in a chat with some veteran female devotees at the Abode, one of them described a recent episode when Cheng Yen's mother spontaneously came to visit her at the Abode and found that she was occupied in a meeting with the hospital construction committee. She waited, but did not let anyone report her arrival to Cheng Yen. The circle of middle-aged women sighed, and the storyteller said that she cried while keeping Cheng Yen's mother's company. Naïvely, I asked why. The storyteller turned to me and nearly screamed: "A mother can't even see her daughter when she wants to because her daughter has very important things to take care of. Don't you get it? How heartbreaking! Don't you get it?"

The salient family ties among goddesses,[22] particularly the filial links as in Cheng Yen's case, suggest that, while a family may strongly object to a daughter's pursuit of the priesthood,[23] a Buddhist woman's relations with her family in the Chinese culture may be flexible enough that her religious pursuits would not to lead to an irreconcilable dilemma. As suggested by the eventual support of Cheng Yen's mother, there may be a resemblance between chujia (leaving the family to become a priest; "ja" is in the first tone, meaning, "family, home, household") and chujia (literally, "leaving for marrying," meaning, marrying; "ja" is in the fourth tone, meaning, "[a woman] marrying [out]"; qü is the word for men) from the family's point of view, since both acts are "leaving the family," whatever the destination.

I have also heard a Tzu Chi female devotee describe the initiation ritual she saw at the Tzu Chi Abode—wherein the novices took the vow and shaved their heads to become nuns—as having reminded her of "a daughter marrying." In the initiation ritual, the novices were accompanied by their families, and the Abode prepared rice cakes (*gui* in Minnan, and *gao* in Mandarin), "as if they were celebrating a happy event such as wedding." A Tzu Chi youth member told me that she felt such "tremendous joy" at her sister's initiation ritual (in a different monastic order from Tzu Chi) that she began crying when the master shaved the last section of hair from her sister's head.[24]

## A Charismatic Nun

Cheng Yen is short, reed thin, and frail: four feet ten (150 c m) and about eighty-eight pounds (40 kg). She is always dressed in typical Chinese Buddhist nun's attire: her head impeccably shaved and wearing a sangha's robe, gray or brown, and footwear. On special occasions—such as when giving a sermon in a large convocation or leaving her Abode—she wears a string of prayer beads around her neck. Her eyes shine; tears seem about to flow from her piercing gaze. Her features are distinctive, but not sharp. Her complexion is often pale and sallow. She rarely smiles and I never saw her laugh. This differs from the iconic look of Buddhist monks who resemble Bodhisattva Maitreya, as depicted in popular Chinese paintings and sculptures: round face, red cheeks, and a big smile.[25]

While she looks like any other Buddhist nun, Cheng Yen has an innate magnetism that both female and male followers often describe as phenomenal beauty. For example, one female devotee of Jiayi first learned about Tzu Chi from a pamphlet she picked up by chance at a train station that described Cheng Yen's legend. She had initially reacted negatively to the title: *The Venerable Cheng Yen and Her Tzu Chi World.* She said, "I felt, huh, how bold she is to claim 'her' world! So I was curious." Cheng Yen's portrait on the pamphlet's back cover immediately caught the woman's eye. She sighed: "What a beautiful nun!" She immediately "fell in love" with Cheng Yen.

Nevertheless, devotees and disciples do not use the common term *piaoliang* (pretty) to describe Cheng Yen; rather, they show their respect with the Buddhist term *zhuangyan* (roughly translated as "solemnly spectacular"). As many disciples phrased it: "*Shifu guangjie shanyuan, shengde feichang 'zhuangyan'* (The master has wide and good binding [with many people in past lives] so she was born looking solemn and spectacular)."[26]

This magnetism is the key to charisma. As in other charismatic examples (Willner 1984: 29), Cheng Yen's magnetism is shown by the strong desire of followers to see her; they cannot help but stare at her whenever she enters a room. For example, at the convocation described in the first paragraph of this chapter, Cheng Yen entered the auditorium quietly in the middle of the procession. An active commissioner, who is a television anchorwoman by profession, was just about to begin her speech promoting subscriptions for a magazine that was newly released by the Tzu Chi publisher. The program did not stop upon Cheng Yen's arrival, but the audience's eyes went from the limelight of the podium to the dim corner where Cheng Yen sat. The anchorwoman had to make an effort to attract the crowd's attention and said:

> I know you all like to see *shangren* [the supreme person, that is, Cheng Yen]. I myself love to see her, too. As soon as shangren enters the room, all of us can't help but turn our heads and look at her. We look and look at her whenever we get a chance, despite what's happening on the stage. But I wish you could bear with me just one moment and look at this magazine in my hands . . .

Sometimes followers showed their desire to see Cheng Yen more directly than by simply turning their heads. For example, on the day of her monthly visit to the Dalin hospital construction site, Cheng Yen moved quickly from her tour of the site to the conference room in order to receive progress reports (see Chapter 3). Only Cheng Yen, her accompanying disciples and devotees, Tzu Chi construction office staff members, and representatives of the subcontractors were allowed in the room. All the local followers (except for a few who served tea and dessert) stayed outside, but they could not help trying to get a glimpse of Cheng Yen. A handful of female commissioners in their *qipao* (traditional Chinese dress) crowded in front of the small window and peeked into the conference room like the teenage fans of a movie star. Those who got a good view exclaimed joyfully: "I can see *shangren*! I can see *shangren*!"

Joy is not the only reaction that people have to Cheng Yen's appeal. Seeing her can be so powerful, especially in person for the first time, that onlookers have become ecstatic and cried uncontrollably. As discussed in Chapter 5, female devotees share the recurring crying experience upon seeing Cheng Yen, in person or in photos. I have also heard a testimonial given by a woman who was overcome by an inexplicable flood of tears at her first encounter with Cheng Yen's phenomenal beauty; and she again began crying when she recounted this experience.

There remains "the possibility," as Geertz (1973: 122) writes, "of articulating just what it is that causes some men to see transcendency in others, and what it is they see." Such magnetism is more than sheer beauty, and, indeed, there are other things that followers "see" in Cheng Yen. One of the characteristics her followers talked about most is her frailty; her apparent physical weakness sharply contrasts with her huge mission. I frequently heard male devotees explain that they felt ashamed simply by the example of how much this tiny and fragile nun had achieved toward the immense mission to which she had dedicated herself. By contrast, they reflected on how little they had done for society, although they were "big men *(da nanren)*." Women often expressed their sense of mission in relation to Cheng Yen's appearance: "We must share the tremendous burdens on her shoulders *(lan tio-ai theh i ta^n* in Minnan)!"

Cheng Yen's delicate appearance was enough to inspire commitment, which grew with her sickness. She was diagnosed with heart disease at the age of forty-two in 1978. A year later, she had a heart attack. Thinking that her years were numbered, Cheng Yen had the idea of building the first hospital as a long-term solution to the continuity of Tzu Chi's mission (Chen [1983] 1998: 35–36). Since then, concern for her health has never left her followers' minds; it is a recurring and widely circulating theme that Cheng Yen is sick, has a cold, or is so exhausted from her backbreaking schedule of sermons and talks that she has to rely on medicinal injections. Cheng Yen once described how she would bite her lips to temporarily overcome the pain in her body in order to carry on with the sermon. Her frailty can cause onlookers to convert to her mission. The founding commissioner of the Tzu Chi hospital volunteer team told me of the "accidental" beginning of her lifelong commitment. It was the day before her departure to study abroad in Japan. She visited Cheng Yen at the Abode to donate money in the name of her mother, who had recently died. The visit made such an impact on her that she never made the trip to Japan and instead became a resident hospital volunteer; she has been living in the Abode for more than ten years (in 1998). When I asked her why she had made such a radical change, she nearly screamed at me: "[Because] she got sick in front of me *(ta bing gei wo kan)!*" A moment later, she continued: "[The Venerable Cheng Yen] was sick on the day I visited. When I was leaving, she came to the door to see me out. She could barely stand straight, leaned against the door, and called to me: 'You must help me! You must help me!' What choice did I have in the face of a call from someone who was so sick and desperate?"

Followers also suffer when Cheng Yen suffers.[27] Moreover, her moodiness worsens her health and consequently deepens the suffering of her disciples, fueling their sense of mission. When Cheng Yen stopped eating and sleeping after it became doubtful that they would acquire land for the first hospital, a senior disciple remembered that they fell on their knees at her feet and tearfully begged her to eat (Chen [1983] 1998: 39–40; also, see Chapter 6 for details of the land acquisition). Another disciple described that they had to "report" to the Venerable Yinshun that Cheng Yen refused to take her medicine regularly. An overseas devotee remarked how she felt about her first experience of dining at the same table with Cheng Yen: "[The Venerable Cheng Yen] does so much and eats so little!" Her followers have, in Lindholm's ([1990] 1993) term, "merged" themselves with the things that Cheng Yen feels and suffers. In this merger, selfless followers project themselves into Cheng Yen's selfless devotion to her mission. When the leader of the premier "sign language song"[28] team described why she felt that she must work for Cheng Yen, tears ran down her cheeks. Cheng Yen told her, "I am just a Buddhist nun. I have no money, no belongings. But I have this life *(wo you zhe tiao ming)*. As long as I am alive, I pursue."

Cheng Yen's verbal appeal touches audiences as well. Her speech alone can have a far-reaching effect on those who have never seen her in person or in a photo. The emotion that is evoked by her words seems to run parallel to the feelings brought on by her appearance.

Except when speaking to Tzu Chi youth or when granting audiences to government officials, Cheng Yen always speaks Minnan, the dialect most widely spoken among middle-aged Taiwanese.[29] She uses simple words. Her speeches consist primarily of small stories in real life, even when preaching and interpreting classic Buddhist texts. She uses the first person in colloquial dialogues with followers and visitors, and when making appeals to her disciples. For example, when she encouraged followers to tune in to the newly formed Tzu Chi television channel, she said: "Remember to watch the Tzu Chi Da Ai *(Da'ai, universal love)* TV. I'll visit your home every day, oh!" She raised her voice almost girlishly at the end, and the audience smiled. Such unmediated communication can feel strongly personal. One devotee, for example, described hearing Cheng Yen's sermon for the first time: "It's strange. I've heard the same advice numerous times before.

But I never listened. Yet when she spoke, I felt she was addressing me. It's as if she knew I was sitting there [among the audience] and she knew that I never took advice."

The quality of Cheng Yen's voice is perhaps more important than the content of her speech. She speaks slowly and lightly, with a nasal intonation. Indeed, her voice somewhat resembles the crying tune that is sung by actresses in tragic Taiwanese operas. The Venerable Zhaohui, one of the most outspoken and activist nuns who speaks forcefully herself, once answered a journalist's question about comparing herself to Cheng Yen: "My image is one of the new women, whereas [Cheng Yen's] is one of the traditional. Those who were frustrated with life found [Cheng Yen] like a mother's embrace. Her voice is tender and slow. It gives me gooseflesh" (Jiang [1994] 1995: 244).[30] Such an emotional voice has great appeal when combined with Cheng Yen's frailty. She often sounds exhausted when pleading for a cause. Seeing her tearful eyes, devotees declare that Cheng Yen "spoke till she wept," although no one ever actually sees her cry. The combination of her voice, her frailty, and her compassionate mission can be powerful and immediate enough to make followers cry when first hearing her preach. As discussed in Chapter 4, some devotees trace their conversions to the tears they shed when first listening to an audiocassette of Cheng Yen's speech. For example, the founding coordinator of Tzu Chi's New York branch was moved to tears solely by Cheng Yen's voice on tape, I asked her why. She could not recall the content of the speech, only how she felt about Cheng Yen's voice: "I don't remember what exactly she said. She was pleading and pleading. And I felt [her] sorrowful heart, very sorrowful (*juede hen beixin*)."[31]

In sum, Cheng Yen's innate magnetism, often described and seen as beauty, can have a strong emotional effect on spectators, causing a feeling of joy and even ecstasy. Such an extraordinary psychological experience transforms one's identity, linking it with the charismatic figure: Followers see themselves in Cheng Yen; they suffer when she suffers and they synchronize their emotions with her "sorrowful heart," as one would tune in to a radio frequency. In such a merger, the selfless follower feels the charismatic figure's feelings and becomes completely devoted to whatever she pursues. The result is to follow her, to "share the burden on her shoulders" (*theh i ta*[n] in Minnan). And the "burden" on Cheng Yen's shoulders is to save humans from suffering. Thus, followers pursue Cheng Yen's mission of relieving human suffering in order to alleviate their beloved master's suffering, which is their own.

## Glorification

In accordance with Weber's notion of genuine charisma, Cheng Yen's extreme emotional expressivity and the excitement it generates make her the object of attention and imitation (Greenfeld 1985; Lindholm [1990] 1993). The charismatic figure is held to possess "superhuman" ability and thus is treated as a leader. Cheng Yen's leadership did not stem from a single event; rather, it first appeared when she attracted a handful of followers and was formalized when she and those followers founded Tzu Chi. She remained the leader of Tzu Chi throughout its growth into the largest formal association in Taiwan: from fewer than forty members in 1966, to about one hundred thousand in 1986, surpassing a million in 1990, doubling in 1992, doubling again in 1994, and finally claiming five million members in 2000. This rapid increase in membership formalized her relations somewhat with her followers.

The first time I saw the Venerable Cheng Yen was in 1993, when I accompanied Professor Robert P. Weller on an interview. In the conference room of the Taipei Tzu Chi branch, we literally "stuck out" when lines of visiting followers prostrated themselves at Cheng Yen's feet—a respectful salute usually reserved for deities. As my research progressed, I eventually became used to seeing waves of bodies lowered to the ground before Cheng Yen—whether on indoor hardwood floors or outside on dirt and sand. More than once, I have also prostrated myself in the correct form I learned in Tzu Chi. At the Taizhong branch, I saw a Caucasian American visitor and the head of the Tzu Chi Foundation's Religion Department prostrate themselves at Cheng Yen's feet three times, on the stage and in front of hundreds of Tzu Chi followers. Those who were at that event proudly sighed: "Even a foreigner would prostrate himself in front of our *shangren!*"

Veteran devotees nowadays still sometimes refer to Cheng Yen as *shifu* (the master, the teacher)—a general form of address toward Buddhist teachers and monastics, especially employed by those who see themselves as followers or disciples of the sangha. When I started my research of Tzu Chi in 1993, *shifu* was the only term followers used to refer to the Venerable Cheng Yen. However, by the time I began my major fieldwork in 1997, *shifu* had been replaced by a much more impersonal term, *shangren* (the supreme person, or, literally, "above human").

The term *shangren* provided a convenient and respectful way for outsiders to address Cheng Yen, who by then was already a nationwide celebrity who frequently granted audiences to a variety of people other than her followers, such as politicians and construction firm representatives. At public events (such as convocations) and when followers or disciples referred to Cheng Yen in conversations with outsiders, I usually heard them use the term *shangren*. In more personal dialogue, such as individual interviews, most devotees, especially veteran ones, still consistently used *shifu*; however, toward the end of my fieldwork in 1999, I began to hear some followers being corrected when they used that term.

One of the reasons given for this change was to avoid confusing Cheng Yen with her monastic disciples, and ultimately with other Buddhist sangha, although no one could explain to me the exact meaning of *shangren* or why it was used instead of other respectful terms for Buddhist venerables.[32] However, a conversation between two nurses I overheard at Tzu Chi Hualian hospital revealed how the term *shangren* and Cheng Yen's leadership were related. A nurse asked her superior why things had to be a certain way. The latter replied blatantly: "Because *shangren* said so." Still confused, the younger one probed: "But, why?" Becoming slightly impatient, the senior nurse lectured her naïve colleague: "Because she is *shangren*, so she knows everything. *Shangren* means above, above, and above people." She raised her hand way above her head to illustrate the lofty status of *shangren*.

In addition to the prostrations and the impersonal, respectful form of address, the recent success and meteoric growth of Tzu Chi have led to the organization's massive dissemination of Cheng Yen's writings, her speeches, and her image, and to her glorification as a living goddess.

Cheng Yen's communications and especially her images appear in a variety of Tzu Chi media: in print, on audiocassettes and videotapes, on television, and on their Web site. This trend perhaps endeavors to meet the inevitable difficulties of a charismatic group that grows largely beyond a small personal circle: contact with the charismatic figure is scarce, along with the extraordinary excitement it generates. Indeed, I heard founding commissioners express their dissatisfaction—and perhaps envy—regarding a few younger commissioners who had the privilege to be near Cheng Yen. In this light, the recent massive issuing of materials that concern Cheng Yen seems to be a solution to the increasing demand (and competition) for proximity to the charismatic leader.

Although for years followers had been taking notes and recording Cheng Yen's sermons on their personal tape recorders and then reproducing copies for circulation, this limited distribution was in no way comparable to the more recent efforts made by the organization. By 1994, Cheng

Yen's sermons were airing through certain private radio stations every morning and evening. By 1997, a personal film crew was created to capture Cheng Yen's charisma for mass promotion. Since then or at least by 2001, except for some private and restricted meetings, Cheng Yen has always appeared with her film crew—a young layman and two novices. Their job is to record every word of Cheng Yen's sermons and capture her every movement and expression. All the shots are then edited to appear on Tzu Chi television, and later to be published as volumes of videotapes. A disciple also transcribes her sermons verbatim to be reproduced in print.

This massive effort has contributed to the glorification of Cheng Yen in three ways: First, followers have gradually adapted to indirect contact with Cheng Yen, much as a deity's statue or image is worshipped—although the result of Tzu Chi's multimedia approach is certainly more vivid than a carved idol. Second, Tzu Chi is protective of Cheng Yen's charisma, especially with regard to its promotion. I heard a follower in Dalin in southwestern Taiwan rebuke his fellow devotees for privately distributing reprints of Cheng Yen's mottos. He explained that Cheng Yen relied on the sale of these reprints in order to give gifts to followers at the year-end convocations and to support her monastic order. Although spontaneous reprinting of religious-moral texts is a conventional merit-accumulating practice in popular religion, it is no longer encouraged or even accepted in a modern organization such as Tzu Chi.

The second explanation, particularly concerning Cheng Yen's close-up photos, is the all-too-often final answer given by the Tzu Chi organization in declining requests: because *shangren* does not like it. This bold reply is sometimes phrased by members of the foundation staff in a more personal way: "because *shangren* would get angry."[33] A more specific and heartfelt reason given by followers is that flashbulbs are very hard on *shifu's* eyes, and that bad photographing may hurt *shifu's image*. Nevertheless, although most Tzu Chi followers carried cameras with them for snapshots, I did not see any pointed at the Venerable Cheng Yen with flashbulbs, except for the few that belonged to the Tzu Chi publisher and which displayed clear Tzu Chi logo stickers.

From my fieldwork, the concerns for Cheng Yen's image seem to be more an act of caring and respect than a result of the bureaucratization of the modern Tzu Chi organization; stories also circulate among followers about the perils awaiting those who attempt to capture Cheng Yen's image for disrespectful purposes. A male devotee, for example, recounted in his testimonial that he had paid for his first visit to Tzu Chi because of pressure from his wife. He was fortunate to see Cheng Yen in person. The first thing he thought about Cheng Yen was: "Oh, this nun doesn't look bad." He then took out his camera and started photographing aggressively, but he claimed that all these photos strangely had been ruined.

Other signs of glorification have appeared recently. For example, Cheng Yen's seats at branch offices and on the Hualian hospital shuttle bus are now exclusively reserved for her.[34] One day in 1994, during my first trip to Hualian as a hospital volunteer, the van was packed with volunteers and I automatically went forward to a seat that was vacant. A commissioner stopped me immediately: "It is *shangren*'s seat!" she said. My reaction was, "But she is not here." Nevertheless, I clearly remember that the commissioner held my arms firmly, in a wordless message. In 1998, when I was again in Hualian on the shuttle bus, I saw a sign above the front right seat: "*Shangren*'s seat. Do not sit." The seat was bigger than the others; it looked like the only first-class seat on the bus. And, again, I was crowded on a bus full of Tzu Chi volunteers. The jammed and lively atmosphere of sign-language songs and playful collective games on the bus served as a back-drop against which the seat appeared to be far more enchantingly sacred.

More overt symbolism of the glorified Cheng Yen is expressed in ritual. In addition to followers' prostration at her feet, a particular dance that uses sign language (for the deaf) has been performed during the last decade as a mandatory prelude to Cheng Yen's sermon in convocations. On most occasions, the performers leave the stage before the Venerable Cheng Yen enters. At the thirty-third anniversary ceremony of the founding of Tzu Chi, however, the performers froze in their final gesture of holding lotus candlelight in their hands and knelt on the stage throughout the sermon. Cheng Yen stood as the point of a human V-shape aimed at the audience. Under the limelight and against the backdrop of performers' bodies, the Venerable Cheng Yen delivered a forty-minute sermon. At one moment, the image struck me as a living Guanyin lifted up by human bodies.

## Conclusion

"Charisma" refers to a quality that appears in the interaction between a magnetic person and others, one that often has a far-reaching impact on those who are engaged in it. As Lindholm ([1990] 1993: 5–6) describes it:

> When such a person enters a room, heads turn, and those who are without this magical attribute try to be close to the one who has it; they want to be

liked by her, to have her attention, to touch her. The hearts of the onlookers race when the attractive other comes near. This capacity is thus a quality admired and envied; and imagined, perhaps accurately, to lead to success in love and work. In the West, we define and 'explain' this magnetic attractiveness of others by referring to it as 'charisma.'

The desire of Cheng Yen's followers to be close to her, in touch with her magnetism, has led to the mass promotion of her personal appeal. Yet this effort has been accompanied by the glorification of Cheng Yen, which has increased the distance between her and her devotees. As Lindholm ([1990] 1993) points out, the purpose of the charismatic group is the extraordinary experience, not its success. Nevertheless, Cheng Yen's rationalized charisma developed from Tzu Chi's success in the 1990s into an aura of individual power, both in the sense of institutionalization as posited by Shils (1965) and in the sense of symbolism as emphasized by Geertz (1983).

The recent glorification of Cheng Yen therefore brings up three issues involved in the routinization of charisma, that is, the transformation of "charisma and charismatic blessing from a unique, transitory gift of grace of extraordinary times and persons into a permanent possession of everyday life" (Weber [1968] 1978: 1121). First, what is being glorified? Many of the followers' emotional commitments toward the charismatic figure as described by Willner (1984: 29) also appeared in Tzu Chi, though not necessarily in exactly the same expressions: "frenzied attempts to see, reach, or touch the person of a leader; according him gestures of worship commonly offered representation of divinity; treating objects he has touched or used as sacred relics." While the objectification of charisma is not new in Buddhism (Tambiah 1984: 335–347), the objects being treated as sacred in Tzu Chi seem to follow Sir James G. Frazer's ([1922] 1950: 12–52) two principles of magic: imitative and contagious. The imitative principle applies to the issue of Cheng Yen's images. The contagious principle applies to the serious concern about her seats.

The second issue concerns the role of the institution in promoting Cheng Yen's charisma. Here, the authenticity of her charisma is not in question:[35] Cheng Yen had immediate personal appeal from the outset and still has; the media promotion is a result of her successful charismatic leadership, not vice versa. Rather, the important issue is the critical yet obscure role of the organization in the process of routinization. On the one hand, the glorification appears to be the organization's management of Cheng Yen's charm.

On the other hand, expressions that glorify Cheng Yen come not only from the organization's bureaucrats but also from followers. The glorified charismatic authority has also become mystified, and hence extraordinary. As a result, Tzu Chi's seemingly modern organization is often less rational-legal than it is personal and obvious, for example in the statement: "because *shangren* said."

The third issue is how tension can be maintained in the followers' emotional connection with their leader. In addition to the promotion of Cheng Yen's magnetism, Tzu Chi also has mechanisms for circulating movements (as discussed in Chapter 3) that keep the dispersed followers in touch with Cheng Yen's personal appeal. Yet, the feelings of followers may also change in the process of routinization of charisma. This structure of emotions is the focus of Chapter 4.

# — 2 —

# Fluid Organization and
# Shapeless Bureaucracy

According to Weber ([1968] 1978: 243), a genuine charisma is opposed to all rational rules. Such charismatic groups are based on an "emotional form of communal relationship"; the administrative staff is chosen in terms of "the charismatic qualities of its members"; and there is "no hierarchy . . . no definite sphere of competence . . . no established administrative organs . . . no system of formal rules." Since the early 1990s, Cheng Yen's "charismatic community" *(Gemeinde)* has become a popular religious group that operates in the form of a modern secular nonprofit organization that runs several multimillion-dollar institutions. This involves a great deal of routinization. How does this modern organization rationalize its charismatic leadership? How does this massive "movement" organize? This chapter endeavors to depict some of the features of the Tzu Chi organization.

## Mapping Tzu Chi

Tzu Chi headquarters is located in Hualian in eastern Taiwan. As of 2000, its congregations and establishments have branched out across Taiwan and around the world. The Tzu Chi umbrella organization consists of three types of establishments: headquarters, congregations, and mission institutions *(zhiye ti)*.

### Congregations

At least by 2001, congregations recognized by the organization's headquarters were found in every part of Taiwan (except for the island of Mazu) and in thirty countries throughout the world.[1] I specify headquarters' recognition in

40

order to make two points about Tzu Chi branches: First, most congregations were spontaneously formed by local followers and later formalized as branches of the umbrella organization. In other words, the way Tzu Chi expands is very different from—perhaps even a reversal of—for instance, the Catholic missionaries. Second, because branches are often initiated locally, it is important to distinguish the formally recognized Tzu Chi branches from those that are still in their grassroots phase of formation. Indeed, in recent years, Tzu Chi authority has made an effort to discriminate between these types of congregations, as part of its ongoing overarching formalization process. Not long ago, Tzu Chi publications might have listed a group as a frontier organization, even if it had only a handful of local followers who would occasionally gather in a member's living room to discuss Tzu Chi affairs, spontaneously collect contributions for Tzu Chi, or sporadically carry out charitable works. Things have changed in the last decade; nowadays, such happenstance gatherings do not automatically represent Tzu Chi authority locally.[2]

Before the beginning of Tzu Chi's rapid growth in the late 1980s, its few locations were indiscriminately referred to as *fenhui* (branches) as opposed to *zonghui* or *benhui* (headquarters). Since the mid-1990s, the congregations that proliferated outside the headquarters have been differentiated into four categories: *fenhui* (branch or region), *zhihui* (sub-branch or branch), *lianluochu* (liaison office or service center), and *gongxiuchu* (assembly place).[3] Table 1 illustrates how many congregations in each of the four levels existed in Taiwan and overseas, based on the directory in the May 2000 issue of *CY* (*Ciji yuekan, or Tzu Chi Monthly*). The great majority (one hundred) of these congregations are liaison offices.

By 2000, none of the Tzu Chi publications I collected explained the distinctions between these four categories. A congregation's level reflects the size and scale of its local development, yet the exact conditions that define each level remain obscure. From my observation, the distinction is made less from fixed assessment criteria than from a relative context, such as how many local resources are provided. There seem to be two basic requirements that any formal establishment must have: local commissioners and a sizable following. However, the minimum number of commissioners (see below), and any other required conditions are never clearly addressed. According to the chronology of many branches, it seems that having a place specifically for local Tzu Chi to function is often the impetus toward formal local establishment.[4] However, many local liaison offices, especially those overseas, were established first and found a regular meeting place later.[5] The specific category that is assigned usually depends on the order of the establishment as compared to neighboring or regional development. Historical background is an important factor, as seen in the example of the Pingdong *fenhui*, which is intriguingly situated next to the Gaoxiong *fenhui* in southwestern Taiwan. Having two branches in the same region appears to be a planned occurrence rather than a spontaneous situation. Although the agricultural branch of Pingdong cannot be compared to the metropolitan Gaoxiong, Pingdong began its history as early as 1977 and received a land donation for local establishment by 1989. By contrast, Tzu Chi in Gaoxiong had a relatively low profile until its rapid local development in the 1990s.

Although it is the norm for each country to have one branch *(fenhui)*, both the United States and Malaysia have more: seven and two, respectively. Malaysia is an example of how the category of a local establishment is affected by that of others in its region. By 2000, the Malacca *zhihui* (sub-branch) had upgraded to *fenhui*, coexisting with the original one in Penang. This, in my view, is due to Malacca's rapid mission expansion and the fact that proliferation of offspring offices in central, southern, and eastern Malaysia since 1997 apparently surpassed the number of those of Penang's *fenhui*. In another example, Tzu Chi in the United States has grown from one branch (located in Southern California) to seven. The reason for this may be because the organization changed structure—from pyramid to plateau shape—when the original head of Tzu Chi in the United States became the head of the Religion Department at the headquarters in Taiwan and the group's leadership changed to a twelve-member board.

Appendix A lists all of the locations of the four congregation levels nationwide and worldwide, according to the directory in the May 2000 issue

**Table 1**  Number of Congregations in the Four Levels of Tzu Chi (2000)

|  | *Benhui* (Headquarters) | *Fenhui* (Branch) | *Zhihui* (Subbranch) | *Lianluochu* (Liaison Office) | *Gongxiuchu* (Assembly Place) | Subto |
|---|---|---|---|---|---|---|
| Taiwan | 1 | 4 | 1 | 21 | 1 | 2? |
| Overseas | 0 | 18 | 1 | 79 | 0 | 98 |
| Subtotal | 1 | 22 | 2 | 100 | 1 | 12! |
|  |  |  |  | TOTAL (including headquarters) = 12( | | |

*Source:* Tzu Chi Foundation.

of *CY*. Tzu Chi authority does not reveal how many members are in each congregation. However, Taipei is commonly referred to as the largest branch and Taizhong as the second largest. The branch in Gaoxiong, the largest city in the south, is a relatively recent establishment. The number of offices under each of the three branches consistently reflects the differentials in development between the three branches. Similarly, the United States has the largest overseas branch, and Malaysia has the second largest.

## Mission Institutions

A *zhiye ti* (mission institution) is a secular nonprofit institution established by Tzu Chi to carry out at least one of the organization's "Four Great Missions" *(si da zhiye):* charity, medical care, education, or culture (in the same order as the Tzu Chi slogan). The word *ti* (literally, "body") refers here to an entity or building, since most *zhiye ti,* such as hospitals, are structures erected specifically for the proposed mission. The rest, including the mission center, are offices set up as operating mission(s). In other words, the *zhiye ti* are Tzu Chi's "hardware."[6] In the strict sense of the term, they materialize the Tzu Chi mission. I specify *zhiye ti* as "secular" institutions for two reasons: First, despite the Tzu Chi spirit that is manifested in these institutions, they are legally, professionally, and technically the type of nonprofit institutions they claim to be. For instance, a Tzu Chi general hospital meets every criterion of a general hospital, though it may distinguish itself from others by, for instance, its free clinics and care for Buddhist *sangha* (monastics) and the poor. The Tzu Chi University, another example, is a standard private institution of higher education, but with distinct programs, such as bestowing great honor on those who donate their bodies to medicine[7] and requiring all freshmen to take a one-year, three-credit course on "Tzu Chi Humanity *(Ciji renwen),*" which consists of reading Cheng Yen's works and volunteering one's services (Hsu and Ho 2007). Second, no one I spoke with in Tzu Chi confused these other buildings with being the same sort as the Abode—the headquarters and the spiritual center of Tzu Chi where the Venerable Cheng Yen and her disciples reside.

Appendix B is a list of *zhiye ti* that were established as of June 2000 in Taiwan and overseas. This list does not include branch halls and offices, which are the agents of the mission of charity. Unless otherwise indicated, most of the institutions of medical and educational missions are in Hualian in eastern Taiwan, where the headquarters is located. The Tzu Chi Hualian hospital, university, high school, and the Still Thoughts Memorial Hall are clustered together on a seventy-hectare splendid complex or mission park in Hualian City near the train station, about eight kilometers and a thirty-minute drive from the headquarters in northern Hualian County. Except for the Still Thoughts Memorial Hall, mission institutions of culture and charity in Taiwan are located in the Tzu Chi branch hall of Taipei, the capital. Mission institutions currently under construction (in 2000), such as the hospitals in Taipei and Taizhong, are not listed in the appendix.

## The Headquarters

Tzu Chi headquarters (*benhui* or *zonghui*) is a Buddhist nunnery in Hualian named the Still Thoughts Abode (*jingsi jingshe*), usually simply referred to as "the Abode" (*jingshe*). In the narrow plain of the agricultural town Xincheng Xiang in northern Hualian, the Abode is quietly situated at the base of the high Central Mountains and across a local highway and the noisy Northern Railroad from the glittering Pacific Ocean.

In contrast to the elaborate and spectacular traditional temples commonly seen in Taiwan, the Abode belongs to an architecture of subtlety. The main

The Still Thoughts Abode—Headquarters and Monastery

hall (*dadian* or *zhengdian*) is a grayish-white one-story house in the traditional Chinese style, a modest space of 3,265 square meters (about 24,576
square feet) that faces east instead of the conventional south.[8] One enters the
main hall by ascending three humble steps to a narrow front platform that is
flanked by four white poles (two on each side) and passing through a well-
worn double door with a wooden-framed screen. Inside, a flawlessly clean
hardwood floor is surrounded above by an array of boards that frame the
tops of the windows on the front and side walls and are inscribed by numerous politicians. Visible at the end of the hall is an altar—minimally decorated
with a wooden background and short canopies—installed with off-white
statues of three Buddhist deities: from left to right, the Dizang Bodhisattva,
the Śakyamuni Buddha, and the Guanyin Bodhisattva.[9] There is no air condi-
tioner; fans are hung from the ceilings and are on the walls. In my first visit in
1994, a big blackboard on the right-hand wall detailed up-to-date annual
contributions and expenses. By 1998—the year I conducted fieldwork in the
Abode—the blackboard had been replaced by two television sets hung from
the ceiling, one on each side of the altar.

The main hall of the Abode is Tzu Chi's oldest building. It was completed
in 1969—three years after the founding of Tzu Chi—and was sponsored by
the Venerable Cheng Yen's mother for Cheng Yen and her disciples. Their
mission building, then a shabby dwelling in the small temple of Dizang
Bodhisattva named *Puming Si,* was located one hundred meters behind the
Abode. Since then, the Abode has constructed at least ten additional buildings, while the main hall remains unchanged.

The Abode, as it existed in 1998, was a compound of buildings in the
same grayish white of the main hall.[10] The following paragraphs illustrate
the spatial arrangement of the Abode in detail (Figure 1) in order to illumi-
nate its complexity and its role in Tzu Chi: the Abode is not a solitary nunnery, but an institution—albeit one that is invisible on the Tzu Chi official
organizational chart—that overlaps and substantiates the Tzu Chi umbrella
organization.

Driving south on the Hualian local route that goes through Taroko National Park, those who know their way turn right at a corner that has no sign
or landmark except for a modest grocery store. This leads toward the giant
Central Mountains by way of a narrow, sloped path along betel nut trees.
Crossing a small railroad track and turning right around rice paddies where
a few Buddhist nuns are sometimes farming, one enters a narrower path,
barely wide enough for one car to drive through. There are rice paddies on

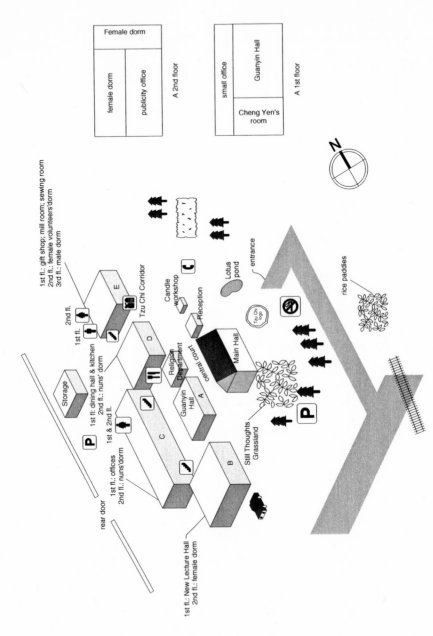

**Figure 1** Layout of the Still Thoughts Abode (1998)

the right and a parking lot for fewer than ten cars on the left, as well as a row of impeccably trimmed cypress trees. Once one is on foot, the tranquil main hall can be seen rising above bushes that have been trimmed to form the Tzu Chi logo. Passing through a small grass yard—the Still Thoughts Grassland (*Jingsi caoyuan*) on the left and a lotus pond in the shape of Taiwan Island on the right—one approaches the front door of the main hall.

To the right of the main hall is a covered corridor where hot tea is often ready on temporary tables, served by a few friendly nuns and laywomen in dark blue uniforms. Next to the corridor is a one-story concrete house known as the reception room (*zhike shi*), a gloomy place filled with old desks, a computer with a black-and-white monitor, a small television set, and several megaphones on iron racks for tour guides. To the right of the reception area is a covered small square space where two or three nuns make candles. Next to this space are a couple of hot tea tanks and four brightly colored recycling bins that stand gloriously on their right. Behind the bins stands a row of pay phone booths, the most popular place in the evening. Next to the recycling bins is the beginning of an inverted U–shaped building, which houses a dining hall (*zhaitang*) that contains more than twenty round tables and the kitchen (*daliao*) on the first floor. At the end of the kitchen, the building extends toward the left. Along the corridor, one passes a women's bathroom on the right, and a long column of offices (the Computer Department, the Finance Department, and the Accounting Office) where nuns and female staff members in uniform work at more than thirty computer terminals. At the end of the office space, the building branches left again into the new lecture hall (*xin jiangtang*), installed with a Guanyin statue. Outside the lecture hall is a driveway where the Venerable Cheng Yen's minivan is parked. Signs that warn "No Visitors" are posted on wire doors leading to the stairways. Upstairs from the lecture hall is a female dormitory for the laity, novices, and some hired staff members who work at the *zhiye ti* in Hualian.[11] A wired door separates this space from the rest of the second floor, which is the nuns' dormitory (*changzhu liaofang*), located above the Accounting Office, kitchen, and dining hall.

A seemingly inaccessible two-story building stands behind the main hall and across a narrow courtyard from the above-described inverted U–shaped building. The upstairs of this central building is divided into two parts: One is an additional female dormitory that accommodates a few nuns and lay female devotees who are close to Cheng Yen. This is the only dormitory inside the Venerable Cheng Yen's personal living quarters. Compared to the specific functions of other female dormitories, it was never clear to me who earns the right to live in this particular building.[12]

The other part of this floor is the Publicity Office *(wenxuan zu)*, where nuns and novices may be found at computer terminals editing for the Still Thoughts Culture Publisher. A private shortcut links this office to the female dormitory upstairs in the inverted U–shaped building. The ground floor across from the new lecture hall is the Venerable Cheng Yen's bedroom, with bamboo fences and plants blocking its windows from view. Next to her room and parallel to the Accounting Office is Guanyin Hall *(guanyin dian)*; in the organization's early days, this was the secondary sutra recital hall, but more recently it has served as the Venerable Cheng Yen's living room for closed audiences. Next to Guanyin Hall is the Social Work Office and the Religion Department *(zongjiao chu,* the former *zongjiao shi)*, where a handful of female and male staff members squeeze in behind a few desks and computers among an excessive number of file organizers and cabinets.

The front door of Guanyin Hall is under a board that is inscribed by former president Lee. Known as the "central court" *(zhongting)*, it is located across a covered courtyard just to the rear of the main hall. In the central court, four conference tables covered with cream-colored plastic tablecloths form a rectangle at the center. About twenty wooden folding chairs skirt the tables, while the side that is in front of Guanyin Hall has only one larger cane chair. This chair is reserved exclusively for the Venerable Cheng Yen when she presides over the daily volunteer morning meeting *(zhigong zaohui)*, delivers small-scale sermons, and grants open audiences.

A three-story building is located on the outer side of, and parallel to, the dining hall and kitchen. On the ground floor of this outer building are the gift shop *(liutong chu)*, the mill room, and the sewing room. All the workers in these rooms are nuns and novices; there are no laypeople in the workshops. At the far corner is the only public men's restroom. The second floor is another laywomen's dormitory *(nüzhong liaofang)* and the third floor is the laymen's dormitory *(nanzhong liaofang)*. These two dormitories mainly accommodate volunteers who work at the Tzu Chi Hualian Hospital and are usually referred to as the "volunteers' dormitories" *(zhigong liaofang)*. Between this three-story building and the one that houses the dining hall and kitchen, is another covered corridor, known as the "Tzu Chi Corridor" *(Ciji zoulang)*, which exhibits the Tzu Chi Four Great Missions in the glass window panels on both sides. On Sundays and holidays, the corridor is filled with visitors following guide nuns who enthusiastically explain the exhibition through megaphones. The Tzu Chi Corridor leads to an open space with a parking lot and construction, and the compound's rear door looks out upon the magnificent panorama of the Central Mountains.

## Structure and Agency

While they are geographically dispersed and categorically differentiated, the congregations, the mission institutions, and the Abode all work as one umbrella organization. The spontaneously formed local congregations did not become independent locales. The mission institutions, although technically and professionally secular, did not depart from Tzu Chi to become self-sufficient institutions, and the name of Tzu Chi on their entrance means more than mere gratitude to their sponsors. The headquarters, the nunnery of the Venerable Cheng Yen and her disciples, did not confine itself to the role of spiritual symbol. Rather, all these establishments coordinate as an umbrella organization, or more accurately, an interlocking pyramid.

Chapter 1 describes the many ways in which the leadership of Tzu Chi is charismatic. The rest of this chapter explains how the Venerable Cheng Yen's charisma is rationalized by this institution. On one hand, it works under unclear authority lines and competence distinctions between staff members and volunteers and among proliferated departments and titled groups, while on the other hand, it maintains a clear outright authority vested in one individual, the Venerable Cheng Yen.

### *The Emergence of the Managerial Staff:*
### *Institutionalization and Bureaucratization*

The primary and initial structure of the Tzu Chi organization—at least for the first two decades of its history—consisted of a leading Buddhist nun and her following of monastic disciples and laity. The primary organizational goal at that time was to supplement medical fees for the poor and care for the needy; and between 1979 and 1986, the organization's concrete task was to raise funds to build a hospital in Hualian. As it approached the completion of its first large-scale mission, the primary structure began to encounter the task of hospital management. Given the high profile of the hospital and its fund-raising campaign (see Chapter 6), the public had high expectations of a humanitarian mission, yet low expectations of a grassroots religious charitable group. People could not wait to discover whether Tzu Chi was prepared and able to manage such a state-of-the-art hospital.[13] As a result of the internal and external pressures, what Johnson (1992) calls the emergence of "a third world," namely, the rise of the staff, was under way.

In fact, Tzu Chi had long considered this new challenge. The Venerable Cheng Yen had been discussing her plan to found a hospital with top-ranking medical practitioners from the prestigious National Taiwan University Hospital. As soon as the hospital entered the blueprint stage in 1982, Tzu Chi formed its construction task force, which consisted of the chair of Taiwan's architect association, several deputy directors of major hospitals, and Buddhist priests, including Cheng Yen herself and her master, the Venerable Yinshun.[14] A month before the ground breaking in 1984, Tzu Chi formed the board of hospital directors, comprised of medical professionals, government officials, and Buddhist monastics, with the Venerable Yinshun serving as the honorary chair and Cheng Yen as the chair.[15] It is not clear whether members of these task forces were all Tzu Chi followers; however, according to the veteran devotee whose husband introduced Cheng Yen to the medical professionals, it is clear that Cheng Yen personally handled the recruitment.

Although these arrangements solely concerned the hospital, the realized need for overall management had a more general impact on the Tzu Chi organization. By the mid-1980s, such words as institutionalization (zhidu hua), routinization (guize hua), and organization (zuzhi hua) had become the stated priority of Tzu Chi. A managerial task force and coordinating structure followed. In January 1985, the organization formed its "research and development committee" to plan, execute, coordinate, and assess all Tzu Chi missions. It was chaired by the Venerable Cheng Yen and consisted of sixteen persons (twelve male and four female)—relatively young compared to the founding and veteran devotees, who were mostly middle-aged women—who were drawn to Tzu Chi through fund-raising events for the hospital.[16] Beginning in November 1987, monthly coordination meetings among the staff members of the Tzu Chi Foundation, branches, and institutions took place in the Abode.[17]

Apparently, Tzu Chi took time to "custom make" the managerial system. In contrast to some other grassroots religious groups—such as *Mazu Chaotian Gong*, which limited its role to sponsorship and let professionals run its hospital independently as a purely secular institution—Tzu Chi wanted to generate its own managerial system. Moreover, besides filling the hospital management positions, the Tzu Chi managerial plan is for all mission institutions—including present missions, missions under construction, and future planning.

The managerial task force, initially comprised of a few devotees, later became a formal establishment that consisted of hired staff. On May 30, 1987, the Venerable Cheng Yen revealed her plan of institutionalization to her devotees in Taipei: the formation of the Tzu Chi management center.[18] In 1990, Tzu Chi founded its general management center *(zong guanli zhongxin).* According to an organizational chart printed in 1993 (Figure 2), the general management center is ranked below the authority of Cheng Yen, the mission planning committee, and the three vice CEOs (chief executive officers), and above the institutions of the Four Great Missions (*CN 1966-1992*: 32-34). The general management center consists of eight offices: secretariat, religion, personnel, finance, construction, general affairs, computer, and assessment; plus one task force for medical development. The initial leader-follower two-tier structure had been bureaucratized with the completion of mission institutions such as its first hospital, on the one hand, and with the installation of the managerial center, on the other.

The 1999 organizational chart (Figure 3) maintains a similar basic structure with a few changes (D. Wang 1999: 136). First, each of the Four Great Missions has obviously expanded, as seen in the increased number of mission institutions. Second, the general management center has been renamed as a mission center *(zhiye zhongxin),* although its horizontal position on the chart remains at the heart of the organization, between the top authority and the array of mission institutions. Third, the several committees that were on the left side of the management center on the 1993 chart have now been compressed into one "mission planning and executing committee." At the same time, the original eight offices of the general management center have now expanded into twelve offices: seven of them continue from the old chart, but have been upgraded from *shi* (office) to *chu* (department); four of them are the mission development departments that were committee task forces on the old chart, plus one new department appears—international affairs. In other words, the managerial aspect of Tzu Chi has become further bureaucratized since 1993 in three ways: upgrading original offices, installing task forces as formal departments, and creating new departments. Fourth, the volunteer association, consisting of two boxes: members and commissioners on the upper left of the 1993 chart has been significantly differentiated into several boxes including commissioners, Compassion Faith corps, eight categories of volunteer association, while its position on the chart remains the same. Finally, and

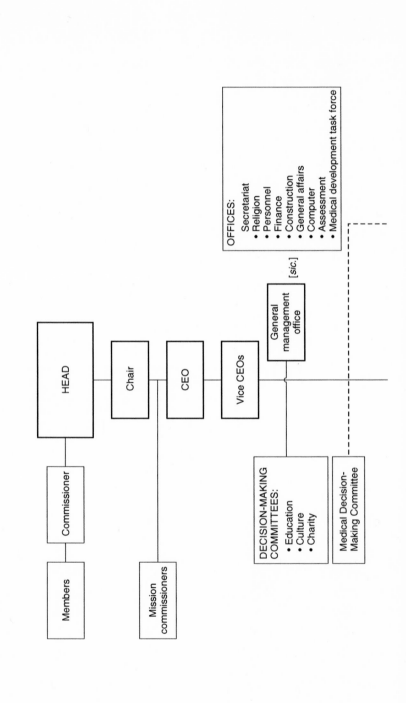

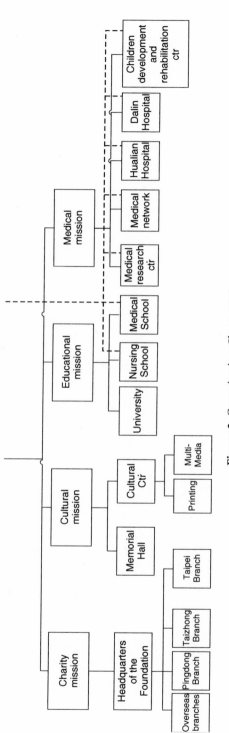

**Figure 2** Organization Chart, 1993

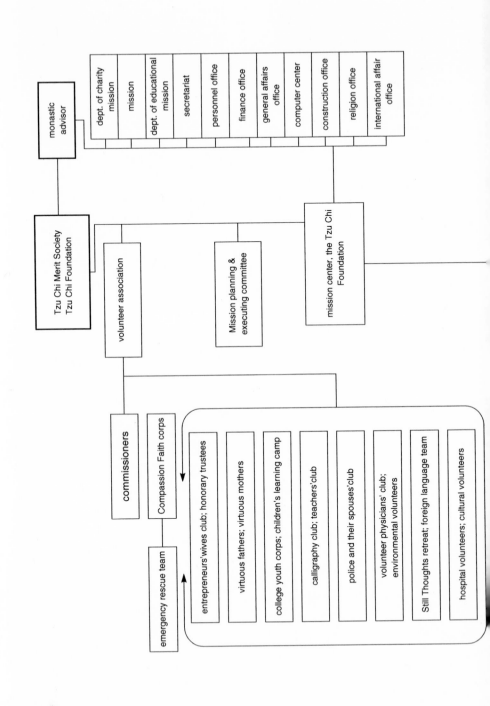

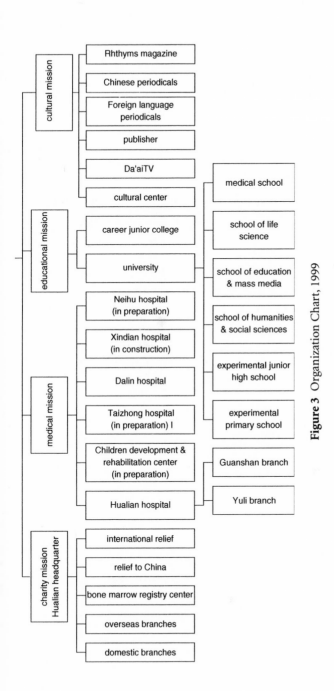

**Figure 3** Organization Chart, 1999

perhaps most important, the top of the organization has changed: all three positions—head of the Tzu Chi Merit Society, chair, and CEO—have been consolidated into one box, "Tzu Chi Merit Association and Tzu Chi Foundation," which no longer indicates its position. A new position, monastic advisor *(zhidao shifu)*, has been created on the upper right. It is horizontal to the central top box and above all the departments of the mission center. This top position is again filled by Cheng Yen.

## Analysis

The section below the vice CEOs (or *fu zongzhixing zhang*) on the 1993 chart, including the institutions of charity, medical, educational, and cultural missions, are self-explanatory bureaucracies. The text explains that there were three instead of four vice CEOs; that is, except for charity, each of the other three missions has a vice CEO who operates above the supervising level, balanced between decision-making committees and the general management center *(CN 1966-1992*: 32). Below the supervising level is a horizontal array of self-explanatory institutions that are divided into four equal-level clusters by each institution's respective mission. While the vice CEOs disappeared from the 1999 chart, they continue in reality to be the leaders of three missions, although their actual authority level within the mission center is unclear.

The rest of the 1999 chart is even more intriguing. An initial question concerns the central top authority. On the 1993 chart, the top three vertically linked positions—the head of Merit Society *(gongde hui huizhang)*, the foundation's chair of the board of directors *( jijinhui dongshizhang)*, and the CEO *(zong zhixingzhang)*—were actually one person: the Venerable Cheng Yen. The multiple top positions being held by Cheng Yen identify Tzu Chi as a typical charismatic organization that vests all authority in one individual. However, the 1999 chart moves Cheng Yen to the upper right position of monastic advisor. As a result, it is unclear whether the monastic advisor or the mission center has direct authority over the twelve departments. Furthermore, the 1999 chart replaces the top central box with "Tzu Chi Merit Association and Tzu Chi Foundation"; ironically, they comprise the exact umbrella organization that this whole chart purports to replace. This critical new top central box, therefore, means everything—and nothing. If the horizontal level indicates hierarchy, then the actual authority lies in the position of monastic advisor, who is the Venerable Cheng Yen.

The multiple charismatic roles identified in the 1993 chart overlap further with two obscure sections: (1) the "charity mission," located at the left bottom; and (2) the two boxes—members *(huiyuan)* and commissioners *(weiyuan)*—hanging on the upper left and related to the whole organization, with an exclusive horizontal line to the Venerable Cheng Yen. In reality, these two separate sections are actually one. The mission of charity is actually led by the Venerable Cheng Yen, and there is no vice CEO for this particular mission, although the chart shows a direct line from the "Vice CEO" box to all four missions, including charity (*CN 1966–1992*: 32). The exact structure for the mission of charity is not as self-explanatory as for the other three missions. As illustrated in the 1993 chart, the mission of charity consists of the headquarters and branches, or, in more tangible terms, the Abode and its congregations. The role of the Abode is discussed below. The congregations, as they exist in reality, consist of devotees who are commissioners and general members (these titles are explained in the next section). The commissioners and members who are the actual agents of the mission of charity on the lower left also fill the upper left of the chart. In other words, the mission of charity, consisting of the Venerable Cheng Yen, the Abode, and congregations comprised of commissioners and members, is, in fact, the initial and primary structure of Tzu Chi. Considering the actual relationship between Cheng Yen, the commissioners, and the members, the mission of charity may simply exist as one self-sufficient system distinct from the whole Tzu Chi organizational chart. An explanation for its appearance in the 1993 chart as two separate parts across the managerial center may be as follows: As a division of the umbrella organization, the headquarters (or, the Abode) and the congregations are subject to the managerial center. In actual interaction, however, the agents of the mission of charity are directly tied to the authority, Cheng Yen, in collaboration with the bureaucratized managerial center. The repeated mission of charity and its unclear relation to the managerial center on the chart diffuses the line of authority—everything leads to Cheng Yen and the lines of actual command are unclear.

The 1999 chart maintains the separation between commissioners and the mission of charity, yet with significant revisions. First, commissioners are located in the top box, above an array of differentiated titles and subgroups on the upper left. Together, these boxes make up the volunteer organization. Second, the volunteer organization no longer links directly to any of the Venerable Cheng Yen's positions. Rather, it links to the spinal cord just below the vague top box of "Tzu Chi Merit Association and Tzu

Chi Foundation," and above the mission committee and the mission center. By skipping the vague top box, the direct authority over the volunteer organization is still Cheng Yen in her new position as the monastic advisor. Third, the charity mission remains separate from the volunteer organization across the managerial or the mission center, yet it now includes new departments—a bone marrow registry center, relief to China, and international relief—in addition to congregations in Taiwan and overseas.

Another question concerns the role of the Abode. In reality, the Abode is the location of Tzu Chi headquarters, where the multifaceted charismatic authority—the Venerable Cheng Yen—resides and is, therefore, the spiritual center of all the followers. At the same time, the sole income of Tzu Chi (that is, members' contributions) is handled by the Accounting Office, and the coordination of millions of followers is handled by the Religion Department, both of which are located in the Abode. In other words, the Abode is the power center of Tzu Chi, encompassing outright charismatic authority, as well as the followers' religious identity, donation, and manpower. Nevertheless, the only place the Abode is indirectly recognized in the 1993 chart is the "headquarters of the foundation" box, located under the mission of charity and above the branches at the lower left; and in the 1999 chart, by "charity mission, Hualian headquarters" at the lower right.

As a monastery, the Abode is itself an institution and its turf in Tzu Chi extends in many ways beyond the mission of charity. The Abode consists of nuns and novices whose status as monastic devotees and as Cheng Yen's disciples in a definitely Buddhist organization are never confused with the laity. And many of the monastic disciples are indeed occupants of distinct positions—for example, in the computer and personnel offices—in the general management center or the mission center. Also, members of the Abode make their living independently by farming and by the income derived from the craft products and published materials of their brand, "Still Thoughts Culture," which are sold at the Abode's gift shop and other Tzu Chi establishments. However, the Abode as an institution is invisible in both the 1993 and 1999 charts.

## Structure of Organization Revisited

A structural redrawing of the Tzu Chi umbrella organization as it exists (Figure 4) would resemble a triangle: On the top is the actual authority of the Venerable Cheng Yen. The large lower level is generally divided into

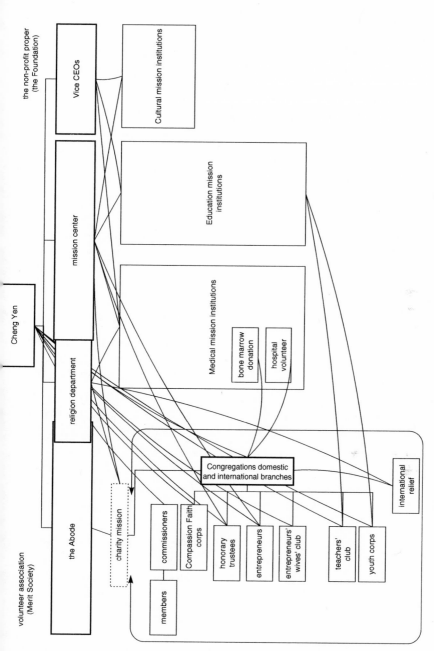

the non-profit proper
(the Foundation)

volunteer association
(Merit Society)

Cheng Yen

Vice CEOs

Cultural mission institutions

mission center

Education mission
institutions

religion department

Medical mission institutions

bone marrow
donation

hospital
volunteer

the Abode

charity mission

Congregations domestic
and international branches

members

commissioners

Compassion Faith
corps

honorary
trustees

entrepreneurs

entrepreneurs'
wives' club

teachers'
club

youth corps

international
relief

**Figure 4** Redrawing of the Structure of the Tzu Chi Umbrella Organization

two parts: the nonprofit proper and the volunteer association. The differences between the official charts and the organizational structure as observed stem, in my view, from the discrepancies between idea and practice: the official charts project what a typical organization would be (according to Cheng Yen), whereas the redrawing depicts what Tzu Chi is in reality (1999)—a charismatic organization. A "bureaucratic" outline with overlapping authority systems focuses attention on the leader. In other words, the official charts are "models for" the reality, and the redrawing, a "model of" the reality (Geertz 1973: 93).

## One Charismatic Authority

The Venerable Cheng Yen is not only the spiritual figure, but also the ultimate decision maker of the Tzu Chi umbrella organization. The power of her charismatic authority is exercised at every level of Tzu Chi, ranging from minute details to multimillion-dollar decisions. Descriptions of the architecture of Tzu Chi establishments always remark on the specific designs that were brilliantly illuminated by the Venerable Cheng Yen. For example, she selected the made-in-Japan brass roof tiles for the splendid Still Thoughts Memorial Hall because brass will eventually turn from bronze to green and, she believes, just as Tzu Chi, will last for hundreds of thousands of years. Construction projects in progress indeed contain technical details dictated by the Venerable Cheng Yen's decisions. For instance, at the end of a brief meeting at the Abode in 1994, a disciple reported to Cheng Yen that the Malaysia branch was waiting for her decision on what type of stereo system should be installed in its main hall. In another example, at the construction site of Tzu Chi Dalin Hospital in 1998, several concrete models of stairs, each with different flooring, stood in an orderly row along the visiting path. According to the head of the Construction Department, they were waiting for the Venerable Cheng Yen to choose one during her next monthly visit.

The Venerable Cheng Yen's authority is not limited to surface technical matters; she controls specific Tzu Chi mission programs. For example, according to a Tzu Chi University administrator, the Venerable Cheng Yen originally declined to include the Department of Communication in the plan for expanding the medical school into a university. She eventually changed her mind after the media reported negatively about the Tzu Chi authority concerning a 1998 students' protest against the required "Tzu Chi humanity course" in its curriculum.[19] Moreover, Cheng Yen's authority is felt in every day-to-day institutional operation. Every Thursday morning, and at other times as well, she comes to her office on the second floor of the Tzu Chi (Hualian) Hospital, which is intriguingly named the Tzu Chi Ministry *(Ciji bu)* and is not listed on the two official charts of Tzu Chi organizational structure. She sporadically tours the hospital without notice. A senior supervisor of the hospital management said that a proposal has a better chance of approval if it is brought to her attention by a doctor rather than an administrative staff member. He explained: "Since doctors are crucial to a hospital, 'up there' *(zai shangmian)* doctors' words weigh more than administrators'." A doctor said succinctly: "The ultimate rule of the hospital is the supreme person's (that is, the Venerable Cheng Yen's) dharma. Who dares to claim a complete comprehension of her immense dharma?"

Perhaps the most important aspect of Cheng Yen's authority is her control over the budget. For example, her deep concern with the media's influence on people's minds has led to the establishment of the Tzu Chi television channel in 1998, which broadcasts without commercials and costs NT$600–700 million a year (the New Taiwan dollar is currently equal to about US$0.025). The head of the Religion Department said in a speech he delivered in Boston in 2000, that the Venerable Cheng Yen has committed to rebuilding forty-five of the eight hundred schools that collapsed in the 1999 Taiwan earthquake. He sighed, "As compassionate as she is, I don't know how many more schools our Venerable has committed to building while I am traveling in the States." Decisions about international relief are also ultimately made by the Venerable Cheng Yen, although she is provided with information from staff members. Each day the Tzu Chi managerial staff members browse the Internet and brief her on the most recent disasters around the world. They then summarize in-depth reports on particular cases so that she can make her final decision as to what action should be taken.

From the outset, Tzu Chi was the Venerable Cheng Yen's creation. And the revolutionary pledge to build a hospital in the then backwater city of Hualian was solely her idea, in order to alleviate the area's poverty on a root level. Her outright control over each step taken by Tzu Chi persists, even as the organization rapidly grows and bureaucratizes. A devotee quoted the Venerable Cheng Yen:

Some veteran followers asked me: "Where are you taking us? Twenty years ago you said to build a hospital. We worked the hardest we could and the dream came true. But it was not the end of story. When the hospital was completed, you then said you wanted to build a university. We worked hard again. There is always another mission waiting for us when we just finish one. We just followed you to complete one after another. There seems to be no end to it."

As the Venerable Cheng Yen said in a sermon: "I shall continue to work until there is no more suffering. If my body dies, as long as this goal is not accomplished, I shall return to continue to relieve the suffering, and return again and again."

The overwhelmingly high goal set by the Venerable Cheng Yen for Tzu Chi may never be reached in her lifetime, and it therefore implies continued devotion. Yet each of the tasks is clear and demands concrete action. The success of each task increases the loyalty of her followers, while their devotion remains, since the ultimate goal of the leader has yet to—and perhaps never will—be accomplished. The charismatic demands total devotion, and therefore needs tasks and activities. Vague goals devalue this life and promote selflessness through collective participation in the mission. Followers sacrifice for the radiant future. The devotees follow the leader in a way that "is not a means to an end but a fulfillment. Whither they are led is of secondary importance" (Hoffer 1951: 116).

### Two Organizations: The Nonprofit Proper and the Volunteer Association

Under the Venerable Cheng Yen's leadership, the Tzu Chi umbrella organization as it pertains to the devotees is divided into two parts that reflect the two titles by which Tzu Chi is often referred: (1) the volunteer association, or the original *Ciji Gongdehui* (Tzu Chi Merit Society), and (2) the more recent nonprofit proper, or the Tzu Chi Foundation.[20] The nonprofit proper is made possible by the contribution of its counterpart, the volunteer association.

The nonprofit proper is generally referred to as "the foundation" (*jijinhui*). It consists of hired staff members at the mission center and in each of the mission institutions. As of 1998, there were about 100 staff members at the mission center, 60 of whom worked in the Construction Department. Each mission institution is staffed according to its scale of bureaucratization. For example, as of 1998, the Tzu Chi Hualian Hospital had about 1,060 staff members: 300 administrators, 160 doctors, 600 nurses, and the rest medical technicians.

The Venerable Cheng Yen is at once the chair of the board of directors and the chief executive officer of the foundation. Next in line as decision makers are the three vice CEOs, each in charge of one of the foundation's three missions: medical, educational, and cultural. Under the leadership of the vice CEOs, each of the mission institutions is headed and organized as a typical bureaucracy according to its secular nature, such as a university or a general hospital. Charismatic characteristics are pronounced: Cheng Yen is very involved in the selection of these top employees. The medical mission's vice CEO is a veteran devotee of Cheng Yen and was said to have been a professional accountant before she took up Tzu Chi as her full-time career. No one had an answer when I asked why she was appointed, except to say that she "has always been with" the Venerable Cheng Yen. The cultural mission's vice CEO is the Venerable Cheng Yen's brother. He was a professional journalist who was quite successful in the mainstream newspaper trade. A few founding commissioners told me that they never knew Cheng Yen had a brother during the early years of development. The vice CEO of the educational mission is rather low-profile compared to the other two, but Tzu Chi publications indicate that he has been a follower of Cheng Yen since at least the 1990s. The heads of the mission institutions, such as the late and current directors of Tzu Chi Hualian Hospital, trace their appointments to Cheng Yen's "personal invitation."

The foundation—which includes Tzu Chi's assets and staff members—is solely supported by the volunteers' contributions. Staff members tend to be younger than the majority of volunteers. They wear uniforms that are distinct from those of volunteers, yet during some outdoor events, such as the hospital's community outreach program in Hualian, they may nevertheless wear the volunteer uniform of dark blue polo shirts and white pants. Except for some specific professionals such as physicians and professors, employees generally refer to themselves—and are referred to by those in the volunteer association—as "of the foundation" (*jijinhui de*), as opposed to "the followers of the supreme person" (*shangren de dizi*).

In principle, the activities of the volunteer association and its mission of charity are under the supervision of, or in coordination with, the mission center. In practice, it is unclear whether the actual relation between the foundation and the volunteer association is hierarchical or lateral; there are overlaps between the two—both in personnel and in division of labor. The only thing that is certain is the outright authority of the Venerable Cheng Yen.[21]

Overall, the foundation is more or less a self-explanatory nonprofit proper. Its significance lies in how it was established in the context of Tzu Chi history: It was created simultaneously with the completion of the first two Tzu Chi mission institutions (Hualian Hospital and Nursing College) and out of a need to institutionalize the primary and initial organization, the Tzu Chi Merit Society. By contrast, the Merit Society consists of, in a nutshell, the religious following of the Venerable Cheng Yen. From the beginning in 1966, her following comprised the monastic disciples and the laity, and was essentially a voluntary association. With the establishment of the nonprofit proper and the substantial number of hired employees, members of the Merit Society claimed their "new" role in their old organization by default: that of volunteer.[22]

The distinction of the role of volunteer came in part as a result of the overall trend adopted by the nonprofit proper: institutionalization as well as formalization. For example, one of the primary tasks of the secretariat was to register copyright for all the uniforms and logos that formerly had been used freely by individuals of the Merit Society. A more general example of this trend toward regulation is when the secretariat began to set up a formal application procedure in 1998 for researchers who wished to obtain authorized data, particularly those who wanted to conduct participant observation. Prior to such measures, members in the Merit Society often had enthusiastically welcomed those who wanted more information about Tzu Chi and particularly those who wanted to participate, regardless of their research.

As in the nonprofit proper, the Venerable Cheng Yen is the highest authority of the Merit Society. Her position is primarily and technically the *huizhang* (head) of the society, although this term has been replaced by the more respectful—and religious—*shangren* (supreme person) since late 1990s (see Chapter 1). Second in authority to Cheng Yen is the headquarters compound, which exists as the Abode and consists of the monastery, some active commissioners, and the Religion Department. Compared to the secondary authority in the nonprofit proper, whereby three vice CEOs head the three missions, the volunteer equivalent is much more obscurely structured. Activities and congregations of lay volunteers nationwide and worldwide are coordinated through the Religion Department, which is an office under the bureaucratic leadership of the mission center of the nonprofit proper, yet its work realistically takes place in the Abode. The head of the Religion Department is a lay male devotee, formerly the head of Tzu Chi in the United States. He left his private business in the United States and returned to Taiwan for this position at the Venerable Cheng Yen's request. He is administratively higher, yet religiously lower, than the monastic disciples he works with at the Abode. Moreover, while coordinating the volunteer system, the head of the Religion Department does not lead the Merit Society's mission of charity, which is instead led by the Venerable Cheng Yen.

The nonprofit proper came into being during a time when the Tzu Chi umbrella organization was undergoing its tremendous expansion. It has since continued to bureaucratize as the Tzu Chi missions have increased in number and diversity. In parallel, the Merit Society has been largely differentiated as its participants have increased in number and heterogeneity. The following section explains the categories of the differentiated volunteer association.

### The Differentiated Volunteer Association

The primary and initial distinction among the laity since the founding of the Tzu Chi Merit Society has been between commissioners *(weiyuan)* and members *(huiyuan)*.[23] By 1993, the number of categories had increased to fifteen. Appendix C is a list of categories and their brief descriptions in order of their formation based on the *CN (Ciji nianjian,* or the *Tzu Chi Yearbook)*. Except for the Still Thoughts sign language team, all the groups founded after 1993 or not dated were from the latest organizational chart of 1999 that was provided by the secretariat.

The overwhelming list of titled positions reflects the increasing variety of activities and heterogeneity of the volunteer association since around 1993. Despite some subtle preferences toward the position of commissioner (see below), the elaborate lexicon is not overtly hierarchical. It is less a sign of bureaucratization than a reflection of the followers' positions in their power relation to the charismatic leader. The proliferation of titles among followers is a phenomenon of the "pseudohierarchy" observed by Victor Turner ([1969] 1995: 190–194) among alternative social movements, where inferiors favor delusory hierarchies. In practice, the actual core consists of only six title groups: commissioners, (male) Compassion Faith corps members, honorary trustees, and members of Tzu Chi's friends' club, teachers' club, and college youth corps. A title group gives its participants a distinct categorical identity within the Tzu Chi context. Coordination among title groups results in the coordination of the Tzu Chi volunteer association. Other categories or subgroups are functions of general members and members of the six title groups. Among the six title groups, commissioners and male members of the Compassion Faith corps are the most essential and devoted, with the former as the primary and initial driving force of the Tzu Chi Merit Society. The 1999 organizational chart places commissioners and Compassion Faith corps on top of the volunteer association, along with the six boxes of the other four title groups and eight subgroups.

The following is a description of the major title groups and their related subgroups and functions as they exist in ethnography. Two of the title groups—the teachers' club and the college students' youth corps—are not discussed here, as they are relatively self-explanatory. Their functions in the Tzu Chi volunteer organization are similar to that of the honorary trustees or their related subgroups (the entrepreneurs' club and their wives' club) in that each organizes activities or events that merge its Tzu Chi identity and its social status, and in so doing, conveys the Tzu Chi mission to its members' social connections.

*Weiyuan* (Commissioners)

At every Tzu Chi event, many women can be seen either standing by the entrance or busily walking around. They all dress in dark blue *qipao* (traditional Chinese dress), elegantly trimmed with a thin red border, a golden ship pin below the collar, and a silver photo ID tag on the upper left.[24] Below the dress are grayish-purple stockings and traditional Chinese women's shoes of black fabric with crimson flowers stitched on the front. Each woman's hair is pulled back from the forehead into an impeccable bun that is decorated with a dark blue lotus hairpin. All are smiling. Most of them are middle-aged; a few of them appear to be in their thirties, but there are hardly any young girls. If you are not in any kind of Tzu Chi uniform, one or two of these women spontaneously come forward, greet you with joined palms and *"Ami tuofo (Amitabha),"* and then cordially offer assistance.

These women are *weiyuan* (commissioners); they form the core of the Tzu Chi volunteer association. Commissioners are the missionaries of Tzu Chi. No branch can be established without local commissioners. The title was established at the time Tzu Chi was founded. There were fewer than ten commissioners among the total of thirty founding lay members in 1966. According to the secretariat, by March 1998, the total number of commissioners had grown to 8,168 worldwide (7,594 in Taiwan and 552 overseas). Table 2 shows the general trend in increasing numbers of commissioners.

(Notice the discrepancy between the numbers provided by the secretariat and those in Table 2. The latter is based on data in the *CN*, 1998 (1999).)[25] The growth rate fluctuated in the first twenty years and then increased rapidly between 1988 and 1991. Since 1992, the growth rate has reached a plateau of almost 20 percent per year.

Commissioners are the religious followers and the devoted "deployable agents" who constitute Tzu Chi mobilization. The total number of commissioners is therefore more meaningful than the conspicuous and elusive total membership, which has been unknown since Tzu Chi authority last revealed it in 1992. In fact, the growth in number of commissioners indicates the growth of membership; for commissioners, the basis for their eligibility and their primary duty is to proselytize a minimum number of households. A Tzu Chi publication states that the mission of commissioners is to: (1) proselytize contributions, exemplifying the spirit of compassionate contribution *(ci bei xi she)* and the spirit of relieving suffering while bestowing

**Table 2** Total Number of Commissioners, 1966–1998

|      | Total | Growth in Numbers | Growth Rate (%) |
|------|-------|-------------------|------------------|
| 1966 | 10    |                   |                  |
| 1971 | 32    | (average per year) 4.4 | (average per year) 44.00 |
| 1976 | 75    | (average per year) 8.6 | (average per year) 26.88 |
| 1979 | 100   | (average per year) 8.3 | (average per year) 11.11 |
| 1983 | 190   | (average per year) 22.5 | (average per year) 22.50 |
| 1984 | 310   | 120 | 63.16 |
| 1985 | 433   | 123 | 39.68 |
| 1986 | 565   | 132 | 30.48 |
| 1987 | 705   | 140 | 24.78 |
| 1988 | 1,024 | 319 | 45.25 |
| 1989 | 1,460 | 436 | 42.58 |
| 1990 | 1,853 | 393 | 26.92 |
| 1991 | 3,106 | 1,253 | 67.62 |
| 1992 | 3,603 | 497 | 16.00 |
| 1993 | 4,074 | 471 | 13.07 |
| 1994 | 4,887 | 813 | 19.96 |
| 1995 | 5,786 | 899 | 18.40 |
| 1996 | 6,936 | 1,150 | 19.88 |
| 1997 | 8,204 | 1,268 | 18.28 |
| 1998 | 9,551 | 1,347 | 16.41 |

Source: *Ciji nianjian 1998 (Tzu Chi Yearbook)* (1999): 491.

joyfulness *(baku yüle)*, in order to educate the well-to-do; (2) investigate and follow-up on low-income households; (3) care for disaster victims and patients; and (4) participate in local branch activities and the commissioners' club, and attend small group meetings.[26] A commissioners' manual, printed in the early 1990s, details procedures of each task, such as how to draw kinship charts and what information to gather when investigating the eligibility of each charity applicant.

How can one become a commissioner? According to a Tzu Chi publication, an individual is eligible for the position of commissioner if he or she:

(1) holds righteous knowledge and perspective, no deviant habits; (2) has time to carry out relief for the poor while teaching the well-to-do; (3) deeply comprehends "Buddha's heart as one's heart, master's missions as one's missions," abides by the master's instructions, behaves elegantly and properly; and (4) abides by the work spirits of *cheng* (sincerity), *zheng* (righteousness), *xin* (faith), *shi* (honesty), and has been *muhou* (interns; literally, "behind the curtains") for half a year or more.[27]

Tzu Chi literature describes the eligibility of commissioners more in a moral and symbolic manner than by tangible rules. It does not discuss the "recipe knowledge"(the knowledge just enough to get through the track)[28] told by my informants from the small town of Dalin in Jiayi County

When you are recommended by your [supervising] commissioner to sign up on the commissioner track, you are a *jianxi* (probationer). Then, if you are serious and proselytize twenty households, you become a *peixun* (trainee). And you have to attend classes and orientation and fulfill a certain number of volunteer hours. You have to proselytize forty households to be able to "come out" *(chulai)* to be awarded *(shouzheng)* as a commissioner.

One remains in the internship until the minimum proselytization is fulfilled. (In some cases, the supervising commissioner "gives" some of her members to her intern to speed up the process.)

Probationer and trainee are the two tiers of the internship *muhou*. A general member enters the internship voluntarily, though most cases I know were a result of the push and pull of their supervising commissioner's "encouragement." *Muhou* makes sense of the common expression, "coming out" as a formal commissioner. It also clarifies how commissioners and interns coordinate as a proselytizing team. My informants in Dalin, Jiayi, explained the "obvious" distinction: "A commissioner holds *ng phoh a* ('hard booklet' in Minnan; literally, 'cloth-covered bookkeeping'). A trainee gets *neng phoh a* ('soft booklet' in Minnan; literally, 'paperback bookkeeping')." The "booklet," commonly referred to as the proselytizing book (*quanmu ben* in Mandarin and *kuan mo pho a* in Minnan), records the personal data of members and their contributions proselytized and collected by the holder. The result of an intern's paperback bookkeeping is a subtotal of that which appears in her supervising commissioner's cloth-covered bookkeeping. The number of interns "behind" each commissioner can range from zero to more than one hundred. Usually at the beginning of each month, the commissioner binds her cloth cover with her interns' paperbacks, updated together, and carries them by hand along with their total contributions (mainly cash) to the local branch to be counted as the monthly total under her commissioner ID number. The branch tallies the proceeds according to the updated records on the bound booklets, submits the accounting sheets to the headquarters, and returns the booklets to each member along with individual pink receipts that are printed from the headquarters' computers. Each cloth cover has space for forty households. In some cases, a commissioner has more than ten booklets in her subsystem—that is, more than four hundred households (or approximately two thousand members, based on Taiwan's average household size of five). At the Accounting Office on the fourth floor of the largest Tzu Chi branch in Taipei, uniformed staff members work at computer terminals, and a handful of commissioners hold rulers and repeatedly verify each entry on the phenomenal number of white accounting sheets. An endless flow of commissioners come with piles of booklets and cash, and leave with booklets bound in pink slips.

Twice a year—in winter and summer—the title of commissioner is granted by the headquarters and awarded by the Venerable Cheng Yen to those trainees who have fulfilled all the numeric requirements, are recommended by two local commissioners (including the supervisor), and are supported by the local district with more than half its votes. The local voting also takes place twice a year. The determining factor in winning the local vote lies to a great extent in the power of one's supervising commissioner over his or her fellows. I know of a case in Dalin in which a candidate failed to win the local vote as a statement of the younger generation's resistance to the supervisor, who represented the older generation. To my knowledge, any delay in earning the full title usually takes place during the stage when the decision is under the supervising commissioner's control. Special cases of expediting the intern to full title do exist; for example, a couple of media celebrities attracted attention when they began to participate in Tzu Chi, usually beginning with a special audience granted by Cheng Yen. These celebrities "became" commissioners after a relatively short period of time—compared to many ordinary interns who struggled with delayed advancement—partly because their professional contributions were said to be indispensable to the Tzu Chi mission. The final selection of commissioners at the headquarters is either too mysterious or too obvious because devotees never revealed how it works. When I first asked the coordinator of the New York branch in 1994 about the evaluation criteria at the headquarters, she said: "They know. They just know. How *sincere* you are."

Commissioners are, in addition to the master, the "walking" definition of Tzu Chi. They embody Tzu Chi individually and collectively. The Taipei branch's local subdistrict commissioners' directory from the mid-1990s says that a commissioner should "carry *Rulai*[29] *jiaye* (Buddha's family vocation) on the right shoulder, Tzu Chi spirit on the left shoulder, and present the elegance of Tzu Chi people in front." The Venerable Cheng Yen recently changed this to "on the right shoulder, carrying Buddhist spirit—compassion; on the left shoulder, the image (or reputation) of Tzu Chi—practice on the Buddha's path; and in front, presenting individual elegance—responsibility for individual behavior."[30] The new version replaces family concern with the more universal concerns of Buddhism, and Tzu Chi identity with individual identity. Apparently, Tzu Chi has been gradually blurring the female/feminine image of commissioners as nurturers of a universal family (Huang and Weller 1998) in favor of a less-gender-specific and more universal way to accommodate the changing gender ratio brought about by the recent rapid increase of male commissioners. The new emphasis on individual responsibility seems to be a strategy to remind devotees of their responsibility for their personal behaviors, in order to protect the collective organization from liability should any of the thousands of its commissioners go awry. Moreover, the new version of embodiment presents quite a "modern" idea of social life: one that consists of just the individual and the universal, with nothing in between.[31]

In fact, although the position of commissioner is a lifelong vocation, there are situations in which one's Tzu Chi commissioner status can be suspended or terminated. The manual states that if a commissioner should fail to submit or report contributions for three consecutive months, suspension immediately follows. If a commissioner is temporarily unable to fulfill her responsibilities for any reason, she should submit all her Tzu Chi identifications and

Template for Female Core Members (Commissioners) —Hairstyle and Dress

take a leave of absence. Suspension persists as long as the cause persists. During the 1996 presidential election, a candidate's daughter requested suspension of her Tzu Chi commissioner status before she joined her father's campaign activities, since participating in political campaigns violates one of the ten precepts of Tzu Chi.[32] Although no standard of proselytization—such as the first forty households—exists after one earns the title, commissioners are expected to keep bringing in new members. A general impression of Tzu Chi commissioners among those who do not follow Tzu Chi in Taiwan is that they proselytize whenever they can. When some of my friends learned that I had been conducting participant observation in Tzu Chi, they said they were surprised that, as close to Tzu Chi as I was, I had not asked them to join the membership.

Commissioners are not only the key to the Tzu Chi proselytization system, but also the core of effective Tzu Chi mobilization, which often impresses the public and outshines the government's response during any emergency.[33] Two coordinating modules operate among commissioners to maintain effective Tzu Chi mobilization. The first module is the commissioners' calling chart, frequently updated and distributed among commissioners of local subgroups, which outlines regular tasks and prepared-for emergencies. All commissioners are divided into three regions (north, central, and south) across Taiwan. Each region is divided into districts *(qu)* that follow official governmental administrative units, each district is divided into groups *(zu)*, and each group is divided into subgroups. Each subgroup is comprised of about ten commissioners and headed by three coordinators. Each coordinator is then responsible for communication with three to four commissioners. This coordinating net lists all the numbers (home, work, cellular phone, and fax) of each commissioner. With such detailed and localized calling charts on hand and constantly used for multiple functions, it is little wonder that in an emergency Tzu Chi can mobilize thousands within one hour, especially since devotees will give up whatever they are doing in a charismatic commitment that is all encompassing.

The second coordinating module is the detailed division of labor at the group level, updated frequently and distributed along with the calling chart. In such a developed branch as Taipei, task allocation is specifically divided into an array of twenty-eight task forces.[34] This detailed division of labor warrants the coordination of commissioners' regular activities and special events, while placing commissioners at the center for coordinating other volunteer title groups, such as the youth corps and teacher's club.

Members of each subgroup meet regularly for monthly briefings and headquarters' updates, as well as for other functions such as sign language and garbage recycling. Subgroup communications also extend to ordinary life, such as gift exchanges for life passages of fellow commissioners' families (for example, weddings and funerals).

*Cicheng dui* ([Male] Compassion Faith Corps)

The male Compassion Faith corps was not formally established until 1990. Until the late 1980s, Tzu Chi was largely a women's group. Just as women in Taiwan often form their gender-based subgroups within the patricentric public arena, men initiated their space in Tzu Chi by adhering to their gender-specific contribution and role as a team of safety guards in 1989. In light of the rapidly increasing number of male participants who did not pursue the commissioner track, the Venerable Cheng Yen created the male Compassion Faith corps, based on a set of eligibility requirements tailored for the ideal men of Tzu Chi.

The first cohort of Compassion Faith corps members received their titles from the Venerable Cheng Yen in August 1992. The total number then was 545, selected from 2,000 applicants (Shaw 1997: 26). According to the secretariat, as of January 1998, there were 3,340 certified Compassion Faith corps members worldwide (3,178 in Taiwan and 162 overseas). Table 3 shows the corps' rapid growth in seven years. (Again, notice the statistical discrepancies between Tzu Chi authorized sources.)[35]

Similar to the commissioner track, to become a certified Compassion Faith corps member, one needs to go through the two-tier internship: *jianxi* (probationer) and *peixun* (trainee). According to the regulations, a man is eligible to be a trainee if he: (1) holds Tzu Chi membership, has been a probationer for three months or longer, identifies with the Tzu Chi mission, abides by the Compassion Faith corps' precepts, and participates in orientation lectures; or (2) is a Tzu Chi commissioner.[36] When he has been a trainee for more than one year, earned the minimum points from participation in lectures and volunteer hours, attended the "Tzu Chi spirit retreat" at least once, and has recommendations from two Compassion Faith corps members,[37] he is eligible to apply to the headquarters for certification. Finally, a certified Compassion Faith corps member is a man who is at least twenty years old, has a proper job, identifies with the Tzu Chi mission, and abides by the Compassion Faith corps' precepts.[38] A qualified trainee is eligible to wear the Compassion Faith corps belt and necktie with his dark blue suit, and to receive the certificate from the Venerable Cheng Yen at the semiannual award ceremony.

While the primary eligibility of commissioners emphasizes proselytization, morality, and Buddhist vocation, the critical criteria for the male

**Table 3** Total Number of Compassion Faith Corps Members, 1992–1998

|      | Total | Growth in Numbers | Growth Ratio (%) |
|------|-------|-------------------|------------------|
| 1992 | 834   |                   |                  |
| 1993 | 1,113 | 279               | 33.45            |
| 1994 | 1,602 | 489               | 43.94            |
| 1995 | 2,096 | 494               | 30.84            |
| 1996 | 2,647 | 551               | 26.29            |
| 1997 | 3,979 | 1,332             | 50.32            |
| 1998 | 5,384 | 1,405             | 35.31            |

*Source: Ciji nianjian 1998 (Tzu Chi Yearbook) (1999): 491.*

Template for Male Core Members (Compassion Faith Corps)—Hairstyle and Dress, holding a traffic wand in hand

Compassion Faith corps lie in *jielü* (precepts and disciplines). The ten precepts consist of two parts: The first five are the basic lay Buddhist precepts—no killing, stealing, adultery, lying, or alcohol. The other five precepts are customized by Cheng Yen to protect the ideal Tzu Chi men from the common bad habits attributed to Taiwanese masculinity. These new precepts are as follows:

- no smoking, drugs, or betel nuts
- no gambling or opportunistic investments [especially in the stock market]
- must show filial piety, be soft-spoken, and have a gentle expression
- must abide by traffic regulations
- must not participate in political activities, protests, or demonstrations

An intern commissioner worries about how to find forty households to fill her proselytizing book, whereas an intern Compassion Faith corps member wrestles with abstinence from the substantial male social habits in Taiwan, particularly smoking, drinking, and betel nut chewing.

Before the Compassion Faith corps was formed, a relatively small number of male commissioners were conspicuously working among the predominantly female commissioners. As one veteran commissioner said: "Until the [Hualian] hospital was completed, we had only 'women soldiers' *(nübing)*. There weren't many different kinds of people." The male Compassion Faith corps accompanied the increasing number of male devotees. The formation of the corps, especially its emphasis on precepts for attaining eligibility, significantly affected the volunteer association. First, it creates a mode of participation that is an alternative to the commissioner track. Social status or attributes, such as male gender, then becomes a plausible basis for forming a subgroup in Tzu Chi. In this way, the volunteer association was aptly transformed from a sorority to heterogeneity. Following the male Compassion Faith corps, other titled groups based on social status or occupation have also been formed: for example, the teachers' club, college students' youth corps, entrepreneurs' club, and, most recently, the police club. An individual can belong to as many of these groups as he or she desires. Since the mid-1990s, Tzu Chi has been a far cry from a women's group; instead, it is a microcosm that represents Taiwan's diverse social strata. Second, the formation of the male Compassion Faith corps initiates a new emphasis on eligibility criteria other than proselytization. Many social status–based title groups legitimate their Tzu Chi spirit by adopting these relatively more mainstream and individualistic qualifiers. The broadening application of precepts on the diversified volunteer association leads to the third effect brought about by formation of the male Compassion Faith corps: the assimilation of a precept-based Tzu Chi culture. Presently, the ten precepts originally tailored for male inclusion also apply to commissioners and the youth corps.[39] The recent emphasis on individual bodily disciplines parallels the embodied expression of orderly collectivity in "sign language song" that is discussed in Chapter 4. When the press asked the Venerable Cheng Yen about her "secret" strategy of managing such an enormous organization, she replied: "There is no need of management in Tzu Chi. If I must name one, then it is 'precepts as the institution, love as the management.' " Put differently, the bodily disciplines and morality of the precepts make each Tzu Chi individual a manageable module of collectivity; and under the canopy of love—however it is defined—tasks are coordinated and accomplished.

If commissioners are the missionaries of Tzu Chi, then the Compassion Faith corps is the guard of the mission. Indeed, the Compassion Faith corps that appeared first in Tzu Chi as the safety guard is now widely referred to as the dharma that defends vajra *(hufa jingang)*.[40] Its major role in Tzu Chi is to collaborate with commissioners by fulfilling the distinct functions mostly identified with male disciplines. At every large Tzu Chi event, corps members with crew cuts or shaved heads appear in their spirited uniforms—blue hats with bright yellow threads tied to a badge above the peak, dark blue suits with yellow arm badges, tidy light blue shirts, and neckties printed with white stripes and the Tzu Chi logo—and use whistles and traffic wands to direct vehicles and pedestrians. Their uniforms for informal occasions look less like those of law enforcers. Compassion Faith corps members also appear in their gray polo shirts and jersey pants when doing construction work for Tzu Chi establishments, or in their blue polo shirts and white pants for carrying heavy loads. Recently, the Compassion Faith corps has formed emergency rescue teams, complete with lifeboat drills.

With regard to organization, parallel to the commissioner system, the Compassion Faith corps system consists of three levels: regional corps or *dadui* (north, central, and south Taiwan), middle-range corps or *zhongdui* (usually at the county level, for example, *Jiayi Zhongdui*), and small corps or *xiaodui* (usually in local districts, for example, a city or township). The regional and middle-range corps have a parallel uniform structure: one leader *(duizhang)*, one deputy administrative leader, one deputy duty leader *(qinwu)*, and fifteen "secretaries" *(ganshi)* in charge of various activities and affairs. The deputy administrative leader supervises eight secretaries and the deputy duty leader supervises the other seven.[41] A small corps in Jiayi consists of ten or fewer corps members, and has one leader with no further division of labor.

The organizational structure of the Compassion Faith corps serves to coordinate corps activities and to conduct corps affairs, while adapting their operation to the module of commissioners. In Jiayi, for example, each of its five small corps groups is paired with a subgroup *(zu)* of commissioners to adapt itself to the commissioners' operation in its geographical district and in other branch work. The task descriptions of filming, environmental, and public relations secretaries at both the regional and middle-range levels specify cooperation with commissioners.

Nevertheless, the optimum goal of the Compassion Faith corps member is to become a commissioner. A male commissioner is eligible to be a Compassion Faith corps trainee without going through the three-month probation. Although the number of male commissioners obviously increased from zero in 1966, they remain a minority among the massive number of female commissioners. One psychology professor who was a participant observer in the Tzu Chi hospital hospice remarked: "I have never seen so many women at the same time anywhere in Taiwan as in Tzu Chi in my life." Although I have no exact numbers to characterize the gender ratio among the 10,000 commissioners worldwide, as of 1998 in Jiayi, only about a quarter of the 1,439 local commissioners were men. At the local Compassion Faith corps subgroup meeting in which I participated, one of the major items on the agenda was to encourage members to proselytize in order to enter the commissioner track. Participants immediately shook their heads in frustration. A few male interviewees also expressed privately that proselytization remains their most challenging task: they perceived obstacles before they actually tried, finding it difficult simply to "open the mouth" to proselytize.

### Honorary Trustees, the Entrepreneurs' Club, and Their Wives' Club

Honorary trustee *(rongyü dongshi,* commonly referred to as *rongdong)* is the second title that appears in the development of the volunteer association. In 1986, upon the completion of the Hualian hospital, Tzu Chi thanked those whose individual donations or individual proselytization equaled NT$1 million or above by awarding them the title of honorary trustee. As the number of honorary trustees rapidly increased, eligibility became more limited: the amount of proselytization no longer earns a hardworking commissioner the title of honorary trustee. Those who wish to "fulfill" (*yuanman*) an honorary trusteeship should now complete the NT$1 million donation level within one year. A "payment plan" stretching several years or even a lifetime—which was so encouraging in the past to some less well-to-do devotees—is no longer acceptable. It is unclear why the option of a payment plan was demoted, but it is a fact that the number of new donors each year has already exceeded the capacity of the auditorium for the honorary trustee awards ceremony.

In contrast to commissioners and Compassion Faith corps members, the eligibility of honorary trustees is solely based on monetary contribution. Whether the contribution is made under the donor's name is a different matter. The most common case is that of a female commissioner who "makes" her husband an honorary trustee, despite his nonparticipation in Tzu Chi. Many honorary trustees are children and deceased parents (in one extreme case, a beloved pet dog). In other words, honorary trusteeship may be given to someone as a gift of love from a family member. Because it may be involuntary, it is hence the most detached title in the Tzu Chi volunteer association. Above all, the ten precepts are rarely addressed when it comes to honorary trustees.

However, there are also active devotees who participate solely as honorary trustees. The major function of an honorary trustee is to contribute money. If commissioners are the missionaries and Compassion Faith corps members the guards, then honorary trustees are the philanthropists. Honorary trustee events often unfold into a spectacle of phenomenal giving. At the honorary trustee awards ceremony in Taipei on December 31, 1997, for example, a long queue of four hundred new honorary trustees crossed the stage one after another, bowed to the Venerable Cheng Yen, and received from her the golden certificate and a prayer-bead bracelet. It took less than ten seconds to award a million-dollar donor. As the fast-paced ritual proceeded, the names of spontaneous donors giving hundreds of thousands of dollars in immediate donations were announced by the emcee. Announcements proceeded as rapidly as the awarding queue; the amount of each immediate contribution rose as high as the corresponding applause and passionate Tzu Chi background music. In less than one hour, taking notes as quickly as possible, I jotted down at least forty-four immediate contributions in different amounts that ranged from NT$100 thousand to NT$10 million, and totaled nearly NT$60 million (about US$2 million, at an exchange rate of US$1 to NT$30).

In addition to individual donations, the function of honorary trustees expands through horizontal association and through extending their Tzu Chi beliefs to their entrepreneurial, professional, or social connections. The honorary trustees' club was founded in 1987 and has branched across much of Taiwan. Once every three months, each regional honorary trustees' club holds a meeting at the Taipei, Taizhong, and Gaoxiong branches when the Venerable Cheng Yen visits on her monthly tour. However, in contrast to the task-briefing meetings of commissioners and Compassion Faith corps members, the honorary trustees' meeting is more like a beneficial dinner party that is combined with the Venerable Cheng Yen's sermon. Except for the devoted and veteran honorary trustees who form the inner circle and take turns chairing the club, many honorary trustees do not know each other, let alone organize or coordinate in a way that is comparable to the commissioners or Compassion Faith corps members.

The key to how the honorary trustees function, therefore, lies less in organizational structure or coordination than in the activities of the core groups of individual philanthropists themselves. A fair number of the core honorary trustees are also actively involved in the authority of the Tzu Chi mission, for example, those who are entrepreneurs in civil engineering or the construction business have formed a construction committee to regularly help the Venerable Cheng Yen in supervising construction for Tzu Chi establishments. Moreover, active honorary trustees also mobilize their social connections and sporadically organize the Still Thoughts Retreat for influential people in different fields—such as members of the chambers of commerce and leading journalists—to give them a taste of Tzu Chi.

In addition to donating their professional knowledge and mobilizing their social connections, active honorary trustees generate further associations based upon their shared entrepreneurship. This has resulted in the formation of the entrepreneurs' club and its offshoot, their wives' club (*Ciyou hui*, Tzu Chi's Friends' Club), with the latter outshining the former as the most active promoter for a philanthropy culture in Tzu Chi. The original criterion for *Ciyou hui* was that a woman's husband be an entrepreneur and a Tzu Chi honorary trustee. In practice, however, the wives of high-income professionals, such as physicians and lawyers, are also members of *Ciyou hui*. As one active member put it, "as long as one does not find hanging out with wealthy women uncomfortable, one is eligible to join us." *Ciyou hui* is therefore a status group based upon lifestyle. Despite their effort to wear the volunteer uniform of blue polo shirts and white pants, members of *Ciyou hui* are distinctively different from the commissioners: they tend to be younger, and many underscore their wealthy lifestyle with designer sunglasses and fashionably highlighted and permed hair. The primary function of *Ciyou hui* is to hold high-end fund-raising events such as charity auctions of used designer and flaunty clothes, valuables, jewelry, artwork, and antiques, often in conjunction with the entrepreneurs' club and the honorary trustees' club. Such flamboyant events, and their successful billion-dollar fund-raising, often attract wide press coverage as well as criticism from other nongovernmental organizations.[42]

No matter how many millions in funds these entrepreneurs may raise or contribute and no matter how well connected they are with influential socialites, the title of commissioner remains the optimal identity and goal for the honorary trustees and their related clubs. Although members of *Ciyou hui* are not required to become commissioners, the leaders are all commissioners and the others are expected to eventually follow suit. When they do, they are announced and applauded in their meetings.

In the Chinese New Year of 1998, a few "big" honorary trustees greeted Cheng Yen in her reception room at the Abode. About ten male honorary trustees in dark blue double-breasted suits sat on the cane couches, with Cheng Yen in the center chair. Outside of this inner circle were female commissioners and nuns, who either sat on the floor taking notes or stood up to get a look at the happenings around Cheng Yen. A male honorary trustee fell to his knees at Cheng Yen's feet, and respectfully presented her with a red envelope. Cheng Yen acknowledged his respect and had her disciple take the envelope. I was in a crowd among the several rows outside of the center and barely heard the man on his knees wishing Cheng Yen health and resolutely vowing that he would better himself by becoming a commissioner. As I exited the room, I heard Cheng Yen speak to the man in a high-pitched voice: "What? You are not a commissioner yet?"

## Conclusion

This chapter has attempted to depict the Tzu Chi organization in three ways: (1) displayed as a geographical tour, (2) unfolded into the official charts, and then (3) expanded into its ethnographic existence. In some way, all three descriptive approaches fail in the sense that none of them draws a clear picture of an organization, let alone of a bureaucracy. Yet, in another way, each approach captures a charismatic organization that is caught between structure and antistructure, or to use Victor Turner's term, between structure and *communitas*.

First, Tzu Chi, as it exists today, is obviously a huge organization. Each of its four missions has greatly expanded in the number and scale of its institutions. Concomitant to the emergence of the managerial section, the Tzu Chi organization has been significantly bureaucratized with naturalizing task forces as permanent departments, on the one hand, and with upgrading and increasing specialized offices on the other. Hand in hand with the bureaucratization is the differentiation and formalization of the volunteer association. The lexicon of the volunteer association rapidly expands. At the same time, the exact ways in which an agent finds his or her way to contribute to Tzu Chi unfolds into a host of eligibility terms and conditions to pursue, procedures to follow, precepts to abide by, allocated functions to fulfill, and systems of modules to coordinate with one another. In other words, being a *Cijiren* (Tzu Chi person)—whether as a follower or a staff member—is to be an agent of a tremendous organization, and requires adaptation to the rules and coordinated structure of the Tzu Chi world.

While espousing regular rules and elaborate hierarchy, Tzu Chi is an organization with an undefined structure. Its modern nonprofit foundation runs parallel to the volunteer association, and the foundation's departments and the titles among followers continue to proliferate in number with obscure hierarchical and authority lines between the different boxes on its organizational chart. The Tzu Chi organization consists of "multiple bureaus and parallel institutions with purposely unclear and competing spheres of influence . . . the bureaucracy was in the process of gradually being reduced to utter shapelessness" (Lindholm [1990] 1993: 112).

Nevertheless, it is evident that whatever title or position is addressed, the Venerable Cheng Yen remains the outright authority of the Tzu Chi umbrella organization. In other words, the bigger the organization, the more obscure the bureaucratic lines become, and consequently, the more all the agents of the confused structure depend on the outright authority. Cheng Yen shows that charismatic leadership *can* be rationalized as a huge organization and bureaucracy by making bureaucracy ruleless but personal; in other words, by making sure that the bureaucracy does not become an autonomous or self-generating monster. Charisma is rationalized as long as its organization attains a twofold nature, as pointed out by Nyomarkay (1967: 26): in the case of the Venerable Cheng Yen, the explicit role of the organization is to carry out her immense humanitarian mission of relieving suffering, and the implicit role of the organization is to "generate, maintain, and enhance" her charismatic authority. In the sociological typologies of routinization, it could be said that Tzu Chi belongs to the type in which the founder prevails and encourages routinization (Wallis 1984) and in which the Venerable Cheng Yen collaborates with the staff members while retaining control by espousing a CEO type of authority (Johnson 1992).

# — 3 —

# Circulation and Transformation

Chapter 2 depicts the Tzu Chi umbrella organization as geographically dispersed and categorically differentiated. This chapter explores the mechanisms that maintain the "geo-body" (Winnichakul 1994) of a charismatic authority. Rather than mapping, the Tzu Chi geobody circulates into repeating centrifugal and centripetal forms of flow. Through patterned flow between the core and branches, the expansive umbrella organization maintains a collective geobody that centers on—and in routine proximity to—the charismatic authority at the headquarters. At the same time, dispersed congregations of differentiated followers share symbols and experience derived from the center, or the heart, which recharges a "sense of mission" for the global geobody.

## Forms of Flow

The global Tzu Chi works as a whole, based upon a system of flow that spans Taiwan and the world. In general, this flow circulates in two directions: one begins from the headquarters, moves around the island of Taiwan, and ends back at the headquarters; the other departs from different regions of Taiwan and the overseas branches and "returns" to the headquarters. The former is characterized by the master's monthly tour around the island, usually referred to by followers as *shangren xingjiao* (the walk of the supreme person).[1] The latter consists of an array of followers' "homecoming" retreats such as the introductory tour *Ciji lieche* (Tzu Chi Train) for general members, the recent variant *xungen* (root finding) for new members of title groups, the "civility" orientation retreat, children's summer camps, and the hospital volunteer retreat.

Cheng Yen is not the only one in Tzu Chi who regularly travels outside the headquarters and tours across Taiwan. There are several minor tours that depart from the headquarters to multiple locations and dispersed congregations. Tzu Chi hospital staff members from Hualian conduct free clinic tours in remote areas of eastern Taiwan. These tours began as early as 1972;[2] however, this is more of a contribution by medical professionals and an extension of Tzu Chi's medical mission than a religious maintenance mechanism. In contrast to the complex and long-distance itineraries of the two major forms of flow, the free clinic tours are usually limited to one region, in Taiwan or overseas.

There are other forms of efferent flow. The head of the volunteer association is an orator in Chinese and English, and a known frequent flyer who represents Cheng Yen outside of Taiwan. Resident veteran hospital volunteers also travel frequently outside Hualian—and sometimes overseas—to eloquently convey their volunteer experiences to followers in different branches. Famed articulate devotees, whose well-attended speeches—or, in most cases, testimonials—draw tears and laughter, are customarily guest speakers at various branches as well as at the headquarters. However, these forms of efferent flow do not involve the charismatic leader, usually have specific tasks, and are barely distinctive as typical Tzu Chi travelers. They are considered minor forms of flow that are supplemental to Tzu Chi missions and therefore are not discussed further in this chapter.

In recent years, a few destinations secondary to the headquarters have been added to accommodate visits from followers of the different congregations. For example, the second Tzu Chi hospital—the Dalin hospital in Jiayi County (southwestern Taiwan)—has been a visitation site since its construction began in 1996 and has been an even more sought-after destination since its grand opening on August 13, 2000. Congregations across Taiwan also organize tours to visit the Dalin hospital: The itinerary often includes local non–Tzu Chi tourist spots, particularly the spacious National Chung-cheng University in Minxiong and the neighboring town of Dalin; sometimes, the northern congregations stop on their way home to visit the Buddhist site Baguashan of Zhanghua.

Ever since Tzu Chi reorganized its congregations into discrete levels (see Chapter 2), local followers of small districts (for example, townships) or lower levels (such as a liaison office) travel to their regional branch (for instance, from Jiayi to Taizhung and Tainan) for Cheng Yen's sermons and for training programs. Large overseas branches also arrange regional tours: For example, devotees of Tzu Chi Boston and other congregations in the United States fly to the Texas branch to attend annual officer's training retreats. Although tours to secondary destinations also serve to create and maintain a shared sense of mission, they are different from the unique symbolic meaning of "homecoming" to the headquarters and therefore are not discussed further in this chapter.

## Centrifugal Flow: Leader's Monthly Tour

Cheng Yen has been a mobile figure since she first embarked on her journey to become a Buddhist nun (see Chapter 1). At that time, she severed her lay family ties and sought the quiet monastic life, eventually finding it in the backwater areas of eastern Taiwan. After she founded Tzu Chi, she resumed her mobility, which then took her in the opposite direction, included followers, and was driven by a clear mission. She returned to the mundane world with a resolve to relieve suffering.

Tzu Chi publications record that, at least by 1968, Cheng Yen had begun to take short trips with her lay followers to visit and deliver relief to poor homes in Hualian.[3] Parallel to the early development of the Tzu Chi mission, Cheng Yen's trips extended to Taidong in southeastern Taiwan by 1970, to Taipei by 1972, and around the island by 1976.[4] Case investigations and in-person delivery of relief and care to charity recipients have been the core practice of Tzu Chi from the outset, so that visiting the poor *(fangpin)* has been on a par with proselytization for commissioners. However, Tzu Chi publications specify only the ten-day tour for visiting the poor: In 1976, Cheng Yen led about thirty-two uniformed commissioners (two male and thirty female, from Hualian by chartered bus to visit 120 families around Taiwan.[5] Except for this historic occasion, Cheng Yen's progress around the island—albeit somewhat overlapping the charity mission to visit the poor—has evolved into a distinctive genre of mobility in Tzu Chi culture. Called "the walk of the supreme person," it is also known among followers as *xuishixing* (following the master's walk), and participation in the tour is called *xuishi* (accompanying or following the master).

The walk of the supreme person is so important to Tzu Chi that it publishes a series, *Zhengyan fashi de nalü zuji* (*The Footprints of the Dharma Master Cheng Yen*), which was first printed in 1987 and comprised twenty-seven volumes by the year 2000, along with documentary videotapes of recent years' walks. At the same time, devotees yearned over those who were fortunate enough to participate in Cheng Yen's walk. For example, when a veteran devotee described how Cheng Yen favored the first anthropologist who came to research Tzu Chi and later became a devotee, she emphasized how "the master took her [that is, the anthropologist] on her walk the next month!" In contrast, when an acolyte of Cheng Yen accidentally offered me a chance to join the tour during an early stage of my fieldwork in Dalin, I naively passed up the opportunity simply because it conflicted with my planned observation of an annual ritual at a local popular religion temple of the goddess Mazu (Chang 1993; Sangren 1993). Since then, followers have reminded me several times of my unfortunate decision to bypass such a precious opportunity, a chance that never came again. When I formally requested that the secretariat allow me to participate in and observe the supreme person's walk, I was told bluntly: "It's impossible!"

Why is the master's walk so important to Tzu Chi? A quick answer is that participating in the walk allows one to be with Cheng Yen constantly for several days. The walk does not have a fixed schedule or route. It may be an around-the-island trip between Hualian and Taipei, departing northbound from Hualian, through southern Taiwan via Taidong in the southeast, and returning to Hualian. Each walk lasts at least three days and sometimes up to two weeks. Participants are physically with their beloved master for every stride of the trip;[6] they hold her hand while navigating the steep paths in poor neighborhoods, put up an umbrella to shelter her from rain and shine, and closely observe her expressions. They listen to every word she utters, whether in formal sermons, as immediate instructions to followers, or at meetings with Buddhist dignitaries, project task forces, politicians, or the press. As the author of the first journal of the master's walk writes in the be-ginning of her preface: "Every Tzu Chi person sees '*xuishixing*' as the exclu-sive Dharma door to being close to the Supreme Person Cheng Yen and to in-depth understanding of the Tzu Chi spirits" (Shi Dexuan 1997).

Yet the walk of the supreme person is not just about acolytes' personal closeness to Cheng Yen. In fact, the detailed journals of the walks reveal the primary history of Tzu Chi's islandwide collectivity through the footprints of Cheng Yen, the bodhisattva of this world *(renjian pusa)*.[7]

While it is commonly termed the "monthly walk," the schedule of the supreme person's walk is not fixed to once every month of the year or to a particular period of each month. For example, Cheng Yen made two trips in March 1987 and there are no records of her traveling in February 1987 or between July and August in both 1987 and 1998. These gaps may be a product of the Buddhist tradition of summer retreat *(jiexia anjü)* that dates back to the time when the Buddha and his disciples retreated annually for learning during the summer rainy season.[8] Whether for traditional reasons or not, Cheng Yen remained at the headquarters in the summer of 1998, although her schedule was nonetheless filled with numerous rites performed for the waves of followers who were there on retreat and interspersed with a steady flow of visitors and interviews. As explained in the 1998 journal, "The supreme person had to give sermons to each of the consecutive camp retreats in July and August and could not leave Hualian for the walk then" (Shanhui shuyuan 1998: 343). In light of her mission to raise secular contributions, it makes sense to view Cheng Yen's walk as a trip that deals with business matters. For example, she took two trips in March 1987 for different reasons. The first was a visit she had long promised followers in southern Taiwan; the opening of the Hualian hospital had kept her from traveling there the previous year. The second trip in March 1987 began with meeting a central official in Taipei regarding the hospital's application for labor insurance (Shi Dexuan 1997: 18, 41). Compared to its fluctuations and abbreviated length in 1987, the walk seems to have stabilized into a routine, taking place once a month except for July and August and generally lasting about ten days.

Parallel to its temporal structure, the course of the walk is not fixed except that it is invariably northbound beginning in Hualian.[9] Nevertheless, it has gradually evolved into a distinct pattern over its decade of expansion and formalization. Generally, the course seems to encompass major branches, although there was some discrimination among areas in 1987. The primary stops since then have been the two largest domestic branches, Taipei and Taizhong, and the Huayü Abode of Taizhong County, where Cheng Yen's master, the Venerable Yinshun, resides. The Pingdong branch of southern Taiwan, which began early in Tzu Chi history, appeared as a secondary stop in 1987.

By 1998, an around-the-island course had emerged, primarily threading one branch to another. It begins northbound via the Yilan liaison office of northeastern Taiwan, proceeds to Taipei, then southbound along the western coast to the Taoyuan liaison office, the Taizhong branch, Dalin Hospital, the Tainan liaison office, down to the Gaoxiong and Pingdong branches of southern Taiwan, and then eastbound to the Taidong branch and northbound along the eastern coast. This completes the tour and makes a full circle back to its origin, Hualian. The Huayü Abode remains an invariable stop whenever Cheng Yen is in the Taizhong area. There are also stops along the fringe and detours between branches that are discussed later in conjunction with the contents of the walk.

The walk is, by and large, Cheng Yen's business trip for the Tzu Chi mission. As she once began her sermon in Taipei by saying: "There are so many things of the Tzu Chi mission to take care of. How can I not go out?" Indeed, a substantial element of her walks in 1987 consisted of fulfilling concrete tasks for the mission, such as meeting with government officials on Tzu Chi affairs or surveying a potential location for building a new branch. During the walk however, Cheng Yen never hesitates to enter into a desolate neighborhood to visit a destitute family or into a seriously affected disaster area to comfort the victims.

In addition to the special tasks required for the mission, events and activities evolve spontaneously around Cheng Yen during the walk, making demands on her Tzu Chi persona as both a spiritual leader and organizational authority. As the organization's authority, she examines progress reports and mission updates from the branches, speaks to domestic and international visitors and the press, and grants audiences to politicians, celebrities, and dignitaries in the different locales. As the spiritual leader, she patiently listens, consoles, and gives practical advice to the ceaseless flow of individual followers and their relations who are disconsolate, distressed, disoriented, or simply dissatisfied. They have various problems that range from worrying about unruly teenage children to grieving over family deaths, to career frustrations and moral quandaries, to doubts about Tzu Chi and confusion about Buddhism. As both the spiritual leader and organizational authority, she presides over ceremonies of different title groups in each congregation, lights the candle held by each local devotee, awards titles to every newcomer, blesses each follower and branch staff member with a New Year red envelope, and summarizes in sermons the comprehensive reports and future direction of Tzu Chi missions as well as interpretations of Buddhist texts. Moreover, she often makes spontaneous stops on behalf of mission affairs. For example, in 1987, her conviction to build the Still Thoughts Memorial Hall as an edifice that reflected both Chinese and Buddhist style led her twice to visit the National Opera House and Symphony as well as the Little World theme park, "to gather ideas of traditional Chinese architecture styles." Other spontaneous visits to followers' homes, to their ailing relatives, and to their families' funerals demonstrate her keen relationship to veteran devotees.

Still other elements of the walk reflect Cheng Yen's individual persona as a Buddhist nun with abundant affection and as a filial daughter in her well-known former lay identity. Whenever she is in the Taizhong area, she visits the Huayü Abode to respectfully update her master Yinshun about the Tzu Chi mission and to touch base with her fellow monastics. She also often makes spontaneous stops at fellow monastic temples for intimate chitchat on her way from branch to branch. During her 1987 walks, she paid a visit to her natal parents and adoptive mother whenever her schedule in the Taizhong area allowed. As recently as 1998, on her way from the Taidong branch back to Hualian, she routinely stopped at the remote Luye and reveled in a brief moment of quiet nostalgia among the woods there—the first stop on her original, relentless journey that led to what she has become: a resolute Buddhist nun for this world.

## A Snapshot at the Dalin Hospital Construction Site

The planned date of Cheng Yen's visit to Dalin Hospital has never appeared in the branch's monthly schedule on the bulletin board in the hallway of the Jiayi liaison office. It was posted instead on the blackboard inside the main office. Local devotees say they would rather keep it low-key lest it encourage a large crowd that would delay Cheng Yen's busy schedule and obstruct the primary purpose of her visit: progress checks on the construction. However, during each of her many monthly visits that I witnessed at the Dalin Hospital construction site, a relatively small crowd never failed to appear.

On the day of her September 1998 walk in Dalin, devotees in uniforms had congregated at the construction site by 8:00 a.m. Women were busy making desserts and tea, while male Compassion Faith corps members directed traffic and organized the space. By 9:00 a.m., when Cheng Yen had completed her tour and reemerged from the hospital building, about fifty men and women of various ages, some in uniforms, had filled the platform in front of the door of the temporary conference room. They were quiet and motionless. As soon as Cheng Yen stepped onto the platform, the crowd immediately flowed toward her, like needles attracted by a magnet. Among them were the Compassion Faith corps members, who at that moment appeared more like part of the crowd than enforcers of order. Those at the front immediately fell on their knees at Cheng Yen's feet with their palms joined, and fixed their gaze firmly on Cheng Yen's face.

Despite the flashing cameras and the intrusion of Cheng Yen's personal film crew's camcorder, the crowd was rather quiet and peaceful—their still postures sharply contrasted with the emotional expressions on their faces. One middle-aged woman of Dalin, in her brand new uniform, presented a red envelope with trembling hands to Cheng Yen. The coordinator of the Dalin Tzu Chi branch accompanied her husband, who also submitted a red envelope to Cheng Yen. (Later, I learned that each envelope contained a check of NT$1 million—the amount required to earn a title of honorary trustee.) Cheng Yen showed her approval with a slight nod. The three withdrew from the crowd with glorious smiles on their faces. A woman told Cheng Yen that she had just had surgery to remove a breast tumor. Cheng Yen replied like a mother comforting a child: "You are done with the surgery. Then it's OK. It's fine now." A thirtyish female commissioner of Jiayi City in her uniform was on her knees, with her back straight, palms joined, and face tense; she was speechless and resembled a praying statue, except for the tears rising in her eyes. The coordinator of the Jiayi Tzu Chi branch spoke to Cheng Yen on behalf of the young woman: Her husband, who was a member of the Compassion Faith corps, suddenly passed away and left behind two young children for her to raise with only a scanty savings. Cheng Yen consolingly advised her to let go of the death and concentrate instead on the children. Like a leaf overburdened by the weight of dew, the young woman dropped her head and finally freed the tears that flowed down her face.

The incident at the platform took about ten minutes, after which Cheng Yen entered the conference room along with her entourage. Among them were the vice CEO of the medical mission, the head of the Religion Department, the vice president of Hualian hospital, a former network television anchorman, a handful of disciples, and a few female commissioners that included one commissioner from each of the United States, the Philippines, and Malaysia. Except for the female commissioners who served tea and desserts, all the local followers remained outside. The representatives of contracted construction companies and architectural firms, staff members of the Tzu Chi Construction Department, and the members of the Tzu Chi construction committee were already waiting in the conference room. The vice CEO of the medical mission called on all to rise and salute (wenxun) Cheng Yen. The Tzu Chi construction staff members then prostrated themselves in front of Cheng Yen, and gave a song performed with sign language. After the opening performance, overhead projections and model

Leader's Monthly "Walk"

presentations outlined the project's progress. All speakers addressed the supreme person. After the briefing, the vice CEO called upon the few over-seas followers to give their reflections on the tour; then came laughter, applause, and a moment of silence. All rose and respectfully invited Cheng Yen to speak. The salute was repeated when her sermon ended.

It was before noon, and the monthly meeting had been completed in just two hours. The coordinator of Tzu Chi Jiayi approached Cheng Yen and updated her on the local mission for a few minutes. He proudly said to me afterward: "See? How efficient!" Cheng Yen left the room and boarded her minivan. Followers who had already formed several rows while waiting on the platform then saluted their valediction. Cheng Yen acknowledged them through the window as the van left the site and headed southbound to Tainan, while several automobiles filled with followers trailed in her wake.

However, this was not the end of the Jiayi locals' monthly encounter with the éclat of Cheng Yen. Shortly after the van and its trail of followers disappeared from sight, devotees boarded a charter bus that waited in the parking lot to take them to a grand stadium across the street from the Tainan liaison office, where Cheng Yen was scheduled to deliver a grand sermon. Not until after the sermon and Cheng Yen's minivan departed from a sea of reaching hands did the Jiayi locals finally settle down to wait for the leader's next monthly visit.

## A Circulation of Persona over Time and across Space

This snapshot of local happenings, which were probably repeated at many different stops, was absent from the lengthy 1998 journal of the walk. The text of that particular day in Dalin instead gives a lucid summary of the construction progress meeting and Cheng Yen's sermon. Indeed, the foci of the records of the walks shifted as the mission expanded along with the number of scheduled meetings and happenings around the island, overflowing the journals' contents. The 1987 volume is written much in the style of ethnography through the eyes of a disciple of Cheng Yen's who participated throughout the walk and "felt compelled to share the unique experience with everyone." The result vividly reveals the leader's persona in a rich description that flows with offhand remarks and spontaneous visits. In contrast, the more recent 1998 volume—ten times the number of pages that were written a decade earlier—folds a lion's share of the walk into lucid mission updates and verbatim transcripts of public sermons. This change of focus may be due partly to the abundance and repetition of events, such as the year-end ceremonies that ran day and night for different title groups in large branches. It nonetheless reflects the shifting loci of the walk in the world of Tzu Chi: from narratives of the leader's personal handling of the mission and her attendance to individual followers in multiple locales, to comprehensive mission constructs built upon the charismatic leader's teachings and authority.

Despite the shifting locus of presentation, the primary functions of the walk persist with proselytization, maintenance of connections, and a centralized authority. Cheng Yen often has been invited to deliver sermons outside Tzu Chi settings in conjunction with her walk. This happened even more frequently as Cheng Yen and Tzu Chi rose to stardom in the national arena with the completion of the Hualian hospital. Many Jiayi followers made an initial commitment to Tzu Chi after their first encounter with the leader on her visit to local areas (see Chapter 5). In addition to proselytization, the walk is a substantial process in which Cheng Yen maintains ties to her followers and to her Buddhist lineage. She not only presides over each important ceremony for different local congregations, but also expresses her concerns for individual followers through personal audiences and even visits to their families. Veteran devotees, especially those in Taipei, remember the old days when Cheng Yen stayed in their homes. Congregations of southern Taiwan said that Cheng Yen came such a long way in person in order to boost their solidarity. At the same time, her master's Huayü Abode remained a routine stop during her walk, and her unreserved briefing of the mission to the Master Yinshun persisted, despite her increasingly back-to-back schedules. Finally, the walk serves to regularly reinforce Cheng Yen's outright authority over each branch of the organization and every phase of its tremendous mission; it is crucial to the maintenance and operation of authority. For instance, Cheng Yen made a walk in the early 1990s specifically to accompany all the newly appointed directors of the Tzu Chi mission institutions; although many of them were distinguished professionals, they had little experience in Tzu Chi. As it turned out, many of these directors expressed how they were impressed by Cheng Yen's participation and moved by her devotion.

The walk personifies how Cheng Yen takes care of the mission and makes it personal. It shares the "symbolics of power" with the royal progress described by Geertz (1983: 125): "When kings journey around the countryside, making appearances, attending fêtes, conferring honors, exchanging gifts, or defying rivals, they mark it, like some wolf or tiger spreading his scent through his territory, as almost physically part of them." Cheng Yen's walk is a routine structure that keeps branches and individual followers in tangible proximity to the central authority. It is therefore a vital mechanism that regularly conveys—in an unmediated fashion—the charismatic leader's personal appeal to multiple domestic congregations, and hence centralizes the differentiated and dispersed umbrella organization in Taiwan.

## The Heart of the Geobody: The Headquarters

Tzu Chi followers are as mobile as their leader. While a primary part of Tzu Chi practice is to engage in daily life, Tzu Chi followers often express their longing for a "return to Hualian" *(hui hualian)* to "recharge" *(chungdian)*, for the heart of their religious pursuit lies there—in the headquarters.

As the trunk of eastern Taiwan, Hualian is a scenic county that consists mainly of the splendid Central Mountains and the dazzling seashore of the Pacific Ocean, with a scant amount of plains in between. The Central Mountains neatly divide the island from north to south into two asymmetrical parts—the prosperous west and the poor east. The wide plain on the west is ideal for agriculture and has been a prime dwelling place since the early history of the Aborigines. It is also across the Taiwan Strait from southwestern coastal China and, hence, the first plantation for the Han Chinese immigrants.

Because of its mountainous geography and consequent transportation difficulties, the eastern coast was historically left behind when the Chinese immigrants brought prosperity to western Taiwan. As the dominant group, the Chinese immigrants occupied the western land and drove the early dwellers—that is, the Aborigines—to live in the undesirable mountains and eastern coast. Because the Aborigines are often victims of discrimination, this peculiar demographic composition further hindered eastern Taiwan both socially and politically. Until the 1980s, Hualian had only two connections to the west: one through the risky, curving road on the cliffs along the Pacific Ocean to Taipei, the capital; and the other the equally difficult path through the axis of the Central Mountains to Taizhong City in west central Taiwan. Until recently, people in western Taiwan referred to the eastern coast as *au soaⁿ* ("backwater" in Minnan, or, literally, "back-mountain"), a term that historically connotes it as a backward and undesirable area that deserves only the Han outcasts and Aborigines. During my fieldwork in

1998, the wife of the director of Tzu Chi Hualian Hospital recalled with awe how people regarded their decision to move to *au soa$^n$*: "Only those who were at large and had no choice would flee to the backwater." It goes without saying how hard it was, and perhaps still is, to recruit doctors—the most privileged professionals in Taiwan—to live on the eastern coast.

It is because of this historical and social background that Hualian, as the location of Tzu Chi headquarters and especially as the original site of its mission, is significant in the broader context of Taiwan (see Chapter 6). At the same time, the peripheral locus of Hualian nonetheless substantiates Tzu Chi's system of circulation. The long distance and relative inaccessibility of the region between Hualian and most of the rest of Taiwan makes a system of mobility between the headquarters and branches necessary, plausible, and significant. On the one hand, it justifies the leader's long descending process from the remote center to her here-and-now incarnation in each local branch. On the other hand, it shapes a follower's trip to the headquarters as a real "getaway" and, hence, a state of liminality that is distinctive from day-to-day life, allowing one to revel in the embrace of the religious "home" and in the ascendance toward a new and renewed Tzu Chi identity.

## The Abode as the "Home"

Followers across Taiwan and around the world call the Still Thoughts Abode their "home." A regular column in the biweekly newsletter *Ciji nianjian (Tzu Chi Yearbook)* and on the Web site that reports updates and events at the Abode is entitled "News from Our Home" (*lan tshu-e siau-sip*, in Minnan). Upon arrival at the Abode, even if you are not a familiar veteran devotee, as long as you are wearing some kind of Tzu Chi uniform, Cheng Yen's disciples greet you warmly: "You are back!" Followers sentimentally recall the nuns' farewell wishes after their first visits to the Abode—"Remember to return often!"—leaving them with a deep sense of longing for their next "homecoming." I have also heard a testimonial in which a permanent inmate of a leper house tearfully recounted that the first time in her decades of desolation that she heard the words, "come home for [Chinese] New Year" they came from the nuns at the Abode.

Although the Abode is widely considered to be the "home," very few lay followers actually live there. The residents of the Abode, as of 1998, were Cheng Yen, her eighty-six monastic disciples, and about twenty novices. Lay female residents included three lifetime hospital volunteers, a couple of women who were too old to join the monastic order,[10] two nuns' mothers, and a few foundation staff members who worked in the mission park of Hualian. There were also a few lay male residents, including the head of the Religion Department, an old man who volunteered as a handyman, and the cameraman of Cheng Yen's personal film crew. All the other residents were temporary male and female visitors who stayed for just a few nights.[11]

Although the great majority of the millions of lay followers do not live there, activities of lay followers are rarely absent from the Abode. At the very least, the volunteer dormitory houses about seventy hospital volunteers each night who stay during their shift of a period between three to seven days. The following is a description of a typical day at the Abode, interspersed with events of special days.

## A Typical Day at the Abode

A "typical" day at the Abode, like those of other monastic orders, begins before dawn. The morning call, *daban* (literally, "hitting wood"), sounds at 3:45 a.m. by the nun who is on daily agenda duty, *xiangdeng shi* (literally, "incense lamp master"), and the residents of the volunteer dormitory immediately jump into action. They climb out of their bunks in the dark, and grab the cleanser and toothbrushes prepared by themselves the night before. Some rush to the two lavatories at either end of the dormitory, while others file to the sinks in the corridor to brush their teeth and wash their faces. The facilities are fewer than the numbers of people who stay in the dorm. There are about twenty toilets for a total of more than eighty women. They must make every move efficient in order to finish their toothbrushing, face washing, using the toilets, hair combing, dressing, and locating their shoes in ten minutes. More important, they are not supposed to make any noise in the midst of this rushed pace. While people still quickly move in and out of the dorm and up and down the bunk beds, the drum sounds intensely, and those who are ready move swiftly downstairs toward the hall for the morning ritual *(zaoke)*.

The intensive percussion is followed by bell sounds. Those who attend the morning ritual are supposed to have removed their shoes while standing still in two columns on either side of the entrance to the new lecture hall and in Chan *mudrā* (palms folded upward and in front of the waist) by the time the bell sounds. The two columns are either one male and the other female or mixed sexes with men in the lead. The two columns carefully file into the hall. Each participant stops at a meditation pillow. All men and women dressed in *haiqing*[12] sit cross-legged in the front rows, followed by women in commissioner uniforms, then by those in volunteer polo shirts, those in gray jersey shirts and pants, and, finally, by those not in uniform. All rise and salute the Buddha. The acolytes and nuns chant in the main hall of the Abode, whereas the laity, except for some special visitors such as overseas followers, chants in the new lecture hall. There are usually one or two nuns who stay in the lecture hall to assist the laity in following the ritual smoothly and to assign seats. Monitors hung from the ceilings in both halls show the sutra page by page, according to the acolytes' lead.

On a summer day, the sun shines through the windows and birds are singing when the class approaches its end. The morning ritual usually runs about one and a half hours, depending on the length of the sutra chanted and whether Cheng Yen gives a sermon at the end. Whether giving a sermon or not, Cheng Yen enters the main hall at the end of the ritual unless she is away for her monthly "walk." With participants forming five rows on two sides, she enters and prostrates in front of the Buddha on a gorgeous round pillow placed at the center of the aisle. Sometimes she gives a brief sermon, which is usually interpretation and narratives of a passage of Buddhist sutras, and then leaves the hall. Sometimes she prostrates, receives disciples' salutes, and leaves.

As the ritual ends, all rise and repeat three salutes to the Buddha—and one to Cheng Yen, if she is present—and then turn toward the central aisle with joined palms. Both sides bow to each other with the greeting "Amitaba." The lay followers exit the hall, put on their shoes, form two columns, and quietly proceed down the corridor on the ground floor along the courtyard. By this time, the smell of food has already pervaded the whole Abode. There sounds another wood hitting: Breakfast is ready! No doubt those nuns who are on kitchen duty have been busy cooking while others were chanting sutras.

All nuns and laity enter the dining hall *(zhaitang)* and sit at round tables. There are about twenty tables, each seating twelve. Nuns, laywomen, and laymen, sit at separate tables; all are silent and motionless except for those nuns who are on kitchen duty and are busy serving dishes to the tables. Individual chopsticks, small plates, and bowls lay surrounding the dishes, the serving chopsticks, and a small metal kettle on the lazy Susan. The central table in the hall is served with off-white plates, and its seats are not yet completely filled. It is the table for Cheng Yen. A handful of Compassion Faith corps members and commissioners stand by the entrance.

A moment later, those standing by the door call all to rise. Cheng Yen appears at the door, a handful of commissioners trailing in her wake, as usual. When she stands by her table, all salute her, then sit down and say the prayer with palms joined: "serving the Buddha, serving the Dharma, serving the sangha. Amitaba *(gongyang fo, gongyang fa, gongyang seng, amituofo."* Eating then begins, while the loudspeaker broadcasts a tape of Cheng Yen's sermons in the background.

The master eats little and briefly. She usually leaves quietly in five minutes without getting any attention. Each diner is expected to finish all the food on his or her individual plate and bowl. When finished, each pours some water from the small kettle to rinse the plate, and then pours that water into the bowl, and drinks it up. With joined palms, each says the prayer "Amitaba" before leaving the table, and then brings his or her plates, bowls, and chopsticks to the kitchen.

After the breakfast, some laypeople, usually women only, spontaneously help the nuns do the dishes in the back of the kitchen. Those who are on chore duty go to their posts to complete their jobs, such as cleaning the lay dormitory restrooms. Other volunteers busy themselves with dressing up for the day. Some sit on the beds in the sunlight and apply makeup with small compact mirrors. Others stand in front of the only two dressers and mirrors in the corridor, penciling eyebrows, blow-drying and styling hair, and fastening back their buns with the help of a colossal amount of clips, gels, and hairspray.[13]

Hospital volunteers gradually move toward the central courtyard for daily testimonials (*zhigong zaohui,* volunteers' morning meeting). Nuns and novices all go to different posts: farming in the backyard, chopping and washing vegetables in the kitchen, making handicrafts in the workshop, preparing the gift shop, working at the computers in the accounting and publicity offices, and a couple of them setting up the camera at the central courtyard for the meeting. By 7:00 a.m., about eight nuns enter to sit in the front rows, while the volunteers zealously practice "sign language song" (see Chapter 4). Cheng Yen appears from the door of her living room at Guanyin Hall. There is silence, and all rise, salute her, and sit down. Cheng Yen delivers a brief speech of the day, usually reflections on the disasters and tragedies seen on the morning television news (see Figure 5). The daily testimonial proceeds with the speakers who have been sitting in queue next to the microphone.

**Figure 5**  A Rendering of the Morning Testimonial for the Hospital Volunteers

The volunteers leave the Abode right after the meeting and before 8 a.m. Nuns continue working at their posts. Cheng Yen may grant a closed audience to special visitors at Guanyin Hall, but this does not affect the daily work of the Abode. The Abode resumes its quiet after the testimonial unless it is followed by special events, which might include mountain worship, commencement rites of special hospital volunteer teams, reception of the Tzu Chi Train on weekends or holidays, and weddings.

On special days such as Tzu Chi's founding anniversary weekend (the second weekend of May), the first wave of "mountain worship" ritual *(chaoshan)* participants arrives at the Abode just as breakfast is ending. A nun stands in front of the main hall and instructs the arrivals to form rows and salute the main hall, followed by the vow bestowing merits to all living things. The arrivals then proceed to have tea in front of the reception room and to the dining hall for a breakfast or desserts. After they rest, some arrivals follow the nuns who carry loudspeakers for a tour of the "Tzu Chi Corridor" (see Chapter 2). Others scatter throughout the courtyards, lingering and chatting while waiting for their charter buses. This procedure is repeated with each new wave of arrivals throughout the day until late afternoon, and again on each day until the anniversary celebration ends.

On Saturday during summer, the daily testimonial turns into the commencement rite, *yuanyuan* (fulfilling the the bond or relation), for a special hospital volunteer team, such as teachers (see below for details), presided over by Cheng Yen. This is a special event in the course of the hospital volunteer retreat. The young woman who is assigned to be the emcee rehearses for two days prior to the event. The setting is also different from the daily morning testimonials. Seat pillows are placed in the central courtyard in lieu of chairs and stools, arranged in rows that arch inward toward Guanyin Hall. The commencement rite begins when Cheng Yen and special guests such as the vice president of the Tzu Chi hospital appear, proceeds with salutes, and is followed by the Tzu Chi anthem when everyone stands up and sings, including Cheng Yen.[14] After volunteers' testimonials and Cheng Yen's sermon, the rite climaxes as Cheng Yen personally places a prayer-bead bracelet on each participant's wrist while Tzu Chi music plays in the background. Although this is the only day during the retreat when volunteers are not in a rush to get to the hospital, the event nevertheless proceeds intensively. When the rite is completed, photos of participants with Cheng Yen are taken in prearranged order, and the volunteers proceed to pack and wait for the shuttle bus to depart.

On every weekend or holiday, several Tzu Chi Trains scheduled to arrive in the morning bring hundreds of visitors to the Abode around the time of the daily testimonials. The quiet and uniform Abode suddenly turns into a pilgrimage center filled with curious visitors in ordinary clothes. Visitors may sit in the rear rows during the testimonial. After the testimonial, while volunteers get ready for departure on the shuttle bus to the hospital, visitors follow the nuns on their tour of the Tzu Chi Corridor and have the opportunity to purchase souvenirs at the gift shop.

In addition to these rotating special events, unusual ceremonies such as weddings—called *fuzheng* (literally, "blessing witness")—take place after the daily testimonial. According to a disciple, there has been no more than one wedding each year of late, for it is presided over by Cheng Yen herself, and is therefore exclusively for, in the disciple's words, "very, very special" people.[15]

Fortunately, a wedding took place while I was there. On the day of the wedding, the bride, the groom, and guests arrived by 10 a.m., while nuns were busy worshipping and setting the altar with gifts inside the main hall. The groom wore a normal suit, the bride wore a simple Western-style dress in untraditional dark green (nearly black), and the guests were either female commissioners in their *qipao* uniforms or non–Tzu Chi people in their ordinary clothing. The eldest disciple of Cheng Yen, the Venerable *Deci*, led the participants as they practiced the entrance rite: the bride and groom leading two columns of guests, proceeding from the entrance of the front courtyard toward the main hall while chanting "*namou amituofuo* (amitaba)." When the ceremony began, the Venerable Deci led the chanting guests into the main hall, where they split into two rows in the same arrangement as the morning ritual. When the chanting ended, the bride and groom prostrated at the altar, and then to Cheng Yen. Cheng Yen gave a brief sermon to the newly wedded, and then gave each one a gift of prayer-bead bracelets. The ceremony was simple yet sublime; it was followed by a "reception," also presided over by Cheng Yen, in the central courtyard where participants were seated in the same arrangement as during the morning testimonial. The reception ended by noon and all were invited to the dining hall for lunch with Cheng Yen.

On a typical day, Cheng Yen appears again briefly at lunch. Those present are usually only nuns and novices, plus a handful of lay residents, visitors, and sometimes construction workers; all return to their posts after lunch. Sometimes open meetings are held in the central courtyard in the afternoon when, for example, special visitors arrive with the press.

The evening ritual *(wanke)* of sutra chanting begins around 3:00 p.m. In contrast to the morning ritual, this is usually attended by fewer than twenty nuns and no laity, except on special days such as the universal salvation in the mid-seventh month of the lunar calendar. Soon after the evening ritual, around 5:30 p.m., volunteers return from the hospital on the shuttle bus and form a few rows to salute the main hall upon arrival. Dinner is already on the tables. There is no wood hitting, nor does Cheng Yen appear. Each one sits and begins eating right after privately saying the prayer. There are usually no dishes used for dinner, only individual bowls with fried noodles or rice. In contrast to the sacred atmosphere at breakfast and lunch, the procedure for dinner is low-key. According to Buddhist tradition, one is not supposed to eat after noon *(guowu bushi)* unless for medical reasons; dinner is therefore called "medicine" *(yaoshi)*.

Those who finish dinner move quietly and quickly to the dormitory to take showers and do laundry. There is usually some free time in the evening. Some nuns and novices sit in the central courtyard watching television, which is tuned to the Tzu Chi channel broadcasting Cheng Yen's sermon of the day. Others continue to work in the publicity office. Outside the courtyard and the main compound, nuns and laity occupy the six pay phone booths. In the summer or during the stay of special hospital volunteer

**Table 4** Types of Retreat (as of 1999)

| | General | Commissioner | C.F. Corps | Hon. Tr. | Teacher | Youth | Child | Staff |
|---|---|---|---|---|---|---|---|---|
| Tzu Chi Train | PP | I/C | I/C | | | | | |
| Mountain Worship | PP | PP, I/C | PP, I/C | | | | | PP |
| Root Finding | | I/C | I/C | PP | PP | | | PP |
| Still Thoughts | | I/C | I/C | PP | | | | PP |
| Civility | | I/C | I/C | | PP | PP | PP | |
| Parent-Child | | PP, I/C | PP, I/C | | | | PP | |
| Officer Training | | PP | PP | | | PP | | |
| Virtuous Parents | | PP | PP | | | | | |
| Disciplines 1 & 2 | | PP | PP | | | | | |
| Hospital Volunteer | | PP, I/C | PP,I/C | PP | PP | | | |

*Note:* Role: PP denotes primary participant; I/C denotes instructor or coordinator.

teams, participants proceed with their evening program after dinner. Some evenings they gather at the new lecture hall for speeches delivered by veteran volunteers or by the foundation staff members. Other evenings, they gather in the front yard and form a circle for lively Aboriginal dances or split into small groups for discussions on their volunteer experiences.

All activities stop by 9:30 p.m., when the first wood hitting sounds. At 10:00 p.m., the second wood hitting sounds and the lights are extinguished. Another day of work will begin in less than six hours.

## Centripetal Flow: Followers' "Homecoming"

The Abode is frequently occupied with crowds of followers that arrive in an organized manner. Indeed, in contrast to Cheng Yen's monthly walk from the headquarters when she interacts with dispersed congregations, followers from different locales organize retreats to the headquarters itself. While the leader leaves her footprint islandwide, the "homecoming" followers are drawn from nationwide as well as worldwide locales.

Table 4 lists the various categories of retreats and their primary participants. They are listed from top down in approximate order from the most general pilgrimage to the most exclusive drill. I participated in only three types of followers' retreats: Tzu Chi Train for general members, civility camp for Tzu Chi youth, and the hospital volunteer program for commissioners and the teacher's association. I chose these three retreats partly because of time limits imposed by my fieldwork, limited permission granted to me by the secretariat's office, and more important, because each of the three categorically represents a different level—the most general, the intermediate, and the most exclusive. The higher the level, the more distinct the characteristics of the retreat become as a liminal stage of rite of passage. The role of participants shifts from onlookers to insiders, and the locus of practice moves from the visitors' trail on the outskirts, to inside the mission institutions.

### Tzu Chi Train

Tzu Chi Train *(Ciji Lieche)* is the most prominent entry-level tour to the headquarters. It is an introductory tour designed for checkbook members and prospects. Participants consist of women and men of various ages from one geographic location. During the trip, participants stay overnight at ordinary hotels rather than being accommodated at any of the Tzu Chi buildings. Except for the staff members, which consist of commissioners, Compassion Faith corps members, and the interns of either, participants do not wear any kind of Tzu Chi uniforms. The roles of primary participants are limited to that of tourists who see, listen, take snapshot photos, purchase souvenirs, honor minimum rules of the host environment (for example, no smoking), and worship only if they wish. They may join in a Tzu Chi sign language song. In a nutshell, they are visiting but not coming home to the Tzu Chi headquarters.

The term "Tzu Chi Train" refers less literally to transportation than to a tour genre; some Tzu Chi Trains actually use charter buses. The present Tzu Chi Train genre appeared at least by 1991, when two trains from Taipei arrived in January, and another train in April brought six hundred people from Taipei.[16] Veteran devotees of Jiayi recounted how they spontaneously organized and led bus tours, *chhoa chhia* (in Minnan, literally, "leading a car"), to the headquarters in the early 1990s before the Jiayi liaison office was developed enough to fill a train.

I participated in the Tzu Chi Train from Jiayi in May 1998, which was a train actually filled with a tour destined to the Tzu Chi headquarters in Hualian.[17] Twelve passenger cars carried a total of 621 people from Jiayi and Tainan in southwestern Taiwan for a two-day, one-night tour. According to a repeat participant, Tzu Chi Trains used to depart from Jiayi twice a year, but had recently been reduced to once a year in either April or May. (This is much less frequent than such large branches as the one in Taipei, where tours depart to the headquarters each weekend.) The mobilization began two months in advance, in April, when a blank sign-up sheet appeared at the local weekly meeting in Dalin, Jiayi. Each commissioner coordinated the event and collected payments from members of his or her proselytizing franchise. Indeed, seats were not randomly assigned or given on a first-come-first-served basis; rather, they were prearranged and divided into cars, or blocks within one car, according to each commissioner's proselytizing network.

On the day of departure, about thirty Dalin locals—including commissioners and members—gathered at the town train stop by 6:00 a.m. and took a communal train via Mingxiong (where more tour participants joined) to Jiayi City train station. By the time we arrived around 6:30 a.m., the entire platform was already filled with columns of women and men of various ages. Most of the participants came with families. Uniformed commissioners wearing bright green badges on their upper arms and holding numbered pennants made up the front row. Each column followed their commissioner to board their assigned passenger car and began the nine-hour journey through southern Taiwan to Hualian. There were no Tzu Chi signs on the train.

Nevertheless, we were soon to be reminded of the purpose of our trip when, upon entering the car, a bombastic loudspeaker greeted us with Tzu Chi music. When the train departed at 7:00 a.m., one of the leaders of our car turned off the music and led a brief "morning ritual." As she explained: "We are Buddhist Tzu Chi, so please join your palms now and follow me." The ritual proceeded with repeating "*nanmo amituofo*" for a few minutes in lieu of a full sutra chanting, and concluded with the normal ending of blessing vows *(huixiang)*. As it turned out, this brief ritual was the only religious ritual throughout the journey. A vegetarian breakfast (buns and soybean milk) immediately followed, and a moment later, in-car programs of songs and speeches began, pausing only briefly at a stop at Tainan to pick up local participants.

The car leaders continuously repeated this cycle of activities for the rest of the nine hours we were on board: serving food and beverages, delivering speeches of personal testimonials and introductions to the Tzu Chi mission, and teaching and leading various songs of sign language and collective rhythms and games. Each passenger had a copy of a pamphlet that listed the two-day agenda with a timetable, a note of dos and don'ts, and nine pages of song lyrics.[18] Despite the leaders' daunting enthusiasm, most of the passengers in my car, except for the few children, seemed to prefer to remain sleepy spectators than join in the songs and games. A female commissioner of Jiayi asked the passengers for support: "Is it because I am not pretty enough? Why are you not responding to me? We must 'lower' *(fangxia shenduan)* ourselves in order to have fun! See? I am just three years old!" A Tainan-based commissioner seemed to have more success in soliciting participation; as entertainment such as singing karaoke is common among tours, including pilgrimages, in Taiwan,[19] an old lady who sat next to me remarked: "She must have worked as a tour guide."

Indeed, the warm and humble way each commissioner and Compassion Faith corps member catered to passengers throughout the trip definitely outperformed any airline's first-class flight attendants' "emotion work" (Hochschild 1983). The participants were there to be served as well as to be educated through each devotee's exemplary Tzu Chi manner, testimonials on the Tzu Chi mission, offhand Tzu Chi Buddhist remarks, and abundant Tzu Chi entertainment, in addition to the primary purpose of the trip: a spiritual gift of Cheng Yen's sermon at the Abode and a visual feast of the array of Tzu Chi edifices at the headquarters.

In other words, the primary participants of the Tzu Chi Train—that is, checkbook members and their families, most of whom had never been to the headquarters—were there to be exposed to both Tzu Chi software (that is, spirit, verbally and physically conveyed examples) and hardware (for example, the mission institutions); their role is to receive. And it is precisely this role that the Tzu Chi Train personifies as the entry level of the symbolic world of Tzu Chi. In Tzu Chi, only action—especially the act of contribution—counts in the last analysis. The humbler one acts and the more one gives, the higher spirit one will attain. Participants of the Tzu Chi Train may be invited to join a sign language song, be reduced to tears by hearing touching testimonials, and perhaps spontaneously help with hands-on garbage recycling. But they are never asked to give; there is no sign of overt soliciting for donations. After participating in various Tzu Chi volunteer practices for many years, I was frankly rather uncomfortable with this "new" role of being served (though they were always welcoming to me on other occasions). I still vividly remember the successful punch line of a young lady's testimonial I heard at the Taipei branch in 1994: "As you all know, in Tzu Chi, only outsiders are pampered with service and compliments. When you get picked on, well, congratulations! You finally found your way in!"

The role of Tzu Chi Train participants much resembles that of pilgrimage tourists. In light of the liminal nature of pilgrimage, however, the two-day collective life and intensive exposure to the symbolic world of Tzu Chi may nevertheless claim some significant differences. No matter how general the content of the tour is compared to other retreats, participants return to their daily lives with the experience of having witnessed the Tzu Chi headquarters and perhaps been influenced by it. For example, after dinner in the dining hall of the Still Thoughts Memorial Hall, a fellow participant spontaneously collected and stacked up the used disposable dinner boxes, as he proudly said to me: "This is one smart garbage recycling trick I learned from this trip." By the time our tour departed the following afternoon, the same passenger car that initially had been the scene of a frustrated leader and a sleepy, passive audience had been replaced by spirited singing and enthusiastic collective sign language songs, cheerfully interspersed with laughter and applause. A couple of participants even took over the microphone to speak about their reflections of the trip. By the time the train finished its nine-hour trip via Taipei to Jiayi, it had completed a full Tzu Chi cycle, similar to the leader's walk, but with a simpler course and reversed origin and destination, completed time and again with fruitfulness and a likely number of prospects for Tzu Chi devotees.

The relation between local and center in the Tzu Chi Train, however, is different from the traditional pilgrimages of popular religion in Taiwan. The most established pilgrimage in Taiwan is that of the popular Mazu (or Ma Tzu, Heavenly Mother) cult, which involves four to five million pilgrims each year, organized by different local cult temples that are connected to the original Mazu temple in southwestern Taiwan (Sangren 1993: 565). Mazu pilgrims compete to represent the identity of their local community in the ritual performances of pilgrimages. Sangren (1987, 1993) therefore points out that the local identity, pronounced in the Mazu pilgrimage, is in contradiction to Victor Turner's interpretation of pilgrimage as an "escape" to an unstructured *communitas*. The Tzu Chi Train takes members from their local branches to the headquarters in a way similar to the Mazu pilgrimage,

Sign Language in a Tzu Chi Train

which "enjoins travel to sacred sites outside the pilgrims' communities" (Sangren 1993: 564). In this sense, the Tzu Chi Train resembles the first two of the three forms of transcendence. Sangren (573) argues that the power of Tzu Chi Hualian comes from being external to the participants' local communities and from being at the top of the Tzu Chi nationwide and worldwide umbrella organization. Nevertheless, the focus of the Tzu Chi Train is on its destination to the charismatic headquarters and on the experience of the visit to the pilgrimage site, rather than as a process of addressing one's local identity or legitimacy by sustaining some sort of pilgrimage relationship to the center. In this regard, the Tzu Chi Train is different from the Mazu pilgrimage wherein "from the point of view of local territorial cults, the specific sites visited on a pilgrimage are less important than that a pilgrimage be undertaken" (576).

## College Youth Retreat

In contrast to the Tzu Chi Train pilgrimage, retreats for youth traditionally engage their participants from the outset. The Tzu Chi youth corps was formed as the result of a few college students initially participating as Tzu Chi hospital volunteers. With special permission from Cheng Yen, the first hospital volunteer retreat consisting of fewer than thirty college students was held in June 1991, followed by another wave the following month. As the experience of Tzu Chi spread among campuses, more and more college students began responding to the appeal with participation and organization. One year after the first college students' volunteer camp, the Tzu Chi youth corps was founded during a ceremony that was presided over by Cheng Yen on May 31, 1992, at the Taipei branch.

There are several different types of youth camps that operate during both summer and winter school recesses. As in other title groups, devotees of the Tzu Chi youth corps often refer to their first visit to the headquarters as a trip of "root finding" *(xungen)*. The root-finding trip is not listed in *The Total Manual of Tzu Chi College Youth Corps Officers (Ciji dazhuan qingnian wanquan ganbu shouce)* and seems to be a pilgrimage-like tour that is organized by local branch or on-campus groups, perhaps overlapping a Tzu Chi Train. Youth camps organized by the Tzu Chi headquarters, on the other hand, include—from the most general to the most exclusive—the Still Thoughts Civility Camp *(jingsi shenghuo ying, shenghuo liyi ying,* or *shenghuo ying)*;[20] the hospital volunteer camp *(zhigong ying)*; the recently developed officers' training camp (*ganbu xunlian ying* or *ganxun ying*);[21] and the newest camp for alumni *(xueizhang ying),* founded in 1999 for those who are no longer in school but remain closely linked to Tzu Chi youth and have yet to take on a new identity (such as commissionership) in Tzu Chi. There is also a civility youth camp for parents and their middle or high school children.[22]

## Civility Camp: Rites of Passage

The civility camp is the entry-level retreat designed for novices and prospective participants of the Tzu Chi youth corps. Eligibility is determined less in terms of participants' Tzu Chi membership than in their student status. The camp features an introduction to Buddhism, Tzu Chi, and traditional values and morality, as well as adaptation to a lifestyle of all the featured discourses. In other words, it is designed to transform youngsters from sybaritic, self-oriented, and morality-free individuals to ones who are ascetic, mindful, civilized, and disciplined. Although it shares the entry-level status of the Tzu Chi Train, compared to the role of observer that is generally played by participants in the Tzu Chi Train, participants of the youth civility camp are the subjects of rites of passage toward a Tzu Chi identity.

In contrast to the Tzu Chi Train, in which participants depart with their families and familiar commissioners, the youth civility camp begins when individual youngsters of different geographical origins arrive at Tzu Chi headquarters for registration. When I conducted my participant observation in a youth civility camp in 1998, some fifty participants had arrived the night before for preliminary registration. Although these early arrivals had gone through a few activities—such as having dinner and breakfast silently, getting up at 5:00 a.m. for group exercise, and taking a pop test on their knowledge of the Tzu Chi mission—they had yet to change from their ordinary clothes. A rite of separation clearly began at the registration counter located in the Still Thoughts Memorial Hall: individual arrivals formed a queue to pay, fill out a personal data form, receive a Tzu Chi youth photo ID tag, get measured for size, and receive a package of youth corps uniforms to change into. At the end of the queue, the youngsters who arrived in their colorful clothes had changed to uniformly light blue polo shirts and white pants. Each one joined the assigned small group and formed a column of ten. Each column had one youth corps officer as the leader and three commissioners as their "parents"—one "papa" (father) and two "mamas" (mothers). When thirty columns were formed, the four-and-half-day retreat was ready to go.

The first program was a welcome performance, *xiangjian huan* (happy encounter), right after lunch. After a brief sign language song, the officers staged a series of hilarious dramas that quickly reviewed the dos and don'ts for the retreat. The welcome performance ended with a sermon by a disciple of Cheng Yen's, who was the former head of the Tzu Chi youth corps. She adamantly lectured the participants to be mindful and work hard in the same way that she had studied in Japan. Participants sat among their small groups in the auditorium, but that was the last time they remained an audience like those in the Tzu Chi Train.

Immediately following the happy encounter was a session of Buddhist civility *(xuefo xingyi)* held in the Gratefulness Lecture Hall, a spacious loft installed with a Guanyin statue. A young disciple of Cheng Yen's who is the head of the Tzu Chi youth corps[23] began the session with a severe speech on how disappointed she felt with the youth. She said that despite all the efforts and money Tzu Chi spent on the thousands of youth camp participants each year, the majority of pupils returned home and soon indulged themselves in pop culture. She pressed her point further by asking: "Are there any business majors here? Raise your hands. Do you think this is a wise investment? Is what we have been doing worthwhile?"

The two opening sermons cross the threshold from separation to transition. After the inspiring—if not shaming—speech, the disciple began teaching participants step-by-step elementary Buddhist etiquette: "Walk like a breeze, stand like a pine tree, sit like a bell," plus detailed table manners, salutes, and prostrations. She walked around and corrected every single participant, and sometimes asked those who did not stand straight, "Haven't you taken the military training class?" Other times, she inspected the girls' hands and said, "It's hip to keep such long nails, huh?" Each team's commissioner "parents" also joined in making corrections. At one point, when I was busy observing and forgot to follow, our team "mama" approached me and asked: "Aren't you a Buddhist? If yes, do it right."

Dinner followed the civility class. As in the previous few meals, the officers performed the wood-hitting ritual seriously and meticulously, handling the piece of wood with raised hands in a sacred manner. Participants formed columns and silently proceeded to the dining hall. The evening program began with orientation of dormitory rules. "Parents" demonstrated the detailed steps of bed making and folding and hanging clothes to dry, among other things, and reiterated the house rules of no hair combing, water, or food in the bedroom, in order to "protect the assets supported by the contributions of millions of followers." Following the orientation, the participants split into small groups, introduced themselves to one another, and filled out safe-arrival cards to be sent to their real parents. The little time left in the evening was for the three hundred participants to finish showering in about twenty shower rooms and retire to bed before lights out at 10:00 p.m.

Discipline, physical trimming, and self-reflection continued on the second day. By 5:30 a.m., all participants were ready, assembled in orderly rows and columns in the front square of the splendid Still Thoughts Memorial Hall. The officers led a kind of morning exercise that any college student might have long forgotten since graduating from elementary school, and then conducted playful collective rhythms and spirited singing of the youth corps anthem. Physical activities continued with housecleaning and ended with getting back in line to wait for the ritual of breakfast. The officers announced that participants would thereafter chant Buddha's names whenever entering the dining hall. The disciplined youngsters indeed chanted in the most solemn and dignified way. During the breakfast, the disciple continued to check on each individual posture as well as long hair and long nails. She picked each deviant participant's ID tag and read the name and school on it aloud. The trimming procedure continued with the officer's announcement of the haircutting schedule with a footnote: "It's voluntary. We won't push you." Nevertheless, the boys cut their long hair and the girls tied their hair in braids with Tzu Chi blue ribbons. With this bodily transformation, the youth camp completed its crucial initial stage of the rite of passage (van Gennep 1960; also see Goffman 1961; Turner [1969] 1995).

Through the first twenty-four-hour physical trimming and hence bodily transformation of previous individual identity, the uniformed participants were ready for the psychological transformation. The program's second day began with a lecture delivered by a psychology professor from Tzu Chi University and focused on filial piety. He showed seven tear-jerking short commercial films he had made—some addressing the unreserved love that parents give to their children, and others depicting the great love of Tzu Chi—and broke the class into small groups to "share" reflections. Sobbing could be heard here and there through the presentation and the small group discussion. One girl ran to the podium and cried gaspingly while confessing to the professor. Our group leader recounted her confrontation with her parents until she was completely overcome with tears and was embraced by

Template for Youth Corps—Hairstyle and Dress

our "mama." The professor finally wrapped up the class with a concluding remark: "Instead of feeling moved, why not move into action *(gandong buru xingdong)?*"

With such moral and emotional devaluation of one's previous being, the participants were ready to receive new indoctrination as a vehicle to a new identity. The following days were filled with an introduction to the Tzu Chi missions, lectures and question-and-answer sessions delivered by many of Tzu Chi's high-ranking staff members and veteran Tzu Chi youth, and a half day in the Abode, where participants attended the daily volunteer morning testimonial and Cheng Yen's sermon. In addition, participants learned to perform sign language songs (Chapter 4) and had a taste of "Tzu Chi Humanity Class," learning how to make tea and traditional handicrafts. Each day proceeded at an intensive and fast pace, and ended with small group "sharing." Except for the trip to the Abode, participants did not leave the camp area in the Still Thoughts Memorial Hall. Horizontal ties apparently formed and rapidly increased as participants who originally arrived as individuals now clustered in circles, chatting and taking group photos during every brief break. Some girls in my room even risked the chance of being caught and whispered conversations for hours after the lights were turned off.

On the fourth day, the same disciple who had spoken severely two days ago now spoke gently to the students: "We see our future in you, and we hope you see us as your direction." Lunch proceeded with discipline. There was no need for correction. In the afternoon, participants were able to discuss their ideas on how to contribute what they had learned here to school and society by carrying on the Tzu Chi mission. The evening was a candlelight farewell party. Participants split into their small groups and again tearfully exchanged reflections and confessions; however, they no longer talked about wrongs in their personal lives, but about their own inconsiderate behaviors during the retreat and gratefulness to their team papa and mamas. The exchanging of greeting cards and phone numbers continued until lights were out and even afterward.

The commencement day finally arrived. After a usual morning exercise and disciplined breakfast, participants assembled in line at the lecture hall. They rehearsed the ritual for an hour until Cheng Yen arrived to give a sermon and light their candles. The severe corrections and disciplines of three days ago in the same hall were replaced with sentiments of appreciation and a sense of mission to "share the burden on Cheng Yen's shoulders." At the end of the commencement ceremony, as Cheng Yen walked down the central aisle on her way out of the hall, participants vowed as they had rehearsed, but with magnificently spirited voices and streaks of tears on their cheeks: "*Shangren,* we will always follow your footsteps!"[24]

The door of the hall remained open while the charismatic leader disappeared from sight, a crew of new youth corps members trailing in her wake. While still reveling in the thrill of collective vowing, the uniformed youngsters suddenly found themselves on the other side of the threshold. All officers disappeared without announcing a schedule for the participants. Straight rows and columns dispersed into running crowds, busily exchanging phone numbers and arranging car pools on their own to the train station. Participants no longer acted as a collectivity, but reverted back to being the individuals they were on the first day. Yet, unlike the colorful lines at the registration counter, they were now homogenized with one another from head to toe in blue shirts and white pants, and would incorporate their new experience, and hence their new identity, into their ordinary lives. As a veteran youth corps member poetically wrote: "So long! I can't take with me the beautiful mountains and wonderful waters of Hualian. I can't take with me a blade of grass or a piece of wood from the Abode. Yet I take with me a body of 'blue sky and white cloud.' "[25]

Similar to the Tzu Chi Train, the youth camp focuses even more on the center of the charismatic power, because the participants arrive home as individuals of multiple locales, not as an organized tour from one locality. Nevertheless, the significance of the youth camp lies less in the symbolism of pilgrimage than in its intensive transformation of individual identity through the Tzu Chi discourse. The youth camp is not just symbolic; it is a highly structured rite of passage that is meant to be a mechanism for producing a new Tzu Chi person from each participant. Its significance is twofold. First, in the Tzu Chi context, the youth camp incarnates the mechanism of commitment through indoctrination or, in Lindholm's term, the "formation of a 'new man' " that was often practiced in large-scale charismatic cases (Lindholm [1990] 1993: 113–116). Second, in the larger context of Taiwan, such a salient large-scale rite of passage for the youth has only been seen in the nationwide youth camps of recreational troupes and militant drills organized by the government-sponsored "China Youth Corps" (see Chapter 4). The officers of the Tzu Chi youth corps adamantly emphasize that their practice is according to Buddhist and particularly the Tzu Chi discourse and is, therefore, distinct from that of the China Youth Corps.

Nevertheless, the organization of the Tzu Chi youth camp does, in fact, resemble that of the China Youth Corps, with its military hierarchical titles of team leaders and the emphasis on physical drills and psychological indoctrination. Similar to Tzu Chi's adopted embodiment of "sign language song" from the China Youth Corps that is discussed in Chapter 4, the Tzu Chi youth camp is a process of transforming the same mechanism from its original discourse of the state to one of a civil society.

## The Nexus: Hospital Volunteer Retreat

Although both the youth civility retreat and the Tzu Chi Train expose different geographically based followers and prospective recruits to the context of the Tzu Chi headquarters, they ultimately differ in that the latter does not mean to transform participants, whereas the former does. The Tzu Chi Train does not extend the role of the participants beyond pilgrimage tourists, whereas the civility retreat transforms the participants through distinct processes of rites of passage, and solemnly expects them to return to their ordinary lives with a new Tzu Chi identity. A participant of the Tzu Chi Train may have snapshots taken at the headquarters and a positive impression of Tzu Chi. In contrast, a "graduate" of youth civility camp holds a certificate that is covered with a photo of his or her small group with the Venerable, and a sense of mission inscribed on this newly achieved identity. With this new identity, the youth is eligible to move along in the structure of the Tzu Chi experience, for example, to apply for one of the most advanced genres, the hospital volunteer retreat.

The hospital volunteer retreat is the most established genre among the circulation of followers' homecomings. It was frequently and highly recommended by my informants in Jiayi as the most revealing experience for an understanding of Tzu Chi. This genre retreat first appeared around the same time as the initial Tzu Chi Train in the early 1990s, when the "old" Tzu Chi Merit Association began to espouse, if not transform, into its new identity as a modern nonprofit proper. According to a "volunteer veteran soldier" (zhigong laobing), Ms. Yan, who had been a full-time volunteer at the Tzu Chi Hualian Hospital for more than thirteen years, the history of hospital volunteering began as early as the hospital's opening in 1986. After having participated in the free clinic that celebrated the hospital's opening, she saw the necessity for a regular supply of volunteers. She then spontaneously worked with those who were willing to participate, and took trips to speak about her particular volunteer experience to different Tzu Chi branches around the island (one of the minor forms of circulation). By the early 1990s, the large number of hospital volunteer applicants from different congregations resulted in a waiting period of a couple of years, despite the fact that, according to several veteran devotees, eligibility to participate was limited exclusively to commissioners.

Nevertheless, the demand for hospital volunteer stints continued to increase despite the limited eligibility. By 1998, Tzu Chi had designed hospital volunteer retreats that specifically adopted such growing title groups as the youth corps and teachers' club—though with some qualifiers, especially for youth, such as prerequisite experience in the general root-finding tour and civility camp. It is nevertheless a retreat exclusive to core title groups including commissioners, Compassion Faith corps members, their trainees, advanced youth corps members, and qualified members of the teachers' club. What is it that makes the hospital volunteer retreat so unusual?

The hospital volunteer retreat distinguishes itself from other Tzu Chi genres by overlapping both the hospital and the Abode: The participants practice in the hospital during the day and have accommodations at the Abode. It is the only retreat in which the primary content is not classes but actual practice in the two Tzu Chi organizations: volunteers practice insides the wards—the milieu of professional practices—and reveal their reflections on the practice to Cheng Yen every morning at the Abode.

The very processional form of "retreat," at the same time, distinguishes the nature of a Tzu Chi hospital volunteer from that of normative secular and religious hospital volunteers. Among the one hundred volunteers who work in the Tzu Chi hospital each day, thirty are Hualian local residents whose practice resembles that of regular volunteers in other hospitals: They come to fulfill their several-hour stints and return to their ordinary lives. Similar to secular volunteers in other hospitals, these local volunteers are not necessarily Tzu Chi followers, let alone core members. Yet the majority of volunteers, a total of seventy-two each day inside the hospital, are nonlocal residents who come to Hualian specifically for the volunteer retreat. Each retreat cycle consists of members of one title group from the same region—northern, central, southern Taiwan, or overseas. From the point when they gather at the train station in Hualian until they return to their train stations at home, they stay together and live completely in Tzu Chi context, twenty-four hours a day for seven days. During this period, the individual volunteer does not leave Tzu Chi edifices unless the whole retreat team visits nursing homes or the Hualian Prison. Different from any normative hospital volunteer practice and similar to other Tzu Chi genres of followers' circulation, the Tzu Chi hospital volunteer retreat is a state of liminality whereby participants bounded together as a collectivity are temporarily secluded from their daily lives and hence from individual status in the larger social context.

### A Fast-Paced Drill: A Day of Hospital Volunteering

The following is an inventory of a day in the hospital volunteer retreat. These activities overlap the above-described typical day at the Abode.
    At the Abode:

- 3:45 a.m. Morning call (wood hitting).
- Rush hours for restrooms and getting changed; move downstairs to the new lecture hall.
- 4:00 a.m. Morning ritual.
- 6:00 a.m. Breakfast.
- After breakfast: Grooming, for example, blow-drying and styling hair, and applying makeup; and doing chores (*chupuo*, literally, "going out to hills"), for example, cleaning restrooms, dormitory, and garden.
- 7:00 a.m. Volunteer morning meeting (*zhigong zaohui*).
- Agenda: Sign language song, salute, Cheng Yen's sermon of the day, and volunteers' testimonials (*xingde fenxiang*, sharing reflections).
- Primary conclusions of testimonials: "The supreme person says, filial piety now and charity now. Or else one will regret like those unfortunate patients."
- 8:00 a.m. Departure ritual.
- Form rows to salute the main hall, and then form two columns to exit the Abode and board the shuttle bus.

In the shuttle bus (fifteen minutes): Announcement, testimonials, jokes, sign language songs, and "follow me." Thank the chauffeur upon arrival at the hospital.
    In the hospital:

- Arrival ritual.
- Form rows to salute the mosaic portrait of "Buddha diagnosing" on the wall between social service office and registration at the hospital lobby.
- Getting ready to work.

- Inside the social service office: Distributing the yellow volunteer vests, known as "mini *jiasha*" (sangha's attires), and helping each other to straighten the attire.
- The work.
- Paired partners proceed to assigned wards, and follow the medical crew's morning rounds.
- Some follow the veteran volunteer to entertain the people at the waiting area with sign language songs and then return to the wards.
- 12:00 p.m. Lunch break.
- At the cafeteria inside the Still Thoughts Memorial Hall: Vegetarian food only; each volunteer dines on the voucher from the social service office, and with one's personal—called "environmental"—wares and utensils; each sits randomly, joins palms, closes eyes, whispers the prayer quietly, and begins eating and chatting. Staff and volunteers usually sit at separate tables.
- Taking a nap inside the dormitory of the Still Thoughts Memorial Hall.
- 2:00 p.m. Returning to assigned wards.
- Or, orientation classes instructed by staff members for teachers, youth, or other volunteer novices.
- And/or, "institutional visits," for example, Hualian Prison and veteran soldiers' nursing home *(renai zhi jia)* or household care *(jujia guan-huai)*.
- 5:00 p.m. Gathering at the social service office.
- Chatting, drinking teas, and sharing snacks while waiting for the shuttle bus.
- Team leader collects, counts, and returns volunteer vests to the administration of the social service office or properly stores them in a locked place.
- Departure ritual.
- Form rows to salute the mosaic of "Buddha diagnosing" at the lobby; dismissal, exit, and boarding.

In the shuttle bus: Announcement, testimonials, jokes, sign language songs, and "follow me." Thank the chauffeur upon arrival at the Abode. Form two columns and quietly walk on the pitch path toward the Abode.

At the Abode:

- Arrival ritual.
- Form rows to salute to the main hall; dismiss to the dining hall.

- Dinner.
- The nuns have set the dinner ready on the tables. Volunteers sit randomly, join palms, shut eyes, and mumble the prayer. Different from the free and relaxing atmosphere at lunch at the hospital cafeteria, there is no chatting at dinner at the Abode.
- Free time.
- Showering, doing laundry (by hand), line up for pay phones, writing, reading, and chatting.
- In the case of novice teachers and youth, evening programs follow free time for personal chores. These programs include, from first to sixth evening: Buddhist civility, small group discussion and preparation for next daily testimonials, senior nun's retrospective of the Abode, Aborigine songs and dances, veteran volunteers' update reports of community service, and foundation staff's update report of international relief.
- Returning to dorm.
- Preparing personal items for next morning's rush hour, getting ready to sleep.
- 9:30 p.m. "Still" (zhijing).
- 10:00 p.m. lights out.

The contents of the hospital volunteer retreat are much more focused than the array of introductions in the Tzu Chi Train and of orientations in the youth civility camp. Except for some of the evening programs for volunteer novices, all collective activities revolve around a cycle: practice at the hospital and reflections on the practice experience when outside the hospital, that is, in the shuttle bus and at the Abode.

### Narrating Volunteer Experience

The exclusiveness of the hospital volunteer retreat is partly a result of the hospital's limited capacity, and partly because of the prestige of its experience. This retreat is prestigious because it is the primary source of revealing stories that have been widely reproduced in oral presentations, printed material, and on tapes distributed among Tzu Chi followers. In other words, it is one of the most narrated experiences.

Yet the reproduction of volunteer experience narratives is the result of the sacredness of the experience. In other words, in Tzu Chi, volunteering at the hospital is not just what they do, it is also what they talk about—repeatedly.

This condition is substantiated by the pivotal mechanism of daily testimonials before Cheng Yen. This is where the nature of liminality in the three genres differs greatly: The participants of the Tzu Chi Train come to Hualian to receive and encounter; the youngsters in the civility camp come to learn and transform; and the volunteers are there to practice, to publicly make sense of their experience, and to affirm and reaffirm their identity in Tzu Chi.

The basic format of the morning testimonials is to describe cases in the wards and reflect upon and interpret them in light of Cheng Yen's teachings. However, the "best" testimonial is expressed in tears: the speaker weeps, and the audience sobs collectively. Tearful speeches tend to be those that relate the individual's reflections on the "true" stories of the hospital experience to personal life confessions. For example, a female volunteer described the contrast between her patience when listening to patients and her avoidance of her mother-in-law; in light of the volunteer experience, she tearfully confessed her mistake in disobeying filial piety. She concluded the testimonial by quoting Cheng Yen's "filial piety here and now."

At the same time, a testimonial is well delivered when it hits the core of volunteer experience: bringing one in close contact with various forms of human suffering. Good narratives reveal the speaker's empathy with the suffering of his or her patients. Such empathy can be drawn only from true stories of personal experiences with the patients. The testimonial should not be simply a categorical report of sickness and death that can be seen in any hospital or even in ordinary life, but a personal narrative of how the patient came to such suffering and how he or she feels and reflects from the sickbed. For example, in one testimonial, a volunteer recounted the recurring stories from the intensive care unit (ICU) that many patients came to their suffering from unsuccessful suicides compelled by family fights. In another example, a veteran volunteer vividly described the tangible "living dead" smell of a patient at the hospice who was suffering from cancer that resulted from smoking and chewing betel nuts. True stories of suffering conclude by signifying the preciousness of life. Volunteers often reiterated their gratefulness to the Venerable Cheng Yen because she grants them the unique firsthand experience of the "living hell" of the hospital while they are still healthy and capable of appreciating their lives before it is too late.[26]

It is precisely in this regard that the hospital volunteer retreat encounters suffering; from this encounter, experience comes to the forefront. With its emphasis on experience, the hospital volunteer retreat seems to be a paradox that contradicts the equally important discourse of Tzu Chi's practical side. On the one hand, an emphasis on addressing causes effectively through secular action (such as addressing the cause of sickness among the poor by building a state-of-the-art hospital) is what most distinguishes Tzu Chi from other religious and secular nongovernmental organizations. On the other hand, while volunteers clearly feel proud of their hospital, their testimonials tend to focus on the suffering rather than the curing. Moreover, in spite of the Tzu Chi focus on activism and tangible demonstrated action (of contribution), narratives of the hospital volunteer experience are about volunteers' personal transformation through witnessing misery, not about ending the misery itself.

In my view, this emphasis on suffering has to do with the linkage between experiencing the emotional expression of suffering and encountering the charismatic moment. As discussed in Chapter 4, the suffering that is witnessed and felt in the volunteer experience often leads to crying, which is exactly the same emotional response to encountering the charismatic appeal. In addition, as discussed in Chapter 1, one of the characteristics of Cheng Yen's charisma is her embodied and extreme emotional expression of sorrow and suffering. Although the ecstatic crying as a result of a charismatic moment may be different from the sorrowful crying that results from empathetic feelings toward the suffering in the volunteer experience, the extreme emotion that is generated and embodied in both is the same: weeping. It is therefore possible that the suffering so emphasized in the volunteer testimonials has to do with followers tapping into this experience for an emotional trigger and that it produces the same result as the extraordinary experience found in the charismatic moment.

This emphasis on experience has ironically become a source of tension inside the world of Tzu Chi. The original purpose of the morning testimonial was to make sure that the volunteers indeed worked mindfully with the patients as caregivers and listeners. However, the mandatory daily testimonial and its sacramental meanings from the chair of the charismatic leader have somehow turned the listening into story soliciting, a peculiar pursuit of misery. At the nexus of the hospital volunteer retreat, the two Tzu Chi organizations—the professional staff members and the religious volunteers—run counter to each other, in a contest over the narratives of patients' miseries.

When asked their views about and cooperation with the volunteers, most doctors began by thanking the volunteers because they are "nice" and "devoted." Some even specified the irreplaceable function and contribution of the volunteers to the hospitals. Nevertheless, as participant observation continued, examples revealed the tension between professional staff members and volunteers. The source of tension, from the staff's point of view, lies precisely in the devotion of volunteers. The religious realization that volunteers glean from the patients' suffering sometimes obscures the line. As a social worker said, "I understand they all have the pressure of 'reporting to *shangren*.' But understanding a patient takes a long time."

## Conclusion

This chapter presents the processional aspects of a charismatic movement in forms of circulation. The primary function of this circulation is to form a vertical tie between the headquarters and individual followers and secondarily to produce a horizontal net among the branches. The nature of Tzu Chi circulation does not lie in daily mundane tasks, but in a state of liminality that is temporarily bracketed from ordinary experience. In the milieu of liminality, the concentric whole unfolds into two major forms of circulating movements: divergence of the charismatic leadership from center to branches, and convergence of dispersed congregations into the center.

Liminality marks transition of status. In the centripetal forms of flow, the charismatic leader descends from the spiritual center, incarnates in person in front of followers of different locales, and exercises and reaffirms her outright authority over the mission of each branch. In the centrifugal forms of flow, followers from different regions immerse themselves in the center of the world of Tzu Chi, where they attest and share the knowledge of the Tzu Chi software and hardware, adopt the array of shared Tzu Chi symbols, render a sense of mission, transform themselves into a new identity within the collectivity, and make sense of miseries through the light of Cheng Yen's teachings.

It is precisely in the liminal power of recurring circulation that Tzu Chi exists time and again as a communitas of a charismatic movement. Here, liminality provides a sphere for identity transformation outside the mundane structure; it is, however, constructive toward a structure of commitment to the charismatic communitas. The leader's monthly walk "marks" her territory similarly to the king's progress described by Geertz (1973). Although the various forms of retreat and homecoming move in opposite directions, they are nevertheless structured toward the construction of identity in the charismatic center of the headquarters. In this regard, while not all retreat genres can be counted as pilgrimage, they echo much of the recent theoretical emphasis on the "structured" side of pilgrimage in charismatic examples (see Werbner 1998).

This combination of liminality and charismatic structure gives a sense of the commitment mechanism's form; the content itself, however, remains obscure. When the retreat or leader's visit concludes, the Tzu Chi identity that is created and reaffirmed in circulation does not become a fable. Such resilience requires a deep and unmediated feeling of shared identity between individuals in addition to the grand circulating system of maintenance. Chapter 4 presents the structure of emotions in the Tzu Chi experience.

# — 4 —

# Weeping and Musical Corporeality

Crying—individually and collectively—is a common experience in Tzu Chi. The first Tzu Chi follower who spoke to me said that she did not become a pious follower until she had an uncontrollable crying experience during her visit to the Still Thoughts Abode. Since then, I have heard many followers mention crying, and I have seen many of them do so. More than once during my stay at Tzu Chi headquarters, I found myself crying along with the followers. Throughout my fieldwork, Tzu Chi followers frequently asked me: "So, how do you like us so far?" I replied with various answers, most of the time receiving sympathetic looks for my anthropological jargon, until the day I said: "I was reduced to tears." The Tzu Chi followers then smiled their approval.

Musical corporeality[1] is no less common than weeping in Tzu Chi. Sign language song or *shouyüge* (literally, "hand-language song") means using sign language to interpret lyrics, while the song is played, sung, or both, in the background. In Tzu Chi, sign language song is less a translation for the deaf than a performance for all, since it is always performed collectively, whether deaf people are present or not. The practice of sign language song is omnipresent and perhaps indispensable to the lay world of Tzu Chi. Every event and ceremony, except for the strictly religious sutra recitals, includes a sign language song performance. Every local branch's regular weekly schedule reserves a day or two for teaching and practicing sign language song. When Tzu Chi volunteers deliver relief to the needy or care for hospital patients, they form a row to sing and mime songs for the recipients and invite the audience to join the performance.

Why are Tzu Chi followers lachrymose? Why is crying so important for them? And why would a group of tearful Buddhists be so interested in sign language song at the same time? Both crying and sign language song are relatively new to Buddhism. They may not be "new" in the sense of invention, but they represent what has remained obscure in Buddhism. No source has said that a Buddhist does not cry; yet few, if any, studies have been done on tearful Buddhists. Because crying is a repeated and shared experience among a great number of followers of such a prominent Buddhist movement as Tzu Chi, the experience itself calls for an explanation. Similarly, *shouyüge* is not found in Buddhist texts or among former Buddhist groups. Certainly, many things that Taiwanese Buddhists do nowadays did not appear in the texts, such as garbage recycling, which is also a "modern" secular practice recently adopted by Buddhist groups, including Tzu Chi and *Fagushan* (Dharma Drum Mountain), a large Chan Buddhist movement in Taiwan. However, only Tzu Chi followers zealously practice sign language song, and only Tzu Chi makes crying central to the experience of religion.[2]

This chapter focuses on understanding crying and sign language song in the Tzu Chi context, not only because both are indispensable to the present practice of Tzu Chi and are unprecedented in Buddhism, but also because in many respects they are opposites and cannot be considered separately. When, where, how, and why Tzu Chi followers cry, and who they are, seems the opposite of when, where, how, and why Tzu Chi followers practice sign language song, and who *they* are. Crying and sign language song, I argue, are the opposite ends of a continuum of emotions between ecstasy and formalization, as they are manifested in present-day Tzu Chi. This continuum did not emerge until sign language song, the formalized collective embodiment, recently became the characteristic performance of Tzu Chi—at exactly the same time that the movement rapidly organized itself to accommodate its burgeoning growth in membership. In other words, the constellation of ecstasy and formalization indicates the emotional routinization of a charismatic movement.

## Crying in Taiwan

In Taiwan, as in other societies such as the United States, sobbing, like laughing, is not uncommon among theater audiences. Legendary tragedies, from *Liang Shanbo yü Zhu Yingtai* (a classic Chinese version of *Romeo and Juliet*) in 1963 to the 1997 hit *Titanic,* have reduced audiences to tears. Such melodramatic crying also pervades the living rooms of many households during some of the prime-time television drama serials.

Individual crying as a performance is a female activity. In Taiwanese opera,[3] there is a distinctive crying tone that an actress employs when she sings in a tragedy. She uses a broken and nasal voice, and frequently stops when her throat closes, sobbing, gasping, and wailing.

In the political context, a woman's tearful orations can be a powerful means of protest. During the repressive period of the authoritarian regime in Taiwan in the late 1970s, when the government sentenced political dissidents to prison, their wives would take revenge by running for parliament. Their campaign strategy was to draw attention to their victim status by delivering tearful public speeches and broadcasting on the street a Taiwanese folk song, "Wang ni zao gui" ("Waiting for You to Come Home," along the lines of "Tie a Yellow Ribbon Round the Old Oak Tree"). The tears of these female candidates brought initial success to the opposition movement (Dangwai fandui yundong): They not only raised considerable campaign funds but also won a great many votes against the ruling party.

In ordinary life, women are expected to cry at both weddings and funerals, often with diverse implications. While Gallin (1966) argues that a bride weeps at her wedding when she leaves her parents as an approved expression of filial piety, Martin (1988) sees a female-gender ideology behind the bride's tears, wherein women perceive weddings to be like death. Wailing is indeed commonly keyed to funerals (Ahern [1973] 1986: 225; Harrell 1979). Widows and children in mourning are expected to cry during the funeral. Many people still consider dramatic crying to be a statement of the widow's chastity and the children's filial piety (for cases in other Chinese societies, see Watson 1988). Women's tearful statements, as in the 1970s political opposition movement, are expected and emphasized in funereal contexts. It is not uncommon—especially in rural areas such as the field site of my major study in southern Taiwan—for people to hire professional female criers in mourning dress to deliver tearful statements.[4] The most dramatic performance is a solo female crier who combines wailing and singing in a crying tone on behalf of the deceased's family members.[5] In listing the members of the family, the crying performance clearly shows onlookers the deceased's status in the kinship system and the strength of the family. Whether the women's crying during weddings and funerals is emotional or formal, their tears are the important "emotion work" (Hochschild 1983) in the ritual whereby the dead are properly remembered by the survivors as part of their family line.

Male crying, in contrast, is not culturally favored in Taiwan. For example, the term *hau-lam min* (in Minnan, "face of a mourning son," meaning "mournful look") denotes an unpleasant person who easily produces tears. This association of lachrymose men with mourning suggests the social undesirability of male weeping, since death, funerals, and mourning are considered polluting (people in mourning, for example, are expected to shun weddings).

As described in the common saying, "a real man does not easily shed his tears" *(naner youlei bu qingtan)*, men are capable of weeping, but they are supposed to hold back their tears by virtue of their masculinity, except in the case of otherwise approved causes. Political concern is an example in point. Male literati may be compelled to express their profound concern for the whole country through tears (for example, the poem of Cheng Ziang of the Tang dynasty, *nian tiandi zhi youyou du changran er leixia* [I think of heaven and earth, boundless, endless, and I am all alone and my tears fall down]). Historic stories such as *xinting duiqi* describe the unbearable sorrow of exiled Han literati for their lost homeland and hence, lost political power. In other words, the prohibition on male crying applies to personal concerns, but not to "higher" causes of emotion in the Confucian ranking, such as nationalism. Even today, particularly in the 1990s it is not novel for male politicians to weep during public speeches; they do so to express their apologies, their repression, and their hopes for resolution. However, in contrast to the women's wailing in political protest that is similar to the dramatization of an actress's theatrical performance, the men lower their faces as they weep, gulp, or simply hold tears in their eyes to be visible in a close-up.

The recurrence of such emotional expression in political oratories has drawn suspicions as to its authenticity and criticisms of its purpose as a performance—political "emotion work," so to speak. A psychiatrist in Taiwan interprets the crying of these men as an act of *sajiao* (Wang 1998: 29–37)—a term that could be loosely translated as "whining" in English and is very close to the Japanese *amae*, which means "to depend and presume upon another's love or bask in another's indulgence" (Doi 1992: 8).[6] Of course, a woman's crying also can be commonly perceived as *sajiao* and can be a manipulative strategy. Proverb has it that a woman gets her way first by crying, then by making a scene, and finally by [threatening] to hang herself *(yiku ernao sanshangdiao)*. Behind these perceptions of adults who use crying as an embodied strategy lies the association between crying and children.

Children's crying is tolerated, but not encouraged. According to the developmental psychologist Heidi Fung's ethnographic research in middle-class families, when children cry in public, parents remove them from the scene to calm them down. While there are some neutral terms used to refer to a crying child—*ai-khau gin-a* (crying baby in Minnan), and *aiku gui* (literally, "crying ghost" in Mandarin), parents in Fung's research tended not to tolerate children's crying and would shame the child who was crying instead of the sibling whose transgression had caused the emotion. While crying by women has vengeful power in politics and demonstrates gender morality at funerals, children's crying is associated with the effects of supernatural forces. I have seen parents comfort a crying baby by assuring it *"Bo oan, bo oan"* (in Minnan, "No one is cursing you! No one is cursing you!"). According to Fung, if children continue to cry, parents of various social backgrounds resort to folk healing—*siu-kia* ⁿ (in Minnan) or *shoujing* (in Mandarin); literally, "removing the shock"—a practice to expel the demon from the body.[7]

In contrast to the impression that Chinese society treats emotion as trivial (Potter and Potter 1990: 180–195), crying in Taiwan is less a display of a single emotion than a means of expression that is rendered meaningful in different contexts. While the conventional understanding of tears as a signal of emotion applies to melodramatic crying, weeping as an expression is often an object of dramatization and interpretation. The cultural construction of tears discriminates domains for women, men, and children. Ideology comes into play in adult weeping, yet the interplay between ideology and crying differ according to gender: Women's tears at funerals help to perpetuate the ideology of patrilineal descent, whereas the acceptance of men's tears is subject to the Confucian ideology that ranks nationalism over personal concerns. In addition, crying is often perceived as a strategic embodiment in both genders. The effectiveness of such a strategy stems from the transformative capacity of crying that allows adults to temporarily adopt childlike characteristics and hence a tacit position of inferiority that fits in well with a soft spot in a hierarchical culture. Furthermore, a kind of dangerous power is perceived in the performance crying of women and in the uncontrollable crying of children.

## Crying in Tzu Chi

Crying in Tzu Chi is not considered to be a ritual. It does not have a clear beginning or ending (in fact, in many cases, the weeping is unstoppable), nor does it have a formal course. Although followers often trace their adherence to Tzu Chi back to their first crying experience, and although crying is common in many Tzu Chi rituals, it is nevertheless a spontaneous experience. It is, to borrow Roland Barthes's description of style, "the private portion of the ritual;" it rises up from the follower's "myth-laden depth and unfolds beyond [her] area of control" (Barthes 1967: 17; cited by Douglas [1970] 1982: 69).

The following is a preliminary classification of the examples of crying collected during my fieldwork.[8] I have sorted the examples into five categories—religious consonance; charismatic appeals; rituals; volunteer experiences; and reproach, conflict, and shock—based on each one's context, that is, when, where, and how. Each category is named by the key element of its context, key in the sense that the element is distinctive and may elicit tears on its own. These categories, therefore, are not exhaustive or exclusive. For instance, weeping due to religious consonance and to charismatic appeals often occurred in a ritual context; and tears were also shed when a testimonial speaker recalled the leader or recounted volunteer experiences. The order of classification generally flows from the most religious instances to the most mundane. Dramatic crying—an unstoppable flood of tears that continues until the person nearly faints—tends to cluster in the religious sphere. Crying in contexts other than the most religious tends to be sobbing or weeping, but may nevertheless overcome the followers in some examples.

## Religious Consonance

Examples of uncontrollable floods of tears mainly occurred in the context of a strictly Buddhist ritual or setting. These examples can be categorized further into two sorts: chanting Buddha's or bodhisattvas' names, and physically facing the statues of Buddha and the bodhisattvas in the main hall of the Abode. The two sometimes overlap. I call this crying context "religious consonance" because the bodily experience of a rush of tears in these situations is immediately consonant with—and unconsciously corresponds to— the purely religious context, for example, entering a Buddhist hall and uttering a bodhisattva's name. Some examples of this type of crying are given below.

The first example occurred in the context of a religious setting. Ms. Li had been a general member of Tzu Chi for many years before she visited the

Abode. As a tourist, she entered the main hall of the Abode with her mother and daughter to pay respect to the three statues—Śakyamuni Buddha, Guanyin Bodhisattva, and Dizang Bodhisattva. Upon entering the quiet and minimally decorated main hall, Ms. Li suddenly began crying uncontrollably until she nearly fainted. Her companions, who were shocked by her outburst, removed her from the scene. This experience led to Ms. Li's lifelong commitment to the Tzu Chi mission.

The second example took place during a sutra recital in the Abode (see Chapter 3 for a description of a typical day at the Abode).[9] Ms. Lu had been a core member of Tzu Chi for years before her retreat in the summer of 1998. She joined the morning class every day during her retreat. One day, as the class was chanting the Eighty-Eight Buddha Sutra, she burst out crying every time she uttered a bodhisattva's name, until she too nearly fainted. She was rather embarrassed, for her uncontrollable crying seemed to have broken the tranquility of the ritual.

This sort of crying during sutra recitals sometimes recurs. As the following example shows, tears of religious consonance may last through a series of sutra recitals. Shugui had never been married. She had been thinking of joining the Tzu Chi monastic order, but instead became a core member while dealing with the ebb and flow of her social and family life. Years later, when her mother passed away, she disposed of her scanty belongings and headed for the Abode to realize her wish of "becoming a nun so as to bestow on my mother the greatest merit." The master granted her permission to stay and she moved into the familiar Abode with a new identity. She had attended the morning class on her countless previous volunteer retreats, yet from the first day she joined the convent, she cried uncontrollably in each daily sutra class throughout the week.

In addition to sutra recitals, tears of religious consonance are shed in some Tzu Chi rituals that involve chanting Buddha's or bodhisattvas' names, a common—and perhaps focal—practice in Pure Land Buddhism as a path to salvation. Although sutra recitals were never the focus for Tzu Chi lay followers, many of their rituals are nevertheless Buddhist rites and therefore involve repeating Buddha's or bodhisattvas' names. The most common among these rituals are *chaoshan* (worshipping the mountain, a short and solemn pilgrimage in which the worshippers walk and prostrate themselves all the way to the monastery or convent) and *zhunian* (assisting with mourning, or "supplement mourning," literally translated as "helping to repeat [Buddha's name]"). Both rituals are common to other Buddhist groups and temples. Tzu Chi followers "worship the mountain" toward the Abode on special occasions such as the anniversary of their founding. "Supplement mourning" is one of the voluntary services that followers provide as a way to support each other in misfortune. In addition to Buddhist rites, Tzu Chi followers repeat Buddha's name throughout a special ritual, *dian* or *chuan xindeng* (lighting or passing the heart candles).[10] This ritual takes place at the end of every relatively important meeting, such as the year-end convocation, and of *yuanyuan* (fulfilling the bond or relation)—the "graduation" from special retreats or camps. It always follows the master's sermon when she is present.

Although a common practice of Buddhism, chanting Buddha's name often results in tears of religious consonance among Tzu Chi followers.[11] Collective crying during the Tzu Chi ritual of heart candles is a case in point. The year-end convocation of the Japan branch in Tokyo in 1997 followed the "normal" sequence of the Tzu Chi ceremony—from mission reports, announcements, and testimonial speeches, to sign language song, and to the closing rite of "heart candle." The space, decorated with yellow draperies at the front with Buddha's portrait hanging in the center, was a temporarily

Ritual—Worshipping the Mountain

converted Chinese restaurant owned by a local core member. The participants consisted of a disciple who studied in Tokyo, local core members and
a few representatives from Taiwan, local general members and Taiwanese
students, and a couple of Japanese. After the disciple's sermon, the meeting
proceeded to the lighting of the heart candles. While candles were distributed among the audience, the emcee called upon everyone to stand. In a
"normal" Tzu Chi setting in Taiwan, the heart candle rite proceeds with a
Tzu Chi song in the background. However, without having had rehearsal
and lacking stereo equipment, the five core members—while they moved
from backstage to the front where a disciple stood by the yellow draperies—
informally agreed to conduct the rite by simply repeating Buddha's name.
When the light was turned off, they stood still facing the audience and
began chanting: "*nanmo benshi shijia muoni fo.*" The disciple lit the candle
of each of the core members, who then lit the candles of the first row of the
audience, and this continued from one row to another, down to the last row.
The crowded little room was dark except for rows of tiny lights from the
candles; there was no sound except for repetitive chanting. I thought the ritual was perfectly tranquil until I noticed the expressions on the faces of the
front core members—they were overcome with tears and struggled to continue chanting and to hold their candles still!

## Charismatic Appeal

Almost every follower who became a devotee before the completion of the
Tzu Chi hospital in Hualian and the organization's ensuing rapid development said they were immediately overcome with tears at their first encounter with Cheng Yen. The setting of their crying experience varied from
the living room in a follower's apartment to the Abode, but these meetings
were more intimate than has often been the case since the 1990s, when
Cheng Yen began to give mainly large-scale sermons. While the crying
experiences of early followers were usually less dramatic than in some cases
of religious consonance, it struck those concerned as inexplicable. In my
conversations with early followers, whenever I managed to ask, "Did you
cry when you saw the master?" their expressions changed. Their eyes
opened wide, they became pensive and sighed: "Yes, I cried."

Many of them said that during the first few years they consistently began to cry whenever they saw the master in person. Although such inexplicable crying generally stopped after a time, some were overcome with

tears whenever they thought about the master. For instance, a founding core member, *Jingheng,* told me she never delivered a speech or testimonial, *gia mai-kut* ("holding the microphone," in Minnan), for fear of dissolving in tears and becoming speechless. "I cried whenever I thought about *shifu* ['the master,' that is, the Venerable Cheng Yen]," she said, "let alone talk about her." In another instance (briefly mentioned in Chapter 1) during our interview, a veteran devotee named *Jingying,* who was also the leader of the premier sign language song team, described the extraordinarily selfless moment she had with Cheng Yen that led to her lifelong commitment:

> It was in the early days of Tzu Chi when *shangren* was still endeavoring to build our first hospital. The circumstance then was not optimistic, but *shangren* was resolute for the mission. When she said, "I am just a nun. I have no money, no belongings. But I have this life. As long as I am alive, I pursue this dream of a hospital," I was compelled by her determination to ask myself, what can I do for her?

At this moment, *Jingying* paused and took out a handkerchief to dry the tears that were pouring down her face.

Cheng Yen's charismatic capacity to induce tears not only lingered over time but also traveled across space. Devotees shed tears outside Taiwan and in the absence of personal contact with Cheng Yen. For instance, Ms. Kang, the former coordinator of the New York branch, said she found herself crying in the kitchen when she first listened to one of Cheng Yen's tapes, which led to her commitment to Tzu Chi without having a personal encounter with Cheng Yen. While carrying out the mission in a foreign country that her adored Venerable Cheng Yen could never visit because of her frail health, the only comfort and encouragement Ms. Kang had whenever her commitment wavered was looking at Cheng Yen's photo. As she moved her eyes away from me, she said: "I looked at her photo and said to myself, 'Didn't you promise her to carry on the Tzu Chi mission, to walk on bodhisattva's path in each life?' Leave Tzu Chi? No way! Just looking at her photo makes me cry."

In addition to individual crying, collective crying in ritual contexts is often related to Cheng Yen's charismatic appeal. For instance, the graduation from a Tzu Chi youth corps summer camp in 1998 ended as usual with the rite of the heart candle. As this took place at the headquarters, Cheng Yen gave a speech before the rite and lit the candles of the two columns along the central aisle. Everyone in these columns then lit the candle of his or her neighbor. In contrast to the happenstance chanting at the Japan branch, the Tzu Chi youth had rehearsed in detail. Against the background music, Cheng Yen lit the candles from front to rear en route to the exit. When everyone's candle was lit and the master was about to exit the hall, all the participants vowed in unison: "*Shangren* [the supreme person], we shall always follow your steps." As I turned my eyes from the master to my fellow participants, I was moved by the sight of so many young faces covered with tears.

## Rituals

The ritual context, as mentioned above, has been a major arena for crying. In many testimonials, tears overcame speakers while audiences sobbed and passed each other tissues. Crying is also common in rituals like "heart candle," "supplemental mourning," and "worshipping the mountain." However, not all these rituals lead to tears. Crying is often found when these rituals overlap religious consonance (such as chanting Buddha's name) and charismatic appeals (such as vowing to the master collectively), as described above. In a slightly different vein, the practice of sign language song, especially to the song "*Mama*" (mother), and during a wedding held at the Abode also drew floods of tears.[12]

## Volunteer Experience

As volunteer work in the hospital and visiting the poor composes the core of Tzu Chi practice and experience, many participants found themselves crying after having contact with miserable poverty, illness, and suffering. For instance, a veteran hospital volunteer described in her speech that a group of Tzu Chi youth who had just returned from their visit to a destitute Aborigine household burst out crying at dinner. They could not bear the striking contrast between their opulent meal and the scanty bite shared among the children of that poverty-stricken household. In another example, a woman once testified to her first mission of "visiting the poor" as follows:

> I wore a tight skirt and high heels, navigating behind my commissioner and team coordinator to visit a poor family. But I cried all the way home from my visit to the poor. In all my life, I have never imagined or seen such

miserable poverty. All I had cared about was enjoying my own life of luxury. I had never cared about others, never cared about what's going on in society.

As mentioned in Chapter 3, hospital volunteers often focused on suffering instead of curing in their testimonials of the hospital experience. Narratives of suffering often led the speakers as well as the audience to weep. For example, during a speech delivered by a veteran hospital volunteer, she described a young boy of a poor family who was burnt to a fatal degree during his work as a laborer. Nevertheless, the first thing he said upon regaining consciousness was: "Can I go back to work now? I must go back to work, or else my little sisters and brothers have nothing to eat!" The speaker paused, and the female commissioners next to me dropped their heads, weeping.

In another example, a new volunteer, who was a relatively ineloquent speaker, reported nervously through the microphone at the morning testimonial that she had been assigned to work at the hospice. Then she continued to report on a patient who had remained quiet, but nevertheless broke the ice and looked happy when he was enjoying ice cream. The next day upon returning to the hospice, she was surprised to find that the patient had passed away. "But he was happy yesterday . . . and he died." She had no words but only tears to elaborate her feelings.

## Reproach, Conflict, and Shock

Tears may overcome Tzu Chi followers after being corrected for mistakes by the master or by fellow followers, or after a long bout of intragroup tensions. For instance, I attended a closed meeting of core members at an overseas branch that was held right after a successful fund-raising dinner party. In contrast to the celebratory atmosphere we had just experienced during the event, the closed meeting turned out to be an outbreak of tensions. The event coordinator began her speech by showing her gratitude to all the volunteers and immediately burst out crying and gasping as she criticized herself for not doing a good job in preparing for the event. Later, I learned that the coordinator had endured a leadership crisis among the core members of her branch during the event's preparation. She had managed to complete the event successfully despite the intragroup tension, but the tense emotion that had been constrained nevertheless had to find its outlet in the postevent meeting.

## Who Are the Tearful Ones?

Almost all the crying examples I have are from women. Although I was told that men also shed tears, especially when giving testimonials and confessions, I have rarely seen men cry.[13] Among the cases I collected, almost all the early followers—only female—share the crying experience. As Tzu Chi grew to its massive scale, the crying experience in the contexts of religious consonance and charismatic appeal became diluted among its countless followers. For example, most of the followers in Dalin—a recent development of Tzu Chi—did not recall a crying experience of religious consonance or charismatic appeal.[14] However, crying continues in the other three contexts— that is, ritual, volunteer experience, and conflict and tension—especially among females.

Does Cheng Yen cry? More than once, I heard followers say: "The master was so heartbroken that she cried [in her speech]." When asked if they actually saw her cry, the answer was rather intriguing: "I couldn't see her closely. But she sounded like she was crying. I felt she was crying." Whether the master indeed weeps or not, her followers believe that she does. Yet Cheng Yen has mentioned in Tzu Chi publications that she has been tearless since her father's death forty years ago—the tragedy that led her to leave home and become a Buddhist nun. In a newspaper interview about earthquake relief in Taiwan in 1999, the master said: "Do you know how much I wish to cry? . . . At the end of the deepest sorrow, one is speechless. Just do it!"

## Why Do Tzu Chi Devotees Cry? Interpretations of Crying

Most people who cried in the Tzu Chi settings could not explain why they did it: "I don't know why, I just cried and cried. And I couldn't stop." Among those who could explain, crying in different contexts had different meanings, as discussed below.

### An Expression of Guilt and Self-Pity

Tears are expressions of guilt and self-pity in the contexts of reproach, shock, and tension. For example, at the end of a Tzu Chi ceremony, the emcee made a mistake in the agenda. To her dismay, Cheng Yen gently reproved her for the error: "Why is it not well prepared?" The emcee spoke to me through her tears afterward: "*Shangren* [the supreme person, that is, the master] contributes every second of her life to the mission. And my mistake wasted a precious moment in her life. How could I?"

Examples are also found in reproaches or corrections between followers. Ms. Chen was a housewife who had a well-to-do family background. Like many followers, she joined Tzu Chi because of her attraction to the charismatic leader, but she was barely aware that she would have to get along with other followers so that they all could collectively fulfill the leader's mission. During her first hospital volunteer retreat, she found it rather frustrating to keep up with the fast-paced schedule and to obey the strict house rules in the Abode dormitory. At the end of an exhausting day, she washed her clothes by hand like everyone else, but she naively dumped them in the dryer and turned it on. A veteran volunteer shouted at her: "How could you use the machine for two to three pieces of clothes? Don't you know you must not use it until you collect at least three persons' loads? What a waste of electricity! Don't you know how precious the resource is and how hard the master and her disciples work to get by?" With shock and regret, Ms. Chen burst out crying. She later recounted: "I had never been yelled at in my life. She was so loud and I was shell shocked. And there was nothing I could do to right my wrong."

Compared to crying in other contexts, those who cried from guilt and shock were rarely comforted, let alone receiving approval from other followers or Cheng Yen; they were simply left alone with their tears. For this reason, tears of guilt and self-pity are the least significant in understanding Tzu Chi. In contrast, tears shed by testimonial speakers that embodied confessions of a sense of guilt—induced by the striking experience of volunteer missions—received the approval of other Tzu Chi followers. Tearful confessions that recount volunteer experiences are reproduced in printed material and audiotapes, and they are aired on the Tzu Chi television channel. The different responses to tears of guilt seem to parallel the discriminated domains of crying by men in Taiwanese culture. In the same way that men's tears are accepted when they are in response to such higher-ranking sentiments as nationalism but despised in response to personal concerns, Tzu Chi encourages confessional tears, since the emotion resonates with more universal humanitarian concerns, and reproaches crying due to an individual's failure in missions.

### Contagious Crying

Crying is contagious, especially in ritual contexts and volunteer experiences. It works very much like the laugh tracks on television shows. Contagious crying is mostly sobbing and is not as dramatic as some cases of crying in the contexts of religious consonance and charismatic appeal. For example, by the end of a "supplement mourning" ritual that I participated in at the Tzu Chi hospital, many volunteers were weeping. One said: "I don't know why I cried. I saw you cry and I saw her cry. A moment later, I found myself crying, too."

Another example took place at a wedding I attended at the Abode. A reception in the courtyard followed the formal wedding in the main hall. Although it was meant to be a party, the seating arrangement was the same as that of the daily morning testimonial: Cheng Yen sat at the center against the front door of her living quarters, facing the back of the main hall, while all the others were seated in several columns at her sides. In the middle of the party, the bride, a professional soprano, spontaneously stood up and sang a song to praise Cheng Yen. While singing, she took the groom by the hand and they fell on their knees at Cheng Yen's feet. Except for the singing, this act very much resembled the farewell to the bride's parents that is traditional in Chinese weddings. As tears streaked down the bride's cheeks, the follower next to me began sobbing and I handed her a pack of tissues. She took one tissue and then handed the pack to the follower next to her. It was passed all the way to the end of my row and then row by row to the front. Afterward, the women smiled and sighed while drying their faces (and thanking me for my well-timed tissues): "Can't help it. [We're] really touched. We are a bunch of weepy people."

## Redemption

Uncontrollable floods of tears are found primarily in the context of religious consonance. Followers' interpret religious consonance crying as a sign of redemption. For example, the woman who cried at morning sutra recitals in the Abode described to me how she felt: "Every time I chanted a bodhisattva's name, I felt I was embraced by someone. Someone I could rely on. Someone in front of whom I could act like a spoiled child. I could cry like a baby."

Interestingly, one of the followers who sobbed while chanting Buddha's name at the heart candle rite in Japan gave me a similar description: "I felt close to Buddha, as if I was taken care of and protected by Buddha. I felt cozy and safe."

The woman who cried at the end of *chaoshan* (worshipping the mountain) spoke to me with tears and sweat glistening on her face, clearly in a state of excitement:

Yes, I cried, especially at the moment of *ru shanmen* [entering the compassion gate; referring here to the gate of the Abode]. You know, it's about the end of *chaoshan*. And our Abode was finally in my sight. I felt as if I was seeing home, as if I had finally returned home. I couldn't stop crying then . . . I also cried at home when I chanted sutras. Sometimes I felt I saw *Guanyin pusa* [Guanyin Bodhisattva]. People said I must have been a nun in my last life. I am so lucky to be a follower of *shifu* [the master, that is, the Venerable Cheng Yen].

## Charismatic Ecstasy

Cheng Yen is frail, short, and often described by her followers as phenomenally beautiful. The experience of encountering her often leads to sudden ecstasy and feelings of disintegration. A woman described her first experience of seeing Cheng Yen in the morning testimonial at the Abode:

It was in this same court and in front of this same door under this same banner inscribed by the president. I was seated like you [the audience]. And I saw a master come out of the door and take the microphone and slowly bow while greeting us: "Amitabha." Her face is so beautiful, her movement so graceful, and her voice so gentle. I have never had such a beautiful moment in my life. At that moment, I cried, I confessed! I confessed!

She began her speech joyously, gradually raising her voice until it became shrill, and then was suddenly overcome by tears. She had to pause for a moment while covering her mouth with her hand and weeping.

While Cheng Yen's charisma left many followers in a state of ecstatic disintegration, as would a momentary contact with divinity, others—especially veteran devotees—spoke of the transforming power of such ecstasy on an individual life. It may linger over decades and eventually crystallize as a lifelong commitment to the master's mission. For example, I asked *Jingheng*— the founding core member who could never deliver her retrospective in public for fear of uncontrollable crying (see above; also Chapter 1)—why she cried whenever she thought about Cheng Yen. Her narrative conveys a subtle reference to Margery Wolf's (1972) notion of "uterine family":

It's *beixin* [literally, "sorrowful heart"]. Whenever I think of the master's *beixin,* I can't help crying. When the master announced [in 1979] that she was determined to build a hospital, most [followers] felt overwhelmed by the difficulty [of raising such a huge sum]. But it was the happiest moment in my life. People said the happiest day in a woman's life is on the day of her son's wedding. On that day, I didn't feel a thing. Then people said the happiest moment would come when my daughter-in-law gave birth to my first grandson. So I waited. Yet when it happened, I didn't feel much at all. But I was never happier than the day the master told us that we would build a hospital together!

## Leader's Interpretation: Lost Family Reunion

Many followers, especially the early disciples, who cried whenever they saw the master, asked Cheng Yen for an explanation. She said it is the *"yuan"* (predestined bond)[15] between them, deeply fixed in a past life or several past lives. "It's like a lost wanderer who finally found his or her family after a long journey," the master continued. "You cry when you finally see your family after a long absence."

The interpretations to this point are consistent. Crying is ecstasy triggered by, and in response to, charismatic and religious appeals. Uncontrollable floods of unmediated tears embody the extraordinarily selfless experience that stands at the core of charismatic movements. Contagious crying and the tearful confessions of guilt are the extended domains of selfless emotion that Tzu Chi distinctly creates by grounding the charismatic appeal in its human- itarian missions. The core of charisma is the pursuit of the extraordinary experience rather than rational concern for the growth of the movement (Greenfeld 1985; Lindholm [1990] 1993; Weber [1946] 1958). For this rea- son, charismatic movements often face the challenge that the extraordinary moment that exclusively stems from contact with the personal appeal of the leader is of a limited capacity. Tzu Chi uniquely extends the domains of self- less feelings into the volunteer experience and its related ritual contexts. The selfless state of emotions can be reached not only through contacts with the religious and charismatic divinity, but also through carrying out the master's mission and in the rituals that draw references from the master's appeal. As a result, Tzu Chi followers—as an army of a humanitarian mission—are a group of people who do not shun misery but instead look for and embrace it. The interpretation of crying as a homecoming—like a child, to a family reunion—suggests that the importance of crying for Tzu Chi people lies exactly in its expressive embodiment of redemption. In the Tzu Chi context, such ecstasy has a transcendental transformative effect on the followers and leads them by the thousands to bind together and carry out the leader's humanitarian missions for the rest of their lives.

Crying in Tzu Chi is strongly associated with religion, charisma, and the mission of compassion. Although it is often contagious, its source is nevertheless individual spontaneous emotion. It has long existed in Tzu Chi and tends to be shared among women. The interpretations of crying by Cheng Yen and her followers draw upon images of the female, motherhood, and family domains.

## Musical Corporeality: Sign Language Song in Taiwan

The theatrical performance and the "follow me" (or the "collective rhythm," namely, collective bodily movements in unison) versions of sign language song differ in their history in Taiwan, although both types had departed from their original function of translation for the deaf before they entered Tzu Chi.

The first collective sign language song genre, or at least the term *shouyüge*, seems to have appeared in the 1977 debut of a drama group that consisted of deaf students from art colleges. They were led by two teachers, one who had just returned to Taiwan with her master's degree in drama from the University of Oregon, and the other an American with a master's degree in language education from the University of California who taught sign language at the YWCA (Young Women's Christian Association) (*Lianhe bao* or *United Daily*, November 18, 1977). After the successful debut, the group was invited to tour for most military entertainment events. Nevertheless, for unknown reasons, the group disappeared in two years, but the genre continues in colleges as an extracurricular activity.

The performance eventually evolved to the "dance" genre and was clearly publicized through a legendary popular television program, "Five Lights Prize" (*"Wu deng jiang"*), around 1983. The show featured various competitions that ranged from singing to juggling. It ran the sign language song competition for a long time. The final champion was an operator at then state-run China Telecom, who wore costumes and danced on the stage while signing the lyrics with dramatic facial expressions.

Many colleges today include a sign language song club among other extracurricular activities. Each year there is a collegiate tournament of sign language song performances. Sometimes, performers who are dressed like cheerleaders dance rock 'n' roll while miming the lyrics.

The popularization of sign language song and its evolution into "follow me" both took place in 1983 and have much to do with the youth culture. The variation seems to have been invented by a teacher of the Boy Scouts known as Teacher Dai who promoted it in a television program, "College Town" *("Daxue Cheng")*. Compared to the more mass-oriented program that promoted the dance genre, "College Town" was part of a "social group" called *Jiuguo Tuan* (China Youth Corps) or by its full name, *Zhonghua Minguo Qingnian Fangong Jiuguo Tuan* (the Youth Corps of Anti-Communism and National Salvation of the Republic of China). Founded by the late president Chiang Ching-kuo in 1952, the China Youth Corps was sponsored by the then-ruling Nationalist Party (Kuomintang, KMT) in order to promote and organize youth outside the classroom. Its motto was "We serve the youth, and the youth serve the country" *(women wei qingnian fuwu, qingnian wei guojia fuwu)*. It came during an era of anti-Communism and represented the KMT's long-term plan for diverting youth from any legacy of student unrest. It promoted a youth culture of patriotism and anti-Communism, and hence was a preparation program for a war against China. Since 1953, its main function has been to organize "self-empowerment activities" *(ziqiang huodong)* based on "research and creativity" *(yanjiu chuangxin)* and the spirit of "stopping only at perfection" *(zhiyü zhishan)* (Li [1982] 1984).[16] The China Youth Corps combined activities used in the Boy Scouts and military training, plus a light mix of games. More important, its goal reflects Duara's (2003) notion of "the regime of authenticity" in making the youth Chinese subjects: "in hope that we could establish a youth activity that fits the style of Chinese youth, let our youth sing their own songs, dance their own dance, and through these activities, evoke *( jifa )* their patriotic passion and belief in the country *(aiguo de rechen ji dui guojia de xinnian)*." As politics changed, the agenda of the China Youth Corps shifted toward that of a recreational and singles' club, which still detoured youth from antigovernment actions. The genre of "follow me" was particularly efficient at turning a gathering into an apt and buoyant drill—a potent combination of cheerful, recreational, and orderly collective embodiment. Thus, "follow me" fit well into the China Youth corps, which then zealously promoted it at various occasions, including the "Self-Empowerment Evening Ceremony" *(ziqiang wanhui)* for the national anniversary of the Republic of China ("Double-Ten," that is, October 10), celebrated by the state.

## Musical Corporeality in Tzu Chi: Prototype, Theatrical Choreography, and Collective Rhythm

In contrast to crying, which has no clear beginning, ending or particular course, the prototype of sign language song as practiced in Tzu Chi is as follows.

The emcee announces, "We now present you a sign language song" followed by the song's name. There are usually five to ten performers, sometimes more, but never fewer than five. Except for the most formal occasions, the performers wear the unisex Tzu Chi volunteer uniforms—white-collared blue polo shirts with white pants. They form a row, bow to the audience with the Buddhist greeting of joined palms *(anjali mudrā)*, and stand facing the audience with their hands in the Buddhist resting gesture of upwardly folded palms (Chan *mudrā)*—that is, both palms facing up and folded together at the waist. In a Tzu Chi setting, their position would be against a backdrop with Buddha's portrait hanging at the top center. The song comes from a stereo, usually at high volume. Typically, the performers do not sing; as the music blares, they begin with a slight movement from side to side. As soon as the words are heard, their hands unfold and sign the lyrics, word by word, synchronized with each word and with each fellow performer. In this typical performance, the performers move only their upper bodies, and their miming is limited to sign language. They do not move from their spot, remaining in the original row throughout the song. When the song is completed, they again bow to the audience with the Buddhist greeting and exit from the stage. Most of the audience remains quiet and seated throughout the performance, except for applauding at the end. Oftentimes some of the audience members join in the performance and sing and sign while remaining seated.

Events of musical corporeality vary in their degree of movement, the songs selected, and the audience's response. Yet the variety of events generally ranges between two extremes: the most formal and theatrical, and the most informal and collective. The most formal event of musical corporeality is the prelude to Cheng Yen's sermon. The songs are limited to Cheng Yen's favorites; they usually praise compassion and other Tzu Chi spirits, and are composed by selected musicians in consultation with Cheng Yen. The performers are members of the premier sign language song team, a select group of female commissioners, who always wear their formal uniforms—dark blue traditional Chinese dress, *qipao*—during the performance. Their number, usually between six and twenty, and their initial positions depend on the particular song and choreography. The performers use total body movements in a theatrical manner, and constantly change positions to form different patterns. They mime the lyrics with elaborate gestures: Not only are their hand movements exaggerated but also their eyes, heads, torsos, hips, and steps are all coordinated with each word that is signed. Nevertheless, all the movements are soft, smooth, and graceful, and to a large extent mimic the feminine gestures common in classic Chinese opera. They use multiple facial expressions, which change according to the word that is signed. When the song ends, the performers freeze in their final posture to form a pattern, such as the thousand-hand Guanyin seated on a lotus. The performance is followed by Cheng Yen's sermon.[17] The audience members remain quiet and seated throughout the performance until they all rise and salute when Cheng Yen enters the stage. Those who spontaneously follow the performance by singing and signing keep their voices and hands low.

In contrast to the serious atmosphere of the most theatrical and formal performances, the "collective rhythm" is done repeatedly in the retreat camps of followers and in activities that are designed for visitors, especially pilgrimage tours to Tzu Chi headquarters and the second hospital. Collective rhythm requires the audience members to move in unison as they follow the performers. In leading a crowd of pilgrim visitors who are novices of sign language song, the collective rhythm performers use simplified movements and often adapt familiar songs from popular culture. This simplified version is called *daidong* (lead into movement)[18] or *daidongchang* (lead the movement and singing). It is basically a form of "follow-me"; in contrast to the serious atmosphere of the theatrical performance, its rhythm is cheerful and somewhat playful. Sad folk songs are never used, nor are the songs that prelude Cheng Yen's sermons.

## Introduction of Sign Language Song to Tzu Chi

Crying appeared in Tzu Chi from its beginning. In contrast, musical corporeality was not present in Tzu Chi until the movement rapidly grew in the early 1990s. The period when musical corporeality—especially in its collective form—became popular in Tzu Chi coincided with many changes in the group: the surge in membership and assets; increasing male participation; a new form of modern bureaucratic organization; and a new trend toward rationalization in various aspects of the organization, from regulations on

Sign Language Song—Theatrical Performance at a Fund-Raising Bazaar in Dalin, Jiayi

Sign Language Song—The Collective Rhythm in a Youth Civility Camp

uniforms to practice and relationships based on rules governed by discipline and orderly collectivity (as opposed to its "old" face of a spontaneous women's community).

According to the veteran core member who was said to have introduced sign language song to Tzu Chi and who is the leader of the premiere sign language song team, its debut in Tzu Chi was in the late 1980s. It was at the opening ceremony of the Nursing College as well as the first anniversary of the hospital. Two songs were performed at the debut: "Preserving the Pure Land in This World" and the "Nursing College Song." She attributed this "invention" to Cheng Yen, who assigned her to organize the event.

The debut was a success, the veteran core member said. By 1992, the Tzu Chi volunteer schedule included a class in sign language song in the courtyard of the Abode during the short break between dinner and bedtime.[19] The premier sign language song team was founded in 1992 and began to establish theatrical choreography as the model performance. The collective form, especially with simplified motion, did not come to Tzu Chi or become popular until 1995 or later.

For a group that aims to help the needy, sign language as a communication skill is necessary to serve the deaf, but one interpreter standing on the stage should be enough. Why, then, do Tzu Chi devotees form a row to sign the lyrics simultaneously? Why do they become involved in theatrical choreography? And why have they more recently included the simplified form of collective rhythm?[20]

## The Practice of Sign Language Song in Tzu Chi

In addition to the premier team in Taipei, each local branch has its own sign language song team and regular sign language song classes and instructors, although performance quality, number of team members, and class frequency varies from branch to branch. Some local branches draw step-by-step illustrations, and copies spread quickly among Tzu Chi followers. Sign language song instruction and performance programs have been shown twice a day on the Tzu Chi television channel since it began broadcasting in 1998. Tzu Chi Press released a series of step-by-step sign language song instruction videotapes.

Many *Cijiren* (Tzu Chi people) love sign language song so much that they spontaneously begin miming when they hear a song they know. More than once I saw a small number of Tzu Chi followers practicing sign language song during a brief break in a meeting or whenever they were free from volunteer duties.

In Tzu Chi, the ability to perform eloquent sign language song is considered a valuable skill. In a group that constantly stresses the importance of "usefulness," the skillful use of sign language song is an appealing option for a *Cijiren* with an able body but no specialty, affluence, or free time to secure a vital membership position. A sign language song teacher is often among the most popular members in a branch. People surround her to practice and learn new songs. There are no standard requirements for becoming a teacher; one does so by learning and actively participating, thereby building a reputation. Usually, a teacher is the one who memorizes the most songs and whose performance resembles the premier team's theatrical eloquence.

The total number of sign language songs is unknown. Any sign language song teacher from any branch may come up with a new performance by translating the lyrics of an existing song from popular culture or from new compositions in Tzu Chi into sign language. The most typical and common of these songs number about twenty to thirty. Often performed are: "Grateful to the Sky, Grateful to the Earth" *("Kam-sia Thi$^n$ Kam-sia Te,"* in Minnan), "Mother" *("Mama,"* in Minnan), "Home" *("Jia"),* "Wish" *("Xinyuan"),* and "Tears of a Leaf" *("Yezi de yanlei").* The song "Wish" is Cheng Yen's favorite and is thus a frequently selected tune for the prelude to her sermon.

The circumstances of musical corporeality are distinct from those of crying. Musical corporeality always occurs before the formal beginning of a meeting, as a "warm-up" for the participants. Whether before the morning testimonials or before the monthly progress briefing at the second hospital construction site, the performance of sign language song precedes the salute to Buddha and to Cheng Yen—that is, the beginning of the religious ritual and Cheng Yen's sermon.

Musical corporeality, especially collective rhythm, is also widely used in pilgrimage tours to the Tzu Chi headquarters and at the end of reception parties for visitors. It often switches the audience from passive listening to energetic participation; and through imitating bodily movements, the distinction between the visitors and the devotees blurs and the two parties blend as one group. Musical corporeality is also a featured event in Tzu Chi volunteer work. For example, hospital volunteers perform and lead sign language song every morning in the waiting area on the first floor and in the courtyard adjacent to the hospice. They also sometimes perform inside the ward for the patients.

In other words, in contrast to crying, which often takes place in more religious contexts, musical corporeality clearly belongs in the lay domain. No musical corporeality has ever been performed inside the main hall of the Abode, where many instances of crying takes place.

## Musical Corporeality and the Tzu Chi People

Musical corporeality is more evenly distributed between women and men than are instances of crying. Yet a closer look at the sociology of musical corporeality reveals its role in the dynamic construction of Tzu Chi identity.

The younger generation apparently favors sign language song, and it has consequently become an indispensable practice of the Tzu Chi youth corps. On the other hand, many senior and veteran followers do not share this zeal; the middle-aged women in Dalin (in rural southern Taiwan), for example, all voted for chanting sutra rather than sign language song when deciding on an agenda for the following week's meeting.

As the premiere team consists of women only, their model for theatrical performance uses feminine gestures. All the local sign language song teachers I met were women. As with many other aspects of Tzu Chi, women initiated the sign language song and mixed it with their gender presentation. Men, as latecomers in the Tzu Chi world, have followed the female model and only recently developed some rare masculine performances. I was first intrigued by sign language song when I saw men practicing it by imitating feminine gestures. A feminist in Taiwan wrote about how she was impressed by the power of Cheng Yen, who "made" some "big men" busy their hands with sign language song (liangshou bi lai bi qü). Some male devotees in Taipei have formed a male sign language song team. At the eventful thirty-third anniversary celebration, a group of men from the United States presented their masculine performance, which combined sign language and martial arts.

The practice of musical corporeality belongs exclusively to the laity. Although nuns, including Cheng Yen, occasionally use simple vocabularies of sign language (for example, clicking the thumb to sign "thank you"), I have never seen a nun practicing sign language song in my fieldwork.

Parallel to the geographical development of Tzu Chi, musical corporeality is a trend that spread first in Taipei and then to the rest of Taiwan. The premiere team is based in Taipei; sign language song is more developed there than in rural areas. The practice in Taipei appears to be the authorized, correct version. I have heard people in Jiayi (southern Taiwan) arguing over which version of a sign vocabulary was correct according to what they had seen in Taipei. The leader of the premier team told me in an interview that she had been planning a reorientation for "standard" sign language song across the country, because there were far too many variations. Her plan implies an emphasis on maintenance of control and order.

Overseas followers are freer in creating new sign language songs, though their creativity is subtly subject to the appraisal of the Tzu Chi spirit. The masculine martial arts performance mentioned above was from Texas. This effort was obviously credited, since it was among only a couple of selected overseas performances that appeared several times on Tzu Chi television. I witnessed a performance at a ceremony in Boston by the Long Island branch. Whether in an effort to improve the performance or to emphasize ethnicity in a foreign country, the performers wore traditional Chinese costumes of the Ming-Qing Dynasty. Despite the team leader's praise of the innovation, the head of Tzu Chi United States who chaired the ceremony did not mention it at all. That was the only time I saw sign language song performed in clothing other than Tzu Chi uniforms. An innovative presentation with unauthentic Tzu Chi identity seems to receive no positive response.

## Interpretation of Musical Corporeality

Very few followers offered their interpretations of sign language song. When asked, they simply responded: "It looks nice" or "It's beautiful" (henmei). A couple of core members said: "Because the supreme person [the Venerable Cheng Yen] likes it." According to the premier team leader, the "follow me" genre stimulates crowd imitation within a few minutes, and thus efficiently initiates interaction among unfamiliar participants.

The premier team leader told me that Cheng Yen has recently equated sign language with Buddhist shouyin (mudrā in Sanskrit), with one crucial difference: Sign language is intelligible to the laity, whereas Buddhist mudrā is intended to remain mystic. Such a linkage to Buddhism obviously provides a perfect raison d'être for devotees to practice sign language song ardently. Indeed, this interpretation was indicated at the thirty-third anniversary exhibition, when the performance of sign language song was symbolized by a large piece of wood carved into ten important Buddhist *mudrās*.

A veteran core member told me that Cheng Yen once sighed her approval of sign language song: "How nice and beautiful the world could be if everyone remained silent as they are in sign language song!" Given all the tensions and conflicts I heard and saw in Tzu Chi, Cheng Yen might have expressed this appreciation as a reaction to the endless arguing among her followers.

Nevertheless, if this quote from Cheng Yen is true, it seems to explain everything at once. In contrast to uncontrollable floods of tears, sign language song in Tzu Chi demonstrates control. It exerts control over the collective bodies in a purely lay context by clearly prescribing bodily movement in a manner that is orderly and pleasurable (and sometimes silent). For the Tzu Chi people, crying is important because it embodies redemption and sign language song is important because it embodies their shared orderly collectivity. When hundreds of hands wave side to side in unison, one experiences the collectivity and feels a power that is greater than the individual. In its larger social context—just as ecstasy has the power to transform and transgress cultural taboos on crying—sign language song also has the power to transform the collective identity orchestrated by the state into a new collective identity in the embrace of Tzu Chi.

## Conclusion

The contrast between crying and musical corporeality is not that the former is emotional whereas the latter is not. Musical corporeality can be happy, and it is often intended to be. I have also seen people cry while miming the song *"Mama"* ("Mother").

Crying in Tzu Chi springs from a spontaneous personal emotion that is experienced in an unpredictable form. Although equally emotional qualitatively, sign language song, in contrast, is a formalized expression. In Tzu Chi, one may burst out crying in situations of conflict, from contagion, or in charismatic and religious ecstasy. Whether an individual weeps uncontrollably or a number of ritual participants are soaked in tears, crying cannot occur without unmediated strong physiological change in each person. In other words, crying embodies an individual's involvement in the context. It does so in a solely individual manner: collective crying is an aggregation of a number of individuals in tears. Sign language song, on the other hand, has a clear beginning and ending, and a defined course. And Tzu Chi followers always perform it collectively and pursue it uniformly. Moreover, Tzu Chi has a system of methodical practice for sign language song. There are performance teams, classes, teachers, special composers, and learning media. But there is nothing that teaches one to cry.

Thus, the contrast between crying and sign language song is one between ecstasy and control, between uncontrollable religious and charismatic ecstasy and organized, formalized collectivity. Both crying and sign language song are the bodily expression of emotions beyond utterance, but, again, the two are different. Crying comes from spontaneous personal emotions. Its source is individual disintegration caused by a striking or revealing experience, which at the same time is embedded in the Tzu Chi mission of compassion as universal motherhood. Sign language song, in contrast, is a formalized expression of collectivity; it is meant to be an orderly and sometimes cheerful presentation of Tzu Chi as a unanimous whole.

This chapter has considered both crying *and* musical corporeality because they are the two ends of the emotional structure in Tzu Chi religious experience: ecstasy and control. Crying, an essentially formless act, presents Tzu Chi as what Victor Turner ([1967] 1994, [1974] 1990) calls "communitas," wherein followers experience a realm of forgiving motherhood and divine compassion. Tzu Chi is a motherhood communitas that is universal enough to found a miraculous welfare movement and transcendental enough to inspire inexplicable and overwhelming floods of tears (Huang and Weller 1998). Using Victor Turner's theory as a frame, sign language song is as opposed to crying as structure is to communitas. Sign language song, which is as formalized as an act can be, is a presentation of Tzu Chi collectivity in Durkheim's sense of collective effervescence. Its uniform imitation is control over the collective body; yet, in so imitating, individuals elevate themselves into the power of collectivity.[21]

Why would a group of tearful Buddhists be so interested in sign language song? The fact that crying and sign language song coexist in the Tzu Chi movement shows that the relation between communitas and structure in a social movement may be coexistence. Their presentations— crying and sign language song—are often interspersed in the Tzu Chi context. In contrast to the power assumed in uncontrollable and spontaneous crying, sign language song also assumes power, not so much in the Weberian sense, but in terms of Bloch's (1975) conceptualization of oratory, insofar as it shapes followers' emotional expressivity into collective uniformity. The very reason that crying and sign language song coexist in Tzu Chi is the movement's ongoing process of formalizing ecstasy. In this formalization from the uncontrollable emotional expressivity of crying into the structure of sign language song, the extraordinary, selfless emotion that is the core of a charismatic movement transforms from formless into uniform collective emotional expressivity. In this way, crying and sign language song—or ecstasy and formalization—are counterpoints in the structure of emotions in the routinization of a charismatic movement.

# — 5 —

# Local Personhood

This chapter describes some of the millions of Tzu Chi followers in their specific local context. Although the term "local" is considered mandatory for ethnography, its applicability seems relatively inappropriate in the case of Tzu Chi. Except for a few years in the movement's early history, the Tzu Chi people have hardly been a "local" religious group grounded in their headquarters. Hualian County contains a relatively insignificant number of Tzu Chi followers and resources. The majority of Tzu Chi lay followers do not live at the headquarters, nor do they practice a solitary religious life at any local branch. Rather, lay devotees follow their normal family and social lives while maintaining Tzu Chi identities. For most of their daily lives, followers do not wear uniforms and they do not live in a Tzu Chi setting. Certainly, they are not secluded in a liminal state, such as in the hospital volunteer retreat (see Chapter 3). In what sense they are still Tzu Chi people (*Cijiren*)? What does it mean to be a *Cijiren* in a context that is distant from the headquarters?

The nuts and bolts of Tzu Chi practice in daily life illustrate what it means to be *Cijiren* in the local arena. Being a *Cijiren* not only implies a cognitive change of religious belief but also entails following concrete practices of the Buddha's path of Tzu Chi during the ebb and flow of daily life. Such practices range from having a tidy hairstyle to following Buddhist courtesies, finding support from family members, and collectively wearing Tzu Chi uniforms in local religious and secular rituals.

Ethnography of the local *Cijiren* may be conducted in any town with a certain number of active followers. Rather than select the headquarters or the two largest local branches—Taipei, the capital, and Taizhong in west central Taiwan—I chose a small town named Dalin (population thirty thousand) in the southwestern county of Jiayi to be my major field site. I selected Dalin not only because no research on Tzu Chi had been conducted in Jiayi but also because it lies in the path of Tzu Chi's future development.[1] Tzu Chi Dalin hospital, the first branch hospital in western Taiwan, had its ground breaking ceremony in 1996 and was opened on August 13, 2000. Moreover, Dalin is distinctive for its background as a "state town." Three military posts are located there. Since the Japanese colonization (1895–1945), a state monopoly, Formosa Sugar, has owned a lion's share of the land and predominated town development.[2] With Tzu Chi hospital—representing a large nongovernmental organization (NGO)—situated in such a state town, Dalin became, to rephrase in Ong's (1987) Foucauldian terms, a "site wherein different discourses compete with each other to address their authority."

Dalin is therefore a perfect site for scrutinizing two "local" issues. First, it serves as a vehicle for understanding Tzu Chi culture at a peripheral position in the umbrella organization. The Tzu Chi Dalin local organization is at the bottom—the sixth level—of the Tzu Chi volunteer system.[3] In contrast to the multimillion-dollar, twelve-story, twenty-hectare hospital, Tzu Chi Dalin and its supervising office of Jiayi County have been relatively "underdeveloped." The total number of commissioners in Dalin (less than 10) among the total of 139 in the Jiayi office is relatively small when compared to the approximately 9,000 nationwide and 10,000 worldwide (1998 figures). Dalin's low organizational position in Tzu Chi and its manageably small number of Tzu Chi devotees allowed me to observe how local devotees practice their Tzu Chi identities when they are not in uniform. For the same realistic reason, the ethnography of Tzu Chi Dalin involves a great deal of description of Tzu Chi Jiayi, since Dalin-based followers frequently intermingle with those who reside in other Jiayi towns.

The second reason that Dalin is a good place to study local issues is the Tzu Chi Dalin hospital—the first Tzu Chi medical mission institution erected in western Taiwan. As a result, Dalin has been one of the Venerable Cheng Yen's regular stops on her monthly tour and a pilgrimage destination for followers—second only to the Tzu Chi headquarters (see Chapter 3).

## Geographical Background: Jiayi and Dalin

Jiayi County is a rectangular portion of southwest Taiwan that is intersected by the Tropic of Cancer. It is located on a delta south of *Zhuoshui* (Muddy Stream) in the center of Jianan Plain, with Taiwan Strait on the west and the *Yü* (Jade) Mountains (with a main peak of 3,997 meters, the highest in Taiwan) on the east. Jiayi County is adjacent to Yunlin County in the north, Nantou and Gaoxiong Counties in the east, and Tainan County in the south.

The agricultural Jiayi has ample land, but has not had much prosperity in recent decades. The size of Jiayi County is 1,902 square kilometers, a medium-sized county among the 16 counties on the island of Taiwan (compared to the largest, Hualian County, which is 4,626 square kilometers). Jiayi makes up slightly more than 5 percent of the country. The 60-square-kilometer Jiayi City is located right in the center of Jiayi County and is the smallest city in Taiwan (compared to Taipei City's 272 square kilometers). The total population of Jiayi County was 566,000 in 1998, an average density of 297.49 people per square kilometer. Jiayi's population density is the sixth lowest among the 20 jurisdictions nationwide. In contrast to the relatively unpopulated Jiayi County, Jiayi City appears to be prosperous. Its total population in 1998 was 268,000, or an average density of 4,382.30 people per square kilometer. However, compared to Taipei City's 1998 population of 2,640,000 and average 9,712.81 persons per square kilometer, Jiayi City is a small town and, indeed, it recently was one of the two urban areas in Taiwan where land price lost value. Jiayi City and Jiayi County combined make up less than 4 percent of Taiwan's total population.[4]

Despite its former name of *Zhuluo* (mountainous),[5] Jiayi is not only an alpine area. Jiayi County is economically, culturally, and politically divided—generally along the north-south railroad—into the mountain and the coastal areas. The plain between the two is filled with rice paddies and other cash crops. The coastal areas grow sorghum and corn. The streets are filled with piles of shells left by oyster workers. Fruits, especially pineapples, are a common crop on the slope lands, while the high-value betel nut trees and tea bushes blanket the mountainous areas. People from the mountain area can tell whether a stranger is from near the seacoast by his or her accent.[6] The coastal and the mountain areas each have one seat in the Legislative Yuan, and they compete over the election of the county magistrate every four years. Jiayi City separated its jurisdiction from Jiayi County in 1982. People refer to Jiayi City as "Jiayi," as opposed to each of the eighteen towns of Jiayi County.

Dalin *zhen* (township) belongs to the mountain area. It is the most northern of the eighteen towns in Jiayi County, across the *Shigui* (Stone Turtle) Stream from Yunlin County, with Meishan *xiang* (township) on its east,

Xikou *xiang* on its west, and Mingxiong *xiang* to the south. Its former name of *Tao-po°-lim* (in Minnan) or *Dapulin* (literally, "great forest" in Mandarin) was changed when Taiwan was colonized by the Japanese government between 1895 and 1945.

Its geographical location at the threshold of the mountains made it the barter center for those from the lowlands and from the mountains. As a result, Dalin was the most prosperous town in the Jiayi area during the Qing Dynasty. In the ensuing colonized period, Dalin's prosperity peaked with industrial and commercial development brought about by the Dalin Sugar Plant, one of the major plants of the Taiwan Sugar Corporation. Residents of the neighboring towns still recall the old stereotype of Dalin as a place where prostitution catered to the businessmen in town. However, as Taiwan moved from agriculture to intensive industrial development in the 1960s, Dalin rapidly declined, especially after the closure of the Dalin Sugar Plant.

In recent years, the population on Dalin's spacious sixty-four square kilometers has barely remained at thirty thousand. Most residents live by farming rice, bamboo shoots, and pineapple. However, Dalin still has economic potential, albeit under the control of the central bureaucracy. For one thing, the north-south highway and the railroad both pass through Dalin, and the town's ample public land is perfect for large-scale planning. In addition to the military posts, Taiwan Sugar Corporation's current entrepreneurial policy of leasing the bulk of its land has gradually changed the immense deserted sugarcane fields into sites of local development. A gigantic pioneer in this change was the Tzu Chi Dalin hospital.

## Local Organization

### Meandering Blue Shirts

Living in Jiayi does not necessarily create encounters with the Tzu Chi people, since they have no neighborhood of their own. I arrived in Jiayi in November 1997, without having had previous contact with any of the local Tzu Chi followers. I sent a letter to the Tzu Chi headquarters informing them of my current research and paid my respects, but did not receive a response. In the same way that I began my research in New York and Boston, I called the phone number of the Jiayi local office as listed in the *Ciji yuekan (Tzu Chi Monthly)*. Through the call I obtained interviews with the coordinators of Dalin and Jiayi County. I then, so to speak, "entered" the field.

I did not ask the coordinators to help me find interviewees, nor did they ever try to control my research. Compared to other researchers' experiences with Tzu Chi, I was completely "free" throughout my research of Tzu Chi Jiayi.[7] I built my local connections through the same method I used in the United States: participating in open events. I did whatever they did, whether they were planting trees or cooking. Although I was fortunate to obtain the directory of Jiayi core members during my first month, I only called a member at home after he or she had personally given me the information and permission.

While I tried to blend in, I never concealed my identity as a researcher. I introduced myself as a researcher, with a strong emphasis on my previous participation in Tzu Chi Boston, and only mildly emphasized that I had a relative in Tzu Chi Taipei. Nevertheless, followers of Jiayi seemed dismissive of my previous participation: They listened to me when I said I was a student researcher and took no notice of my history in Boston, but looked relieved and smiled at my kin relation to Tzu Chi. Many of them concluded: "So you won't hurt us."[8]

## Early Low-Profile Charity Relief, 1979–1988

There were no Tzu Chi followers in Jiayi until 1979, when Mr. Wang, the first local commissioner and the present head of the local liaison office, moved from Taidong to Jiayi and began to proselytize in his wife's hometown of Xingang. Born in 1953, Mr. Wang is the son of two of the Tzu Chi pioneer commissioners of Taidong. His mother was the forty-sixth commissioner, and his father was the fifty-seventh among the now more than ten thousand worldwide.[9] He began practicing Tzu Chi at the age of twenty-five, when he passed the recruitment exam of Tai Power and was assigned to work in Jiayi. He said he remembered how his parents had worked for Tzu Chi when he was growing up and, therefore, when he moved to Jiayi to begin his career, he also began practicing Tzu Chi. For the most part, he delivered charitable relief as a "meaningful thing to do." In his view, the Venerable Cheng Yen is "like mother," who cares for the disaster victims like a mother cares for her children: "You have need and she provides. Only mother to children could be as such."

While the total number of local relief cases increased each year, Mr. Wang remained the only commissioner for the whole Jiayi area for nearly nine years. The significant increase in the number of core members did not occur until 1990. Jiayi's slow, if not stagnant, local development may have had to do with the background and emphasis of its pioneer commissioner, Mr. Wang. As a new young man in town, he proselytized using the local connections of his wife—who was born and raised in Xingang—and among his in-laws and colleagues. He emphasized charity relief. Tzu Chi began to provide relief to local recipients as soon as he moved to Xingang—a town closer to the costal area than to the mountain area. His relentless charity relief efforts not only made him an experienced independent social worker, but he literally led the early history of Tzu Chi Jiayi as a one-man charitable organization. Each month he rode more than 150 kilometers on his motorcycle to deliver charitable payments and supplies to geographically scattered recipients—mostly in the coastal area.[10] Mr. Wang's emphasis on charity seemed to contrast with the preference of some female pioneers for proselytizing in Hualian, Taipei, overseas (see Chapter 7), and particularly in the Jiayi mountain area. Nevertheless, the extent to which gender played a role in determining different patterns of Tzu Chi development is still a question that needs further empirical examination.

Moreover, slow local development of Tzu Chi was common in rural areas or, more precisely, in areas other than metropolitan Taipei. Jiayi had two reasons for slow early development—it was an agricultural area located in the south.[11] Until its rapid growth in the 1990s, Tzu Chi had been very much a northern Taiwan phenomenon or, more specifically, a Taipei phenomenon.[12] Although its headquarters is on the eastern coast, Tzu Chi's major expansion began with Taipei. This was, in part, because the most convenient transportation route from the eastern coast was to Taipei rather than to the south. More important, the capital of Taipei was until recently the primary political, economic, and cultural center of Taiwan. Thus, Tzu Chi initially entered the national arena when its first grand-scale mobilization—building a hospital—directly engaged the central government that was located in Taipei.

The significant increase in Jiayi's local Tzu Chi membership came at the same time that membership increased countrywide. In this sense, Jiayi's development was very much in tune with the growth of the whole Tzu Chi movement.

*Women's Proselytizing in the Mountain Area, 1988–1991*

Jiayi Tzu Chi continued for nearly a decade with Mr. Wang's low-profile yet concrete charitable practice in Xingang and the coastal regions. Members of

Tzu Chi had nowhere to gather until 1987, when the Wangs moved to Jiayi City and converted their new residence into a Tzu Chi meeting place. There were no followers in Dalin and the whole mountain area until the late 1980s, when a couple of local women joined—not through Mr. Wang—and became skilled at proselytizing.

One of these women, Mrs. Jiang (or Mama Jiang, as she is commonly referred to) of Meishan County became the first Tzu Chi commissioner of the mountain area in January 1989.[13] After her first visit to the headquarters in 1987, she immediately began proselytizing and organizing tours to Hualian. She sent the collected membership dues to her contact in Taizhong.[14] Among those who joined through Jiang or were later referred to Jiang by their original contacts were two active members, Ms. Chen Meijin and Xu Xiuzu (or Teacher Xu, as she is usually called) of Dalin. Immediately after Chen taught Xu about Tzu Chi in 1989, they together proselytized more than seventy new members in and around Dalin in only one month.[15] Subsequently, they held the first outdoor event in front of the temple in Dalin downtown to introduce Tzu Chi to more people in 1990. According to Teacher Xu, Ms. Lin Shujing or Ajing of Dalin attended this outdoor event. She also became skilled at proselytizing. Ajing later became the head of Jiayi's second group, which—at least at the time of my 1999 departure from Taiwan—comprised Dalin and four neighboring towns.

In contrast to Mr. Wang's emphasis on charitable relief for the poor in the sea area, these three pioneer women of the mountain area focused their enthusiasm primarily on proselytizing. They only started doing charitable works when they became commissioners. By the time I spoke with them between 1997 and 1999, Mama Jiang, Teacher Xu, and Ajing, each had succeeded in filling more than ten booklets—that is, the recruitment of more than four hundred households in each individual franchise.[16] In addition, Mr. Xu Qinhe, the brother of Teacher Xu, and his friend, Mr. Chen Jingyuan, a Dalin-based entrepreneur who joined Tzu Chi on his own and was referred to Mama Jiang by the headquarters, also became active commissioners by 1991. These two men were not as focused on proselytizing as were the three female pioneers.

Mama Jiang did not know about Mr. Wang and his relief practice until 1990. As a novice commissioner, she felt rather frustrated with her first attempt to visit the poor. She then sought help directly from the Venerable Cheng Yen, who referred her to Mr. Wang for instruction. Other early devotees of Dalin and the mountain area were either recruited by Mama Jiang or signed up through family and friends (not necessarily Jiayi locals) and later referred to Mama Jiang or her franchise. In other words, Tzu Chi's development in Jiayi did not occur because of structured missionizing; rather, it began with clusters of individuals proselytizing and later merged into one local organization through the headquarters.

A great number of current devotees came to the movement in the 1990s, especially toward the middle and end of the decade. An authorized Tzu Chi source recorded a total of 139 commissioners in Jiayi County in 1998.[17] Mr. Wang said during our interview in 1997 that the combined total of commissioners and male Compassion Faith corps members then was 160. Among them, seven to eight commissioners were based in Dalin. (Regular activities at Dalin were attended by about twenty regular participants, with special events attracting up to a hundred people.) Table 5 shows the annual increase of core members in Jiayi.

Parallel to the female pioneers' significant proselytization in Dalin and in the mountain area was the creation of Tzu Chi Dalin hospital. On the one hand, the late development of Tzu Chi Jiayi is understandable, since Tzu Chi mobilization had remained very much a Taipei- and urban-based phenomenon until its rapid islandwide growth in the 1990s. On the other hand, Jiayi Tzu Chi should have been different from other rural areas since the Tzu Chi headquarters had announced its plan to build Dalin hospital by early 1991. A proposition to build a general hospital should be a boost for local membership growth. As we see in Chapter 6, Tzu Chi gained its first national momentum when its plan to build the Hualian hospital received

**Table 5**  Total Number of Commissioners in Jiayi County, 1979–1998

| Total | [Total of Males][1] | Growth in Number | Growth Ratio (%) |
|---|---|---|---|
| 1979 | 1 [1] | | |
| 1988 | 3 [1] | Average 0.22/year | |
| 1992 | 25 [5] | Average 5.5/year | |
| 1993 | 36 [10] | 11 | 44.0 |
| 1994 | 50 [13] | 14 | 38.9 |
| 1995 | 65 [17] | 15 | 30.0 |
| 1996 | 74 [19] | 9 | 13.8 |
| 1997 | 111 [26] | 37 | 50.0 |
| 1998 | 139 [32] | 28 | 25.2 |

1. Total number of males derives from obviously male names on the lists in *Ciji nianjian*.
Source: *Ciji nianjian* (*Tzu Chi Yearbook*).

wide press coverage and government endorsement. Why, then, didn't the Dalin hospital lead to a greater mobilization in Jiayi?

Chapter 6 details the mobilization process for Dalin hospital in the context of Tzu Chi development at the national level. Here, I provide two short explanations. First, despite its expected local benefit, the issue of Dalin hospital was barely discussed at the local grassroots level. It was a matter between the authority of a nationwide NGO, Tzu Chi, and the central government; it rarely involved decision making among the local folks. Second, the successful funding of the first Tzu Chi hospital was actually raised from national resources. Tzu Chi Hualian Hospital was not built upon the scanty resources mobilized within the Hualian locale, nor did its Jiayi hospital count much on the relatively nonaffluent Jiayi.

Despite the efforts of the handful of local pioneers and the publicity of Tzu Chi Dalin hospital, the local office in Jiayi was not formally established—or, in Mr. Wang's terms, *koa pai* (in Minnan, to put up the sign or banner)—until 1994, and then in a temporarily borrowed space. Two years later, the Jiayi office moved to its current address, which is located on Tzu Chi property in the southeastern part of Jiayi City. It used to be a private high school and consists of two buildings separated by a field.

In other words, Jiayi Tzu Chi did not look like a local organization until the mid-1990s. As discussed in Chapter 2, intensive differentiation and bureaucratization did not occur in Tzu Chi until the 1990s. Jiayi become a local post at the time when Tzu Chi transformed itself into a new modern organization. Indeed, soon after Jiayi assumed its formal status as a local office, its organization differentiated intensively and became more formalized in the ensuing few years.

## Recent Reorganization

In 1998, three years after the granting of its formal status, and one year after it acquired its own local office, Jiayi Tzu Chi went through a six-month reorganization that resulted in the creation of its current three subregional groups (see Map 2). One group (the second) consists of the northern mountain towns: Dalin, Meishan, Minxiong, Xingang, and Xikou. The other groups vertically divide the rest of Jiayi County, including Jiayi City. The first group consists of the eastern side of Wenhua Road, including the eastern part of Jiayi City and five southeastern towns—Zhuqi, Fanlu,

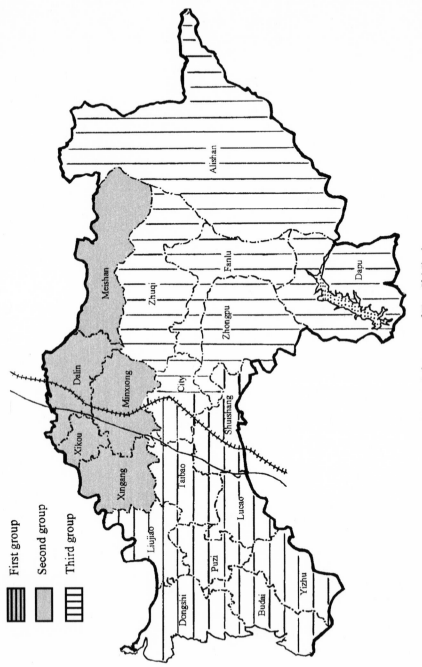

**Map 2**  Subgroups of Tzu Chi Jiayi

First group

Second group

Third group

Alishan

Fanlu

Dapu

Meishan

Zhuqi

Zhongpu

Dalin

Minxiong

City

Shuishang

Xikou

Taibao

Lucao

Xingang

Liujiao

Puzi

Dongshi

Budai

Yizhu

Zhongpu, Dapu, and Alishan. The third group consists of the western side of Wenhua Road, including the western part of Jiayi City and the so-called sea areas of eight towns—Shuishang, Taibao, Liujiao, Dongshi, Budai, Yizhu, Lucao, and Puzi.

This reorganization process was arranged and supervised by Tzu Chi headquarters. In January 1997, the commissioners anonymously voted for the group coordinators, the names of whom were subsequently announced by the headquarters. Similar to the review process for the title of commissioner described in Chapter 2, the headquarters had the authority over of the final decision. It was not clear how much the democratic procedure— that is, the vote—determined the final result. Nevertheless, the local devotees I spoke with believed that the headquarters had made the final decision based solely on their vote.

According to an active commissioner who was relatively young and new in his position, this six-month reorganizing process changed the local group from old and personalistic to a more neighborhood-based—and perhaps democratic—structure:

> Before the reorganization, the old and veteran led . . . After the reorganization, it is completely community based. Why did it have to be done? To implement the institution of community volunteers. For example, I may have joined Tzu Chi through a commissioner in the sea area. Although I myself live in the mountain area, I belonged to and participated in the sea area because of my connection to the supervising commissioner. Shangren saw this pitfall. So she broke it down. Yes, broke it down to make volunteers community based. It was hard in the beginning. But by now, everyone said it's a great idea and it really helps. You know the head of the Religion Office, brother Sixian, graduated from law school. So, he really knows social dynamics. He sees things clearly so he totally rearranged the whole Tzu Chi organization. By July 1997, all the group coordinators changed to younger people!

Put in a relatively larger context, Jiayi was not alone in going through this fundamental structural change; it was a nationwide process. Prior to the reorganization, Tzu Chi was a perfect product of informal social ties. The most veteran commissioner led each subgroup through her personal connections. Each group was a "natural" network that centered on its leading commissioner, who was informally referred to as the "hen" (*ke bok*, in Minnan, *muji*); the interns of her subgroups were referred to as "chicks" (*ke kia ⁿ*, in Minnan, *jizai*). The leader-follower relationship in each subgroup functioned like a mother-child relationship—and was sometimes sisterly—as suggested by the informal "hen" and "chicks." The 1997 reorganization changed the personal networks and completely divided the groups according to government administrative districts. This process of reorganization had to do with the Tzu Chi umbrella organization's overall transformation, as mentioned in Chapter 2. Followers have mixed feelings about this severing of personal ties: Some were glad to be free from the rather matronly old network, while others still spoke of the cozy and warm feelings of the old days. One female commissioner of Taipei described her adjustment to the new system:

> It was hard in the beginning. It's like leaving your home and being married into a new family. You don't know anyone there and have to learn on your own to get along. Some people couldn't make it with the new group and eventually disappeared. I couldn't get used to it in the beginning and often ran back to see my old folks. But looking back at it from now, I think it's good. At least I don't need to travel far to attend a group meeting.

The recent reorganization has had three effects on Jiayi Tzu Chi: (1) the organization is now restructured in accordance with the administrative district; (2) the leadership has changed from the more personal style to a more democratic procedure, from generally older devotees to younger ones (especially for the second group); and (3) following the change of leadership, the division of labor was reorganized in each new group. For example, while it more or less fulfilled all the functions of a local office, the second group did not have a clearly differentiated structure. Each of the few active core members took on more than one task. On June 2, 1998, in the regular weekly meeting of the second group, participants filled out their preferences for tasks on a questionnaire. There were a total of nine options: *wenxuan* (publicity), *fangshi* (case investigation), *caiwu* (accountancy), *zongwu* (supplies), *xiangji* (cooking), *jiaotong* (traffic), *yingshi* (documentation), *huanbao* (environmental), and *zhunian* (supplement mourning).

The list of tasks is much less differentiated than it would be at a larger branch (for example, Taipei; see Chapter 2). In fact, the local devotees had been practicing a similar structure of labor division prior to this. At the same meeting, they also selected coordinators for each of the nine tasks;

each coordinator was someone who was particularly interested in, or already had been handling, that respective task. In other words, the function of this meeting was less a reorganization than a formalization of the ongoing division of labor.

## Regular Activities

Regular activities of Jiayi Tzu Chi are held in three places: (1) the Tzu Chi Jiayi local office (*Jiayi Lianluo chu*, usually referred to as *Lianluo chu*) in Jiayi City, (2) the Dalin Study Hall (*Dalin Gongxiuchu*, usually referred to as *Dafahang*, the shophouse's former factory name),[18] and (3) the Dalin hospital construction site (usually referred to as *gongdi*). These are the three places I frequented. Small meetings of the title groups—especially the male Compassion Faith corps—are held at the members' homes. Large-scale special events, such as fund-raising bazaars, take place in temporarily rented places, such as Jiayi High School in Jiayi City and the recreational park in the town of Dalin. Other events, such as introductory parties or *chahui* (literally, "tea meetings"), and small group meetings for title groups take place in either a temporarily rented public space (for example, town halls, and schools) or in core members' homes.

The two main regular activities for Tzu Chi followers in Jiayi are biweekly meetings at the Jiayi office in Jiayi City and weekly meetings at Dafahang in Dalin. Both are open to everyone, but the meetings in Jiayi City usually consist of the first and third groups, whereas the ones in Dalin are mostly for members of the second group, especially for those who reside in the town of Dalin. The biweekly meeting is one of the many regular activities at the Jiayi office. It has large audiences and often welcomes guest speakers from other branches. Here, I describe only the Dalin Dafahang meeting.

### Weekly Meetings at Dalin Dafahang

Dafahang is a three-story shophouse, a building of a commercial-residential style that is typical in old town Taiwan. The ground floor has no front wall but a wide open commercial facade that is indented with a roofed sidewalk separating the indoor area from the street. Dafahang is adjacent to two other similar buildings and located about a third of a mile from Dalin's downtown. The current coordinator of the second group owns the building. She and her family lived and ran their small factory there until they donated it to Tzu Chi and moved to a much bigger house and factory farther away from town. People refer to this location by its former name, Dafahang.

One would hardly associate the ordinary appearance of Dafahang with the high-profile Tzu Chi, if it did not have the sign of *Ciji Dalin gongxiuchu* (Tzu Chi Dalin Assembly Place) hanging in front. The sidewalk, characteristic of similar buildings across Taiwan, was used for multiple purposes. The Tzu Chi garbage recycling pickup truck parked there at night. On meeting days, a few mopeds occupied half of the sidewalk. On some Sundays, it was filled with women busy washing and chopping vegetables, and cooking on two huge stoves. On days in which no event took place, the sidewalk was covered with boxes of unsorted donations for fund-raising.

Inside the front sliding doors, there is a living room full of chairs and coffee tables on the left, and on the right, an "office" circled by some tables and filled with a few rather unkempt cardboard boxes of Tzu Chi publications. A few feet further, shoe racks and a bulletin board are against the left wall, behind which is the restroom. On the right, a panel outlining the "History of Tzu Chi Dalin Hospital" covers a wall that separates the kitchen from the central aisle. As the flooring changes from concrete to green tiles, one's shoes are removed to enter the religious hall.

The religious hall is about six hundred square feet. An altar of Guanyin stands at the center against the rear wall, overlooking the front door. Two of Cheng Yen's portraits are hung on the rear wall next to the altar. Facing the altar, a blackboard stands on the left and, on the right, is a television and stereo set. On both sides, a few images of the Dalin hospital are the only decorations. Stacked up meditation pads and folding chairs cover the wall on the right, adjacent to the kitchen. The second and third floors consist of the dormitory and a few bedrooms. The dormitory was built to accommodate the foundation's construction staff, and the bedrooms are for the master, her disciples, and the foundation's vice CEOs. Despite this, no one lives there except for one nonlocal volunteer receptionist for the hospital construction site.

The weekly meeting at Dafahang generally consists of the following activities: a salute to the Buddha and to the Venerable Cheng Yen's portrait; a briefing and an announcement of activities and events; the featured activity—scripture chanting or sign language song practice or a special meeting or discussion (such as the survey of the division of labor); and watching the Venerable Cheng Yen's sermons taped from the Tzu Chi television channel. Attendance at these meetings averaged around twenty and occasionally reached fifty. The number varied only in terms of male participation: At least twenty middle-aged women showed up at every single meeting, whereas usually fewer than ten men participated. Scripture chanting and specially organized meetings tended to attract more people.

In other words, the weekly meeting at Dafahang was very much a women's gathering. Two women—Adiu and Xie Huifeng—led the meeting every week from the front of the hall; men and women in ordinary clothes sat cross-legged and separated by gender. The primary regulars were some middle-aged women who lived just a couple of blocks away. A teenaged daughter of a local follower referred to them as *"Xiangji mama"* (cooking mothers) because they were also the primary volunteers for every event that involved cooking. Except for special meetings, there were always some children who came along with their grandmothers. This is in contrast to the regular meeting in Jiayi City, at which a few female devotees were assigned to take care of the participants' children in a separate room. In Dafahang, the children usually tried to stay in their seats but typically ran out of patience with the sutra chanting, and often started running around and throwing the meditation pillows at each other. Women held sutra books in their hands while making faces at the children in hopes they would go back to their seats and quiet down, but this effort was usually futile. Normally one of the women would give up chanting and take all the children outside to play.

## Cooking Up a Women's Community

Although the Dalin office has very few commissioners, it impressively mobilized for every cooking event, by exemplifying hosting in "event production" (Chau 2006: 125–129). Local followers prepared lunch boxes on the days when a large number of followers from different parts of Taiwan arrived to view the progress of Dalin hospital. For example, on a Sunday in 1997, more than fifty buses were expected. By 7:00 a.m., about thirty local women and a few children had already shown up at the construction site. Most of them had not been seen at weekly meetings and did not wear Tzu Chi uniforms except for plaid scarves on their heads. Those who arrived at 5:00 a.m. already had been busy cooking red bean sweet soup and boiling fruit tea in the kitchen tent. They frequently delivered trays filled with bowls of soup and cups of tea to the working women, and warmly invited everyone to enjoy them. About twenty women divided themselves into three circles, each surrounding a banquet-sized table, and started rolling dough by hand into rice cake balls.

By 8:00 a.m., the working team had increased to about one hundred women and men. All the men wore uniforms and took on "heavy-duty" jobs—directing traffic, moving conference tables, or just standing around chatting and appreciating the hospital. A man in uniform joined one of the rice cake circles and immediately the women started giggling and teasing him as the "single green among ten thousand reds."

About ten women in blue uniforms stood between the gate and the conference room; each of them held a sign that read "Follow Me." The rest were part of the cooking team. Most of them were middle-aged women in ordinary clothes, except for a few in gray shirts. Not all of them knew each other; one woman in my circle said her neighbor called her for this event the night before and this was her first time at a Tzu Chi activity. Another woman immediately said: "You must have had great merit reward (*tsok u hok po*, in Minnan, *henyou fubao*)." The other woman noticed my presence and remarked: "Oh! We have a young lady *(xiaojie)* here today!"

By 9:00 a.m., a few busloads of visitors gradually filed into the construction site. While those in uniforms began to give their orientation tours and reception speeches, those in ordinary clothes gradually disappeared on their mopeds, leaving trays of rice cake soup and tea behind for the visitors' reception. I thought they were going home, but they had instead moved to Dafahang to prepare the lunch boxes.

On the front sidewalk of Dafahang, some women were washing, selecting, and chopping vegetables, while others stirred professional-sized woks. A handful of men occasionally stopped by in different vehicles to drop off and pick up various items. Inside on the first floor, the space usually used for meditating was converted to a lunch-box-packing floor, with columns of tables standing parallel to the two side walls. Each column was an assembly line that began with a huge pot of white rice and piles of paper boxes and ended in front of the altar with bundles of chopsticks and rubber bands for the final wrapping of each lunch box. As more and more trays of food were moved to the tables, women began to fill each lunch box with dishes in exactly the same pattern.

By 11:00 a.m., about three hundred lunch boxes for the visitors were ready for the men to pick up. Some women brought out china bowls from the indoor kitchen. All the women began eating the food that remained in

Cooking (Dalin Hospital under Construction in Background)

the trays. Some went outside to do the dishes, and one after another, they disappeared on mopeds.

## Local Body

Although a cooking event could mobilize nearly one hundred local women, the number of primary active followers of the second group—including both commissioners and ordinary followers—was only about thirty, almost equally divided among Dalin, Minxiong, and Meishan, plus a few individuals from Xikou and Xingang. The gender ratio of women to men was about two to one. Except for the current coordinator, Ajing, who was in her thirties, all of the active followers were older than forty; about one-third of them were over fifty. About one-fifth were public schoolteachers or worked in state-run enterprises such as Tai Power; the rest were self-employed. All the members I talked to spoke in Minnan.

How did these local devotees act out their Tzu Chi identity in the ebb and flow of daily life? The following are some of the domains in which individuals embodied the construct of *Cijiren* in a local context.

## Vegetarianism

Although a vegetarian diet is not an exclusive practice of Buddhists, people in Taiwan nowadays still speak of Buddhism as "the vegetarian" (*tsiah tshai-e* or *tshai-e,* in Minnan, *chizhai de*) as opposed to Chinese popular religion. Such common identification of Buddhism with a vegetarian diet is a result of the Taiwanese indigenous Buddhism, *tshai-tng* (in Minnan, *zhaitang,* vegetarian halls) (Weller 1987).[19]

Tzu Chi is a Buddhist group. All the diets in the headquarters (including the food for hospital patients) are strictly vegetarian. The cafeteria at the mission institution sometimes serves scrambled eggs, but the food for nuns on any occasion and for everyone (including the lay residents) at the Abode is completely orthodox Buddhist vegetarian, which excludes meats and eggs as well as scallions, garlic, and onions. The relief food that Tzu Chi delivers to disaster victims never contains any meat. One of the ten precepts of Tzu Chi is the Buddhist one of "no killing"—this is the original source of not eating meat in Chinese Buddhism. However, Tzu Chi never clearly mandated a strictly vegetarian diet for the laypeople in the manner practiced by such religious groups as the Unity Way *(Yiguan Dao)* and the followers of the Master Ching Hai's *Guanyin Famen.*

Many Tzu Chi people I know are vegetarian in their daily lives, but a great many of them are not. Since I approached them as Tzu Chi followers, they would never have suggested a nonvegetarian meal when we dined together. Thus, whether or not they were strictly vegetarian could only be determined in individual interviews. Among those I spoke with in Jiayi, the distribution of vegetarians appeared to be an issue of gender: more men than women were vegetarian.

This does not necessarily mean that males are more pious than females. In fact, many vegetarian Tzu Chi males stopped eating meat before they joined Tzu Chi. Whereas a man might remain a vegetarian while the rest of his family members continued to eat meat, I have not met a woman who did the same. The only strictly vegetarian woman I know was Mama Jiang, and her whole family does not eat meat—from her husband to her toddler grandchildren. In addition to Mama Jiang, only one female devotee told me that she avoided meat since her body seemed to have become adapted to a meatless diet. However, she was the only local female devotee who had never been married. In other words, practicing vegetarianism is a gender issue insofar as such a choice depends on one's role in the family. For a man, it is primarily an individual conviction and secondarily a family lifestyle. By contrast, a married woman has to worry about whether such a diet is practical for her body and for her family. For example, Teacher Xu addressed the two concerns of body and family as she explained her "failure" to become a vegetarian:

> When I was a child, someone said I'd better become a vegetarian. But my mother didn't follow the instruction, because, you know, we women will eventually get married. What if your future family doesn't allow you to continue so? *Hui khi* [in Minnan, *huiqi*, unpleasant, troublesome] *lah!* Since I got married, I have suffered miscarriages, childbirth, and a head injury. I had several surgeries. Because I suffered so many crises, people said my body couldn't stand a strictly vegetarian diet. That's why I never became a pure vegetarian. All I can manage is a vegetarian breakfast.

While most Tzu Chi people were not vegetarian in their ordinary lives, they were very careful to keep any violation of Buddhist food taboos from harming the image of Tzu Chi. For example, when a devotee announced a miscellaneous checklist in preparation for the incoming Tzu Chi Train, he specifically reminded people not to bring any nonvegetarian snacks for the trip. As he explained, the transportation was not a charter train and it would "look bad" if other passengers on board saw Tzu Chi people indulging in snacks like squid jerky (a popular snack in Taiwan). When Tzu Chi followers participated in a local religious festival by putting up a food stand on the street, even though they were in ordinary clothes, they sold steamed corn and peanuts—no nonvegetarian food—to raise funds for their mission.

### Family Support

While women took family as well as health concerns into serious account when considering a commitment to vegetarianism, family appeared to be less of a barrier for women than for men in their pursuit of a broader Tzu Chi identity. Among the local devotees I spoke with, the pattern of family participation in Tzu Chi suggests much about women's autonomy in this matter. Among the veteran locals, wives usually joined first and then sometimes were followed by their husbands. Among those who joined in the mid- or late-1990s, the pattern tended to be couples, some even with their children. In contrast, I did not encounter a case in which a husband joined first and then brought in his wife.

Such an interesting pattern along gender lines further illustrates the different ways that men and women work out their Tzu Chi identity with their family members. A few male devotees expressed their difficulties in this matter. Mr. Xu, the brother of Teacher Xu, for example, lowered his voice and explained this issue grimly during our interview in his living room. He used to be so active that he would drive up to Taizhong for each of the Venerable Cheng Yen's sermons and other events. Although the establishment of the Dalin meeting place has saved him from trips, he did not participate as much because his wife did not like him spending time on Tzu Chi. Mr. Xiao of Jiayi City had a similar "double burden" of family and Tzu Chi during his initial participation, when Jiayi Tzu Chi had yet to develop as a local office. As enthusiastically as Mr. Xu, Mr. Xiao had driven two to three hours each way to Pingdong for Tzu Chi events, and left his wife alone with their small business and two children. Now the young couple has become a model Tzu Chi family, happily participating in each local activity.

Family tension for men who pursue Tzu Chi may come from members other than their wives. Awan of Jiayi City, for example, is a young man who has never been married. He joined Tzu Chi because of his mother's patient persuasion and encouragement. As he and other followers described, Awan had been a hopelessly "bad boy." He miraculously transformed into a model hardworking Tzu Chi man, helping in the family noodle factory and enthusiastically volunteering for seven shifts at the Hualian hospital. To his dismay, his father still adamantly objected to his participation in Tzu Chi. The same man who was rather indifferent to his wife's participation in Tzu Chi reacted strongly—and somewhat violently—against his son's following suit. He put a curfew on Awan in order to stop him from coming to the local office's evening activities, and denied Awan's new identity by destroying his Tzu Chi uniforms. The father ultimately broke Awan's heart by detaining him on the day that he was to be awarded his certificate as a Compassion Faith corps member. In contrast to most Tzu Chi males who appeared in uniforms or street clothes during our scheduled interviews, Awan showed up at the local office dressed like a homeboy, with a bag of tea in hand. By dressing this way, he made his father believe that he was not going to Tzu Chi but rather to hang out and drink tea with friends. Awan still had no clue about the reason for his father's objection. At one point, he complained: "I really don't know what he wants. Would it make him happy if I go back to being a lo mua$^n$ (gangster, in Minnan)?"

Awan's example of family disapproval may be an extreme case. Neverthe-less, the fact that he was unable to discern or vocalize the reason for his fa-ther's reaction seems to have to do with men's relatively inept handling of confrontation or negotiation for compromise. Mr. He of Meishan was an-other interesting example. Somewhat similar to Awan's case, Mr. He joined Tzu Chi as a result of his wife's careful cajoling. Since he joined the Tzu Chi male Compassion Faith corps, he had changed from a drunkard into a sober man. One would automatically assume that his wife must appreciate Tzu Chi for changing her husband as she had wished, and would hence sup-port Tzu Chi in its "efficiency," if not its "efficacy." Yet to my surprise, when I asked him what his next goal would be, he replied grimly that he deeply wished his wife would be willing to join Tzu Chi. Although she was the one who had initiated his commitment to Tzu Chi, she chose to remain a gen-eral Buddhist and Tzu Chi member while her husband moved along on the path of a Tzu Chi devotee.

The reason that men have difficulty in joining a lay organization is not the same as for a monastic order in Chinese Buddhism. It is more difficult for men to become monks because by not marrying they do not produce heirs and thus fail to continue the family line. According to my local infor-mants, men encountered resistance from family with regard to Tzu Chi be-cause of time—their wives felt that they spent too much time on Tzu Chi and not enough time with the family.

Compared to how men deal with a lack of family support, the women who had encountered family disagreement in their pursuit of the Tzu Chi mission seemed to have resolved the situation through communication. Compared to the frequency with which men mentioned family disapproval of their participation in Tzu Chi, only one woman ever expressed this con-cern. Teacher Xu mentioned that during her initial stage of practice, her husband, who is also a teacher and her colleague, once expressed slight dis-agreement with her collecting membership dues. He felt rather perplexed about the involvement of money in her profession as a teacher. Neverthe-less, Teacher Xu cleared up the misunderstanding by explaining to him that the money was not for her personally, but for Tzu Chi's charitable mission. In other words, some misunderstanding or tension in the family during one's initial commitment to Tzu Chi is not unusual for both female and male devotees, but how the person dealt with the misunderstanding dif-fered according to gender. During a casual conversation at the hospital con-struction site, two female devotees of Jiayi City—both over thirty—easily replied to my question about family support: "It's not a problem at all. All you need to do is to talk to your husband gently. Then you'll get your way." Both women smiled triumphantly. After a brief pause, one of them joked about their strategy: "Isn't what we have been doing some kind of "*baoli*" ("violence"; possibly an exaggerating expression of "aggressiveness" or "manipulation" here), huh?"

Although both women and men persisted in their participation in Tzu Chi without drawing in their family, the result of compromise differed between men and women. Among the equally small number of women and men who mentioned tension from their family, men never vocalized how they solved the problem aside from cutting down the time they spent on Tzu Chi. Almost all the women, however, told me the specific solutions they found to stop family objections and continue their individual religious pursuits. Ms. Cai of Jiayi City, for example, simply took a part-time nursing job at a nearby hospital to create a separate income solely for her contributions to Tzu Chi. In so doing, she has successfully stopped her husband from having a negative opinion of her religious pursuits. Ms. Cai of Minxiong traced her conversion to Tzu Chi to the tearful experience she had on her first Tzu Chi Train. She clearly remembered that a woman fell to her knees at Cheng Yen's feet and submitted a donation with trembling hands. "So it must be a good group," she said to herself, and decided to join. Her husband was not happy that she collected money for the mission, and complained that she spent too much time outside working for Tzu Chi. She nevertheless succeeded by demonstrating her commitment to childcare: she took taking their then five-year-old son with her whenever she went to Tzu Chi.[20]

Aru, a young intern commissioner in her thirties, is the only less-successful example. Her husband always drove her back and forth to Tzu Chi events, but her mother-in-law was grumpy about her spending time there. Nevertheless, she was able to convince her mother-in-law to attend a few Tzu Chi events and make a donation. One day after the weekly meeting at Dafahang, Aru explained to another female intern commissioner that she could not participate regularly due to the pressure from her mother-in-law's discontent. Because she had set her goal on pursuing the title of commissioner, she made sure that, although she could not attend frequently, she participated in those training activities that counted for her records. She concentrated on proselytizing among her coworkers' and natal families to achieve the minimum number of forty households required to earn the title. She did not even attempt to proselytize among her husband's family.

## *Uniforms*

The issue of Tzu Chi uniforms is related to the distinction of vegetarianism. When Tzu Chi followers attended the wedding banquets of other followers' children, they appeared in uniforms and sat together at a few vegetarian tables that were often placed at the corner most distant from the central table of the bride and groom and their families. When a person wears a Tzu Chi uniform, he or she is not only supposed to refrain from eating meat in public but also to avoid the behaviors that pertain to a nonvegetarian diet. I have seen women go to the restroom to change from their uniforms into ordinary clothes after an event at the hospital construction site, but I never saw men bothering themselves with such trouble. Either the men did not have a problem navigating different contexts while wearing their uniforms or they, like Awan, did not choose such camouflaged self-presentation. The choice of when and where to wear the uniforms, similar to the choice of becoming a vegetarian, correlates with the gender difference in family roles. During one meeting at Dafahang, a male devotee suggested that all speakers at the Sunday visitors' reception at the construction site wear uniforms in order to "represent Tzu Chi." The Dalin coordinator, Ajing, immediately objected: "We squeeze time from chores to give a hand at the reception. Oftentimes we stop by the construction site when we are on our way to the grocery market in the morning. How can we wear uniforms and blatantly shop at butcher shops?"

Uniforms present a real concern when navigating contexts outside Tzu Chi because they represent the Tzu Chi collective identity: a Buddhist group as well as a large charitable organization. I was surprised that Tzu Chi devotees wore ordinary clothes when conducting their mission of charity investigation. They also never revealed their Tzu Chi identity throughout the interrogation with a prospective charity recipient. They only introduced themselves vaguely as a "charitable group." As one male devotee explained to me, "Of course we could not let them know who we are at the first investigation. Everyone knows Tzu Chi. What if the case turns out to be not eligible? It will be very hard to say 'no' to them if they already know that we are Tzu Chi people."

In other words, followers only put on their uniforms when they wanted to present themselves as part of the Tzu Chi collectivity. In addition to obvious Tzu Chi events such as Cheng Yen's sermons, Tzu Chi followers wore their uniforms to ordinary rituals such as wedding banquets and funerals. Such an orderly presentation was appreciated at the one funeral

I attended. The host family asked the Tzu Chi followers to stay after the mourning ceremony and serve as the flower team because their uniforms "look very nice in leading the parade to the grave."

Detailed dress codes regarding which uniform to wear for specific occasions were usually announced days before each event, including the color of the socks and kind of shoes. Even when there was no advance dress code announcement, followers still showed up wearing the same selection from their variety of uniforms. The three major concerns in matching uniforms with occasions seemed to be formality, purpose of the occasion, and the nature of the work involved in the occasion. Women usually wear the traditional dress of *qipao* and men wear suits for the more "formal" Tzu Chi events (such as Cheng Yen's monthly visits to Dalin) and for fellow followers' ritual occasions. Men wear suits and women wear the (hospital) volunteer dress—commonly referred to as *ba zhengdao* (the eight righteous paths) within Tzu Chi—to attend all trainings, such as hospital volunteer retreats and Cheng Yen's sermons in nearby branches. Both women and men who are interns and commissioners wear the unisex polo shirt uniforms for occasions that entail more labor, such as gardening, and for less-formal events like the weekly meeting at Dafahang. Active general members wear the gray jersey pants and polo shirts to cooking events. However, the gray uniform is not enough for a more "formal" occasion, regardless of how much labor is involved. For example, when a local general member was to submit her donation for the title of honorary trustee, she specifically obtained a brand new blue polo shirt uniform that morning from Ajing, and wore it to submit the donation to the Venerable Cheng Yen during her monthly visit (also see Chapter 3).

The concern for formality may override the concern for laboring work. For example, on a hot summer day in southern Taiwan, I wore the gray uniform to the Jiayi City fund-raising bazaar for Dalin hospital because I was not even an intern commissioner and I thought it was a "laboring" event since it involved a lot of activities. However, as soon as I showed up, the first reaction I got was from a Jiayi City devotee: "Such a big event and you wear this gray uniform? Don't you know how big the event is?"

### Morality

As discussed in Chapter 6, moral certainty serves as a positive force for Tzu Chi mobilization in the national arena, yet it seems different when boiled down to the numerous moral quandaries of day-to-day reality. I have heard of situations in which Tzu Chi people were rudely "forced" to give their seats to able-bodied passengers when the latter protested: "Aren't you Tzu Chi people supposed to 'help' people?" Teacher Xu once told me that she could not argue with her neighbor who occupied several inches of her property simply because she is known in Dalin as "the Tzu Chi teacher." A young couple of Jiayi City described the difficulties that Tzu Chi followers had to cope with in daily life:

> *Kha su lang* [in Minnan, *bijiao shuren,* loosely translated as "you just can't win"] *lah!* Once one knows that you are a Tzu Chi commissioner, one knows for sure that you *are* a good person. Sometimes neighbors took advantage of us. We knew it's not fair to us, but we nevertheless stepped back when people said bluntly, "Hey, aren't you guys *Cijiren?*" [sigh] *Kha su lang lah!*

In the case of any serious incident, Tzu Chi identity also plays a role in an individual's resolution of right and wrong. Mama Jiang's youngest son was unfortunately killed in a car accident a few years ago. Despite the fact that the accident was completely the fault of a speeding driver, Mama Jiang signed the case-settling agreement outside the court and did not ask for compensation for her daughter-in-law and three grandchildren. In response to her forgiveness, the guilt-ridden driver had since delivered three relatively small gifts of money to Mama Jiang: NT$11,000, NT$20,000, and NT$1,800 (about US$367, US$667, and US$60). The last time, the sum was the red-envelope money for the three children on the Chinese New Year. Mama Jiang accepted the money and donated it all to Tzu Chi in the name of the driver. She explained calmly with a poised facial expression:

> I couldn't have let go had I never become a Tzu Chi follower. My son's life is priceless. No amount of compensation could bring my son back to life. I'd rather the driver learn the lesson from this incident, drive carefully, and become a useful person to the society . . . My little son was half a Tzu Chi person: he drove me around to collect membership dues and investigate cases. All I wish is that he could return to be a Tzu Chi person in his next life as soon as possible.

The identity of a person as a Tzu Chi follower also indicates individual moral deeds. One evening during the usual postmeeting chat at Dafahang, perhaps because the event of that day was chanting the Lotus Sutra, a woman said firmly: "Having a copy of *Dizang Wang Jing* (the Sutra of the Dizang King) at home can prevent robbery. Really, that's what happened to my sister." Her anecdote about Buddhism and crime obviously drew the attention of others and began a focused discussion on this topic. Adiu, the organizer of the weekly meeting, took the floor and resumed her leadership in the conversation with her usual soft-spoken manner: "Yes. There are several true stories. A thief broke into a commissioner's home, took all her personal savings but not a penny of the stack of cash of *kong tiok hui*[in Minnan, *gongde fei*, "merit fees," that is, Tzu Chi membership dues]. The other commissioner found her home was broken into. Yet the thief seemed to have moved around in her home and decided to leave without taking anything."

The circle of listeners remained quiet and concentrated. In response to the demand, Adiu continued with a true story of an attempted rape of an acquaintance. The heroine in this story is a pretty young lady, who is a relative of Adiu's and a Tzu Chi member. One day, the young lady's cousin drove her to a remote streamside and attempted *bu jiok* (literally, "humiliating," in Minnan; *wuru*, referring here to sexual harassment or rape). The girl resisted and desperately screamed to the quiet sky and stream: "Where are you, *Kuan yim pho sat* (in Minnan, Guanyin Bodhisattva)? Where are you, *O mi to hut* (in Minnan, Amitaba)? Where are you? Help! Where are you? Help!" The girl continued to scream until the man finally gave up and said begrudgingly: "Okay, Okay. You are really a follower of the Venerable Cheng Yen's. A Cheng Yen follower you are, huh?" He drove her home safely.

After most of the women had left, Adiu explained to me the moral of these stories:

> There are still many other examples. But I didn't want to talk about this during the [formal] *gongxiu* (study session), because I didn't want to confuse people's minds and lead them to think there are some magical powers. Actually, as long as one has a righteous mind and no evil thoughts, one will not be harmed. Those who think about evil things, their minds are not righteous and bad things will eventually come visit them.

Living in a social world in which disputes and crimes are not unusual, the "efficacy" of Tzu Chi identity seems to lie within a morality that accommodates disputes and hence resolves situations in harmony, on the one hand, and that defies crime and avoids harm, on the other. In this vein of thought,

Tzu Chi identity—being a Buddhist as well as a follower of the Venerable Cheng Yen—works in the same way as popular religion, which protects people from harm or at least helps them to find a way to deal with the tragic accidents that happen in ordinary life.

## *"Taking a Break" from Tzu Chi Identity*

While deployment of Tzu Chi identity may result in a moral protection from harm, awareness of individual responsibility for Tzu Chi's collective and moral image sometimes requires taking precautions while living with one's Tzu Chi identity. The strategic choice of the volunteers in not revealing their Tzu Chi identity during initial case investigations was one example. The vulnerability of commissioners when it comes to their Tzu Chi identity in handling disputes also indicated an awareness of individual responsibility. The underlying tension or pressure from such prevailing precautions seems to be demonstrated, albeit somewhat in reverse, by occasional instances when Tzu Chi followers "took a break" from the mission.

After the biggest local event of the year, the fund-raising bazaar on June 28, 1998, members of the second group celebrated their accomplishment by going picnicking together on a Sunday. They took a charter bus that was paid for by the coordinator, Ajing, to one of the popular tourist sites in central Taiwan, *Xitou* Forest Park, in Nantou. Similar to the Tzu Chi Train described in Chapter 3, participants came with their families and did not wear uniforms; neither were there any references to Tzu Chi. However, in contrast to the Tzu Chi Train, there were almost no "collective" activities, except for a brief announcement of the schedule of the trip, some dos and don'ts upon the departure, and some testimonials; there were no sign language songs, games, or mission introductions throughout the trip. Participants were "free" to sleep or chat throughout the bus tour.

It was therefore rather quiet inside the bus. In comparison, the locals' charter bus from Dalin to Tainan that trailed in the wake of the Venerable Cheng Yen during her monthly tour was also quiet, and there were not many collective programs to attend to (see Chapter 3). Nevertheless, the atmosphere during these two bus trips was different. The trip to Cheng Yen's sermon in Tainan was rather serious so that one could tell it was a trip with a mission: devotees wore uniforms, there were no children on board, and one or two brief speeches or reflections were delivered at the beginning. In contrast, the trip for picnicking was relaxing, as it was meant to be.

The leaders of the picnicking tour reiterated at least three times at the beginning of the trip that its purpose was to relax. The leader of the Tzu Chi Train described in Chapter 3 reminded participants at the beginning of the tour to forget who they were and enjoy the Tzu Chi presentations that included speeches, songs, and other collective activities. In contrast, one of the leaders of this picnicking tour specifically reminded the participants: "Let's not call each other *shixiong* (brothers) and *shijie* (sisters) today. Or else people might be curious about what we are."

Concealing their Buddhist or Tzu Chi identity does not necessarily mean that Tzu Chi people intentionally violate their commitment. Although teenage children participating in the trip brought their nonvegetarian lunches such as tuna sandwiches that were purchased that morning from the 7-Eleven, the food made available for distribution among all participants was nevertheless completely vegetarian. Other than the semi-limited food code, participants behaved like any moderate tourists: taking snapshots and chatting while enjoying the forest and the picnic.

## Bodily Discipline and Benign Social Life

Whether they are in uniform or ordinary clothes, followers embody their Tzu Chi identity in their personal appearance and norms of behavior. The template of the female commissioner indicates a hairstyle—pulling hair straight back from the forehead and fastening it in a back bun—that neatly reveals the forehead and a warm and modest closed-mouth smile; and minimalist personal ornamentation: no colored or permed hair, no nail polish, and no jewelry, but a simple hairpin is accepted, usually a ribbon lotus in black or dark blue. The template of the male devotee includes a crew cut hairstyle or shaved head.

In practice, not every female follows the hair template. In Jiayi, hairstyles generally varied between age groups. Middle-aged female devotees combed their hair to conform to "Tzu Chi head" *(ciji tou)*, yet some younger women, especially those around age forty, still wore their hair short with a slight perm—more typical for women of that age group in Taiwan. These women nevertheless were aware of their variant appearance and would pin their perm flat when wearing uniforms for Tzu Chi activities. In comparison, female devotees in metropolitan Taipei seemed to be more strategic in this matter. I accidentally discovered that a few women attached wig buns to their short colored and permed hair. One woman simply wore a wig of straight hair with a bun in the back on top of her real hair that was glamorous perm.

Like the female devotees in Jiayi, the men also did not necessarily follow the hair template. While keeping their hair short, only a few men had crew cuts and none shaved their heads. One Compassion Faith corps member of Meishan had a perm. Compared to the pattern of women's hairstyle variations, the way men varied their hairstyles from the template did not fall into a clear pattern, let alone one of age difference. However, unfashionable hairstyles by virtue of embodied Tzu Chi identity does not matter as much for men as for women. Rather, the more critical bodily expression for male devotees lies in their rigorous abstinence from such "normative" Taiwanese male social activities as drinking, smoking, and betel nut chewing.

As described in Chapter 2, such bodily discipline is essential for male Tzu Chi identity. Among the twenty-five local devotees and followers I interviewed, the answer to my question of "What characteristics of Tzu Chi males do you think distinguishes them most from non–Tzu Chi people?" is interestingly consistent: no drinking, smoking, or other bad habits. A few women also mentioned that Tzu Chi men are more soft-spoken than most Taiwanese men; some specified that Tzu Chi men do not use profanity.

Put in the Taiwanese cultural context, abstaining from smoking, drinking, and betel nut chewing concerns etiquette more than health. At every social event, such as frequent banquets for all kinds of occasions, from rites of passage to religious ceremonies, one expects to see men drink extensively and distribute cigarettes and betel nuts by virtue of their smooth connections and masculinity. Most local Tzu Chi men I interviewed had already been avoiding alcohol, cigarettes, and betel nuts before they joined Tzu Chi. Only four men recalled previous lifestyles of excessive drinking; among them, two came to Tzu Chi at the point when they felt that continuing such a lifestyle would be meaningless, and the other two did not learn to change until joining Tzu Chi. Only one experienced difficulty in quitting alcohol in the beginning, but he said that it was more of a struggle with his bodily addiction than with social pressure. My small number of samples is not enough to suggest that Tzu Chi tends to attract men who do not adapt to "normative" Taiwanese masculinity. But the consistent emphasis on the outstanding bodily discipline of Tzu Chi men is enough to suggest the significance of Tzu Chi male etiquette in Taiwanese culture.

The importance of etiquette in Tzu Chi identity is further supported by my informants' answers on what distinguishes Tzu Chi women from others. Most replied immediately that Tzu Chi women are tender and smiling. One devotee summarized it in Tzu Chi's terms: "They all wear Tzu Chi cream on their face" *(ciji mianshuang)*—that is, contentment *(zhizu)*, gratitude *(ganen)*, consideration *(shanjie)*, and forgiveness *(baorong)*. A few also mentioned practicality *(tashi)*. One female devotee said she felt the need to improve herself as a Tzu Chi person by exercising more control over her occasionally ill temper.

Compared to the domains of male etiquette, female etiquette seems to involve more emotional control than pure bodily discipline. Nevertheless, etiquette as an essential Tzu Chi distinction is significant for both genders. Although Tzu Chi is clearly a religious movement, no follower mentioned that they are different from others because of Buddhism or any particularly religious interpretation. And, in contrast to the commonly held impression of Tzu Chi followers in Taiwan as enthusiastic do-gooders for merit accumulation, no follower perceived their shared distinction in this light.

## Conclusion

This chapter shows how Tzu Chi developed its local organization in the area where one of its recent monumental mission institutions is established, and the domains in which local individual followers express their Tzu Chi identity in daily life. There are two themes that parallel the development of the local organization and the construction of local individual identity. The first theme is how gender matters in Tzu Chi practice. Women's skillful proselytization played a critical role in the development of local organization. The relatively large number of women gathered at each cooking event also shows how a seemingly invisible women's mobilization powerfully furnishes certain tasks in Tzu Chi events. The construction of individual identity shows no distinctive female or male domains. Nevertheless, the expressions in most domains, except for morality, tend to differ between men and women. It seems that women tend to encompass more complexity in their negotiation for a Tzu Chi identity than men. Choice of diet and rules for uniforms are sometimes not a purely individual choice for women. They tend to be more aware of the necessary negotiation for their Tzu Chi identity and therefore seem to encounter or feel fewer family objections than men do. Although etiquette is an essential characteristic for both Tzu Chi female and male devotees, the expression of female etiquette addresses more emotional control, whereas men's etiquette is almost all about bodily discipline.

The second theme is formalization. Such a general theme in Tzu Chi's process of routinization did not change the local organization dramatically, but the face of the organization—including leadership and the division of labor—is clearly formalized. While I am unable to show the construction of individual Tzu Chi identity diachronically, the model I have tried to sketch suggests that much of the Tzu Chi identity in ordinary life is expressed as an embodied model of a person. Being a Tzu Chi person seems to be less about what one believes than about how one behaves in the ebb and flow of daily life. Tzu Chi people act out their identity by presenting the Tzu Chi identity properly and in the right context, and by changing themselves through bodily discipline, emotional control, and morality—that is, the second body, the followers' body, in the local context.

# — 6 —

# A Genealogy of NGOness

In 2003, I was invited to the China Foundation for Poverty Alleviation in Beijing to give an informal general introduction to Tzu Chi of Taiwan. My friend, who had extended the invitation and was chairing the meeting, introduced me and the subject of my talk to his staff: "I was told by many Taiwan friends: 'One must understand Tzu Chi in order to understand Taiwan' *(yao liaojie taiwan yiding yao xian liaojie ciji)*."

Tzu Chi's success came at a time when the growing number of groups glossed under the term "nongovernmental organization (NGO)" created a "political space" (Fisher 1997) around the globe and across Taiwan. Not only does the profusion of NGOs constitute the global "association revolution" (Salamon 1994) but the "global infatuation with NGOs" (Weller 2005) itself also shows the pros and cons of globalization (Bhagwati 2004). Meanwhile, the sociopolitical transformation of postwar Taiwan has been marked, among other things, by the changing landscape of NGOs since martial law was ended in 1987. For example, the number of registered national social organizations *(quanguoxing shehui tuanti)* increased from slightly more than eight hundred in 1988 to more than two thousand in 1996, and to nearly four thousand in 2000 (Kuan 2002). The newly expanded NGO sector has also become increasingly active, pluralist (Hsiao 2005), and transnational (Chen 2001).

It is worth noting that Tzu Chi has been practicing humanitarian services as a lawful civil association in Taiwan since the 1960s—nearly four decades before it "came out" as an NGO and before the term "NGO," and its counterpart, "NPO"(nonprofit organization), became common in Taiwan. The NGO, joining the "diaspora" of a set of related concepts from "the West" such as civil society, public sphere, and, of course, democracy constitutes what Appadurai (1996) calls "ideoscape" in his model of transnational flows.[1] Since deterritorialization is simultaneously a reterritorialization (Inda and Rosaldo 2002), when the concept of the NGO travels around the world, it creates local and idiosyncratic examples of itself. In doing so, the original concept may be reified or confounded.

Although on a very different subject, consider the idea that the long-existing male-male sexuality in South Africa, identified as "gay" in the processes of modernization, should be reexamined as two identities against the intersection of local and global context (Donham 1998). In a similar way, the career of Tzu Chi—from a grassroots group of fewer than forty women to an NGO on the global stage—develops against the genealogy and history of positioning NGOs in Taiwan and globally. The identity of Tzu Chi in the ideoscape of an NGO needs to be repatriated: How Tzu Chi has been situated in the public sphere in Taiwan and globally is patently intertwined with the formation of a new Taiwanese cultural identity in modernization. This chapter substantiates this thesis.

The anecdote at the beginning of the chapter introduces the idea that the salience of Tzu Chi lies deeper beneath the glitter of its large scale and kudos: There is something intrinsically "Taiwan" in Tzu Chi. Just as many theorists have called for an approach to studying the process through which an NGO emerges and becomes legitimate (for example, Keck and Sikkink 1998), this chapter examines the cultural dimensions of *NGOness* by focusing on the positioning of Tzu Chi in Taiwan's public sphere from grassroots to globalization. NGOness, as defined by Conrue (1999: 75), is "to suggest that organizational structures, forms, relations, and operational methods of . . . NGOs in general are . . . sets of practices through which individuals enact relations and through which varying logics in Pierre Bourdieu's sense are reinforced." The analysis of Tzu Chi practice follows Weller's (2000, 2005) theories for civil association in Taiwan and China, and of the relationships between NGOs and the governments in Taiwan, Hong Kong, and China. This chapter addresses the issue of the ideoscape of the NGO: What does the Tzu Chi experience tell us about the relationship between the NGO and democracy, and between the NGO and the state? To what extent might a prominent grassroots NGO be a representation of its society? What do people see about Taiwan in Tzu Chi? Does Tzu Chi foster a certain Taiwanese cultural identity? It seeks to argue that the making of Tzu Chi's NGOness over the last four decades is a process of freeing Taiwan's civil society and of crafting a Taiwan cultural identity in modernization that is poised to absorb capitalism and democracy, while simultaneously being patently local and intractably global.

This chapter delineates the mobilization for the first Tzu Chi hospital in the 1980s and the second in the 1990s.[2] It analyzes how each of the two processes evolved in the public sphere and proceeded with resource mobilization through the pivotal event of the 1987 lifting of martial law. The mobilization for building hospitals, particularly acquiring the public land, was the key to the politics of Tzu Chi development. Its novel appeal as the builder of the first Buddhist hospital in Taiwan initially engaged the state in Tzu Chi's welfare pursuit. At the same time, the hospital brought Tzu Chi into the national limelight and eventually transformed the movement from a grassroots effort into a huge national association. The striving for the second hospital, however, revealed how—in the course of only twenty years—the mechanism for Tzu Chi's operation in the public sphere and its resource mobilization had changed, both in terms of Taiwan's political context and Tzu Chi's organization.

## Phase One, 1966–1978: Grassroots Charitable Women and the Regime of Civil Morality

The genesis of Tzu Chi from an "out-of-the-way" (Tsing 1993) place in 1960s Taiwan is exemplary of gender, religion, and charismatic leadership. Cheng Yen conceived the idea of "doing something for the society" after she was triggered by two events—the so-called pool of blood and an interfaith conversation with three Catholic nuns (see Chapter 1). The founding of Tzu Chi enabled Cheng Yen to combine her monastic order with the laity to create her humanitarian mission. Although local and low-profiled, its appeal in its first decade was already distinctive. The economic autonomy of this monastic order contrasts Tzu Chi with conventional Buddhist livelihoods in Taiwan, and its concrete goal of raising supplemental medical fees for the poor further distinguishes Tzu Chi from traditional ad hoc and spiritual charitable practices. In this first phase, Tzu Chi nevertheless remained a local grassroots movement. Because of its good reputation for clear bookkeeping and tangible contributions to welfare, it received awards up to the level of local magistrates. Resources were mainly drawn from the money and volunteer energy of its followers with cooperation from other local Buddhist charitable groups.

As Hsiao (2005) writes, from the 1950s to the 1970s, Taiwan had "no genuine NGO sector that could have engaged in any legitimate or genuine state-civil society dialogue or exchange." There were only local associations highly controlled by the ruling Kuomintang (KMT), rich and powerful people's foundations, "transplanted" Western philanthropic organizations, and middle-class social clubs (Hsiao 2005); Tzu Chi did not belong to any of these. Ironically, Tzu Chi was able to survive the KMT authoritarianism because it did not take the route of an NGO.

Tzu Chi embodied "civility" under the *regime* of civil morality—the word regime used in Michel Foucault's sense and in Ong's (1999) application in the Chinese case as schemes of power/knowledge by appealing to certain truth. The KMT's efforts in "harnessing the image of a 'civil' society to [its] not-so-civil state" could be traced back to the New Life Movement (Weller 1999: 44–45), which resurrected in Taiwan from its failure in mainland China (Dirlik 1975). In the 1950s and 1960s, the KMT state attempted a regime of civil morality to discourage such popular religious ceremonies as Universal Salvation, as Weller (1985) coherently analyzes, in order to promote a model of frugality for state ideology that the money for ceremonies could be used instead to help people in the mainland, improve Taiwan's economy, assist the needy at home, or contribute to local construction. In 1976, the Ministry of Interior Affairs instituted a reward code for religious contributions to society.[3] From then on, Tzu Chi received the first prize from the Taiwan provincial government in honor of its social contribution—*xingban gongyi cishan shiye* (running philanthropy and charity)—and has been endorsed each year as the country's model temple. These awards positioned Tzu Chi within the conventional domains of religion and charity, portraying it as a traditional do-gooder that exemplified the proper conduct of religious people under the regime of civil morality. Consequently, Tzu Chi was left outside the state corporatism and was poised to pursue its career of *gongyi cishan* (philanthropy and charity)—the two local terms most frequently used to describe NGOs two decades later in Taiwan (for example, Hsiao 2000).

## Phase Two, 1979–1986: Engaging the State

While perpetuated on the ground of a model temple under the KMT authoritarianism, Tzu Chi further engaged Taiwan's state by actively soliciting public land to build the first Buddhist general hospital in Chinese history. At the same time, Tzu Chi crafted a conduit for a nascent civil society under authoritarianism by rechanneling the social capital for building temples toward building hospitals.[4]

By the late 1970s, Cheng Yen felt compelled to build a hospital after she suffered a heart attack following fourteen years of devoting herself to the Tzu Chi mission (see Chapter 1). This health warning compelled Cheng Yen to institutionalize Tzu Chi and to find regular funds for the mission (Chen [1983] 1998: 35–36). To the dismay of her followers, in May 1979, Cheng Yen revealed her idea of building a general hospital in Hualian. Resolute, Cheng Yen proceeded to seek public land and raise funds.[5]

A year and a half passed and Cheng Yen had pursued seven different parcels of public land in Hualian; however, all of these efforts were in vain. The turning point came in October 1980, when the chairman of Taiwan provincial government, Lin Yanggang, and now late president Chiang Ching-kuo each visited Cheng Yen in Hualian. Then chairman Lin had long been paying attention to Tzu Chi.[6] A posthumous article says that Chiang had known about Cheng Yen and Tzu Chi for a long time, and that when he was still the premier of the Executive *Yuan* (Ministry) he praised Cheng Yen's contribution as the model for all civil servants.[7] This visit marked the dawn of Cheng Yen's dream of building a hospital. With the state's endorsement, local government finally began to actively resolve the land problem.[8]

The second turning point again involves a high-ranking official.[9] In May 1981, provincial chairman Lin announced at the annual ceremony—in which Tzu Chi was again one of the recipients of the award for model temple contributions to social welfare—that the government had assigned an approximate eight-hectare riverside parcel of land in western Hualian City to the Tzu Chi hospital and that its legal transfer was under way.[10] On February 5, 1983, then provincial chairman Li Denghui and the Venerable Zhenhua of Xianggaung Abode performed the ground breaking for the Tzu Chi general hospital, but the hospital was never constructed on this ground.

To everyone's dismay, two months after celebrating the ground breaking, the military notified Cheng Yen to halt the construction and to return the land for defense purposes. With this crisis came the third turning point, which again featured a high-ranking civilian. Soon after the dreadful news, provincial chairman Li assigned to Tzu Chi hospital an 8.9-hectare plot of land that was the site of an experimental farm of the Provincial Hualian Agricultural School, while he and Lin (then minister of the interior and formerly Taiwan provinicial chairman) each negotiated with the military to release alternative land for the school farm. Li's endorsement had clout; despite a little resistance from the school principal, legal procedures at different levels went smoothly (Chen [1983] 1998:

39–41).[11] The ground breaking ceremony took place on April 24, 1984, featuring the president of the Judicial Yuan and the Venerable Yinshun. Two years after the second ground breaking, and seven years after Cheng Yen first revealed her dream, the long-embattled Tzu Chi General Hospital was finally erected on this latest "promised land."[12]

The acquisition of land for the Tzu Chi hospital shows how important a role the state played in determining the success of an NGO at that time in Taiwan. Moreover, the ups and downs in the process show the highly centralized political structure; the first determinant push came from the central authority of the president, and although the first futile ground breaking demonstrated the differentiated power between the military and the civilian, the problem was nevertheless solved by the central authority.[13] As an NGO, Tzu Chi had to depend on favors from the top central power to pursue its goal.

But why would the central power, especially the late president Chiang, be willing to support Tzu Chi in the first place? There are two possible answers to this question. One is pragmatism; Tzu Chi's proposal for welfare reform did not demand policy change from the state, but rather requested partial aid for a self-sponsored plan. The location of the proposed hospital was in one of the most marginalized areas of the country. For such a centralized government, granting a piece of public land meant nearly zero cost, considering its enormous holdings, especially along the mountainous eastern coast, where most of the lands were public. In short, Tzu Chi's plan appealed to the state as more of a contribution than a cost.

This pragmatic appeal becomes particularly clear when one looks at how little money the state spent on social welfare at that time. Until the rapid sociopolitical change of the 1980s, social welfare was never a priority for the KMT regime, which saw its stay in Taiwan as temporary and as preparation for its future "liberation" of mainland China. The total social spending in the central government's annual budget in the 1950s and 1960s accounted for less than 5 percent of its expenditures; and then slowly increased to slightly more than 15 percent throughout the successful economic development of the 1980s (Copper 1996: 76; Zheng 1990: 7).[14] The amount in 1989 was only 4.2 percent of the gross domestic product (GDP). This was not even one-fourth of the welfare expenditures of any member of the Organization for Co-operation and Development (OECD) (Zheng 1990: 7).[15] In this light, Tzu Chi's proposed hospital was nearly a "gift" for the state to improve its welfare at an extremely low cost.

There is another reason why the state was willing to help. As powerful an authoritarian regime as it was, the state could have simply ignored any welfare concern for the ordinary citizen and never even bothered to convert its land from warfare to welfare. Tzu Chi was once again upheld by the regime of civil morality. Tzu Chi had earned its solid reputation during its first phase, building on the idea that it was already a model temple by the time it proposed the construction of a hospital. This project would promote a two-faceted positive model: one of social contribution for religious practice and one of volunteerism for the society as a whole. It was so positive, in fact, that when the construction was halted after the first ground breaking, then minister of the interior and former Taiwan provincial chairman Lin tried to persuade General Song with a "bureaucratic talk": "People have shown their intention to contribute to the society. We, as government, should encourage this" (Chen [1983] 1998: 40). The state saw this "encouragement" in the practical model that Tzu Chi projected as a factor in its own long-term future gain.

Nevertheless, the land acquisition provided a necessary but insufficient condition for Tzu Chi hospital. Besides some donations made by the provincial government and by individual political figures, and despite the fact that the amount of money Tzu Chi saved by purchasing the land at its lowest value rather than at market price merely equaled the cost of construction, the Hualian hospital was *not* built with the government's money. Donations increased slowly in the first few years after 1979. By its first ground breaking in 1983, Tzu Chi had raised only about NT$30 million to meet a total construction cost of NT$800 million.[16] Donations significantly increased after the first ground breaking, and skyrocketed after the second, when news coverage on Tzu Chi in the press intensified rapidly. In other words, Tzu Chi's appeal for its hospital did not have financial ramifications until the plan actually had the prospect of succeeding. Donations did not begin to flow until the construction was in process after the second ground breaking. Contributions came from different parts of the country and in various forms—such as gold, jewelry, and money. In other words, Tzu Chi's national momentum came very much in tandem with the government's support.

What was the role of the mass media? Although people in Taiwan in the 1990s often thought of Tzu Chi as a savvy media player, records of Tzu Chi's news coverage show that the mass media did not initiate contributions to Tzu Chi's first national push. Although Tzu Chi made its pleas for the first hospital as early as autumn 1979 in its *Ciji yuekan (Tzu Chi Monthly)*, the public press did not give any coverage to this later-celebrated appeal until the 1980 visits of Provincial Chairman Lin and then-President Chiang.[17] Although Tzu Chi literature retrospectively attributes the successful fund-raising mostly to the attention received from high-ranking officials and the press, a closer look at the news stories shows that Tzu Chi did not receive wide attention from the press until the first ground breaking in 1983, namely, the impending creation of the hospital. The amount of Tzu Chi's news coverage in general for each year averaged 0.9 stories between 1966 and 1980: The annual total number of stories was zero until 1972, remained below 10 until 1982, and suddenly reached 73 in 1983, followed by 106 in 1986, the year the Tzu Chi Hualian Hospital was completed.[18] Moreover, prior to Lin's and Chiang's 1980 visits, news stories about Tzu Chi tended to be perfunctory coverage of awards ceremonies with no mention of the hospital plan. Although Chiang once instructed the Government Information Office to give more coverage to Tzu Chi and Cheng Yen, the particular issue of the hospital was kept low-key until the land acquisition problem was resolved in 1982.

However crucial the government's endorsement was to Tzu Chi's initial national momentum, Tzu Chi eventually raised funds from society for its first hospital and its subsequent rapid growth. Inasmuch as Tzu Chi made its appeal as simple and straightforward as "building the hospital to save more humans' lives," and because the eventual completion of the hospital was based on individual donations, it can be said to have embodied a collective moral effort by the society. Two issues are involved in this embodiment of the Taiwan collective: One is a backdrop of changing the state-NGO relationship under liberation, and the other, the cultural identity of the Taiwanese collective that emerged in the mobilization.

During the same period from 1980 to 1987, Taiwan witnessed "the mobilization of civil society as represented by the rise of social movements and civil protests" (Hsiao 2005: 43). Similar to these new social movements and NGOs, Tzu Chi negotiated for the state's support of its cause. However, in contrast to many of these contemporaries which were, in Hsiao's words, "very contentious in nature, and demanding various concessions from government" (43), Tzu Chi remained positioned under the regime of civil morality. Nevertheless, the successful mobilization of money from the emerging civil society bespeaks the "localization and indigenization of NGO initiatives," which, according to Hsiao, characterizes that period of change.

In my view, the localization and indigenization in the case of Tzu Chi have to do with the making of the Taiwanese collective identity.

A famous story as described in Tzu Chi literature underlined the linkage between the hospital and the Taiwan collective. During the most difficult time of Tzu Chi fund-raising, in 1981, a Japanese citizen offered to donate US$200 million (at that time, about NT$8 billion) for the hospital's construction, "in order to show his gratitude toward the Nationalist *yidebaoyuan* (a virtue for a grievance, as the opposite of 'an eye for an eye') and because he is a Buddhist" (Wang 1997: 35). To her followers' dismay, Cheng Yen declined this generous offer, "in part because of *minzhu zezun* (the dignity of the nationhood)" (35). "I am a Chinese citizen . . . after eight years of war with the Japanese . . . it's very hard for me to accept help from a Japanese . . . if the hospital is built on government's land and with Japanese money . . . how could we have a say in the hospital?"[19] " '*Futian yifang yao tianxia shanshi* (we invite all benevolent people under heaven to the land of merit),' there should be more people to do good than just one person" (35). The same quote resurfaced in Tzu Chi's recent global development.

Cheng Yen's political identity continues to be ambiguous throughout its recent controversies of relief to China (see below). Considering the political situation in 1981 and the importance of war memories in her childhood according to her hagiography, it is not surprising that she refers to Chinese instead of Taiwanese identity. This story demonstrates that Cheng Yen already had the idea in her mind that the hospital was not simply a project to be done; rather, it was meant to be a platform for grassroots collectivity.

Many devotees in southern Taiwan in the late 1990s still remembered the initial appeal of Tzu Chi: "There is a nun in Hualian who builds a hospital instead of a temple." The contrast between temple and hospital indicates a shift in the cultural idea of practicing NGOness that upholds Tzu Chi's mobilization: a pursuit of concrete welfare based on local and indigenous religious resources. As I have argued elsewhere, the hospital cause alone was not sufficient for wide mobilization, as the continued minority status of welfare-contributing Christians in Taiwan may suggest. Tzu Chi's hospital cause struck a chord because it provided a path to embody bodhisattva by saving more people's lives (Huang 2003b: 225).

Was the hospital, then, a collective redemption for Taiwan, particularly against the backdrop of Taiwan's capitalist development? A Buddhist historian in Taiwan, Jiang Canteng (1997), argues that Tzu Chi's Hualian hospital project appealed directly to the guilt-ridden Han Taiwanese, especially those who lived in western Taiwan. He maintains that Tzu Chi provided an opportunity for the majority of Taiwanese, especially those who have benefited from economic development, to repay people on the eastern coast, who had been largely left behind by the national development policy. This harkens back to the tragedy of the Aboriginal woman who had a miscarriage. The event triggered Cheng Yen to found Tzu Chi (Chapter 1). Indeed, from the perspective that the hospital was built conceptually in lieu of a temple and that it provides a way to be bodhisattva, the donation of money suggests redemption. Nevertheless, it seems inadequate in explaining the ensuing "modernization" of Tzu Chi's NGOness.

## Phase Three, 1986–1999

The late 1980s marked a watershed in both Tzu Chi's development and Taiwan's political history. In 1986, then-President Chiang declared from his deathbed the startling news that nearly four decades of martial law would finally end the next year. Years before the order was enacted, a tsunami of social discontent had built up under the authoritarian era. Social protests from nearly every sector of society displayed their discontent over many issues. Such incidents tallied in the hundreds between the mid-1980s and the early 1990s. They included students' petitions for changing the university law, and farmers' riots against the government's unequal trade agreement with the United States.

The first real opposition party, the Democratic Progressive Party (DPP) was founded in 1986 (and took over the presidential office in the year 2000). The rants and raves in the parliament and the Legislative Yuan not only provided frequent scenes of rambunctious lawmaking for the Cable News Network (CNN) but also culminated, along with other social pressures, in the 1992 election of national representatives—a second election that had long been awaited since the founding of the Republic of China in 1911. Parallel to the political transformation, the "Taiwan miracle" of economic development unfolded into unprecedented expressions of the culture of money: a meteoric surge and a plunge in the stock market, nationwide gambling that involved "amoral" religious oracles (Weller 1994), and popular burlesques that celebrated all sorts of rites from weddings to funerals; at the same time, the crime rate rose and numerous social problems became pronounced. At the time, it was commonly said that "Taiwan was being drowned by money" (*tai oan tsi*[n] *im kha bat,* in Minnan).

## The Ascendance of a Buddhist NGO

In this collective milieu of "anomie"—with too many values competing during the same period of structural transition—Tzu Chi's practical humanitarian appeal ascended to its hallmark of morality, and Cheng Yen became the moral and religious savior of the era. Amid the noise and intensity of sociopolitical change, in exactly 1986, Tzu Chi opened its hospital on the quiet and scenic eastern coast. Coupled with the publicity celebrating this "Tzu Chi miracle," Tzu Chi's total membership increased to slightly more than one hundred thousand in 1986, surpassed a million in 1990, doubled that in 1992, and doubled it again in 1994. The hospital opening therefore marked the prelude to a transformation of the Tzu Chi organization, culminating in the birth of a super and moral NGO.

While Tzu Chi had its moral certainty from the outset, the particular timing of its success highlighted its persona as the conscience of Taiwanese society. Its moral presentation was on a far wider scale and more organized than the more generic presentation of its moral values had been during its early grassroots period.

One of the major and obvious expressions of Tzu Chi's model practice, and particularly the Venerable Cheng Yen's powerful leadership, was a series of national and then international awards bestowed on Cheng Yen. Awards that followed the completion of Tzu Chi's first hospital expressed much wider references and higher honors than the previous "model temples" and "good person." Among the new awards that Cheng Yen received were: the highest national honor from Taiwan's government *(huaxia yideng jiangzhang)*; the 1996 highest honor in contribution to diplomatic affairs *(waijiao yideng jiangzhang)*; and the honor of leader of "harmonious social movement" *(shehui yundong hefeng jiang)*. International awards followed; among the first were the 1991 Ramon Magsaysay Award from the Philippine government (an Asian version of the Nobel Peace Prize) and the 1993 nomination for the Nobel Peace Prize.

In addition to recognition through awards and honors, both Tzu Chi's publicity leader and the government overtly began to promote the image of Tzu Chi as the savior of civil morality in the present peculiar era with its "amoral" social atmosphere. For example, Mr. Wang Duanzheng, the leader of Tzu Chi publicity and publication and also Cheng Yen's brother from her lay identity, identified Tzu Chi in 1993 as the "clear stream in society" *(shehui qingliu)*. In another statement, he said that Tzu Chi would bring benign influence to the current society that has been infected by a bad atmosphere *(buliang fengqi)* of prevailing religious money frauds. The same year, celebrating the Tzu Chi anniversary, the head of the Ministry of Interior Affairs announced to the press that he had invited Cheng Yen to lead the ministry's new series that was devoted to "correcting the bad social atmosphere."

At the same time, Cheng Yen was reintroduced to the society as a great moral leader through a series of large-scale speeches around the island. These speeches were sponsored and organized by the government in conjunction with other nonprofit foundations and the Tzu Chi organization.[20] They not only increased Tzu Chi publicity in the national arena[21] but also firmly established Tzu Chi's role and Cheng Yen's leadership as the pillar of civil morality as it functions in the public sphere and between the state and family. Whether it was Cheng Yen's sermons during the early years of the series or the commissioners' confessions as the series continued, the speeches were less religious preaching than moral lecturing. They taught and showed people how to be good, how to live a wholesome life in the modern world, and, above all, how to be exemplary citizens.

Former President Li once praised Tzu Chi, saying it "purifies people's minds and leads to a harmonious society" *( jinghua renxin, xianghe shehui)*, and that Tzu Chi is the most touching chapter *(zui ganren de yizhang)* in Taiwan's development. On January 1, 1998, at the splendid opening ceremony of the Tzu Chi Da'ai television channel at Chiang Kai-shek Memorial Hall, Cheng Yen led thousands of followers in the square to take the vow of the year: "Purify people's minds, harmonious society, no more disaster in the world *( jinghua renxin, xianghe shehui, tianxia wu zainan)*." The first two, coincidently, reflect former President Li's words.

The regime of civil morality continues to uphold Tzu Chi amid the rapid political, social, and economic change. Yet with the rise of civil society, the regime of civil morality works from the bottom up rather than flowing down from the state under martial law. This change bespeaks a certain Taiwanese cultural identity in the currents of roving commodities and burgeoning democracy. Weller (1999: 100–102) rightly argues for a split market culture, wherein Tzu Chi and other Buddhist revivals stand at one end of the spectrum, and money-seeking ghost worship stands on the other—both have roots in tradition, and both are reflexes of the market itself. I want to add one aspect of Tzu Chi for consideration. Tzu Chi's appeal to the Taiwanese people during the period of rapid economic and political changes lies in that it provides a model of civility to regain a sense of order and control in an increasingly disorienting modernity.

The meteoric membership growth and rapid institutionalization have had significant consequences in the organization itself. One of the major changes is gender distribution. Up to the dawn of opening the hospital, Tzu Chi was predominately a women's group, "a kingdom of housewives." While women continue to comprise 70 percent of the membership, the 1990s success resulted in increased male participation and expedited institutionalization. The two trends somehow converge with an emphasis on precepts. With the forming of a male auxiliary, *Cicheng dui* (the Compassion Faith corps), Cheng Yen instituted the ten Tzu Chi precepts, which consist of the traditional five Buddhist precepts and another five that are specially designed for modern life—wearing a safety belt; speaking gently and abiding by filial piety; no betel nut chewing; no gambling or opportunist investment in the stock market; and no participation in demonstrations or political campaigning (see Chapter 2). The ten precepts initially were meant to discipline male devotees, and soon become mandatory among the increasing heterogeneous Tzu Chi followers. In other words, practicing Tzu Chi in the 1990s means not only contributing time and money for the causes but also leading a new lifestyle: ascetic, disciplined, and staying away from exciting politics and overwhelming money games (see Chapter 5). The micropower somehow reminds one of the New Life Movement; discipline, in a Foucauldian sense, is productive of civil morality and of collectivity—as well as the avoidance of money games and political arenas vis-à-vis the concurrent rapid economic and political change.

## Doing Good and Doing Well: Criticisms and Backlash

Parallel to Tzu Chi's increasingly high profile was the rapid expansion of its mission and its tremendous success in fund-raising. The result was a near avalanche of success and the grandeur enjoyed by a super NGO in Taiwan in the 1990s.[22] In addition to the striking five million members it claimed worldwide and the US$0.6 billion in funds, the total budget for all of Tzu Chi's ongoing projects—not including the second Tzu Chi hospital—as of 1998 was NT$24 billion (about US$800 million).[23]

Moral certainty led to Tzu Chi's support from both the government and society, yet it is quite another thing for morality to work in tandem with democracy. Parallel to the grandeur of Tzu Chi, the rapid sociopolitical change and economic success in postmartial-law Taiwan have resulted in a proliferation of nonprofit foundations, as well as social-welfare NGOs. As Weller (2005) points out, such a profusion of NGOs is mainly the result of legal change, of lifting of martial law, and hence of democracy. As Hsiao (2005) indicates, the NGO landscape in Taiwan has also gone through a transformation from social movements to organized legal persons and civil associations. Tzu Chi has benefited from the legal change in that it finally registered as the first Buddhist—and the first religious—nationwide legal person *(faren)* in 1994. At the same time, the new identity of a nonprofit foundation that Tzu Chi endeavored to adopt under the new circumstances, suffered the connotations of its more traditional and old identity of Merit Society *(Gongdehui)*. Wittingly or unwittingly, as a do-gooder, Tzu Chi joined Taiwan's new NGO landscape, which was filled with secular, local, and international service providers, and advocacy groups that subscribed to a certain modern—and Western—discourse of NGOness. The fact that most NGOs are relatively autonomous financially means that they primarily depend on donations from the public (Hsiao 2005). Amid increasing competition for donations among the proliferated NGOs, Tzu Chi's enormous assets are a conspicuous target.

The "do-good" image of Tzu Chi that was held over from its last phase still prevails among people in Taiwan. This image has its good and bad sides. Tzu Chi is *the* helper of society. For example, a 1999 popular prime-time television series on the misery of a poor single mother adds a new character, a Tzu Chi devotee in lieu of a social worker, who gives the destitute family help. On the other hand, people tend to think that charity, in its most traditional sense, is what Tzu Chi does. Religious people say that Tzu Chi followers do good work, but know little of the Buddhist scriptures. Social welfare people say Tzu Chi is *the* traditional charity and must be replaced in time by modern social welfare.

By 1994, people had begun to speak out against Tzu Chi's size. After a large-scale art and jewelry benefit auction that was reported to have raised about US$10 million, journalists and activists began to call Tzu Chi a "money vacuum" and a "religious monopoly of social welfare." While it was not the only religious—Buddhist, in particular—group to hold multimillion-dollar fund-raising events, Tzu Chi was the most successful and hence the most conspicuous (for example, Xie 1994). As a result, in 1993, Tzu Chi curtailed its routine of revealing the exact amounts of annual donations and many other statistics, such as total membership. As a Tzu Chi Foundation staff member said: "People only look at how much money we have. No one cares how much we have done." This conflicts with clear and open bookkeeping, which was one of the most crucial Tzu Chi practices in building the foundation's reputation during its early phases. For example, during my first visit to the Still Thoughts Abode in 1993, there was a big board in the main hall that clearly displayed detailed income and expenses. That board had been permanently removed by 1994, indicating the tremendous pressure on Tzu Chi.

In the late 1990s, in the context of rising social welfare consciousness, Tzu Chi was a "problem" that I was often personally confronted with as a researcher. One example occurred in 1998 at a two-day conference on social welfare movements that was held at National Taiwan University in Taipei. Despite the variety of social welfare movements presented at the conference, Tzu Chi, though not the subject of my paper per se, was the most talked about topic. Practitioners and students of social welfare movements went to great lengths, sometimes emotionally, to discuss the "Tzu Chi problem" of receiving the lion's share of society's resources for social welfare. A man in the audience adamantly called attention to the important role of Cheng Yen's brother, Mr. Wang, in controlling Tzu Chi, and how "inhumane" Tzu Chi was in that it only delivered relief to one specific village. A young student worried: "Is there any way to stop Tzu Chi from taking so much money and stubbornly putting it in the traditional charity?" Nevertheless, there was no criticism addressed specifically to Cheng Yen; all were about Tzu Chi as a whole. The "Tzu Chi issue" occupied nearly the whole general discussion session until the moderator took the microphone and asked: "Is there any question or comment that is not about Tzu Chi?"

"Pro–Tzu Chi" people are similarly vocal. For example, one day in 1999, I was with a friend of mine at a teahouse in Taipei. After I mentioned what I had learned about how people criticized Tzu Chi, a man who sat in the opposite corner of the teahouse suddenly stood up, pointed at me, and made a scene: "You must understand Tzu Chi! I am not a Tzu Chi person myself but I have a friend who is a Tzu Chi commissioner. I can introduce you to my friend for you to get a better understanding of Tzu Chi!"

The "Tzu Chi issue" was exacerbated when the conspicuous Tzu Chi "monopoly" encountered the uproar inspired by Taiwan's nationalism. Tzu Chi international relief began its fund-raising efforts for flood victims in China in 1991. Such an initiative was a big step in the foundation's internationalization, yet, at the same time, a catalyst for its domestic challenge. Tzu Chi devotees at Jiayi in southwestern Taiwan consistently told me that they had never encountered any difficulty in proselytizing for Tzu Chi since it is "doing good," with one exception: the relief to China. People in Taiwan began to accuse Tzu Chi of "having so much money that it began to help our enemy [that is, Beijing]." However, it was unclear whether the antagonism was against China or against Tzu Chi's size, since devotees in Taipei also described the hostility they received when fund-raising in 1999 for the earthquake victims in Turkey.

Moreover, Tzu Chi devotees responded to the suggestion that their organization is "too big" as something beyond question. A typical answer is echoed in the response given to the press by Mr. Wang, Cheng Yen's brother and the vice CEO in charge of the cultural mission: "It is a good group. Why should people be afraid of a good group becoming too big?" (Xie 1994: 67). According to the secretariat office of the premier of the Executive Yuan, Tzu Chi's representative assumed special privileges in dealing with the state. They always called to meet the minister's secretariat on short notice, often from a mobile phone while they were driving, only minutes away from the Executive Yuan. And they reiterated that "we are doing good (women shi zuo shanshi)" when they negotiated—often effectively—with the minister's secretariat for their request.[24]

Morality that is combined with nondemocratic possession of massive resources often makes outsiders uncomfortable, especially intellectuals. As a senior journalist at Lianhe bao (United News)—one of the three largest newspapers in Taiwan—said emotionally, "Tzu Chi does not open its decision making to the outside. We can't do anything about it. And what really gets you is that Tzu Chi always appears with such strong morality. They are doing good. What can you say about people who do good? They do good, and if you criticize them, then you are the bad guy."

The "Tzu Chi problem" is one that is common for NGOs: they claim to represent the common good, but their means are not democratic (Weller 2005). However, one needs to look closely to distinguish the unique Tzu Chi issues from the common problems of NGOs and democracy.

One of the controversies concerns accountability, which should be handled as a legal issue. Indeed, this issue concerns not only Tzu Chi and other religious foundations but also such reputable and more intellectual-oriented NGOs as the Consumers' Rights Foundation (Chang and Zhang 2003). The issue of conspicuous size specifically concerns Tzu Chi, but it is also where the power of legal solution falls short. The law in Taiwan, and perhaps in most democratic countries, requires minimum thresholds in assets for membership associations and in funds for foundations (the two categories are usually referred to as NGOs in other countries). No upper limits are set, nor is there any kind of antitrust law for NGOs.

Overlapping the size issue are the cultural and historical aspects of the controversies. In a nutshell, Tzu Chi is a grassroots writ large—so large and so fast that it outgrew the normalizing power of Taiwan's civil society, which has just begun to mature. The relationship between Tzu Chi and civil society is dialectical: Tzu Chi pioneered civil society; there could be no Tzu Chi miracle without the rise of civil society (compare Weller 2005). Nevertheless, the strong and pluralist NGO sector brought about by a maturing civil society eventually turns against Tzu Chi. In some ways, the controversies of Tzu Chi and democracy may parallel the recent debates over faith-based welfare services in the United States (Wuthnow 2004).[25]

An infamous civil lawsuit—known as the "pool of blood" (yitanxue) defamation case—against Cheng Yen in 2003 seems to have climaxed the backlash against Tzu Chi. The "pool of blood" refers to the genesis of Tzu Chi (see Chapter 1). The family of the doctor in question, who was said to turn away an Aboriginal woman because she had insufficient funds, sued Cheng Yen after a devotee revealed his identity in 2001. Cheng Yen lost the civil lawsuit and was ordered to pay NT$1 million and one (US$29 thousand) to the doctor's family. To everyone's dismay, Cheng Yen decided not to appeal: "The wound won't heal if we continue to appeal." It was said that the family would later donate the payment from Cheng Yen back to Tzu Chi. This lawsuit made headlines at that time. The family and kinsmen of the poor Aboriginal woman, who supported Cheng Yen, tearfully recounted the tragedy and hence the miserable living conditions of the Aboriginal people. Former patients of the doctor, almost all of them Han Chinese, testified that the doctor often gave treatment for free. The evidence shows that the woman visited the clinic and left without receiving treatment, but it is unclear what drove her out of the clinic. The doctor's family believed the whole "tragedy" was fictional.[26] This case was still discussed with strong emotion in 2005 by both followers and nonsupporters of Tzu Chi.

The case was handled strictly as a legal matter. It is reminiscent of the Amadou Diallo case in New York City in 2000, in which four white plainclothes policemen were charged with killing an unarmed West African man—with forty-one bullets—in the vestibule of a Bronx apartment building, when the man reached his hand into his pocket. Similar to New York's due process of law, in the "pool of blood" case, the issue of ethnicity was not raised. Perhaps the stakes were too high: like "the elephant in the middle of the courtroom that no one wants to talk about."[27]

The "pool of blood" lawsuit summarizes much of the "Tzu Chi issue": It is less a legal issue than a history that is retold in a modern setting and through a variety of mass media. It is a rerun of a series of social and cultural memories that reference a now-savvy NGO that everyone in Taiwan can relate to in one way or another. Unique in the Tzu Chi issue is the ever-hyped attention from the also perpetuating public sphere in Taiwan. What lies at the core is perhaps the idea that the brief history of Tzu Chi somehow captures the Taiwanese imagination in the processes of modernization. Tzu Chi espouses modern NGOness while Taiwanese civil society is "freeing" itself from political and economic constraints. People in Taiwan like to talk about Tzu Chi in the same way that Geertz (1973) interprets the Balinese and their cockfighting: the cockfight is a "deep play" of Balinese culture, and people come to cockfights to look at a representation of themselves, and "saying something of something," that is, interpreting culture as a text. As Geertz puts it, "societies, like lives, contain their own interpretations. One has only to learn how to gain access to them" (453). In my view, Tzu Chi somehow became the access point to "Taiwanese" cultural identity.

## Resource Mobilization for the Second Hospital

With its new image of a super NGO, Tzu Chi launched the mobilization for its second hospital in the 1990s. As with the first hospital, it made the appeal that the foundation's mission was to save more human lives and that land acquisition was the first and foremost necessity for the hospital. Yet, in contrast with the case for the first hospital, both the larger context and Tzu Chi itself had changed a great deal. On the one hand, the political structure after the lifting of martial law had become much more democratized than the authoritarian one that Tzu Chi had dealt with ten years earlier. While acquisition of public land was still a process of political negotiation, the determinant for success was no longer an outright endorsement from the top authority, but instead an involved negotiation with the much more differentiated political landscape brought about by the recent democratization. On the other hand, building the second hospital was quite a different experience from that of the humble grassroots group that struggled to build the first one. Tzu Chi had become the largest national association with a conspicuous wealth of resources,

and mobilizing for its second hospital was the first step toward forming a nationwide medical network.

### Selecting the Location

Tzu Chi publications describe the story of how the second hospital began in
1990 and how the government was immediately involved in its early planning, especially the site selection. On September 24, 1990, in her speech delivered at the Tzu Chi Cultural Center in Taipei, the Venerable Cheng Yen
proclaimed the long-term goal of the Tzu Chi medical mission: a nationwide medical network of branch hospitals in each metropolitan area.[28]
Three months after the announcement, in December 1990, Zhang Boya,
head of the Department of Public Health, Executive Yuan, visited the Tzu
Chi headquarters in Hualian. On behalf of the central government, Zhang
expressed her support of the Tzu Chi medical network plan and suggested
to Cheng Yen the priority sites based on an official survey of the regions that
were most in need of medical resources. These counties were Jiayi, Yunlin,
Tainan, Gaoxiong, and Miaoli.[29] Between November 1990 and March 1991,
local politicians (including county magistrates and parliamentarians),
township heads, and representatives from four of the priority regions visited the Tzu Chi headquarters and received audiences with the Venerable
Cheng Yen to improve their local prospects for acquiring a Tzu Chi hospital.[30] At the same time, Cheng Yen continued to travel across the island, personally investigating possible sites for branch hospitals.[31] By March 1991,
the first priority was identified to be the Yunlin-Jiayi region, which had an
average 2 beds and 1.7 physicians for every 10,000 people,[32] as of Cheng
Yen's visit in February 1991.[33]

Yet for the veteran local followers of Dalin, where the second hospital was
eventually built, the story of Tzu Chi's second hospital, or the Tzu Chi Dalin
hospital, involved local followers' initiatives that began before Cheng Yen's
declaration and consultation with the government. Who primarily initiated
Cheng Yen's eventual selection of Dalin as the hospital site? There are two
slightly different answers among the Dalin locals. The first version emphasized the efforts of the coordinator, Ajing, as I was told repeatedly by her
during the numerous reception meetings at the hospital construction site.
This version is also the statement of the "Dalin Hospital Chronology" that is
posted in the Tzu Chi Dalin meeting place, Dafahang (see Chapter 5)
(translation and emphases are mine):

The Origin: With her conviction of a compassionate mission *(beixin yuanxing)*, the Supreme Person has long planned on a medical network across the country and instructed to build branch hospitals in regions that were short of medical resources. Around 1989, *because of* Sister Lin Shu-jing's [the full name of Ajing] commitment of "land donation" *(juandi)*, the Supreme Person visited Dalin to investigate the land for the [Tzu Chi] local branch office. The Supreme Person then deeply empathized with Yunlin and Jiayi's deficiency of medical resources, and commiserated with the locals for having to endure travel and delays in seeking treatments at distant hospitals. As a result of many people's efforts [the Supreme Person] eventually found the nineteen-hectare land of Formosa Sugar located behind the Dalin train station, and proceeded to acquire the land for the branch hospital.

This version emphasizes that Ajing's spontaneous donation of a piece of her family land was the first thing that led Cheng Yen to pay a visit to Dalin. When she first met Cheng Yen at the Taizhong branch, Ajing asked her commissioner, Mama Jiang, to tell Cheng Yen her wish to donate land so that Cheng Yen would build a Tzu Chi branch office in Dalin. In reply, Cheng Yen said she would soon pay a visit to Dalin to "look at the land." When she arrived, she asked the local followers if they knew of any bigger and better land. This story of the land acquisition was not clearly stated in Ajing's version. It focused on the fact that Ajing was so completely devoted that she volunteered to donate a piece of land from her poor family's scanty property in hopes that her master might eventually come to her village, Dalin.

The other local version briefly mentioned Ajing's contribution to Cheng Yen's first visit to Dalin, and then elaborated in detail about the ensuing search for proper land and the efforts made by the local elite, who were not Tzu Chi followers. Teacher Xu is the primary advocate of this version. She recounted how she and the other local elite had enthusiastically reported all the possible lands to Cheng Yen and accompanied her on every investigative trip, in her words, *kandi* (or *khoa$^n$ te*, in Minnan, literally, "viewing land").

Despite the slight differences involving individual credits, the two versions are in agreement on two things: (1) it was the local followers' original idea to help their charismatic leader come to their town, and (2) none of them knew from the beginning that Cheng Yen was looking for land on which to build a hospital. After Cheng Yen had been disappointed several times by the size of the land they showed her, in February 1991, she announced her idea of building a hospital at a public meeting that was held at the Dalin town hall. Local elites and politicians who participated in the meeting later formed an association and continued to support the mobilization.[34]

### Land Acquisition: The Politics between Sweetness and Morality

Despite the discrepancy between the Tzu Chi central authority and the local followers' rhetoric with regard to the original decision of selecting Dalin as the site, as soon as Formosa Sugar's land in Dalin was selected to be the hospital location, the legal restriction on the assets of state-run companies became the major issue, and local followers no longer had much say in the decision making. The mobilization soon entered the negotiation for land acquisition. From the cascade of print and individual interviews, the mobilization for Tzu Chi Dalin hospital may be divided into five stages:

(1) Between 1990 and 1991, Tzu Chi finalized Dalin as the site for the first branch hospital in conjunction with its long-term mission of establishing a nationwide medical network plan. The issue at stake was to find a plot of land large enough to be suitable for the hospital. Despite the local emphasis on efforts and influences leading (or cajoling) Cheng Yen to Dalin, what primarily attracted the Tzu Chi authority seemed to be the size of the land, its location adjacent to Yunlin County, and access to a highway. From the point at which the Dalin site was selected, Tzu Chi anticipated the problem of land acquisition, for Cheng Yen made it clear that Tzu Chi wanted to purchase, not rent, the land.

(2) From 1991 to 1993, when all the signs pointed to the land acquisition and building of the hospital was likely, Dalin local elites formed a "mobilization association" *(cujinhui)* to help change the legal zoning of the land at both the county and provincial government levels. The political system up to the level of Taiwan provincial government approved the bill that changed the usage of the land in question from agricultural to medical, and reserved it for Tzu Chi, which was required to begin hospital construction within three years. This legal change was announced in 1992. The Department of Public Health, Executive Yuan, approved Tzu Chi's proposal for the Dalin hospital in principle, but with the condition that Tzu Chi first resolve the land problem. While fund-raising for the Tzu Chi medical network took place across the nation, the difficulty of land acquisition became obvious as the newly elected legislator representing Jiayi County, Zeng Zhennong, began to involve himself, according to his

promotional pamphlet, "out of Tzu Chi's and Jiayi locale's request." Indeed, on June 12, 1993, the Ministry of Economy declined Tzu Chi's proposal to purchase the land for the following two reasons: (1) the land in question was designated for Formosa Sugar's agricultural usage and therefore could not be sold; and (2) as a civic association, Tzu Chi was not eligible to purchase land owned by a state enterprise.

(3) Between 1993 and 1994, two weeks after the rejection of the proposed purchase, Legislator Zeng proposed to the Bureau of Economy that they amend the rental regulations of land owned by a state enterprise by deleting terms that excluded industrial usage and by including usage for medical facilities. While the bureaucracy processed the amendment proposal, the negotiation between Tzu Chi and Formosa Sugar continued. As the amendment moved on to the Executive Yuan and was pending, the issue at stake shifted from whether Tzu Chi could rent the land from Formosa Sugar to how it would do so. A new crisis arose when Formosa Sugar massively decreased the size of land being offered for rent from eighteen hectares to six hectares. Political negotiation once again came into play as Tzu Chi's vice CEO Lin and Legislator Zeng sought help from the head of the Department of Health, Zhang Boya. Zhang promised to issue an official document to Formosa Sugar and its two supervising bureaucratic divisions—the Ministry of Economy and its Committee of State Enterprises—to persuade them to accept Tzu Chi's proposed request for eighteen hectares.

During this stage, the Dalin local elite's "mobilization association"—consisting of township-level politicians, local entrepreneurs, schoolteachers, and realtors—also traveled north to meet with the head of the Committee for State Enterprises in Taipei to show their concern about the land rental code issue.

(4) In October 1994, the Executive Yuan passed the new rental regulation of land owned by a state enterprise. On behalf of the Venerable Cheng Yen, vice CEO Lin of the Tzu Chi Foundation went to thank Legislator Zeng at his office in Jiayi County. However, more difficult issues on the lease began to emerge. By December 1994, the issue at stake shifted to the amount of rent. The Tzu Chi authority insisted that since the foundation was charitable in nature, the rent applied should be lower than the legal rate applied primarily for industrial purposes. (According to the legal rate, which was based on the announced estimate of the land value, Tzu Chi would pay a total of approximately NT$6 million in rent each year. The Tzu Chi authority felt this would be an excessive burden in addition to its already enormous costs

for the hospital construction, that is, between NT$6–10 billion.) The rate issue apparently so dimmed the prospect of Tzu Chi Dalin hospital that the county magistrate, the head of Dalin Township, and Tzu Chi began to propose several alternatives to the land of Formosa Sugar. Rumor had it that some locals threatened to protest against Formosa Sugar. None of the several alternatives passed the first step of policy change at the county government level. And there was simply no other public land in Dalin large enough to fit Tzu Chi's plan of a grand hospital other than the one in question, since Formosa Sugar owned one-third of the Dalin district. Nevertheless, by the end of February 1995, at a meeting held at Zeng's office in the Legislative Yuan, Formosa Sugar agreed on the size of the land for rent and the lowest rate, under the condition that Tzu Chi would give priority to hiring its ex-employees and purchase Formosa Sugar products.

(5) By May 1995, before anyone could celebrate the newly reached agreement, negotiations regarding the rental terms and conditions ran into another snag: what to do with the existing buildings upon termination of the lease. Tzu Chi could not authorize the version that was drafted by Formosa Sugar, which gave the latter the right to destroy the establishment at the expense of the former. At the same time, Formosa Sugar could not agree to Tzu Chi's version, which required whoever was responsible for the disposal of the buildings to pay for the cost. A considerable number of private negotiations that involved Legislator Zeng and the Bureau of Economy failed to bridge the disagreement. The problem was once again resolved as politics came into play. On September 30, 1995, twelve days after Legislator Zeng and his wife had their meeting with Mr. Lian Zhan, then the head of the Executive Yuan, Formosa Sugar's board of trustees agreed to accept Tzu Chi's draft version.

On October 14, 1995, Tzu Chi and Formosa Sugar signed the contract at Formosa Sugar's Beigang factory in Yunlin. Tzu Chi now rents the approximately eighteen-hectare parcel of land from Formosa Sugar at the lowest rate for a maximum legal period of fifty years, according to the rental regulations governing land owned by a state enterprise. And Tzu Chi has two priorities: The first is to renew the lease while the buildings are still in usable condition when the lease terminates, and the second is to purchase the land should it become salable under the approval of the Executive Yuan.

Except for Cheng Yen's original wish to purchase the land, every obstacle was resolved according to the wishes of Tzu Chi. The land acquisition for the second hospital was similar to the case of the first hospital in that it required a lot of political intervention, but the intervention appeared to work in a very different way. Under martial law, Tzu Chi only needed the blessings from the top officials. For the second hospital, we see the complexities of adjusting to democracy—especially the key role of the local legislator. Nevertheless, it was still the involvement of top political leaders (Lian Zhan) that made a difference. Therefore, the pattern of top government leader patronage remained salient.[35]

## Local Efforts

The mobilization for the second hospital differed from the first hospital in its pronounced local county-level involvement. The local legislator was just one of the actors in the local efforts. His role was particularly emphasized in the above-mentioned cascade of publications for two reasons: (1) his political and legal influence at the central level as a legislator representing Jiayi in the Legislative Yuan, and (2) at the local level as nearly the "king" of the mountain area of Jiayi County—as opposed to the other local legislator, Wong Chongjun, whose influence is in the coastal area (see Chapter 5 for this distinction). The second Tzu Chi hospital, Dalin, was located in the mountain area. And it just so happened that Legislator Zeng's major involvement in Tzu Chi's negotiation for the land occurred only a few months before the election in December 1995. One of the sources of the above chronology was based on a special pamphlet that detailed Zeng's and his wife's contribution to the legal negotiation for the Tzu Chi Dalin hospital that was printed by Zeng's campaign office. Zeng was reelected in that election.

In addition to the local legislator, Dalin local elites were also actively involved in the mobilization of the second hospital.[36] They formed an association to help lobby for the legal change of the land acquisition and also contributed individual donations.[37]

Local followers' accounts of the hospital mobilization usually end in 1993, when Tzu Chi finalized its decision to pursue the land of Formosa Sugar. Their participation at the level of decision making and land acquisition was rather limited, if not absent. They nevertheless resumed their roles as volunteers after the closing. Beginning with the land clearing in 1996, followed by volunteer work at the construction site (which included reception and sometimes gardening or clearing), and the present mission of hospital volunteering, local followers have been the primary volunteers in the process of building the Dalin hospital.

Local efforts continued in the form of fund-raising after the signing of the lease and also with the construction. In 1997, the Dalin Women's Association organized a fund-raising bazaar for Tzu Chi Hospital. Through the mobilization of the KMT local political system that was usually used for election—that is, including public schoolteachers and the mother organization of the Women's Association, "Service Center for the People" (*Minzhong fuwushe*)—the bazaar raised more than NT$8 million. The head of the Women's Association was elected to be the head of Dalin Township in December 1997. The next year, in June 1998, she hosted the second fund-raising bazaar in conjunction with local NGOs other than Tzu Chi, especially the club for local young businessmen (JAYCEE). Yet, by this time, the Tzu Chi Dalin hospital had already become a current mission for all Tzu Chi followers across the nation. Despite the fact that the Dalin town hall had mobilized all organizations in the KMT local political system, in the end, Tzu Chi followers from all over Taiwan were in charge of 136 stands, which comprised 68 percent of the total 200 stands.

The process itself shows how a national NGO localizes its project in a specific site. In each stage, the level of the forum and the issue at stake shifted, as did the political landscape of this particular NGO shuffle. The first stage was between a charismatic leader and her local female followers. When the acquisition of specific land was at stake, the local elite were drawn onto the scene, while the forum gradually shifted toward the central political level. As the land acquisition finalized, the locals, including both the followers and the nonfollowers, resumed their active participation and, at the same time, revealed the landscape of NGOs in local politics.

## The Nexus of the Global and the Local

The earthquake on September 21, 1999, which killed more than two thousand people and collapsed more than forty thousand houses across Taiwan, marked another turning point for Tzu Chi. Its volunteers' efficient and devoted relief work for the victims, including those who were stuck in the most remote areas, outshone the government's efforts and impressed society. The vibrant criticism against Tzu Chi international relief works disappeared as thousands of Tzu Chi volunteers persistently and powerfully embodied the organization as a pillar of Taiwan's civil society.

The about-face that Taiwanese society showed to Tzu Chi after the quake marks the unique position held by this NGO in Taiwan's public sphere in the late twentieth century: a nexus of the local and the global. Much of Tzu Chi's development in the 1990s focused on broadening its "global ecumene" (Hannerz 1989) overseas expansion, in terms of its proselytization within Taiwanese diaspora and its international outreach (see Chapter 7). By the year 2000, the Tzu Chi diaspora had more or less become one of the "four faces of globalization," like Christian Evangelicalism (Berger 1997) and the Sai Baba movement from India (Srinivas 2002). Different from these examples, Tzu Chi's transcultural practice resulted more in the shaping of religious diaspora within the overseas Taiwanese and Chinese communities than a vibrant mixture of cultures, or creolization (Hannerz 1996). Meanwhile, its cross-border charitable work won its leader a growing list of international awards. Its growing network among its overseas branches and with international NGOs indicates that Tzu Chi might be moving in the direction of a transnational advocacy network (Keck and Sikkink 1998), although Tzu Chi tends to remain within the traditional charity rather than advocating for such "modern" issues as human rights.

While becoming increasingly global, Tzu Chi continues to be a quintessential local concern for Taiwan. Many social scientists continue to view Tzu Chi as a "monopoly," which claims more than its share of social welfare donations. Despite Cheng Yen's adamant reiteration of her apolitical stance, the press never ceases to be interested in her position in Taiwan's political spectrum. The border crossing of Tzu Chi's practice is in part a realization of the bodhisattva's universal ideal of relieving all beings from suffering regardless of ethnicity or nationality, and in part a result of Taiwanese transnationalism straddling two or more countries. Such deterritorialization of a "grassroots NGO" shows the government's diplomatic predicament in sharp contrast. Rather than being antagonistic or even repressive toward this NGO, the government—both the KMT and the DPP since 2000—has attempted to recapture Tzu Chi by collaborating with, if not riding on the coattails of, its outreach beyond borders. For example, President Chen of DPP used Tzu Chi as an example of Taiwan's global engagement, although it is not a member of the United Nations (UN).

## Conclusion

This chapter looks at Tzu Chi as it evolved within Taiwan's national arena. It makes three points:

First, Tzu Chi entered the public sphere with moral certainty. Such a moral image was what first engaged the state to be involved in its humanitarian welfare mission. With the critical endorsement from the state, Tzu Chi's appeal soon resulted in social ramifications until it grew into the largest formal association in Taiwan. As it grew to its huge scale during Taiwan's rapid sociopolitical change, the moral image of Tzu Chi and its charismatic leadership was ever more highlighted—both by itself and by the government.

Second, the relationship between NGOs and democracy is complex and involves many tensions. Tzu Chi achieved its first large-scale mission of building a hospital with help from the authoritarian regime. Yet, as it grew along with rapid democratization in Taiwan, its mobilization for a second hospital, especially concerning the issue of land acquisition, had to deal with the already differentiated political structure and the meticulous legal change and negotiation. In this light, the extent to which a democratized polity provides a "better" environment than an authoritarian one for NGOs seems to be a question that needs more ethnographic investigation. Moreover, the correlation between NGOs and democracy is not unilateral. On the one hand, Tzu Chi's appeal for social welfare reform and the result of its mobilization for the first hospital demonstrates how an NGO might contribute to the formation of an active civil society. On the other hand, as the successful NGO continues to claim public goods by virtue of its moral certainty, its nondemocratic means nevertheless result in harsh criticism and a backlash from the same democratization change that once contributed to the NGO's national momentum. While many scholars see NGOs as a positive contribution to democracy (compare Fisher 1997), whether such a contribution is definitive is perhaps another question for comparative researches.

Third, neither an NGO nor its sociopolitical context remains unchanged. The brief history of Tzu Chi within and along with Taiwan's public sphere shows that the positioning of Tzu Chi NGOness is itself a process of freeing Taiwan's civil society and crafting a Taiwanese cultural identity in market value and democracy, while being simultaneously local and cosmopolitan— a binary distinction of world culture posited by Hannerz (1996: 102–111). As Taiwan was experiencing modernization, Tzu Chi itself changed from a grassroots organization to a large and global NGO with branches within Taiwanese diaspora and UN recognition. The regime of civil morality for Taiwanese NGOness as experienced by Tzu Chi shifted from a model temple to a welfare infrastructure cause, to micropolitics of civility, and to deterritorialization and globalism. By the year 2000, Tzu Chi had become a nexus of the local and the global. As Weller (2000) argues, its organized charity is one of

Taiwan's religious responses to capitalism and the island's status of nonnation/nonstatehood. On the other hand, both government and society attempt to reterritorialize Tzu Chi while its practice expands globally. The hype surrounding Tzu Chi captures a palpable Taiwanese imagination: The career of Tzu Chi's NGOness from grassroots to globalization against a shifting backdrop from the regime of civil morality to a public sphere went hand in hand with the crafting of Taiwanese cultural identity in modernization and the positioning of Taiwan on a global stage. The "deterritorialized, diasporic, and transnational" (Appadurai 1996: 188) world as presented by Tzu Chi seems to have, in turn, facilitated what Appadurai calls the "production of locality" for Taiwan—"as a structure of feeling, a property of social life, and an ideology of situated community" (189). In so doing, Tzu Chi highlights a "cultural intimacy" of Taiwan.[38] Tzu Chi and Taiwan stand as a critique of the salience of modern nation-states (for example, Wang 2000).

Is the Tzu Chi case Taiwanese or global? This chapter explores this question by positioning Tzu Chi in the Taiwanese context, and ends up revealing global issues. The next chapter takes an opposite angle, and discusses Tzu Chi's transnationalism and global aspects.

# — 7 —

# On a Global Stage

This chapter examines the characteristics of Tzu Chi as an example of a global Buddhist movement. More specifically, it seeks to describe the forms and content of the movement's globalism and to examine the ways in which the worldwide spread of a Taiwanese Buddhist movement may represent both the importance of diaspora communities in the globalization process and the desire to move beyond ethnic confines. First, I describe the external and indigenous sources that have blended in Cheng Yen's creation of the movement. Second, I provide an overview of the structure of Tzu Chi's expansion worldwide, which consists of two overlapping parts: mission and missionaries, and, more specifically, their global outreach programs and their overseas branches of devotees. The closing section summarizes the characteristics of Tzu Chi's religious diaspora and the possible implications this example has for the interplay between religion and ethnicity in the global context.

Tzu Chi is distinct from traditional religious practice among overseas Chinese. Despite the mistakenly common label of "Buddhism," the most widely practiced religion among overseas Chinese communities has been Chinese popular religion (Wee and Davies 1999: 80). "Canonical religions, in particular Christianity and Buddhism," did not significantly rise until the 1990s, when a majority of overseas Chinese communities were comprised of well-educated people instead of the earlier laborers and sojourners (82).

From the beginning, Tzu Chi has retained its Buddhist identity—symbolically and legally.[1] However, unlike most Chinese (Mahayana) Buddhists who focus on sutra chanting, Tzu Chi emphasizes building a "pure land" in this world through secular action—namely, making concrete contributions to humanity. Perhaps more important, Tzu Chi is a formal association compared to (although not completely separate from) informal social ties such as personal connections *(guanxi)*, and it operates under a new form of transnational organization in contrast to (although, again, not completely separate from) familism. To be a Tzu Chi person *(Cijiren)* is to identify oneself as a "deployable agent" of Buddha's universal compassion for all the living by contributing to the Tzu Chi mission.[2] Through this contribution, one becomes a member of the group and involved in its "religious community." Such engagement in Tzu Chi, as shown by the present case study, helps to "retain a sense of plausibility" of one's new religious identity (Berger and Luckmann [1966] 1967: 158) and simultaneously offers a vision of Buddhist global community among Chinese and particularly Taiwanese diaspora.

## Pluralism in the Creation of Tzu Chi

Cheng Yen is the key to understanding Tzu Chi, not only because she is charismatic but also because all Tzu Chi missions are very largely the result of her vision of Buddhism. She states how and why Tzu Chi is a reform of traditional Chinese Buddhism:

> In the past, Buddhism in this world had sounds but no forms, and was hardly "practical" *(shiji)*. The so-called Buddhism saw only temples and masters speaking of texts. This was the image of Buddhism in the past 2,000 years, and the reason why most people misunderstood Buddhism as only about chanting sutras and worshipping Buddha, a religion of old ladies . . . I founded Tzu Chi for Buddhism and for all the living,[3] with the hope that Buddhism shall not only exist on [people's] lips, but also manifest itself—to demonstrate the spirit of Buddha through practical action; to pursue "involvement" *(shi)* (the spirit of Tzu Chi) and "truth" *(li)* (the spirit of Buddha) in tandem. (Shi Cheng Yen 1990: 11, 110; quoted in Li 1996: 43)

What Cheng Yen meant by "practical action" and what she saw for Tzu Chi engagement generally consisted of contributions to social welfare carried out by both the monastic order and the laity. On the one hand, in contrast with most Chinese Buddhist priests who rely for their livelihood on alms and chanting scripture *(sutra)* for donations, Cheng Yen and her disciples not only completely support themselves independently from donations but also contribute to the relief funds. On the other hand, the main practice of the lay followers is not chanting scriptures, but contributing their time and money to proselytizing, raising funds, and volunteering for Cheng Yen's mission.

Cheng Yen's mission has expanded from uplifting the poor and caring for the needy in the 1960s and 1970s, to building a Tzu Chi hospital in the 1980s on the impoverished, eastern side of Taiwan where most Aborigines reside, to the "Four Great Tzu Chi Missions" and the four "footprints" *(jiaoyin)*. The Four Great Missions *(si da zhiye)* are: charity (that is, on-site investigation, evaluation, and long-term care); medical care (for example, building hospitals); education (for example, building a university and organizing the Tzu Chi teachers' club and youth corps); and culture (for example, Tzu Chi publications and television). The additional four "footprints" are: international disaster relief, bone marrow drives (that is, collecting bone marrow samples for an international database and transplantation), environmentalism (for example, sorting garbage for recycling), and community volunteers (for example, cooperating with public social workers to provide local elders with long-term care). In contrast with the often ad hoc nature or emphatically spiritual practice of Buddhist charity in Chinese societies, Tzu Chi has established a reputation for searching out causes and mobilizing for effective implementation.

The breakthrough that Tzu Chi has made in Chinese Buddhism is very much the result of the reformism that Cheng Yen developed through her own reflection upon various religious traditions in Taiwan. Tzu Chi literature describes how Cheng Yen came to conceive of the organization through a series of events that spanned her life, both as a lay person and a nun. A closer look at the major events reveals clues to the pluralist influences on Tzu Chi from Japanese Buddhism, Taiwanese folk Buddhism, reformist Chinese Buddhism, and Catholicism (Li 1996).

Japanese Buddhism inspired Cheng Yen to establish an economically independent priesthood. As described in Chapter 1, after her father passed away, Cheng Yen sought help in Buddhism and began to frequent Buddhist temples in her hometown in central Taiwan, where one of the nuns told her that she could no longer agree with the dependency of Chinese priesthood after she had studied Buddhism in Japan. Cheng Yen said to herself, "I shall change the circumstances and build the dignity of Buddhist priests if I become a nun one day" (Chen [1983] 1998: 10–11). Ever since she embarked on the journey toward becoming a nun, Cheng Yen has been abiding by the Chan Master Baizhang's teaching: "A day without working is a day without eating" (Fojiao ciji jijinhui (Buddhist Tzu Chi

Foundation) 1994: 5). Cheng Yen further established three "noes" for her monastic order: no scripture chanting for a fee, no dharma ceremony for a fee, and no begging.

In addition to Japanese Buddhist influence, Taiwanese folk Buddhism (*Zhaijiao*, literally, "vegetarian religion") played a role in Cheng Yen's early years as a priest.[4] After leaving home at the age of twenty-four to become a nun, Cheng Yen wandered to different temples. Eventually, she took refuge with a lay Buddhist in Hualian on the eastern coast. Cheng Yen shaved her head by herself and meditated on and studied the Lotus Sutra alone in a humble house (Chen [1983] 1998: 11–20). Li (1996: 37) argues that both her following a lay teacher and her solitary meditation without formal ordination accord with the tradition of Taiwanese folk Buddhism, the most prevalent form of Buddhist practice in Taiwan until the Japanese colonization (1895–1945).[5]

A link to a reformist Chinese Buddhism came when a well-known reformist monk, the Venerable Yinshun, agreed to be Cheng Yen's tonsure master for her ordination in 1963. Yinshun has made his mark in the contemporary religious-political arena. Inspired by the Venerable Taixu in mainland China during his early years as a monk, Yinshun fled to Taiwan after the Communists took over in 1949 and has long advocated Buddhism of the Human Realm (*renjian fojiao,* also referred to as "Humanistic Buddhism").[6] Because Yinshun's this-worldly approach challenged the then Buddhist authority's otherworldly approach, he was silenced in the 1950s, when they suggested that his position constituted Communist agitation (Jiang 1996; Yang 1988; also see Jones 1999: 131–133). Yinshun was later vindicated and became one of the most respected masters in Taiwan. Tzu Chi and other large Buddhist groups (for example, *Foguangshan* and *Fagushan*) have adopted his reformist notions since the late 1960s.[7]

Catholicism, among other things, compelled Cheng Yen to think of a lay organization as the way to save the lives of those who are too poor to receive medical treatment. One of two major events in 1966 that led her to conceive of Tzu Chi in this way was an interfaith conversation with three Catholic nuns, who criticized Buddhism for looking only to self-fulfillment while ignoring the larger problems of society (see Chapter 1). Cheng Yen then began to contemplate the possibility of *organizing* the widespread "anonymous" Buddhists.[8]

Tzu Chi is therefore a creation that draws inspiration from the religious pluralism in Taiwan. In his historical analysis, Li (1996) argues that Tzu Chi is a religious transformation of postcolonialism. It resonates with Taiwanese folk Buddhism, which barely survived the repression of Japanese colonization and the coercion of the Chinese Nationalist regime, and incorporates elements from foreign traditions—Japanese Buddhism, Chinese Buddhism, and Catholicism, which experienced significant growth under the above two regimes. Li's analysis grounds Tzu Chi in Taiwan's history of Buddhism and shows that it is not merely a reflection of Taiwan's political history, but a new religion that organically combines elements of different religious traditions and which is distinct from, and cannot be attributed to, any of its indigenous and external sources.

Yet Li does not explain why Tzu Chi's distinctive appeal received such a tremendous response from women and why it did not achieve a massive following until Taiwan's economic and political change in the late 1980s. In spite of its monastic leadership, Tzu Chi is essentially a lay movement. A comparison of Tzu Chi women with charitable women in the nineteenth-century West shows the cross-cultural similarities between the two cases. It points to the powerful, shared effects of modernity, the new opportunities women may achieve from rapid structural change, and, in turn, the social ramifications brought about by women's activism. The equally important differences between Tzu Chi and the Western case show that the significance of Tzu Chi lies in its unique expression of Buddhism among people,[9] in the emerging role of women in the public sphere worldwide, and in the development of civic associations in postmartial-law Taiwanese society, as Weller and I have argued elsewhere (Huang and Weller 1998: 392–395).

Tzu Chi is therefore significant in Taiwan's historical context as well as in its modernization. On the one hand, it cuts through the religious pluralism in Taiwan and reveals a dialogue between indigenous and external sources. On the other hand, it opens a space in the public sphere for Buddhism among people, for women's activism, and for the formation of civil society in Taiwan. Moreover, placing it in the larger context of the global arena, Weller (2000: 496) points out that the particular timing of Tzu Chi's rapid growth also coincides with significant change in the global context, especially communication, including both the media and transportation. The significance of Tzu Chi in the global context lies in its breakthrough in manifesting the active role of religion—Buddhism, in particular—on a global stage. The following pages show Tzu Chi's religious transnationalism in terms of three approaches (Huang 2003b): (1) the civil society approach presents Tzu Chi's service-oriented mission, which results in international outreach programs; (2) the religious diaspora approach presents Tzu Chi's overseas growth among the Chinese, especially Taiwanese, diaspora leading to a mobilization of overseas Chinese that will center on Taiwan as a new religious pilgrimage; and (3) in so centering, the Tzu Chi Buddhist travelers mark the third approach, border crossing.

## Global Outreach and Transnational Development

Concomitant to its rapid growth in Taiwan in the 1980s, by 1990, Tzu Chi had broadened its vistas in the following three ways: dedication to both international and domestic relief projects; the organization of worldwide bone marrow donation drives; and the development of overseas chapters. Both international relief and bone marrow donation drives are usually initiated by the headquarters in Taiwan, and receive support from overseas chapters through their fund-raising publicity in host societies.

Four overarching motifs seem to emerge from Tzu Chi's global efforts. One is the vision of a global community, in which people from different parts of the world are considered possible prospects for becoming Tzu Chi followers, who will then join together to build a better world through their collective good work. In Tzu Chi's words: "[We] invite all benevolent people under heaven to the land of merit; with hearts pure, like ten-thousand lotus buds, we will create a world of Tzu Chi" *(futian yifang yao tianxia shanshi, xinlian wanrui zao Ciji shijie).*[10]

The second motif, especially for international relief projects and worldwide bone marrow donation drives, is based on the Buddhist notion of the universal connection of, and empathy with, all the living, regardless of any mundane category such as race, ethnicity, or nationality. In Tzu Chi's words: "Great compassion for those who are known and unknown, boundless mercy for all beings" *(wuyuan daci, tongti dabei).*

Overlapping the first and second motifs is the pursuit of "making benevolent connections" with people around the world, especially the charity recipients of different races, ethnicities, and nationalities. This motif, akin to Master Hsing Yun's *(Xing yun's)* emphasis on links of affinity (Chandler 2005), is highlighted by the priority of direct contacts in its practice of global outreach. One of Tzu Chi's principles for international relief is that it attempts in whatever way possible to personally deliver the relief directly, rather than through other international or local organizations.

The final, yet perhaps the most crucial, motif is the leader's charismatic appeal. Cheng Yen, like a lightning rod, finds herself at "ground zero" for international projects, giving the personal push for the urgency of these missions. "When other people are hurt, I feel their pain; when other people suffer, I feel their sorrow" *(renshang wotong, renku wobei)*.[11] Cheng Yen embodies the suffering of disaster victims and, in her spellbinding speech, evokes the followers' response. As it is shown in the third part of this chapter Cheng Yen's personal appeal has also played a crucial role in inspiring new converts to start proselytizing, which later resulted in the founding of overseas branches.

## International Relief

The first international relief that Tzu Chi delivered was to flood victims in the People's Republic of China (PRC) in the summer of 1991. In four months, Tzu Chi raised more than NT$400 million (approximately US$13 million) (Wang 1998b: 6).[12] Cheng Yen set up the principles for all their international relief efforts with this first project: on-site investigation and delivery without delegating to or going through mediating organizations or institutions, in order to "make benevolent connections" *( jie shanyuan)* with the victims; giving priority to the most seriously affected locations; and respect for local people and culture by not discriminating among recipients (Shaw 1997: 25). Cheng Yen later added another three principles: no wastage of contributions, timely delivery, and gratitude expressed to the victims for the opportunity to help (Wang 1998a: 2–4).

From the Taiwanese perspective, the issues involved in relief to the PRC and to other countries are different. The relief to the PRC is more frequent than to other countries, and Tzu Chi literature presents their PRC project as distinct from other overseas outreach projects. For example, by 1998, Tzu Chi had delivered relief to major disasters in the PRC at least once a year— building houses, schools, and elders' nursing homes. These are inscribed with the name of Tzu Chi. The result has impressed people in the PRC (Huang 2003a), although it does not translate into influences on the government's religious policy (Laliberté 2003).

In addition to the PRC, since 1992, Tzu Chi has provided aid to the victims of natural disasters and warfare and other disasters in more than thirty countries.[13]

## Bone Marrow Donations

In order to embody the bodhisattva's ideal of "giving one's head, eyes, marrow, and brain for the benefit of others," Tzu Chi has also channeled its organizational, medical, and manpower resources into bone marrow donation projects.

In respect to a request by the Taiwan government's Department of Health, Tzu Chi founded its Marrow Donor Registry in October 1993. To combat a common misunderstanding of alleged ill effects experienced by marrow donors, Tzu Chi followers held promotional events and gave blood tests across Taiwan. The drive collected data on more than 140,000 volunteer donors between 1993 and 1997, and increased the number to 242,039 in 2003. The registry is currently the largest databank in Asia and the third largest in the world. Tzu Chi has helped to carry out 559 cases of nonrelative transplants. Among these cases, there were more than 300 international donations to countries such as the United States, Australia, Japan, and Germany.[14] Likewise, almost every overseas branch has held promotions and marrow donation drives in their local community.

## Overseas Branches

The first overseas branch, Tzu Chi United States (*Fojiao Ciji Jijinhui Meiguo Fenhui;* its official name in English is the Buddhist Tzu Chi Foundation, United States), obtained legal status in California in 1985 and was formally founded at the turn of 1990 in conjunction with the opening of its chapter house, the Still Thoughts Hall, named after Cheng Yen's monastery, the Still Thoughts Abode. In the ensuing ten years, Tzu Chi devotees in other countries opened their own branches. Among the more than one hundred countries where there are Tzu Chi members, twenty-eight had formed local chapters by January 2000 (see Table 6).

Most chapters have only one congregation in the country, but the scale of local development varies considerably. Local membership ranges from less than 100 to several tens of thousands. Tzu Chi United States is the largest branch, with 50 offices in 2003. As of 2000, it had 50,000 of the total 90,000 overseas members, and nearly 400 commissioners among the overseas total of 552.

All Tzu Chi branches are located in the major cities of their host countries. According to Mr. Huang Sixian, the head of the Department of

**Table 6** The Tzu Chi Diaspora

| Number of New Branches Each Year | Branches | Africa | Asia | Oceania | Europe | Middle East | Latin America | North America |
|---|---|---|---|---|---|---|---|---|
| 1990 | 2 | | Japan | | United Kingdom | | | United States |
| 1991 | 2 | | Singapore | | | | | |
| 1992 | 7 | South Africa | | Australia<br>New Zealand | Austria | | Argentina<br>Brazil | Canada |
| 1993 | 2 | | Hong Kong<br>Malaysia | | | | | |
| 1994 | 2 | | Indonesia<br>Philippines | | | | | |
| 1995 | 1 | Lesotho | | | | | | |
| 1996 | 1 | | | | | | Paraguay | |
| 1997 | 5 | | Thailand<br>Vietnam | | Germany<br>Spain<br>Netherlands | | Mexico | |
| 1998 | 2 | | | | | Jordan | | |
| 1999 | 3 | | Brunei | | France | | Dominican Republic | |
| 2000 | 1 | | | | | Turkey | | |
| 2001–2005 | 2 | | | | | | El Salvador;<br>Guatemala | |
| Total | 28 | 2 | 9 | 2 | 6 | 2 | 5 | 2 |

Religion as well as one of the highest lay representatives of Tzu Chi, participants in all the branches consist primarily of overseas Taiwanese, secondarily of overseas Chinese. Tzu Chi does not, at any rate, prevent non-Chinese from joining; rather, the foundation makes efforts to go beyond ethnic boundaries. However, there were hardly any non-Chinese among Tzu Chi overseas followers at the time of my fieldwork. During our interview in 2000, Huang Sixian listed three exceptions. The coordinator of the Orlando, Florida, chapter is a Caucasian, but his wife is Taiwanese, and he himself also speaks Chinese. One of the volunteer doctors in the Phoenix, Arizona, chapter is a Caucasian, but this does not necessarily mean that he is a Buddhist or a Tzu Chi follower. And one Caucasian volunteer in the Hawai'i chapter, a hospital administrator by profession, has been a Tzu Chi devotee to the extent that he proselytizes for the organization and received the title of Tzu Chi commissioner in 2000. Recently, *Ciji yuekan (Tzu Chi Monthly)* devoted two pages to a profile of a Christian Zulu woman of Tzu Chi Durban, South Africa. She was a Tzu Chi charity recipient for seven years and became an active Tzu Chi volunteer in 2002, wearing a uniform and delivering speeches about her experience of Tzu Chi as well as her pilgrimage to the headquarters in Taiwan.[15] The same literature also reports that four hundred out of the fourteen thousand Zulu trainees at the Tzu Chi Durban career center have begun to participate as volunteers in the local branch's AIDS relief programs.[16] The special attention given to these exemplars suggests that they are still somewhat exceptional. The majority of Tzu Chi devotees worldwide are Chinese or, more specifically, Han Chinese, according to my fieldwork up to 2000.

Ideally, all overseas branches work toward the model of the headquarters, that is, the "Four Great Missions" plus the four "footprints." In practice, the scope of the overseas branches varies and may be generally divided into three levels: basic, intermediate, and the most active. The interplay between participants' Chinese ethnicity and their practice varies at each level. Practice in the least-active level consists of the initiates' proselytizing efforts, volunteering at local social service institutions and/or hospitals, and providing emergency help to Taiwanese and Chinese immigrants and travelers. There is significant overlap in Tzu Chi overseas branches at the basic level between ethnic boundaries and the scope of practice; they function pretty much as ad hoc ethnic associations based on a shared belief in the Tzu Chi path of Buddhism.

At the intermediate level, services extend beyond ethnic boundaries, even while there is increasing attention to shared cultural heritage. A chapter at

this level has a regular schedule of recruitment meetings, with teas and vegetarian buffets, specific volunteer services, intragroup activities, and special
events such as bone marrow drives, free on-site clinics, and fund-raising for
the headquarters' international relief projects and local projects. Regular
volunteer services reach out to the local community and include visits to local institutions (for example, seniors' houses), support for other charitable
organizations (for example, homeless shelters), street cleaning, and a system for the provision of care to individual charity recipients. Intragroup
activities include regular weekend (usually Sunday) scripture chanting
and meetings regarding the branch's affairs; a study group on Cheng Yen's
teachings; retreats; and community activities such as chorus, sign language
(Chinese) for the deaf, and Chinese (Mandarin) language classes for the locally born second generation. Branches at the intermediate level also have
chapters of the Tzu Chi youth corps among Taiwanese students at local
colleges. The corps functions as an auxiliary to local chapters. In sum,
intermediate-level branches are ethnic Buddhist associations that reach out
to the wider community across ethnic boundaries while creating social ties
and establishing secondary socialization among participants based on a
shared cultural heritage.

Branches at the most active level tend to institutionalize their efforts both
in reaching out to a variety of ethnicities and in preserving the Chinese cultural heritage. On the one hand, large branches take further steps toward
transcending ethnic boundaries. They not only establish medical institutions and charitable systems for serving the local poor of all ethnicities but
also initiate the delivery of disaster relief to neighboring countries. For example, Tzu Chi United States runs a free clinic in Alhambra, California,
which provides most of its services to local Hispanic communities. At the
same time, Tzu Chi United States provides substantial relief to Mexico and
other countries in Latin America, whereas the Australia and Malaysia
branches play leading roles in relief to countries in Southeast Asia.

On the other hand, large branches establish secondary socialization institutions that preserve Chinese cultural heritage and spread Tzu Chi teachings. These institutions consist of Chinese schools for second-generation
immigrants and the youth corps for Taiwanese college students. Large
branches in Western societies—the United States, Canada, and the United
Kingdom—have founded seventeen "Tzu Chi Humanities Schools" (Ciji
renwen xuexiao)[17] and currently have a total of more than two thousand
pupils (in 2000), whose parents do not necessarily participate in Tzu Chi.

Every weekend, youngsters up to the twelfth grade learn Chinese characters through the official textbooks of the Taiwan-based Committee for Overseas Chinese Affairs, as well as Cheng Yen's "Still Thoughts" teachings, using the pedagogical methods formulated by the Tzu Chi Teachers' club in Taiwan.

The Tzu Chi youth corps is important to the education mission, for it brings students outside of Tzu Chi institutions into contact with Cheng Yen's teachings. The Tzu Chi youth corps of some chapters in the United States (for example, Berkeley, California, and Boston, Massachusetts) have their own separate pages on the Tzu Chi Web site, and also organize activities and function as a distinct group in cooperation with local Tzu Chi followers. In comparison, the Tzu Chi youth corps of Malacca, consisting of local-born Chinese rather than Taiwanese college students, has become the branch's focal source of mobilization.

In addition to the obvious importance of introducing the younger generation to Tzu Chi values and practices, the Chinese schools and youth corps are felt to be important because of their potential for bringing Tzu Chi to people who do not have a Chinese ethnic background. When asked if Tzu Chi has a particular plan to draw in non-Chinese, Mr. Huang immediately replied, "Tzu Chi youth are our future, because they study [abroad] and have their cross-ethnic social connections. When they are out of school and start working, they may draw in their classmates, colleagues, and friends."

Meanwhile, Tzu Chi is not waiting for the future to come with the next generation. Recently, it has significantly increased its use of a variety of languages in the media. In addition to holding special meetings completely in English for local non-Chinese,[18] it has been distributing an English quarterly since 1993 and including English pages in its monthly newsletter, along with publishing a series of English translations of Cheng Yen's teachings and children's books. In addition, it has been publishing a monthly journal in Japanese since 1997. A Tzu Chi Web page, in Chinese (traditional and simplified), English, and Spanish, not only covers its daily news and each branch's profile around the world, but also airs the programs of its Taiwan-based television channel. English subtitles have been added to each of Cheng Yen's televised sermons since 2000.

While extending communication beyond the Chinese language and excelling in the use of global media, Tzu Chi has been knitting together its dispersed congregations into a transnational system since 1995. Every January, core members from North and South America and Southeast Asia participate in a "Tzu Chi Spirit" retreat in Houston, Texas. In addition to horizontal ties between branches, the headquarters maintains direct ties to overseas branches. On the one hand, Huang Sixian, sometimes accompanied by one or two of Cheng Yen's disciples, represents the headquarters and presides at every important ceremony of each major branch, such as the year-end thanksgiving party. On the other hand, overseas members (including mainland Chinese) visit the headquarters as part of the "homecoming" ceremonies. Moreover, overseas followers take individual trips to the headquarters in the name of "root finding" *(xungen)*, often obtaining a special audience with Cheng Yen and priority in the long waiting line for volunteer opportunities at the Tzu Chi hospital in Hualian. In addition to these occasional individual links to their religious "roots," representatives of each branch join in an annual retreat in conjunction with the anniversary ceremony at the headquarters; the headquarters also has vacation camps exclusively for the overseas youth and followers' school-age children. A system of transnational itineraries that centers on Taiwan has therefore emerged in the Tzu Chi worldwide organization.

In sum, Tzu Chi's overseas development is an ongoing process of transforming an ethnic religious association into both localized community service and an international nongovernmental organization (NGO) that are not limited by ethnic boundaries. At the same time, the linkage among Tzu Chi congregations has created not only itineraries that bring dispersed overseas Taiwanese and Chinese, in Peter L. Berger's (1967) terms, under the "sacred canopy" of Tzu Chi Buddhism but has also strengthened ties to Taiwan as a pilgrimage center for overseas Chinese. To some extent, Tzu Chi has created a new "homeland" of religious identity in Taiwan in lieu of the traditional cultural homeland in mainland China. In this sense, Tzu Chi worldwide development can be seen as a Tzu Chi diaspora (compare Vertovec 2000: 3).

## A Ceremony for Buddhist Travelers

A good example of how Tzu Chi emphasizes global development was the ceremony for its thirty-third anniversary held in May 1999. One week prior to the anniversary ceremony, seven hundred representatives of various overseas branches arrived at the headquarters and joined an additional three hundred local followers to begin the core members' training retreat being held at the Still Thoughts Memorial Hall. The retreat consisted of various programs that included speeches delivered by, and questions and answers with, Cheng Yen and lay leaders of each of the Tzu Chi missions; intensive small group discussions; and a celebration concert of performances presented by each branch. The corridors to the auditorium in the Still Thoughts Hall were converted into a photo gallery for a "global tour" of overseas branches. Several hundred additional overseas core members arrived on the day of the anniversary ceremony, for the event and a retreat during the following week.

The televised anniversary ceremony on the evening of Sunday, May 9, 1999, began with overseas followers entering the auditorium via the central aisle. All were dressed in the Tzu Chi volunteer uniforms of blue polo shirts and white pants, with the first person of each national branch holding the flag of his or her host country. Each branch sat in a column, with the branch leader in the second row, holding the flag. Meanwhile, the local followers entered the hall through the rear corridors and sat in the balconies. When the second row formed an array of flags and the hall was filled with blue-and-white uniforms, about forty monastic disciples of Cheng Yen entered by the central aisle in two columns and sat down in the first row.[19] Cheng Yen entered via the central aisle, followed by two columns of male corps members in uniform suits, each holding a lighted candle. Cheng Yen sat among her disciples. The emcee called for everyone to rise, face the stage, and salute three times (san wenxun) to the Buddha. The stage backdrop was a six-story-high portrait of Śakyamuni Buddha compassionately looking at, and laying his hand above, the globe. A ten-foot-high panel of the world map stood in front of the backdrop on the stage.

The program included the three essential parts of all Tzu Chi rituals: a sign language song performance, a sermon by Cheng Yen, and the heart candle. Sign language song preceded the sermon. When the sermon ended, with the lights out, representatives (mostly women) of each branch slowly came to the stage, each holding a candle and his or her respective national flag. They formed a row and fell on their knees at Cheng Yen's feet. Cheng Yen lit each representative's candle. One by one, each representative approached the world map panel, placed the candle and the flag below the map in a row, turned on one sparkling light on the map to indicate the location of his or her branch's host country, bowed to Cheng Yen, and exited the stage. They followed in this fashion, one after another, until the world map shone with sparkling lights representing all the Tzu Chi overseas branches.

This anniversary ceremony symbolized Tzu Chi's perception of its future as a global Buddhist movement. The vision was portrayed in the grand backdrop of Buddha overlooking the globe. The ritual of candles and lights on the world map embodied how this vision will be realized: the lay followers who approach Cheng Yen for teaching shall carry those teachings to the world. Overseas followers are therefore central to the Tzu Chi future; yet, these central carriers of Tzu Chi's future, as present at the anniversary ceremony and in the Tzu Chi official description, are primarily Taiwanese and secondarily Chinese. Why are overseas Chinese so interested in Tzu Chi Buddhism? How may such an ethnic constituency contribute to the globalization of Buddhism?

## The Tzu Chi Diaspora

Based on my ethnographic research and supplemented with Tzu Chi literature, the following is a case study of four overseas branches: New York, Boston, Tokyo, and Malacca. Each case is presented with three foci: the process of formation, the description of the membership, and their major practices. The goal is to provide a comparative framework of Tzu Chi overseas development and hence to shed light on the interplay between the Tzu Chi diaspora and the globalization of Buddhism.

### New York

An hour after departing from Times Square in Manhattan, the eastbound L train arrives at its destination in Flushing, Queens. Distinct from the old Chinese community in Chinatown, Flushing is a relatively new Taiwanese community that merged into the multiethnic Queens around the 1980s (Chen 1992). About a ten-minute walk through the busy streets from the subway station, on the top of a ten-story office building, many Taiwanese find a path for their belief in Buddhism.

On April 4, 1991, under the supervision of Mr. Huang Sixian, who was then the chief executive of Tzu Chi United States, Ms. Kang and her friends founded the New York branch at a core member's home. The branch has maintained slightly more than twenty core members since then, but has developed a total membership from two hundred in 1992 to twenty-five hundred in 1994. In September 1992, the branch moved to its rented space. It was a sunny thousand-square-foot office space, divided by file cabinets into two parts. The larger section was a multifunctional hall, as well as a shrine room with a statue of Guanyin on the altar and a portrait of Śakyamuni Buddha on the wall. The smaller part of the room contained two desks, one computer, stationery, and cardboard boxes filled with Tzu Chi publications. At least one core member sat at the desk as a volunteer receptionist every day.

In early 1990, a commissioner, Ms. Qiu, migrated with her family from Taiwan to the United States. Ms. Qiu brought several Tzu Chi publications from Taiwan and distributed them to local Taiwanese through her cousin, Ms. Jian. Among those who received the materials were Ms. Jian's daughter and their family friend, Ms. Kang, who responded by spontaneously proselytizing for Tzu Chi. Both Jian and Kang have been pious Buddhists. Ms. Kang in particular, who later became the founder and first coordinator of Tzu Chi New York, had long participated in Buddhist teachings and many weeklong Chan meditation retreats at local temples since a family crisis that occurred a few years earlier. She described why she eventually chose Tzu Chi to be her path:

> You know, temples are always separated from home, where you and your family actually live, and where your life really is. You may drop everything that bothers you for the time while you are cultivating yourself at a temple. You feel peace of mind at that time. But the problems come right back as soon as you return home, or step out of the temple and back into real life . . . One day I got some tapes of the Venerable Cheng Yen's speeches. I was so touched by listening to her compassionate voice that I found myself crying in the kitchen. I finally found the master with whom I really wanted to work.

Ms. Kang began to collect money from her local Taiwanese friends and sent the contributions to Tzu Chi United States in California. Until the next year,[20] Ms. Kang and her friends remained an informal circle of charitable women. This nascent group consisted of Taiwanese women, many of them Ms. Kang's friends at the Grand Temple *(Zhuangyan Si)*—a Buddhist monastery in Carmel, New York. The New York branch therefore began with a few Taiwanese Buddhist women who later drew in their husbands. In fact, all of the first six local commissioners were women and their husbands who had known each other in Taiwan and had been regulars of the Grand Temple until they became actively engaged in Tzu Chi.[21]

The linkage to the Grand Temple is one aspect of the Tzu Chi branch's embeddedness in the diverse yet lively Buddhist community in and around

New York City. According to Qin's (1992: 5–6) research, in and around New York City there existed more than twenty-three Chinese Buddhist organizations. Eighteen of them were temples and the rest were lay organizations. Almost all the active members of Tzu Chi New York that I spoke with said they already had been pious Buddhists prior to their participation in Tzu Chi. In addition to the Grand Temple, Tzu Chi members had frequented the Great Enlightenment Temple *(Dajue Si)* in the Bronx, the Compassionate Temple *(Ciyin Si)* in Flushing, and the Buddha's Gratitude Temple *(Foen Si)* in Chinatown, for Buddhist teachings. Moreover, both the Venerable Abbot Sheng Yen *(Shengyan)*[22] of the Chan Meditation Center *(Dongchu chansi)* in Elmhurst and the Learned Senior Xianming (a former abbot) of the Grand Temple, attended the founding ceremony of the Tzu Chi New York branch on June 16, 1991.[23]

According to Qin's report (1992: 13–6), local Buddhist temples and associations adhered to the "traditional" practices in Chinese societies. Their major activities included Buddhist festivals (such as Buddha's birthday and the Ullambana Festival), retreats, and the fairly ritualistic practice of "releasing living creatures" *(fangsheng)*. Although most Buddhist temples have scheduled their major activities on Sundays according to the Christian calendar, their Sunday services consisted mainly of scripture chanting, teaching, meditation, and vegetarian feasts. In contrast, Tzu Chi in New York distinguished itself by its secular practice toward concrete goals of engaged Buddhism.

This "practical" approach, in local devotees' parlance, was embodied in the branch's activities. Some of the Tzu Chi practices were similar to those at local temples. For example, members met every Sunday morning to recite scriptures and to watch the videos of Cheng Yen's speeches, and again on Wednesday afternoon to study Cheng Yen's writings. Unlike the Buddhist temples, Tzu Chi New York offered scripture chanting and text study with no Buddhist priests presiding or leading. Tzu Chi further distinguished itself by working for concrete causes. Fund-raising bazaars that supported the headquarters' specific international disaster relief were held occasionally. Each month the branch hosted a public meeting—a "tea party" *(chahui)*—featuring an introduction to Tzu Chi missions, core members' testimonials, and vegetarian desserts. Other days in the month, core members researched and delivered relief to eligible recipients, volunteered at local hospitals, held bone marrow drives, visited local nursing homes and prisons, delivered blankets to homeless people on the streets, and swept streets and shoveled snow in Flushing and sometimes in Chinatown. Tzu

Chi New York also ran a weekend Chinese school for members' children to learn Mandarin and Cheng Yen's teachings, and held other activities (for example, chorus and sign language) for members.

Active branch participants, as of 1994, were middle-aged, upper middle-class Taiwanese couples living in Flushing or around New York City. Such shared origins and lay constituency seem to mark Tzu Chi New York as an ethnic immigrant association that practices Buddhism. However, as cosmopolitan as New York City can be, there are far too many secular and religious options—including Taiwanese Christian churches—other than Buddhism for one to join if he or she only wants to reinforce ethnic identity; moreover, Flushing itself is a distinct Taiwanese community (Chen 1992). Tzu Chi is only one of the many Buddhist lay organizations in New York. The shared social ties and Buddhist identities of the branch's founding members came prior to their Tzu Chi membership. In the context of New York, therefore, Tzu Chi appeals less as an association that caters to Taiwanese ethnicity in the name of Buddhism than as a congregation that emphasizes this particular form of this-world Buddhism. On the one hand, many followers talk about how their lives have changed in light of Cheng Yen's teaching of Buddhist discipline. For example, husbands quit their longtime habit of smoking upon joining Tzu Chi; wives no longer hire maids in order to lead an ascetic lifestyle and to save money for the Tzu Chi mission; and couples no longer fight with each other, making themselves a model for their children. On the other hand, followers see their practice for community and humanitarian causes as individual experience in Buddhism and as the mission of Buddhism in this life. As one convert from Christianity said, "We are not giving. We are benefiting." Personal participation in the Tzu Chi mission is the concrete way toward peace and harmony in spirit. And in so doing, Buddhism is embodied and realized in this world. As one member put it, "I still sometimes go to the Grand Temple . . . where we "speak" of Buddhism, whereas in Tzu Chi we "do" Buddhism . . . I only come [to Tzu Chi] to do work. If I don't work for the mission, I don't come here [Tzu Chi New York], for if I just want to worship Buddha, I can do that at home. Why bother coming here?"

## Boston

Among the four cases, Tzu Chi Boston is the only one that did not begin with Taiwanese immigrants. As in the other three cases, the early formation of Tzu Chi Boston began with Buddhist laywomen's efforts. Ms. Cai, a Vietnamese Chinese, was the first person in Boston to proselytize for Tzu Chi. Born in 1941 in Saigon, Ms. Cai took refuge with a Buddhist monk at age thirty and participated in several Chan meditation classes. She and her family fled the Communist Liberation to the United States in 1979. When her circumstances finally improved after her first ten years of hardship as a refugee, she encountered a series of family crises—her husband's death and the household's division between her married children. She sought help in Buddhism. She first felt inspired by the video of a Taiwanese Buddhist monk's speech[24] and began frequenting the Chan Meditation Center *(Dongchu chansi)* in Elmhurst, New York, because she found no Buddhist temple in Boston. As she continued to procure videos through the Buddhist community in New York, she received some videotapes of Cheng Yen's speeches by mail from a woman of Tzu Chi New York. In the tape, Cheng Yen spoke about Tzu Chi's relief to flood victims in south China. As Ms. Cai recounted during our interview:

> [The Venerable Cheng Yen] built so many houses, one school, and a nursing home [for the victims]. I found myself crying while watching the tape. Although I was born in Vietnam, I always see myself as Chinese . . . What I want to say is that my heart is always with China. I always care about China. So, what the Venerable Cheng Yen has done in China really touched me. Although she is a master in Taiwan, she helps China.

Both Ms. Kang of New York and Ms. Cai of Boston responded to Cheng Yen's appeal. But the consonance they found in Cheng Yen's message differed: While Cheng Yen's personal appeal was the key to Ms. Kang's first encounter of Tzu Chi, a Chinese diasporic sentiment led Ms. Cai to identify with Tzu Chi. Tzu Chi's emphasis on contributions, however, critically resulted in the proselytizing efforts of both Ms. Kang and Ms. Cai.

While continuing her visits to Buddhist temples in New York, Ms. Cai proselytized in Boston for the Tzu Chi mission and sent the money to the New York branch. With the close geographic and cultural link between Boston and New York, Ms. Cai and seven of her women friends worked as an extension of the New York branch, introducing Tzu Chi to their local Chinese friends, and slowly finding eligible charitable recipients—mainly Chinese. In the meantime, Ms. Cai visited the Tzu Chi United States base in California and revealed her goal of founding a Tzu Chi Boston office to the chief executive.

The formation of Tzu Chi Boston eventually materialized when resources other than Ms. Cai's local Chinese friends gradually came along. In 1995, a Taiwanese woman, Ms. Fong, came to Ms. Cai and proposed to form a Tzu Chi youth corps. She had been a schoolteacher in Taiwan and her husband had a doctorate degree from the Massachusetts Institute of Technology (MIT). On September 9, 1995, under the supervision of the Tzu Chi United States base and the New York branch, Ms. Cai, Ms. Fong, and their friends founded Tzu Chi Boston.

In contrast to the Taiwanese constituency of the New York branch and most of the others (except for San Francisco) in the United States, Tzu Chi Boston combines Chinese and Taiwanese immigrants. Soon after its establishment, in 1996, Tzu Chi Boston was divided into two groups or, vaguely, two "districts." Yet the distinction was barely as geographically clear as that between the local Chinese leadership in Penang and the Taiwanese leadership in Malacca across the north and south straits in Tzu Chi Malaysia (see below). The only geographical distinction between the two Boston groups was rather vague in that the so-called first district centered on Chinatown and included South Boston, and the rest of Boston belonged to the so-called second district. However, a closer look at the participants' backgrounds reveals the line between two districts as less geographic than linguistic and lifestyle-oriented. As of 1996, the first group was led by Ms Cai and consisted of the Cantonese-speaking Chinese. Most of them had migrated from Southeast Asia, China, and Hong Kong, resided in Chinatown, Quincy, and Dorchester, and held restaurant-related or Chinatown-based occupations. Ms. Fong[25] led the second group, which consisted of Taiwanese immigrants who spoke no Cantonese, resided in relatively affluent suburbs (for example, Andover and Lexington), and made their living by either self-employment or professions that require high levels of education (for example, engineers).

The two groups were roughly divided between the Taiwanese and other Chinese. A handful of Taiwanese who worked in Chinatown and spoke Cantonese—the lingua franca of Chinatown—joined the first group. In fact, many participants of the first group, including Ms. Cai, did not speak Cantonese at home. They nevertheless were fluent in Cantonese because their social life centered on Chinatown. The first group was therefore the Cantonese-speaking group rather than the Chinese or the non-Taiwanese. Its primary network appears to intertwine with the complicated social ties centering on Chinatown. The social network Ms. Cai built up from her many years of working in different stores and restaurants in Chinatown not only made her grocery shopping convenient but also provided her resources to proselytize nearly five hundred Tzu Chi members.

In contrast, the Taiwanese group led by Ms. Fong had a great deal of overlap with the parents at the Sunday (Mandarin) Chinese school at the Lexington High School. Every Sunday morning, more than one hundred parents drove their children to Chinese school and socialized in the cafeteria for the three hours of class time. The school cafeteria provided a haven for Ms. Fong to spread information about Tzu Chi and to organize further Tzu Chi programs and affairs with her fellow followers.

Related to the difference in background networks is the distinction between the participation patterns. Overlapping with the parents of the Chinese school, the second group appears to be a nuclear-family pattern of participation, as they are young, suburban, professional couples with school-age children. In contrast, although most of its members were middle-aged married women, the Cantonese-speaking group remained women whose spouses rarely came along.

It is hard to say whether the Cantonese speakers and the Taiwanese have different approaches to Buddhism; both are equally devoted to Tzu Chi. Yet within the context of the Buddhist community of the Boston area, the two show differences. Most of the Cantonese-speaking Tzu Chi members also participated in the teachings and festivals at the Thousand Buddha Temple *(Qianfo Si)* in Quincy, where a Cantonese-speaking Buddhist nun presided. By contrast, religious affiliation prior to or other than Tzu Chi among the members of the Taiwanese group appeared to be variable. Many of them attended lectures at the intellectually oriented lay Buddhist study hall (Samantabhadra Hall, *Puxian Jiangtang*) in Lexington;[26] yet many others had no clear link to any local Buddhist temple or organization. In addition, there were also Taiwanese Christians who volunteered for Tzu Chi.

Despite these differences, in 1997, the two districts were reunited under the leadership of one Taiwanese man, Mr. Guo. Although many small meetings, study groups, or scripture-chanting meetings continued separately between the Cantonese speakers and the Taiwanese, the branch's mission has drawn all members together. The branch's activities include: visiting nursing homes (not necessarily Chinese); holding fund-raising concerts, banquets, and bazaars for the headquarters' projects; bone marrow drives in different neighborhoods; and providing help to Chinese who had serious accidents and to Kosovo refugees in Boston. Members of the two linguistic groups also mingle at other functions, such as a dinner party at a core member's home on Chinese New Year.

Between 1996 and 1997, the Taiwanese group relied very much upon the parental network of the Chinese school in Lexington. By 1997, Tzu Chi Boston had formed its own (Mandarin) Chinese school in Malden and gradually centered its association on the Chinese school. In 2000, the school had one hundred pupils whose parents did not necessarily participate in Tzu Chi. Since the branch has no formal meeting place or office, core members now technically meet every Sunday at the school. Taiwanese (including college youth) work as teachers and administrative volunteers along with those who are not Tzu Chi followers. Cantonese-speaking volunteers sell groceries and handicrafts to raise funds for the Tzu Chi mission. The principal, who is a Taiwanese Tzu Chi follower and a social worker by profession, adamantly states that the Tzu Chi branch affairs are separate from those of the school. Tzu Chi followers often handle newsletter distribution and other branch tasks while waiting for their children to finish class.

Although the branch itself appears small and inactive compared to other Tzu Chi overseas branches, due to the high density of colleges in this area, the Boston branch has a relatively active chapter of the Tzu Chi youth corps. The Tzu Chi Boston youth corps—mainly consisting of Taiwanese graduate and undergraduate students—had less than twenty core members as of 2000, yet its activism is clearly demonstrated in that it has a separate page on the Tzu Chi Web site and by its capability to organize activities on its own—though with support provided by the two linguistic groups. For example, the Tzu Chi youth corps of the Boston chapter organized an outdoor concert in Chinatown to raise relief funds for earthquake victims in Taiwan in 1999. The youth corps arranged the performance while adult branch members of both linguistic groups handled the street fund-raising. The youth also organized their own separate training retreat, while adult branch members supported it with food and accommodations, as well as other facilities.

The Boston branch is therefore a lay Buddhist association with relative diversity: the distinction between the Cantonese speakers and the Taiwanese group reflects the diversity of "overseas Chinese" in Boston. At the same time, the rather independently active youth corps and the focus on the Chinese school turn Tzu Chi Boston into a socialization mechanism for Chinese Buddhist culture. The two linguistic groups identify themselves with the Tzu Chi mission, but slightly differ in their emphasis. Members of the

Taiwanese group speak of Cheng Yen's teachings as guidance for their personal and family lives and see the very experience of participating in the Tzu Chi mission as both a task and the learning of Buddhism. In comparison, core members of the Cantonese-speaking group value the practice of Tzu Chi as a Buddhist mission that is equally important to, and the way to realize in this life, what they learn at a local temple. They nevertheless see Tzu Chi more as a disciplined, humanistic movement that embodies Buddhism than as an association that pertains to their family.

## Japan

Tzu Chi Japan, as in the other three cases, began with women's efforts. The founder and coordinator, Ms. Xie, a Taiwanese in Japan, had long been a pious Buddhist before her encounter with Tzu Chi. Ms. Xie's conversion to Buddhism is related to a significant change in her personal life. Her story began in a near-fatal car accident seventeen years ago. She was driving with her mother-in-law and children when her brakes failed on a steep hill in Taipei. Immediately before the car crashed onto the roadside, she prayed to Guanyin Bodhisattva to let her redeem her family. Just as she had prayed, her family was only slightly injured; but she went into a coma. What appeared to her as a miracle and her eventual recovery led Ms. Xie to pursue serving Guanyin with a vaguely conceived mission of compassion. Enthusiastically, she tried her hand at organizing the parental group at her daughter's high school in Tokyo. Lacking experience and a concrete goal, Ms. Xie soon found her first effort rather disappointingly adrift.

It was not until 1991 that Ms. Xie found the "right way" to fulfill her religious pursuit. Through a shopkeeper in Taiwan, she first learned about Tzu Chi and soon discovered that her father-in-law had long been paying membership dues to a veteran commissioner, Mrs. Song, the wife of one of his ex-employees in Taiwan. Through her father-in-law, Ms. Xie contacted Mrs. Song, who then took her to visit Cheng Yen in Hualian. As with many Tzu Chi devotees, Ms. Xie burst out crying when she finally found the "right" master to follow after a long search. She became determined to develop Tzu Chi in Japan.

Ms. Xie first turned to her husband, who consented to support her forming Tzu Chi Japan with one condition: It must be legal. Compared to Ms. Kang of New York, who works as a cashier for a living, and Ms. Cai of Boston, who is a worker at a school meal plan factory, Ms. Xie is from a

wealthy and prestigious family. After consulting with—and receiving positive responses from—several family friends, including a hospital director
from Taiwan, Ms. Xie applied for legal status for Tzu Chi Japan. In contrast
to the overt confidence of Mr. Liu of Malacca, who legalized Tzu Chi in a
Muslim society, Ms. Xie, even during our interview in 1997, was persistently in awe of the liability she and her family would bear should Tzu Chi be
accused of wrongdoing. "If anything goes wrong, not only me, but all my
family will be in trouble. It's no kidding in Japan!"

The Japanese government granted its permission in June 1991. With the
presence of a few Taiwanese Buddhist nuns who had no personal relation to
Cheng Yen, Tzu Chi Japan was formally founded at Ms. Xie's apartment in a
prestigious neighborhood where many diplomats reside. A few years later,
Tzu Chi Japan moved to an office in Sanganjiaya, a relatively less-crowded
area a few stops away from Shibuya—one of the major subway stations and
shopping districts in Tokyo.

The office in Sanganjiaya was a three-hundred-square-foot two-bedroom
apartment that Mrs. Song purchased while her two daughters went to college in Tokyo. The two bedrooms were filled with cardboard boxes of Tzu
Chi publications. One of them had a computer squeezed in among the
stored items. The main room was a small space designed for multiple uses,
which was typical of expensive Tokyo. A table stood near the kitchen for reception, dining, and meetings. The rest of the main room was outfitted with
tatami[27] on the floor and a statue of Guanyin on the altar against the wall.
The tatami room was the worship hall, conference room, or classroom during the day and a bedroom at night for the two full-time volunteers. Other
members came to help with bookkeeping and cooking once a week or to attend special meetings.

Since 1994, helping a Spanish Roman Catholic nun with her food project
for homeless people had been one of Tzu Chi Japan's weekly activities.
Every Thursday, two Tzu Chi devotees helped Sisters Mose and Maria and
their male volunteers with cooking and making rice cakes for the homeless
people during the day, and sometimes helping with the evening delivery at
the park and on the street. Other Tzu Chi followers participated occasionally. One of the two regular Tzu Chi volunteers said she tried to bring her
teenage niece into the project, "but young people just can't stand the hardship here."

The other weekly activity was at the seniors' nursing home in Sanganjiaya, several blocks away from the Tzu Chi office. Tzu Chi volunteers folded

diapers in the basement laundry room of the nursing home. One regular volunteer said she prayed "Amitabha" once on every diaper folded, as a blessing to those seniors whom she, as a volunteer, was not allowed to have contact with in person. In contrast to the personal service found in the Boston and Malaysia Tzu Chi projects, Tzu Chi followers in Japan had to channel their enthusiasm and compassion within the institutional policy of segregating volunteers from licensed practitioners. A core member at the branch interpreted this policy in terms of the background relations between Japanese and non-Japanese. She said, "Most Japanese do not like to accept help from 'lower' people." In her view, Taiwanese immigrants, like Korean and other non-Western minorities, have been historically categorized as "lower" people in Japan.

As in Boston and Malaysia, Tzu Chi Japan often helped Taiwanese and Chinese people who fell victim to accidents or disasters in Japan; they moved quickly, for instance, to help the Taiwanese victims of the 1994 China Airline crash in Nagoya.[28] Tzu Chi volunteers comforted the victims' families and provided them with translation services and other aid. They also helped with relief delivery to the earthquake victims in Kobe in 1995 and provided financial aid to Taiwanese and Chinese students in reduced circumstances after the quake. Local followers have also visited prisons in Japan.

Tzu Chi Japan began to form its youth corps in 1997. The corps consisted of only Taiwanese college students in Tokyo who occasionally participated in the homeless food project and frequently attended special events, such as the year-end thanksgiving party. Japan's youth corps is not yet as independently active as those in Boston and Malaysia.

Compared to the other three branches, the Buddhist clergy has been relatively active in Tzu Chi Japan. As in the other three branches, a handful of non–Tzu Chi Buddhist nuns were often invited to major events. Yet, unlike the other three cases that had one or two of Cheng Yen's disciples visit once a year, the Venerable Dexun, a disciple of Cheng Yen, acted at once as the branch's on-site consultant and the head of the local youth corps, since she was then pursuing her college degree in Tokyo. Dexun led the branch's formal ceremony, gave a brief sermon, and lit the candles at the year-end convocation. Other than the ritual context, Dexun has greatly limited her role to a leader of the youth corps—by virtue of her status as a student in Japan. Tzu Chi Japan maintains its layperson-led Buddhist organization, as do other overseas branches.

Tzu Chi Japan, at least up to the time of my visit in 1997, consisted only of women. Similar to the common background of restaurant workers among the Cantonese Tzu Chi Boston group, women in Tzu Chi Japan worked for a living, except for the coordinator Ms. Xie. Six out of the nine core members in 1997 shared a previous background of a lucrative occupation at hostess clubs. Their common life history was coming from Taiwan to Japan alone in their early twenties and enduring a decade-long struggle for survival. Many of them eventually became successful breadwinners by running their own businesses. In contrast to the family participation among the middle-class members of the New York and the Taiwanese Boston branches, both the Cantonese Boston and the Japan branch persist through only female participation, mainly among those who have a shared, lower social status. Different positions in social stratification somehow foster different participation patterns, as well as a different gender distribution.

Tzu Chi Japan appears to be an ethnic religious congregation that endeavors to navigate its secular action in the host society. Ms. Xie points out the two major difficulties for Tzu Chi development in Japan. First, the above-mentioned institutional policy of segregating volunteers from licensed practitioners is critical to Tzu Chi's focal practice of direct service as the means for realizing the Buddha's path. Second, the Taiwanese constituency of the branch seems at a disadvantage. Ms. Xie was very concerned with the competition between Tzu Chi and the "new religions" and the "new new religions" in Japan, inasmuch as the latter are often aggressive in proselytizing and providing an adaptive channel for immigrants into the host society. Against these difficulties, the few local devotees carried a redemptive undertone; these women have renounced previous bitterness for a new identity as pious Buddhist followers of Cheng Yen.

## Malaysia

Tzu Chi Malaysia is one of the largest overseas branches in terms of the number of local chapters.[29] Tzu Chi Malaysia currently has two branches. The Penang branch runs a dialysis center and a cultural center in Penang and coordinates local chapters in Ipoh, Kelantan, and Kedah of northern Malaysia. The Malacca branch has a splendid assembly hall and leads a total of nine local chapters in central, southern, and eastern Malaysia. By 1997, Tzu Chi Malaysia had a total of thirty-three commissioners (about two-thirds of them women) and a total of twenty male corps members. Except for a handful of Taiwanese, all core members and participants are Malaysian Chinese.

Tzu Chi Malaysia has a relatively full-fledged "Four Great Missions"—charity, medical care, education, and culture. Medical care refers to the dialysis center and local support for bone marrow donations; education refers to the activism of both the Tzu Chi teachers' club and the youth corps; and culture includes the distribution of Tzu Chi publications (including the branches' Web pages) and the presentation of cultural events such as speeches and sign language performance.

Practice of these three missions more or less overlaps with their participants' Chinese ethnicity. As in the United States, Tzu Chi Malaysia moves beyond Chinese ethnicity mainly in the mission of charity. Following the headquarters' categorization, Tzu Chi Malaysia distinguishes "international relief" from "charity." Charity refers to local practice. Across Taiwan and around the world, charity has been the cornerstone of local Tzu Chi practice. Both the Penang and Malacca branches see finding and caring for local, eligible charity recipients as their core practice. Although Tzu Chi is always the first one to respond, and the first to be called, for helping with Chinese or Taiwanese, their charity recipients belong to all ethnic groups. In fact, the charity recipients of the Malacca branch have been primarily non-Chinese, given that the Chinese are relatively the better-off minority in Malaysia. With regard to international relief, Tzu Chi Malaysia has not only raised funds for every appeal from the Taiwan headquarters but also joined their fellow Tzu Chi followers from Taiwan and Australia to help local relief delivery in Indonesia and Vietnam.

### Penang

Penang Island is the state where the Chinese form a significant percentage of the population. In contrast to the Islamic landscape of Kuala Lumpur, streets in Georgetown tell much about the culture of Malaysian Chinese: temples and various Buddhist associations, such as a charitable medicine association *(shiyao xiehui)*, are scattered among lineage halls, Chinese schools, and, of course, arrays of shops with signs in Chinese characters. Although the Tzu Chi cultural center and dialysis center are not far from prosperous areas, in my first visit in 1999, none of the local Chinese I randomly spoke with had heard of Tzu Chi. By 2007, the branch had become much more elaborate with three dialysis centers in Penang, Butterworth, and

Kedah, operating a total of twenty-three machines. The manager of the Penang center said on the branch's Web site: "RM18 million (US $5,130,000) had been spent since 1997 to maintain the three centers and provide financial subsidy to another 180 patients for their dialysis expenses at other dialysis center."[30]

The story of Tzu Chi Penang began in 1989 when a commissioner, Ms. Ye, moved from Taiwan to Penang for business reasons. She continued to practice Tzu Chi during her time off from her full-time job by drawing in local Chinese and by visiting correction institutes and nursing homes for the elderly and the handicapped. Tzu Chi in Penang remained informal and low-profile until a local Chinese businessman, Mr. Guo, joined and became the protagonist.

In May 1993, accompanied by seventeen local followers, Mr. Guo visited Cheng Yen at the headquarters and vowed to develop the Tzu Chi missions in Penang. Three months later, with the help of a few of Cheng Yen's disciples from Taiwan, the Penang liaison office was formally founded and later became the Tzu Chi Malaysia main branch. The office is in Jesselton, one of the most affluent areas on Penang Island (in 1999). It is a converted 0.165-hectare residential house with a roomy backyard that is surrounded by beautiful mansions and private gardens. A young woman in a Tzu Chi uniform works with a handful of middle-aged local volunteers in the two-hundred-square-foot reception office. The backyard has been converted to a garbage recycling post—quite a contrast to its fancy neighborhood. In addition to caring for charity recipients and disaster victims, core members collect garbage in their own neighborhoods for recycling, meet every week for chorus rehearsal or sign language practice, support annual children's and college students' retreats, and sponsor Tzu Chi speeches and fund-raising events.

Similar to the pioneer Tzu Chi followers in Ipoh (the capital of Perak state, north to Malacca), the majority of those who have responded to Tzu Chi's message are Malaysian Chinese students. In the early 1990s, a few students of Universidi Deknologi Malaysia in the Johor State formed their own charitable group, "Love Link," in conjunction with the Buddhist Association on campus. Each student contributed two to three ringgits a month and mailed their contribution to the poor. Through the newspaper, members of "Love Link" contacted Tzu Chi Singapore and began their Tzu Chi practice by caring for the local poor and by visiting nursing homes and orphanages. In 1993, the students sought instruction from Mr. Guo at Tzu Chi Penang, which resulted in the first Tzu Chi collegiate retreat held by the Penang branch. The corps currently consists of students from eight colleges[31] and has been the main thrust of volunteers for local Tzu Chi missions.

## Malacca

In contrast to the rather "invisible" Penang assembly house set among gardens and mansions, the Malacca branch is a splendid edifice with a façade imitating that of the Tzu Chi Abode in Taiwan and is conspicuous in the export-manufacturing industrial park in Batu Berendam, Melaka (Malacca)—several miles away from the Dutch colonial-style downtown. The location of the Malacca branch office says much about the background of its founders, Mr. and Mrs. Liu, an overseas entrepreneurial Taiwanese couple.

Like the founders in the other three cases, Mr. and Mrs. Liu had long been pious Buddhists, and yet they saw Tzu Chi's appeal as more "practical" *(shiji)*. The Lius immigrated to Malaysia in 1988 to set up their garment factory in Malacca, at exactly the same time that most of the labor-intensive factories began to move abroad due to the change in Taiwan's labor market. On one of her visits to Taiwan, Mrs. Liu read a Tzu Chi newsletter and hence took a trip to its headquarters. She was very touched and wanted to begin fund-raising in Malaysia, but her actual initiative did not begin until two years later, when she learned from local Malaysian pioneers about starting with services instead of fund-raising. She and her workers began their regular volunteer work by cleaning at a local poor seniors' house (which consisted of mostly Chinese and Indians).

Mrs. Liu took her husband to visit the Tzu Chi headquarters, where he felt deeply touched by Tzu Chi's autonomous "way of cultivation" in this world. The Lius held the first charitable relief distribution at their factory in 1994,[32] and built the Still Thoughts Hall in 1997 in the current parcel of land located in an industrial park.

Entering the façade, which imitates the Tzu Chi Abode, one sees in the lobby a documentary history of the branch, such as followers feeding the elderly and bathing Aborigines. When asked how the Malaccan locals responded to a conspicuous Buddhist assembly hall in the industrial park, Mr. Liu pointed to the array of photos and said triumphantly: "They can see! We are actually doing things." Next to the lobby is a large auditorium and worship hall with a hardwood floor the size of two basketball courts. The statues of Śakyamuni Bodhisattva, Guanyin Bodhisattva, and Bodhisattva Dizang Buddha are installed against the rear wall of the main hall in exactly the same fashion as those at the Abode in Hualian. The space is big enough for the annual Tzu Chi youth corps retreats of twenty-four hundred students. Adjacent to the altar is a studio, where a few young staff members were editing a documentary of Tzu Chi Malacca. Mr. Liu said, "I prefer hiring Tzu Chi youth who have just gotten out of school." Opposite the main hall is the foundation's office. Its thousand-square-foot space is filled with about twenty desks for staff, bookcases, and file organizers, with the Venerable Cheng Yen's epigrams hanging on the walls.

The second floor consists of a conference room, dorms for retreats, and a master suite exclusively for the Venerable Cheng Yen. Despite the fact that the master is unable to travel abroad due to her heart disease, Mr. Liu had people clean this room every day in preparation for the master's visit.

In 1997, the Malacca branch had twelve thousand members across south, central, and east Malaysia; among them, four hundred volunteers for Tzu Chi missions. Although the Lius are Taiwanese immigrants, the Malacca branch is primarily local Chinese. None of the staff members I met at the foundation office were from Taiwan. On one evening of my stay, about twenty male volunteers came to the branch. Some practiced percussion performance in preparation for their branch presentation at the Tzu Chi thirty-third anniversary concert in Taiwan, whereas others worked on cardboard recycling. All of them were local Chinese who worked during the day and contributed free time to Tzu Chi. Mr. Liu pointed out the difference between the participants' background in Penang and Malacca: "Most of the people in our branch are not employers but employees." Recently the Malacca branch has also begun to include immigrant workers from China (PRC).

The youth corps of the branch also consists of only local-born Chinese. This is similar to the corps in Penang and different from the Taiwanese college students in Boston and Japan. Nevertheless, the Malacca branch not only shares with other branches the recently growing attention to campus and youth but it also has shifted its local development to education. When Mrs. Liu began to feel stuck in Tzu Chi local development, she consulted a commissioner in Taiwan, who said, "Go to campuses." The result of introducing Tzu Chi into the historically developed Chinese educational system in Malaysia has been impressive. The branch has been able to hold Tzu Chi collegiate youth retreats of more than two thousand students in recent years. And many of the foundation staff members are former Tzu Chi youth who have turned their volunteer participation into a professional career. In addition to the youth corps, the Malacca branch has succeeded in gradually influencing Chinese high school students. Despite her lack of teaching experience, Mrs. Liu has been demonstrating Tzu Chi "Still Thoughts Pedagogy" in local Chinese high schools. Her efforts resulted in the formation of the Tzu Chi teachers' club in Malaysia, the first one of its kind outside of Taiwan, whose members include Tzu Chi teachings in their students' curriculum.

Except for its leaders, the Malacca branch has few Taiwanese. Although there are many Taiwanese small shopkeepers and entrepreneurs in Malacca and in other cities that have local chapters under the Malacca branch, they tend to contribute money rather than participate in Tzu Chi activities. Both Mr. and Mrs. Liu spent time with the Taiwanese circle when they arrived twelve years ago, and it was then a relatively small group. The Lius eventually became distant from it because of different lifestyles. Mrs. Liu said she was too busy helping her husband's business to fit in with the leisured lifestyle of local Taiwanese housewives. Mr. Liu, who, like many Tzu Chi male devotees, already shaved his head and wore a Tzu Chi uniform suit every day, raised funds among Taiwanese entrepreneurs for Tzu Chi but did not find further social involvements appealing.

These four case studies share the following aspects: First, overseas Tzu Chi is a rather recent phenomenon. Its first overseas branch in the United States began in 1989 and all the four branches above were not founded until the 1990s. Second, Tzu Chi overseas development, at least from the cases described above, stemmed from the support of overseas Taiwanese and Chinese from societies other than Taiwan (for example, Tzu Chi Malacca consisted mainly of locally born Chinese; and Tzu Chi Boston began with the support of Chinese immigrants from Vietnam), and the participants in overseas Tzu Chi have so far remained within this ethnic group. Third, they have always extended charity beyond ethnic Chinese. Fourth, the founders were already pious Buddhists prior to taking up Tzu Chi practice. Fifth, all the four branches began with women's efforts in response to the appeals of Cheng Yen's charisma and her emphasis on social service. Women continue to play an active role in overseas Tzu Chi. No overseas branch is created, led, or, staffed by Tzu Chi monastic disciples. The pivotal role of women in the organization's development is similar to that in the Japan-originated, grassroots lay Buddhist organization, Soka Gakkai (see Clarke 2005 and Learman 2005a for a comparison between the two cases).

Tzu Chi overseas development not only reveals but also contributes to change in the associations of overseas Chinese. First, its significance for Chinese transnationalism lies in its contribution to the role of Buddhist women in overseas Chinese formal organizations, in which, until recently, women have been underrepresented (Wickberg 1999). Women were more visible in two genres of organizations: First, the vegetarian halls of mainly sectarian religions have thrived in Singapore since the 1930s and continued to be active at least by 1955. These halls were mostly for "socially unattached" women from Guangdong, that is, "widows and wives who had been separated from their husbands" and "spinsters who had vowed not to marry and women who were married 'in name only'" (Freedman and Topley 1961: 20). According to Freedman and Topley, vegetarian halls provided women high status in the religion they belonged to and membership in a religious "family" that helped in fulfilling anniversary celebrations, funerals, and ancestor worship (21–22). Second, associations—what Duara (1997) called "redemptive societies"—mostly originated in China during World War I and subsequently developed overseas. These associations sought spiritual solutions to a world that suffered war and moral degeneration in Buddhist and/or Confucian universalism (1033–1038). Many of these societies pioneered Tzu Chi's charity transnationalism: They were committed to "benevolent works and philanthropy *(cishan shiye),* including traditional charities such as soup kitchens and poorhouses, and also modern hospitals, schools, and contributions to relief works. In these efforts, there was an insistent urge to break through national barriers" (1034).

Different from the vegetarian halls and redemptive societies, Tzu Chi has a distinctive formal Buddhist identity. Nonetheless, Tzu Chi emulated upon the agency of religious women in the two predecessors, especially the redemptive societies (Duara 1997: 1037–1038, 1998: 305–306). The fact that all four branches of Tzu Chi discussed above began with women's efforts confirms that Chinese women are not socially inept but have the informal ties that enable mobilization for civic associations (Weller 1999). Moreover, women's initiatives in their host societies are a direct response to Tzu Chi's appeal for Buddhists to contribute to this world through secular action: in each of the four cases, we see women taking action—proselytizing and finding a local niche for Tzu Chi practice—immediately after being exposed to Cheng Yen's appeal. Although the formal establishment often was brought about by a push from others, the formation of each branch would have been unlikely without the women's enthusiasm and early mobilization outside their homeland. Like their sisters in Taiwan, who in the last three decades have developed a small local group into an islandwide movement, overseas Chinese women were the carriers for the ongoing worldwide growth of Tzu Chi Buddhism.

The second significance of Tzu Chi in the context of Chinese transnationalism lies in its contribution to the emerging study of Taiwanese immigrants and Taiwan. Taiwanese immigrants in each host society have been indispensable in the formation of local Tzu Chi branches. These four branches either received their first Tzu Chi information from Taiwanese immigrants or were founded by Taiwanese. Indeed, the timing of Tzu Chi overseas development is not only linked to its headquarters' growth on a massive scale in Taiwan but is also grounded in the phenomenon of Taiwanese emigration during the 1990s. According to the Ministry of the Interior, from 1990 to 1996, the number of emigrants from Taiwan increased more than fourfold, from 25.5 thousand to 119.1 thousand. As Horng-luen Wang (1999: 214) points out, the majority consisted of "middle-class businesspersons, investors, and professionals," and "no matter where they settle a majority of them continue to be integral members of the society from which they originated."

The spread of Tzu Chi during the Chinese and especially Taiwanese diaspora demonstrates the interplay between Chinese transnationalism and Buddhism. On the one hand, increasing Taiwanese transnationalism—in terms of number of people and intensity of mobility—provides the resources for the overseas development of a Taiwan-based Buddhist organization. On the other hand, the differential appeal of a Buddhist nun's charisma and her mission of social service to overseas Taiwanese reveals a changing aspect of the Chinese diaspora: overseas Chinese from Taiwan, rather than the PRC or the host society, are demonstrating their influence in their local communities, both in the associative life among Chinese communities and in the contributions that reach beyond ethnicity.

Moreover, transnational as they can be, the emerging pilgrimage route between Tzu Chi overseas followers and the headquarters essentially promotes Taiwan as a new "homeland" of religious identity for the Chinese diaspora. In contrast to other Taiwanese transnational Buddhist organizations, Tzu Chi overseas adherents focus on Taiwan as embodying an idea of "home" by first identifying with its Buddhist charismatic center, rather than as a "bridge to cultural heritage," as in the case of Foguangshan (Chandler 2005). Whether the overseas Chinese, defined as "Chinese not residing in China," ever constituted what Maurice Freedman ([1970] 1979: 414, 416; quoted by

Nonini and Ong (1997: 7) calls "a residual China," or, as Nonini and Ong (7) rephrase it, "an imperfect replication" of "real 'Chinese culture' in China," overseas Tzu Chi reveals not only the diversity of Chinese descendants living outside any Chinese society but also the Buddhist influence on the changing identities among "the" overseas Chinese. In the context of Chinese transnationalism, the Tzu Chi diaspora therefore shows an alternative face of diasporic community among Chinese descendants in the global context.

## Conclusion

In this chapter I have described and analyzed the respects in which the Tzu Chi movement may be termed "global": first, the creation of the movement was a synthesis of external and indigenous sources, and the timing of its rapid domestic growth was brought about by both an intensive social change and a breakthrough in interplay of women, religion, and civil society; and second, the global vision of its mission was an adaptation to, and a manifestation of, the role of religion in intensified global communications and increasing Chinese/Taiwanese transnationalism. The result of Tzu Chi's global mission has been to put Buddhism on the world map of border crossings in the fields of international relief and bone marrow donation drives. Another outcome of its global mission has been to organize and highlight the resources of the Chinese, and especially the Taiwanese, diaspora in such a way as to channel it into an active religious movement that is universal in terms of its causes but particularistic in terms of its ethnic constituency, as it focuses on Taiwan as a new religious pilgrimage center for Chinese transnationalism.

Tzu Chi is international yet ethnically specific. The Tzu Chi case shows (1) the importance of culture in terms of both the unique context of the movement's origins and the salience of ethnic identity; and (2) the power of world-affirming religious charisma. First, the trajectory of Tzu Chi's development—from a grassroots women's group to an islandwide movement, to an international nongovernmental organization—is closely related to Taiwan's cultural context. Taiwan is a postcolonial society that is culturally hybrid. It is also a newly developed and democratized society that has ample space for social change. And finally, it is, as an ambiguous nation-state, endowed with wealth and a pool of transnational people.

Second, inasmuch as Tzu Chi's trajectory can be attributed to the cultural context of Taiwan, the fact that its overseas development has drawn upon the Chinese-speaking people from societies other than Taiwan suggests strongly that ethnicity is a salient cultural boundary. However, it is not enough to point out that Tzu Chi appeals to the Chinese diaspora. The question remains: Just why are overseas Chinese so interested in Tzu Chi's particular path of Buddhism?

The answer perhaps lies in the power of Cheng Yen's world-affirming charisma: Her personal appeal serves as a catalyst for a practice that emphasizes concrete contributions to human welfare; that appeal is unique in the context of Chinese Buddhism but is still embedded in the Buddhist canon of universal compassion. Her charisma has led overseas followers to take the initiative to start local missions; and it has also moved people in Taiwan to contribute toward relief projects on the mainland, despite cross-strait political tensions. The fact that she does not travel outside of Taiwan—whereas the leaders of the other two equally transnational groups, Foguang-shan and Fagushan, are globe-trotting (Chandler 2004, 2005; Laliberté 2004; Learman 2005b)[33]—is crucial to Tzu Chi's unique Taiwan-centered transnationalism.

# — 8 —

# Tales from Malacca

Seven kilometers north of picturesque historic downtown Malacca at the entrance to the industrial Free Trade Zone (FTZ) of Batu Berendam, and amid the bustling traffic of Malaysia-made Proton compact cars and streams of blue buses shuttling veiled girls from factory jobs to their *kampong* (villages), stand two huge signs: on the right, *"SIRIM Berhad,"* the industrial development research organization under the Malaysian Ministry of Finance Incorporated, and on the left, atop a huge pole, sits a now-familiar logo—the blue and white sign that depicts a boat and two Chinese characters encircled in a lotus.

One Monday evening in January 2006, about two hours after the broadcast of the fifth Muslim prayer of the day, two men in blue shirts and white pants directed cars entering a front gate marked with a sign in Malay that read *"Pertubuhan Buddhist Tzu Chi Merits Malaysia."* Beneath it was another sign, this one in Chinese, bordered by the lotus logo. It read, *Ciji yuanqü* (Compassion Relief Park), followed by a line in larger font, *Fojiao ciji gongdehui maliujia fenhui* (Buddhist Compassion Relief Merit Society, Malacca Branch).

Inside the gate to the right was a white one-story building with blue signs that indicated in both English and Chinese: "Tzu Chi Free Clinic." To the left stood a two-story compound, with a gated entrance covered by an inverted V-shaped roof supported by four white columns.

Two middle-aged women in dark blue dress uniforms greeted each arrival to the compound with the Malay phrase, *"Selamat Datang!"* (Welcome). Around 7:00 p.m., about twenty volunteers in blue and white or gray uniforms stood at the door of the main building. By 7:30 p.m., their numbers had increased to more than fifty. Visitors were given a navy blue shoe

The Malaysia Branch in Malacca—Modeled on the Abode

bag and instructed to remove their footwear before entering the building. They were also given a small transparent silk sack with a ribbon bow tie that contained a short candle and a tangerine. The candle was made in the group's headquarters in Taiwan, and the tangerine was from Yongchun, Fujian—the ancestral place to one of largest Chinese hometown associations in Malacca. The tangerine signified luck, as the pronunciation of the word tangerine, *ji*, is the same as the word luck, *ji*.

A book exhibit filled the center of the lobby, surrounded by a photographic display that showcased an array of social services delivered to non-Chinese recipients, among them aid to a Catholic nun to help rebuild a house for a Portuguese Malaysian typhoon victim. A white statue of Guanyin Bodhisattva, the Goddess of Mercy, stood at the end of the lobby. More than five hundred participants, all Chinese, were seated on white lawn chairs that faced the stage over which hung an artistic representation of Śākyamuni Buddha looking downward with his palm wrapped over a globe. A video showing a nun, the Dharma Master Cheng Yen, played in the foreground on a large screen. The hall was filled with the sound of the nun's voice preaching in Mandarin Chinese about righteous thought *(zhengnian)*, and except for her voice, the only sounds heard throughout the hall were whispers. A woman next to me reminded her children to be quiet. Two white men appeared, accompanied by a Chinese man and sat in the back row; their conspicuous appearance caused many heads to turn, breaking the silence, but it was immediately quiet again. By 8:00 p.m., an emcee speaking through a microphone greeted the audience with the word, "*amituofo*", and announced that the 2005 end-of the-lunar-year convocation had formally begun.

The 500 participants in this audience constitute only a small part of the roughly 5,000,000 members of the Tzu Chi movement in about 117 countries (as of 2000). The Malacca branch is one of 126 establishments of Tzu Chi among 28 countries holding similar year-end convocations—from Taipei to Boston to Tokyo—roughly simultaneously, according to the Chinese lunar calendar. Yet, very few of the worldwide synchronized ceremonies parallel this one's unique setting in the FTZ.

Its setting reflects a strategy of flexibility for capitalist accumulation through the processes of time-space compression brought about by globalization (Harvey 1989). The compound where this event took place was once a garment factory, owned since 1988 by the branch coordinators, a Taiwanese couple. Like the other 390 manufacturers (out of 435 Taiwanese-owned factories in Malaysia as of 1998; Hung 1999: 124), the entrepreneurs in question moved southward to lower production costs and hence raise profits. Indeed, Malaysia championed Taiwanese southward investment, which between 1989 and 1998 (the years of major accumulated growth realized by Taiwanese businesses) totaled US$1,205,058,000 (Jou and Chen 2001: 430).[1] By 1999, Taiwan had become the third-largest foreign investor in Malaysia, following Japan and the United States (Hung 2000: 24).

However, the preceding vignette is an example of flexibility with a religious twist. The same decade of southward movement by manufacturers saw a major Buddhist revival in Taiwan. One symbiotic aspect of this latest revival was the flourishing of large-scale, modern, and well-endowed Buddhist nonprofit social service programs run on a worldwide basis within the Chinese diaspora.

Tzu Chi exemplifies this global movement. Among the twenty-eight countries where Tzu Chi branches are located, the Malaysian division is most resourceful in terms of manpower, closely following the United States. The Malacca branch was established in 1992 and was the first and the head of what are now seventeen offices (as of 2004) across Malay Peninsula and East Malaysia.

The development of bodhisattvas within an FTZ presents a transnational conundrum, in which two fundamentally opposite motions are manifested—one consists of the drive toward rapacious maximization of profits by navigating the global capitalist system, and the other engages in proactive efforts toward creating universal humanitarianism by relieving suffering in this world. How does the bottom-line goal of foreign entrepreneurship fueled by local state development policy dovetail with the aims of local lay Buddhists who draw their inspiration from a legendary nun of the foreign entrepreneurs' home country?

Deterritorialization is a key characteristic of cultural globalization. It refers to a general thinning of the glue between culture and place, a critical observation that the concept of culture as a bounded entity grounded within fixed boundaries no longer holds true (Appadurai 1996; Gupta and Ferguson 1997; Inda and Rosaldo 2002: 11; Tomlinson 1999: 106–149). While it is a truism that people, culture, and place never were isomorphic to each other, current globalization takes deterritorialization to an extreme (Inda and Rosaldo 2002; Kearney 1995). Inda and Rosaldo (2002) summarize two theories for deterritorialization: Harvey (1989) offers a picture of time-space compression. Low cost and high technology in transportation shorten distance in space, enabling offshore production and outsourcing, and accelerating turnover. Giddens (1990) conceptualizes the processes as time-space "distanciation." In this interconnected world, links and modes of interaction are intensified, and ties across borders are not sporadic but regularized.

Recent anthropological reflections are geared toward bringing roving cultural subjects and objects back down to earth, and an increasing number of studies have heeded the processes of reterritorialization (Inda and Rosaldo 2002; Louie 2000). Reterritorialization refers to a drive to create a cultural "home" or to feel "at home" with global modernity; and, it stresses the importance of locality since, after all, human beings are "*embodied and physically located*" (Tomlinson 1999: 148–149, emphasis in original). What is at stake is not a zero-sum game between the seemingly dichotomous deterritorialization and reterritorialization. Rather, it is about how certain people, things, and ideas in a world in motion are put together in a specific place at a specific time and how a set of concerns for the people in question are formulated (compare Ong and Collier 2005).

Drawing from my fieldwork conducted in Malaysia in 1999, 2004, and 2006, this chapter attempts to delineate the double processes of deterritorialization and reterritorialization in the transnational, seeming like a paradox of bodhisattvas within an FTZ. This chapter describes the multiple flows woven in Tzu Chi's tales from Malacca: the arrival in Malacca, the thickening of Malacca locality, and the conduit back to Taiwan.

## Deterritorialization

The Malacca Tzu Chi branch was founded and continues to be led by Mr. and Mrs. Liu. The Lius had long been considered pious Buddhists, taking refuge in Taiwan Buddhism with two popular monks. Mr. Liu distinguishes Tzu Chi from his previous Buddhist practice: "Our 'Pure Land' practice used to involve only chanting scriptures every day. The Dharma gate of Tzu Chi, which we now identify with, is more 'practical.'"

I first met the Lius in 1999. As soon as I arrived at the branch office, before I could even find my notebook and pen, Mr. Liu began showing me the different departments of the local branch. Prior to my departure for a second trip to Malaysia in the summer of 2004, Mr. Liu called my cell phone to say that he had figured out my flight number and had begun filling in my schedule for the week. The next day, when I arrived at his branch office in Singapore, he was juggling multiple phones, stopping only for a minute to tell me that the British Broadcasting Corporation (BBC) had been there to film their mission in Indonesia. Moments later, he raised his head and commanded that I follow him throughout the first fortnight of my field trip.

The Lius moved to Malaysia in 1988 and set up their garment factory in Malacca. Their two daughters came with them, but were sent to study in the United States soon afterward. The first two years were difficult, they told me. They once mentioned in passing that the earlier arrivals would take advantage of the newcomers (*lau-kio thai sin-kio* in Minnan, literally, "old expatriates 'kill' new expatriates"). When asked whether she spent time with other Taiwanese entrepreneurs' wives, Mrs. Liu answered bluntly: "I was too busy." She told me that she had wanted to do social work ever since college. According to one of her early employees, Citian, Mrs. Liu brought back Buddhist audiotapes, sutras, and images each time she visited Taiwan. She also took the initiative to do charity work by mobilizing employees to donate money to needy people whose plights were reported in local Chinese newspapers. On one of her visits to Taiwan, Mrs. Liu took a fact-finding trip, *xungen* (root finding), to Tzu Chi headquarters in Hualian on Taiwan's eastern shore. She consulted with a commissioner there on how to handle the contributions she collected and asked whether she should begin practicing Tzu Chi in Malaysia. The answer was that she must send all the money back to Taiwan. Mrs. Liu hesitated, since she knew that it would be rather difficult in Malaysia to raise funds solely for use abroad. "You know, people will talk," said Mrs. Liu.

Two years later, Mr. and Mrs. Liu were introduced to the pioneer Tzu Chi practitioners through their lay Buddhist teacher in Kuala Lumpur. From these practitioners, the Lius learned how to perform locally. While Mr. Liu hesitated, due to the legal residence code and their business in Malaysia, Mrs. Liu asked the workers in their garment factory to provide the names of people in need of help. She and her ten workers began volunteering by regularly cleaning a local indigent senior citizens' house (consisting mostly of poor Chinese and Indians). As she recalled: "In three years, we turned the place from miserable filth into spick and span."

In January 2004, Mr. Liu launched a speaking tour across Peninsular Malaya to promote his new book, *The Aesthetics of Life (Shengming de meixue)*. Hours before the first speech in Kuala Lumpur, the Lius and I went to a nearby Japanese noodle house with two Taiwanese entrepreneurs. Mr. Liu, with his shaved head and standard suit and tie and Mrs. Liu, with her hair tied in a back bun and wearing the dark blue *qipao* uniform, contrasted greatly with their fellow Taiwanese entrepreneur friends who sported designer clothes. The two entrepreneurs, both men who owned electronic enterprises, said to me: "We can tell you everything about his past! [Mr. Liu] was our comrade *(nanxiong nandi)*. But he 'left the suffering sea *(tuoli kuhai)*.' He can't even find his golf clubs now."

After dinner, Mrs. Liu went straight to the rear of the stage while the rest of us went to the front row of the ballroom in the Federal Hotel in Kuala Lumpur. I asked her why she declined to join us and she smiled: "Let him [Mr. Liu] do the speaking. I have no time."

In his speech, which elicited frequent laughter and applause, Mr. Liu described how his wife "set him up" to join Tzu Chi:

> She showed me the photos of their volunteer work, and I shook my head over the bad shooting. So she asked me to be the photographer . . . Ladies, if you want your husbands to join, you'd better use some strategy. My Sister (wife) asked me to go to Hualian [the Tzu Chi headquarters] with her, and I really didn't want to go because I couldn't imagine how I could survive a week without meat [in the Abode, the headquarters]. So I told her that I've booked a golfing trip. She challenged: "What kind of successful

entrepreneur are you? You can't even find time to go on one trip with your wife! Never mind." Well, she got me!

He accompanied his wife to the headquarters, where he felt, as he said to me in 1999, deeply touched by Tzu Chi's autonomous "way of cultivation" in this world. In our 2004 interview, he said he had also been moved by the Venerable Cheng Yen's personal moral model *(deheng)*.

By 1994, Mr. Liu was as devoted to Tzu Chi as to his business, and indeed, today he applies much of his skill as an entrepreneur to doing good works. The Lius held the first Tzu Chi charitable relief distribution in Malacca at their factory in April 1994. Mr. Liu realized that having a chapter house was a priority: It was needed both for Tzu Chi development and for making a distinction between his business operation and his religious mission. Two years later, Mr. Liu vowed to the Venerable Cheng Yen that he would build a hall for Tzu Chi. In May 1997, the Still Thoughts Hall was completed right next to—and dwarfing—his factory on a two-hectare land parcel in the FTZ. Coincidentally, when I was at the headquarters shortly before the final foundation was laid, one of the disciples told the Venerable Cheng Yen that Mr. Liu of Malacca had just called to ask her to choose the brand for the auditorium's stereo system.

By 2004, the factory has been torn down and replaced by a new one-story complex that consisted of a kindergarten, an auditorium, a classroom for Tzu Chi humanities, a bookstore café, and a free clinic. This new arrangement says much about the change in the Lius' life: They closed down their factory and devoted themselves and their assets full-time to Tzu Chi's mission.

Put in a larger context, the Lius' migration to Malaysia was part of the Taiwanese capital outflow and regional division of labor in Asia. Since 1987, the pressure from a strong Taiwan dollar and the rise of environmentalism and labor movements had resulted in an increasing number of enterprises leaving Taiwan. This trend reached a crescendo between 1988 and 1993. The textile and garment industries were the most prone to exit the country because of advantages offered by cheap labor and production. By the year 2000, the wage standard for general labor in Taiwan was the second highest among the Four Dragons, second only to Singapore (Hung 2000: 30). Moreover, preoccupied with labor-intensive industries and fettering rapid capital outflow to mainland China, in 1993, Taiwan's government championed the "Southward Policy" *(nanxiang zhengce)* and further encouraged investment in Southeast Asia (24). At the same time, after twenty years of import-substitute and export-oriented development, Malaysia launched the Industrial Master Plan for 1986–1995, further pushing export-oriented development by speeding up the growth of manufacturing. In 1986, Malaysia implemented new investment regulations, established the Free Trade Zones, which attracted billions in foreign investment, and encouraged export (Hung 1999: 123).

What marked the Lius as peripatetic Buddhist entrepreneurs was Tzu Chi's distinctly portable model for local practices. As many have pointed out, part and parcel of the increase in Taiwanese transmigration in the 1990s[2] was the practice of "two-legged existence"—the frequent shuttling back and forth between Taiwan and one or more countries (for example, Tseng 1995).[3] As with the founding of the Tokyo branch, Tzu Chi's Malacca branch began with frequent visits to Taiwan by an overseas Taiwanese entrepreneur's wife concomitant with her belief in Buddhism. In contrast to the lonely computer widows in Silicon Valley depicted by Ong (1999), in the case of Tzu Chi, women have taken the initiative to be the carriers of transnational Buddhism and global humanitarianism. As discussed below, women's agency personified by the middle- and working-class followers in religious deterritorialization and reterritorialization bears a strong relevance to—if not a contrast with—class differential gendered transnationalism (Nonini 1997: 215).

It is clear that Mrs. Liu and the founder of the Tokyo branch were both pious Buddhists as well as transnationalists. Mrs. Liu disseminated Buddhist information from Taiwan prior to her visit to Tzu Chi headquarters. Her first instinct to carry out Tzu Chi in Malaysia by collecting money locally and sending it back to Taiwan was in line with her hitherto "traditional" practice of Buddhist charity; that is, through donations either to those in need or to those who could carry out the charity's mission. But soon they found the traditional Buddhist approach unfulfilling and found solace in Tzu Chi. As recounted by the Lius' former accountant:

Many people would feel the merciful heart (lianminxin) when they see others suffer! But they don't know how to help them, where to begin. When we were working in her office, Ms. Jian [that is, Mrs. Liu] had already started collecting charity money and sending it to the newspaper. We read about people who suffer and who need money for surgery. Mrs. Liu told us to start the drive and she'll put in the rest to make ends met.

Each one of us put in five or ten [ringgit]. We're all in one office, so we could influence one another. I was in charge of the clipping and book-keeping [of this charity fund] . . . I just reported to her the clippings, she rarely checked the source. Just told me to go ahead to send in fifty [ringgit] (to the newspaper). It's very little *lah!* But because we're mindful *(women hen youxin)*, the cases increased to so many that we couldn't handle them all. Then we found Tzu Chi, and learned that the money we sent in was of-ten insufficient. And, money really can't do much, they easily spend it all. But Tzu Chi is different! It does the fundamental work! It goes to the re-cipient's home to understand/investigate, and it comforts their minds and consoles them. So we switched to Tzu Chi, carrying out deeper work.

In this way, Tzu Chi's portable and ecumenical "do-it-yourself" model for charity landed in the Malacca FTZ. It started out as a team of a few office staff members led by Mrs. Liu. Through the staff members' network, they learned about the nursing home that needed volunteers. In addition, the fe-male factory workers informed them of individuals and families that were in need of help. "Because of their own living environment, they're more likely to know people who have been suffering, and they reported to us," Citian explained. Each day at 5:30 p.m., the team members hopped into one or two cars. As Citian explained:

We followed the address as reported to us. Once we got there, we were re-ally touched, felt very sorry for them. We felt inspired *(huanxi),* because we could be of help. We cared for them, and delivered money and material relief. It's a consolation to them. You can feel it. And when we visited one house, their neighbors were curious. Because we just got out of the office, we were still wearing high heels, and hadn't yet put on our uniforms. We were all dressed up, and of course we attracted attention. Why had this de-serted household suddenly gotten so many visitors? We told them we're here to help. They would report other families who also needed help. So we have more and more cases . . . Then we held a reception *(chahui,* liter-ally, "tea party," Tzu Chi's term for reception) at Mrs. Liu's office, and told everyone to bring their friends and family here to learn about Tzu Chi.

Tzu Chi's "action dharma"—to borrow Christopher Queen's (1996) term—of "Do it, then it's right!" *(zuo jiouduile,* or perhaps even better translated into "Just do it!" which connotes Tzu Chi as a kind of "Nike" Buddhism) also works in a deterritorialized context. It is a "model of" and "model for" Buddhism, as we have argued in the Taiwan example, according to which only actions count in the final analysis (Huang and Weller 1998). However, the attribute of entrepreneurship philanthropy often associated with the upper-middle-class devotees in Taiwan is less pronounced in the Malacca branch than the other attribute of phenomenological social work—an experience-centered practice carried out through encountering human suffering in its realistic context, sometimes boiled down to blunt advice to a novice: "Go see the poor!" (Huang and Weller 1998). Mr. Liu mentioned in our 1999 interview that the Penang branch has more "bosses" or entrepreneurs, whereas Malacca has a constituency of working class or lower-middle class.

The leitmotif of the Lius' factory gradually shifted from export garment manufacturing to charity groundwork for the local population. In the aftermath of the 1999 economic crisis in Southeast Asia, Mr. Liu closed down his business, tore down the factory, and replaced it with a second compound of missions, thus completing its transformation from a center for capital outflow to one working on behalf of Tzu Chi's diaspora. By 2004, he went south, per the order of the Venerable Cheng Yen, to take over the Singapore branch office, while Mrs. Liu went north to spearhead the Kuala Lumpur office. As he said in his speech, "Each one of us has one *po* ("hill" in Chinese, here is a transliteration of 'pur' in Kuala Lumpur and 'pore' in Singapore)." Both don Tzu Chi uniforms seven days a week, are busy on cell phones throughout the day, and continue to travel between Southeast Asia and Taiwan, with only a couple of personal trips to visit their daughters in the United States each year.

## Localization

### Who Are the Local Followers?

Among the fourteen local adherents this chapter refers to (not including the Lius) were ten females and four males. Seven were born between 1931 and 1956, four between 1960 and 1965, and three between 1972 and 1977; seven first came to Tzu Chi before or during 1997 (the year when the local branch building was erected) and the rest after 1997 (age groups are distributed equally between the two periods). Except for the one Caucasian from Australia, the thirteen Chinese-ethnic interviewees included only one Taiwanese and the other twelve were born locally with no relations in Taiwan.

Four were from relatively lower-income backgrounds, the Australian was unemployed, and the other three had retired from jobs as a nurse, a tailor, and a barber. Seven were from middle-class backgrounds or had spouses who were small shopkeepers or professionals (accountant/secretary/educator/preschool principal), and three were either from the upper-middle class or their spouses were (physician and entrepreneur). The Taiwanese was a first-generation immigrant and the twelve born locally were at least second- and mostly third-generation migrants from mainland China. Except for one straits-born Chinese who didn't know her ancestors' hometown, the ancestral origin or dialect group (language spoken at home) of the other eleven locally born interviewees were: five Hokkien, five Cantonese (four Teochu and one Hakka), and one Hainan. Three out of five Cantonese descendants were from outside Malacca. The sample, therefore, reflects the local Chinese population quite well: predominantly progeny of nineteenth-century immigrants of Hokkien descent.

All of the thirteen Chinese-ethnic interviewees worked for Tzu Chi more than one day a week, and the Australian had worked for four months. In fact, as they listed their activities, all of them worked for Tzu Chi every day, either coming to volunteer at the branch or participating in activities such as sorting garbage for recycling and visiting the charity recipients and nursing homes, or going out individually to collect membership dues. Three of the interviewees were full-time staff members who also spent their free time as volunteers.

## How Did They First Come to Tzu Chi?

Ten of the fourteen local followers first signed up for membership or volunteer work through public events held by the Malacca branch. This is in contrast to the major mechanism of direct recruitment through family or friends deployed in Taiwan, especially prior to Tzu Chi's rapid growth and bureaucratization in the mid-1990s. In other words, most local followers were self-motivated to spontaneously join or convert to Tzu Chi after seeking out information about the group through public media, rather than by the usual route of becoming a general checkbook member through initial personal networking and gradually entering the group and converting.

The recruitment through public events says two things about localization: First, it shows that Tzu Chi is a "new" religious group of "foreign origin" that has yet to be embedded in the local network. With this said, the religious policy of local Tzu Chi has never advocated the use of mass media for publicity, not even the local Chinese newspapers that are the major mass media for the local Chinese communities and indeed regularly and widely cover events of local Buddhist and charitable groups. As one follower compares: "What we have done . . . we never asked to be posted in the newspapers for people to see! Like we visited the nursing home, but we didn't ask the press to come to take photos."

The followers nevertheless knew about the public events through the local Buddhist associative network. Two former Tzu Chi youth contacted Tzu Chi when they were already participating in the Buddhist Study Club in college. The founding member, the Taiwanese entrepreneur's wife, the straits-born Chinese nurse, the elder environmental volunteer, the current social work staff member, and the computer retailer all learned about Tzu Chi through public speech events that their fellow Buddhist friends took them to. In other words, the existing local Buddhist community allows Tzu Chi to be adaptive to prospective members, and the prospective members are already Buddhist converts who have taken refuge with one or more Buddhist monastics elsewhere prior to taking refuge with the Venerable Cheng Yen (except for the Taiwanese).

During my fieldwork in Flushing, New York, in 1994, I found a similar scenario among converts there who also had a Buddhist background (Chapter 7). Like the religious landscape in New York, Malacca has a lively variety of Buddhist associations and a few temples. However, in contrast to the rather horizontal or general variety among the New York Chinese Buddhists, and the existing temple from another Taiwanese Buddhist institution, the associative life of Buddhists in Malacca—as well as Malaysia in general—is highly organized. Local followers there come from four sources: (1) Buddhist study groups in neighborhoods or, in local terms, gardens (*huayuan* in Chinese, or *taman* in Malay), (2) Buddhist study groups at colleges/universities, (3) the sutra chanting classes and dharma events at local popular temples (mainly, *Cheng Hoon Teng* and *Seck Kia Een*), and (4) a variety of Buddhist associations. These range from the most organized, active, nationwide monastic network, Malaysia Buddhist Association (*Malaixiya fuojiao zonghui*, commonly referred to by its abbreviation, *Mafozong*) and the equally organized yet far more secular, intellectual, and publicly outspoken (especially on issues of Chinese civil rights) Young Buddhist Association of Malaysia (YBAM, *Malaixya fojiao qingnianxiehui*, commonly referred to by its abbreviation, *Mafoqing*), as well as other groups of smaller scale, such as *jingzong xuehui* (Pure Land Study Association).

The significance of the role of Chinese Buddhism in Tzu Chi's localization lies more in nurturing the idea for Tzu Chi's action-oriented practice than in providing an existing network for recruitment. Local followers spoke forcefully about how Tzu Chi provides a meritorious land for them to cultivate, a way to realize the meaning of Buddhist texts they have studied, and embodies "walking scripture" *(xingjing)*. The local followers can be divided into roughly three groups according to their occupations and livelihoods: (Chinese) education system, professionals, and retirees of craftsmanship working class. All three groups spoke about the importance of Tzu Chi's practice, yet in slightly different ways.

The distinctively resilient Chinese education system in Malaysia has been one of the major sources for Tzu Chi's development.[4] This source includes the Chinese school system from elementary school to high school, and the Buddhist studies clubs at colleges.

Lixia had been active in the Buddhist Study Club at college. She organized volunteer services to the New Villages[5] and other community services. She encountered Tzu Chi in 1997, when she invited a few core members to give a talk on how they carry out social work. Lixia suddenly thought through what she had been reading about Buddhism:

As soon as I started participating in Tzu Chi's activities, I immediately identified with [Tzu Chi's goals]. It is because I was already in the Buddhist studies class; in addition to community services, I lectured in the Buddhist Studies class. That's why I felt [Buddhist teachings] immediately proved *(yingzheng)*, that I could feel *(ganshoudedao)* [Buddhism] in action; I felt what I lectured in the Buddhist studies class, because the Buddhist studies class teaches the students impermanence *(wuchang)*, but at that time I never experienced *(tihui)* what impermanence is, so, after visiting the nursing home, I soon deeply felt-understood it, and I immediately identified with what this group is doing.

She and a couple of friends started Tzu Chi on campus. Because the Buddhist Studies Club was already registered as "the" Buddhist extracurricular group, Lixia and her friends had to rent a place off-campus as their residence and the meeting place for Tzu Chi activities. She then began mobilizing for the summer youth camp by knocking on every door at all the dormitories on campus. In retrospect, she was amazed by her own courage: "I felt my courage *(yongqi)* was coming from [the faith]: You give me two days (for the summer camp) and I'll give you the whole world! . . . even though I didn't know much about Tzu Chi at that time." In a few days, the friends mobilized more than one hundred participants.

Some of the professionals spoke about the revealing experience of social work and began to realize how fortunate they had been. Yuchang had only just earned the title of commissioner when we met in 2004. He was born and raised in Malacca and left home at the age of eighteen to begin his own career. He traveled through Kuala Lumpur, Singapore, and finally Johor Baru, where he eventually ran his own computer retail shop. He was devoted to the business and was on call for services twenty-four hours a day. By that time, he had heard about Tzu Chi because the local office was just across street from his shop, but all he knew was that Tzu Chi recycled garbage. Then, two years ago at a reception, he watched a documentary about Tzu Chi's delivery of goods to Afghanistan and was impressed by the "internationalization" and the scale of its mission. About the same time, he had a health crisis, and realized that health is something money can't buy. He said in our interview:

> I reflected, what have I earned? Money or health? Then I chose health, even though I had a goal that I shall return to Malacca once I earn a certain amount of money. But the problem is, you know, maybe it's just for ordinary people, once you achieve your goal, you want more and more and more. There is . . . *no end lah!* So when I became ill, I told my wife that we'll sell everything and move back to Malacca, because the quality of life in Malacca is better. I hoped I could slow down because it's Malacca. It's impossible to slow down in Johor Baru, because everyone surrounding you is . . . very competitive.

Yuchang and his family moved back to Malacca eighteen years after he had first left home. He went straight to sign up at the Tzu Chi branch and Mrs. Liu took him to investigate charity cases *(fangshi)*. Through the experience, he reflected upon his lifestyle and what he had just gone through: "It wasn't really hardship! Compared to the recipients' lives, I 'discovered' that I grew up in a very happy family, was very lucky . . ." Like many other devotees, the more he participated, the more he felt inspired. Ironically, although he moved back to Malacca to pursue a family-centered lifestyle, he ended up working nearly full-time for Tzu Chi—literally seven days a week:

I came back to slow down. But in Tzu Chi, you just can't slow down. You are busy from Monday to Sunday, from morning to evening. I come to Tzu Chi whenever I find free time. Can't slow down, either. But the feeling is very different! In Johor Baru, every morning we woke up and first thing was to do [customer] services, it's another day for making ends meet. It's for a livelihood! Back in Malacca, I am busy for Tzu Chi, but when you are busy, you have that dharma joy *(faxi)!* What is dharma joy? I can't explain. You simply like coming here! You don't get anything in return for what you give, but you just give happily. I myself feel strange, too. A friend asked me, what do you get from Tzu Chi? I can't. I couldn't give him an answer. I just know that I like coming here, I like giving. It's that simple. I don't really know the reason. It's strange . . . I like participating in these activities . . . when we give we feel, it's meaningful. It's not just for one's own livelihood.

Yuchang began taking up Tzu Chi as his "career" when he eventually recruited fourteen members after a dire zero for the first nine months. Like Mr. Liu, he applies much of his entrepreneurship spirit to doing volunteer work, in the sense of being relentlessly proactive. Nevertheless, he has distanced himself from charitable or social groups that resonate with the business world. He was aware of other social welfare or charitable groups in Malacca, but he was reluctant to join them because he felt people in the social groups tend to be "calculating and manipulative" *(gouxin doujiao)*.

Devotees with a working-class background expressed a strong commitment to doing good as complementary to sutra chanting. This is in accordance with my findings among the working-class-background Cantonese speakers in the Boston branch during my fieldwork in 1995 (Huang 2003a). Like the devotees from the education system, and unlike the professionals, the working-class devotees reflected upon the gap between scriptures and practice. At the same time, the working-class devotees shared with the professionals a common revealing experience when they first participated in visiting a charity case.

Qiu Jinnian was seventy-three when I interviewed her in 2004. She had received no education: "Never even set foot at the school's door, because we have eight brothers and sisters, only two younger brothers could go to school." She was married at the age of seventeen and began working as a tailor until her eyes no longer permitted. She has been retired since the age of forty-one. She first heard about Tzu Chi when her Buddhist friend took her to a tea party held at the Lius factory, and she was moved by Mrs. Liu's speech. She remembered:

> I can see what Tzu Chi has been doing. At that time, I attended 'worshipping Buddha' (*baifuo* or sutra chanting). I said to myself, worshipping and chanting I can do, but charity I have done nothing. I went to the speech the next month. Mrs. Liu talked about the elders in the nursing home. They have cancer! I felt, wow! Mrs. Liu can do this even though she is the wife of a wealthy entrepreneur (*laobanniang*). She served the elderly. She wiped the blood off their faces. I could never do that. She showed us the photos. I was really touched . . . I felt, if even wealthy Mrs. Liu could do it, why can't we ordinary people?

She then made every effort to ask other volunteers to help her with transportation and prayed to Guanyin Bodhisattva to help her find a ride to work for Tzu Chi:

> And a sister [fellow member] called to give me ride. I felt I was happier than winning the lottery! . . . I went on a house visit (case investigation) that day, and I continued the following week. I saw those people suffering as if they were living in hell. I came home, and I couldn't sleep. It's suffering. Their family really suffered. Our house is so much better than theirs. I asked him, what do you eat during the day? He said his grandson has to work, so he left him a cup of tea and a piece of toast or cookie, because he is blind. That's all for the day until his grandson returns.

One day she saw a commissioner deliver money to the office, and she learned that it was a collection of membership dues. Mr. Zhang, the educator, explained to her that the money was to support charity. So she started proselytizing on her own. She wrapped each of the membership dues with paper, and asked Mr. Zhang to write the member's name on it. By 2004, she had proselytized more than five hundred members.

A common theme running through the interviews conducted with Tzu Chi local members regardless of their class background is the commitment to socially engaged Buddhism. All seemed to view their engagement as important to self-actualization as opposed to obligations of livelihood, profit, or peer-group approval. Apparently, they see the significance of hands-on charity born out of their earlier beliefs and practices in Buddhism. Why do they have such strong urges for socially engaged practice? Two possible explanations might be considered. One is that all devotees interviewed spoke about how thorough and systematic Tzu Chi's missions are compared to other local charitable groups. In other words, scale and standardization matter in localizing a global Buddhism. Beyer (2006: 243–244) points out that the failure of the Venerable Taixu's efforts in "modernizing" Buddhism in pre-1949 China had much to do with a lack of organizations bearing the distinct transnational component necessary to carry out the project. Chinese Buddhism continues to present "an enigma depending on how it fluctuates between its characteristics of Chinese 'culture' and its 'partial foreign-ness'" of a world religion. Taiwanese Buddhism as present in Tzu Chi provides such a transnational organization *par excellence.*

The second explanation might be the nature of socially engaged religious charity in providing a path to the public sphere for those who have been categorically excluded by gender or ethnicity. Elsewhere we have examined the similarities between the appeal of Tzu Chi to Taiwanese women in the twentieth century and the appeal of volunteerism to Christian women in the West during the nineteenth century (Huang and Weller 1998). Religious-based charitable organizations allowed women in the two modernizing societies to wield power in the public sphere and respond to rapidly changing social structures under advancing industrialization. In the case of Malaysia, the minority status might have contributed to the structural constraints in compelling the Chinese to pursue a socially engaged Buddhism as a nonpolitical means for participating in the local public life and in response to the social change and problems in the environment (Embong 2001; Nagata 2005; Shamsul A. B. 1994; Tan 2000). As the educator, Mr. Zhang explains how careful they should be in practicing social work in a pluralist society (compare Embong 2001):

> Even when we discuss our Buddhism with [a Malay], we'll be very careful not to mislead him, oh, for example, if I am talking to a Malay friend, oh, I talk about why Buddhism is good, and he talks about why Islam is good. What if, in the end, he says, oh, what you say about Buddhism sounds really good, I think I'll go with you! Then, you are in trouble. You are in trouble.

## Reterritorialization

When asked about their ties to Tzu Chi's headquarters in Taiwan, all of the local followers appeared to be surprised and confused. After probing, they said it's only through Mr. and Mrs. Liu, and perhaps also through the secretariat staff members.

Such exclusively bureaucratic protocol with respect to headquarters is in stark contrast to the frequency of their visits to Taiwan and to their emotions for Cheng Yen and the Abode. Ten out of the twelve local Chinese followers have visited the headquarters on average three times, each time for at least one week. Except for the Taiwanese immigrant, all of the locals visited Taiwan solely for Tzu Chi purposes and never stepped outside of the Tzu Chi context throughout their stay in Taiwan. This is in line with my interpretation of Tzu Chi's retreats as liminality (Chapter 3). In contrast to the argument of transnational "social space," wherein values and ideas in addition to money and goods are circulating between the two ends of the transnational social life (Levitt 2001), the protocol reterritorializing the Malaysian followers in Hualian, Taiwan, remains characteristically Tzu Chi's own. As one core member said: "I have been to Taiwan eight times! I've never been to places outside of Tzu Chi." Participants of the "root finding" departed together from Kuala Lumpur, were picked up by Taiwanese followers at the CKS International Airport, immediately boarded their around-the-island tour of Tzu Chi mission buildings (Chapter 2), and ended the visit with Taiwanese followers seeing them off at the gate at the CKS International Airport:

> All Tzu Chi persons are nice . . . with smiley faces . . . Their culture is very simple and they love helping people. They give you the best, serve you the best food. They are very considerate. It feels like at home . . . I feel very safe. If I go 'outside,' rarely but I did . . . they are not like Tzu Chi people, they are like ordinary people. They don't know me and I don't know them. We have no relation . . . I have been to Hualian, Taipei, Tainan, and many places, I don't know their names.

To the Malaysian locals, Taiwan means not much more than where Tzu Chi headquarters are and where Cheng Yen lives. In contrast to the disembodied geography and sociology of Taiwan, the Malaysian followers' emotion for Cheng Yen is distinctly embodied. All the interviewees who visited Hualian said they cried when they first saw Cheng Yen. As Yulan recounts:

> It was in the ceremony of touring around the Buddha *(raofo)* about 4 o'clock in morning at the Abode. We followed the monastics *(changzhu),* walking while chanting sutras . . . There she came . . . she entered the hall from outside . . . and my tears kept dropping . . . kept dropping and

dropping. Like that. Oh! This woman is the Venerable Cheng Yen. How tiny she is! Look at the way she walks. Lightly like floating *(qing piaopiao)*! Guanyin Bodhisattva *(Guanshiyin pusa)*! She just floated in like that. No sound. No one noticed . . . I saw her face and my tears dropped naturally. It's a very strange feeling. It must be because I had good bonding with her in a previous life that we could be reunited. That's why I cried.

This account vividly resonates with the notion of the leader's body (Chapter 1) and the collective body (Chapter 4). The three bodies of charisma are thus unbound on the global stage.

Yet, the locality continues to be salient in followers' practice and commitment. The mission they perceived is firmly locally grounded, and unaffected by the reterritorialization of their emotions for the leader. In some way, their local concerns parallel, if not complement, their transnational emotions. A founding member, Citian, narrates the striking moments of her lifelong commitment after the first year of practicing Tzu Chi in Malaysia:

[I went back for "root finding."] Yes, I was so touched when I saw the supreme person. Naturally, very naturally, I cried and cried . . . I felt like I saw someone I haven't seen in a very long time. My tears just kept dropping and dropping. Just like that. Very strange. Oh! Then there was this cassette tape of a testimony of a Sister who changed from a juvenile delinquent to a Tzu Chi person. I was thinking, we have more and more problems here in Malacca. Students skip school and hang out doing bad things . . . If Tzu Chi can develop here, maybe it will reduce or even solve the problems. So I vowed! I shall carry out Tzu Chi . . . I believed I have this predestined boding . . . I was alone at home, I burst out crying. I cried hard and loudly.

## Conclusion

The multiple flows woven into Tzu Chi Malacca began with profit-seeking migration, merged with Buddhist inspiration from the homeland and charitable women's initiatives, grooved through a local need for Buddhist reformism, crisscrossed the local ethno-religious pluralism, and repatriated the diasporic Chinese back to Taiwan as a religious homecoming. The competing leitmotifs included in this narrative remark that the dovetail of foreign entrepreneurship and foreign religious movement is just a node between the long history of Malaysian Chinese and the brief history of Tzu Chi in Taiwan. The tales from Malacca are simultaneously locally engaged and transnationally embodied, and flesh out the three bodies of charisma on a global stage.

# Conclusion

In this book I have presented Tzu Chi, a spectacular Taiwanese religious movement, as an example of charisma. I have shown that the leader, the Venerable Cheng Yen, is a genuine charismatic who was born with personal magnetism and endowed with emotional expressivity that can generate extreme excitement from those who surround her.

Charisma must be rationalized for a movement to grow large and survive. The question is how to rationalize it. In the preceding chapters I have shown that Tzu Chi exists as a successful modern organization while retaining, if not perpetuating, its leadership that is based upon the personal appeal of the Venerable Cheng Yen. This is achieved through two major mechanisms: The first mechanism is a shapeless bureaucracy whose organizational structure consists of unclear authority lines among its different parts, a lexicon of proliferating titles that presents a pseudohierarchy among the followers, and a clear outright authority bestowed upon one individual—the Venerable Cheng Yen. Crucial to the success of such a shapeless bureaucratic organization is the unique form of charismatic commitment. Charisma's demand of followers' complete devotion is rationalized by high goals with clear tasks: on the one hand, the leader's mission of relieving all human suffering is extremely ambitious and requires continued devotion; on the other hand, devotees abide by codes of discipline and demonstrate—and increase—their commitment through the completion of each concrete task given by the leader. In my view, Tzu Chi's existence and success as an organization is due to the combination of shapeless bureaucracy and the self-generating, progressive commitment mechanism of high goals and clear tasks inspired by the leader's selfless devotion.

267

The second mechanism is maintenance of the followers' commitment through forms of circulation, particularly the leader's monthly movement around the island and a variety of followers' retreats to the headquarters. Charismatic appeal and the commitment it entails are to be repeated as lived experience among the now geographically dispersed followers. Each month on her tour, the Venerable Cheng Yen incarnates herself as a living bodhisattva in the face-to-face reality of local followers. She maximizes the distribution of her charisma by personalizing the business trip, by attending to followers' family concerns and individual suffering, and by delivering large-scale sermons as well as receiving her followers' prostration at her feet. The followers' renewal of commitment, shared symbolism, and integration, as well as the process of recruiting prospective devotees, are carried out in another form of circulation—a variety of "homecoming" retreats to the headquarters, where the charismatic leader resides. This form of circulation serves to keep the dispersed followers, to borrow words from Shils (1965): "near the center of the thing." In the liminal state of intensive collective life at the headquarters, charismatic authority is embodied both in the sublime ritual and in the splendid institution. Collective symbolism is learned, missions are internalized and reinforced, and commitments are, in the followers' words: "recharged" *(chongdian)*.

Moreover, the commitment that is generated and renewed in the collective context of the organization is to be lived by individual followers in their ordinary lives. In the local context of Jiayi of southern Taiwan, the meaning of "Tzu Chi person" *(Cijiren)* is manifested in the formalization of local organization and mobilization, and, more importantly, a distinctive expectation of personhood constructed with morality and etiquette with a suggested gender difference in aspects of etiquette and mobilization. In the current era of globalization and increasing Taiwanese transnationalism, the Tzu Chi charismatic movement continues to thrive as a living reality. Women continue to play active roles in the forefront of Tzu Chi transnationalism, yet these roles are slightly different from the strong morality and etiquette found among followers in southern Taiwan. The major appeal of Tzu Chi to its overseas followers lies in its unique concrete approach to practice that allows overseas Taiwanese as well as Chinese to redefine their activism in a variety of host countries.

Related to the local construction of Tzu Chi personhood, particularly in regard to Tzu Chi's conduct with Taiwan's national arena, is the importance of morality in Tzu Chi's development in the public sphere. As discussed in Chapter 6, the rapid growth of Tzu Chi in Taiwan has occurred hand in hand with rapid sociopolitical change: the meteoric expansion of Tzu Chi around the year 1990 is, coincidentally or causally, closely linked to the nearly "anomic" state in Taiwan wherein a postmartial-law society with its successful economic development unleashed much of its energy and discontent in waves of protests and lavish consumption. Amid such a situation of overloaded values and changes, the moral certainty of Tzu Chi that was once promoted and endorsed by the authoritarian regime, time and again is upheld as a model of conduct for nongovernmental organizations (NGOs) in the democratizing political structure. The crucial role of morality in the development of Tzu Chi speaks to the negative stereotype of "charismatic cults." It is true that charisma demands unrelenting devotion to whatever mission is given by the charismatic figure, as long as he or she gives an order. As Cheng Yen and Tzu Chi have demonstrated in their humanitarian mission, the charismatic mission can be highly moral, containing much value for humanity, and can even be adaptive to the state's constraints.

Tzu Chi's success suggests that the charismatic phenomenon is not a single event that explodes in an extraneous collective crisis. Related to the moral certainty of Tzu Chi in Taiwan's national arena is the changing sociopolitical context that Tzu Chi has had to deal with, insofar as it continues to be rationalized as an NGO that pursues goals with necessary resource mobilization. At the same time, the boundaries of "society" in Tzu Chi's case also show great fluidity as Tzu Chi's most recent trend is to thrive among overseas Taiwanese and Chinese communities and, hence, to engage the resources of transnationalism and the issues of globalization. The democratizing political structure in Taiwan after the lifting of martial law has led Tzu Chi to no longer benefit from the authoritarian regime's favor—as was the case in the mobilization for its first hospital; but, instead, to deal with local politicians and meticulous legal change for its more recent monumental mission of building its second hospital. The milieu of this charismatic movement's social background has also been gradually shifting as the Taiwanese people become increasingly transnational and as the charismatic appeal appears to have "traveled" along with the dispersion of overseas Taiwanese. In other words, charisma as a collective phenomenon is to be examined as a process that continually negotiates with the ever-changing social context. A "crisis" may catalyze the social ramification of a charismatic leadership. However, the charismatic movement, at least in the case of the Venerable Cheng Yen and Tzu Chi, is not only a spark at a moment of crisis but also a fire that continues to burn.

While I emphasize that the charismatic movement is a social fact not to be treated as a happenstance event, the charismatic moment, in its phenomenological sense and as seen among many individual Tzu Chi devotees, is indeed a moment. This brings us to the second question, how are the charismatic emotions expressed in Tzu Chi? As discussed in Chapter 4, the ecstasy of the charismatic moment is experienced by many devotees as beyond utterance, expressed only in the unmediated form of crying. Such an extreme embodied expression and the leader's and followers' interpretation of this expression (experienced as a homecoming, family reunion, and feeling like a baby) prove that the charismatic moment, as posited by Weber ([1968] 1978: 401-402), is indeed an extraordinary moment of emotion with high psychological redemptive value to the extent that crying is common and important to Tzu Chi devotees. Moreover, the multiple contexts of pervasive crying in Tzu Chi, and its coexistence with an equally emotional form of sign language song, suggest a possibility of transforming the charismatic emotion into musical collective corporeality. The extreme emotional expressivity of crying that "opened up"[1] in the extraordinary experience of charismatic ecstasy may appear and recur in other such "approved" contexts of religious consonance, rituals, and volunteer experiences—contexts that are relevant to the core of Tzu Chi's Buddhist humanitarianism. At the same time, the coexistence of the uncontrollable crying and the orderly yet equally emotional expressivity of sign language song shows Tzu Chi as a synthesis of the two ends of the emotional spectrum in the rationalization of a charismatic movement—a continuum between the uncontrollable and controlled, between ecstasy and formalization.

The charismatic commitment stems from a process of searching and negotiating identity through dialectic between emotional experience and meaning-seeking social action. Emotion is what makes the relationship between a magnetic individual and those who surround her charismatic in the first place, and rationalization follows to transform their relationship into a charismatic domination with significance in the social world; as this relationship crystallizes into routine and institution, the intensity of the relationship may be maintained as long as the group succeeds in finding new forms of expressivity and new sources of extraordinariness. Charisma is, as succinctly written by Feuchtwang and Wang (2001: 172): "the expectation of the extraordinary."

Tzu Chi has succeeded in perpetuating its emotional form of commitment, though not without tension, by expanding the compassionate-sorrow emotion of charisma to a general emotion toward the experience of suffering built into its humanitarian practice, and by paralleling its original charismatic ecstasy of crying to the collective effervescence of sign language song. Such transformation not only perpetuates commitment in its emotional form but also rekindles the interplay between emotional experience and subsequent meaningful symbolization.

The three-body model in the multiple levels of social world I propose in the introduction allows an analytical approach that not only transcends the three dualities in considering charisma but also puts the charismatic moment as well as movement in an empathetically progressive and transformative perspective. To recapitulate, the leader's body accounts for the personal appeal and the phenomenological embodiment of extraordinariness and the followers' body hinges on a framework of organization and symbolization, and on the practice and ideal of identity; while the collective body or the musical body is the means of transformation from an inchoate and formless emotional "communitas" to a choreographed and formalized interpretive community within the finite yet multiple-leveled social world. It is beyond the scope of this book, yet I would suggest future comparative research in analyzing the three bodies in the Buddhist examples of new and the new-new religions in contemporary Japan.[2]

Does charisma, as in the Tzu Chi example, have a limit? First, inasmuch as charisma makes sense as lived experience interpreted as a source of inspiration and extraordinariness, it is prone to certain cultural limits. The fact that the majority of Tzu Chi's overseas followers remain within the Chinese community seems to suggest a cultural limit on Cheng Yen's global charisma. A similar ethnic constituency is also found in the overseas expansion of other Taiwan-originated Buddhist movements with charismatic leadership and universalist mission such as Master Hsing Yun's Buddha's Light Mountain (Chandler 2005). In some ways, going beyond a particularistic context is a common issue for globalizing religious movements (for example, Beckford 2000; Weller 2003). In the Chinese cases, it may suggest that a diasporic community may hinder transcultural expansion, not only for Buddhism but also for Christianity (for example, Chen 2002).

Yet, what hinders Tzu Chi is not the diaspora. Tzu Chi's focal practice of service often strikes outsiders as secular social work. It appears "too familiar" to the westerner (Learman 2005a) because it lacks monastic characteristics and does not build temples (Chandler 2005). Nevertheless, there remains a possibility of reaching past the ethnic walls through Buddhist ideas inspired by charisma. Tzu Chi literature highlights non-Chinese volunteers who maintain their Christian identity.[3] I do have one example, albeit anecdotal or exceptional, from my fieldwork. The only Caucasian adherent in Malacca shared with the local Chinese followers a long Buddhist background prior to joining Tzu Chi. He learned about Tzu Chi through a book by Cheng Yen that he picked up at a cosmopolitan café in the tourist historic district of downtown Malacca. He sighed: "Wow! There is this nun. She built a hospital! And I thought I would like to learn more." He first converted to Buddhism in Australia out of dissatisfaction with what he called Sunday religion, namely Christianity. He went to Thailand and was again disappointed because it's not Buddhism "in the community." He eventually found Cheng Yen's teaching in Malacca and had been working as a regular volunteer for four months when I interviewed him in 2004.

The second limit is mandatory and critical for each and every charismatic group, especially a successful one, such as Soka Gakkai (Seager 2006: 206–207)—the problem of succession. Like Ikeda of Soka Gakkai, as of 2007, there appear no clear heirs to Cheng Yen in Tzu Chi. Tzu Chi's official response to the question of succession is to remind one that Buddhism continues to thrive thousands of years after Buddha attained nirvana. In this book, I have captured as much as possible the ongoing institutionalization of Tzu Chi. In light of its current scale, Tzu Chi's nonprofit organization runs deep and solid legally and financially, and may not immediately run into a crisis unless otherwise challenged or debilitated externally. As my analysis of the mechanism of embodiment and commitment also suggests, emotional salience might be measured but is not immediately diminished.

In 2005, at the end of an international conference on engaged Buddhism organized and hosted by the Tzu Chi Foundation, all the participating scholars were invited to the Abode for an audience with the Venerable Cheng Yen. After we were all seated, we waited in silence. Moments later, Cheng Yen entered the newly renovated reception room, accompanied as usual by a crew of acolytes, received our bowing, and sat on the designated master's seat behind a table that faced rows of about thirty Buddhist scholars from Japan, North America, and Taiwan, seated among the select devotee-escorts. She looked tired, and her eyes were spacey and preoccupied. She briefly greeted the roomful of scholars and told the emcee, a bilingual fe-male commissioner, to open the floor for questions and comments. A Japa-nese professor approached the microphone, saying that he was impressed by the small size of the Abode, which is in stark contrast to the groups' gigan-tic mission, and also a contrast to the spectacular buildings of some large religious groups in Japan. The emcee smiled and thanked the professor for his comment. Then an American professor took the microphone and asked the Venerable Cheng Yen point-blank: "Many of your followers talk about how much they love you. What do you make of this?" The room suddenly sank to a silence and we soon felt tension and unease from the controlled commotion among the devotees sitting among us. The emcee jumped in to answer the question, but it only made the situation even more self-serving. Finally, the Venerable Cheng Yen spoke, slowly and lightly: "They want to love me. There's nothing I can do [to stop them from loving me] *(tamen yao ai wo, wo ye mei banfa)*! [The audience laughed.] But I do want them to develop this love into great love, universal love. The world of Tzu Chi is built on love, the love for all living beings."

In the end, a nun's tale is never just about one nun.

# Locations of the Four Congregation Levels in Taiwan and Overseas

## Taiwan

*1. Fenhui: Taipei, Taizhong, Gaoxiong, Pingdong*

*2. Zhihui: Taoyuan*

*3. Lianluochu:*

- Under Taipei *fenhui:* Jilong; in Taipei City: Songshan, Neihu; in Taipei County: Shuanghe, Haishan, Sanchong, Xintai (in Xinzhuang); in Taoyuan County: Zhongli, Xinzhu, Miaoli
- Under Taizhong *fenhui:* in Taizhong County: Dajia, Gangqu; in Nantou County: Puli; Yunlin
- Under Gaoxiong *fenhui:* Jiayi; Tainan; Penghu
- Other: Yilan, Taidong

*4. Gongxiuchu:* In Taipei City: Zhongshan; in Taipei County: Xizhi, Luzhou; in Taizhong County: Gangqu; in Jiayi County: Dalin (Dalin was not listed in the source, *Ciji yuekan,* yet exists at least during my fieldwork between 1997 and 1999.)

## Overseas

### North America

- *Fenhui* Canada

- *Zhihui* Toronto

*United States:*

- *Fenhui* Southern California—*Lianluochu:* Diamond Bar, Santa Monica, Torrance, Cerritos, Orange, Northbridge, San Gabriel, San Diego, Phoenix (Arizona), Flagstaff (Arizona), Tucson (Arizona), Albuquerque (New Mexico)
- *Fenhui* Northern California—*Linaluochu:* San Francisco, Modesto, Seattle (Washington), Fresno
- *Fenhui* Chicago—*Linaluochu:* Indianapolis, Dayton, St. Louis, Kansas, Detroit, Lansing, Minnesota, Des Moines, Madison, Columbus.
- *Fenhui* Hawaii
- *Fenhui* New Jersey—*Lianluochu:* Washington, Pittsburgh, Cleveland
- *Fenhui* New York—*Lianluochu:* Long Island, Boston
- *Fenhui* Texas—*Linaluochu:* Arlington, Dallas, Austin, Comfort, Atlanta, Miami, Orlando

*South America*

- *Lianluochu* Argentina (in Buenos Aires)
- *Lianluochu* Brazil (in Sao Paulo)
- *Lianluochu* Mexico (in Tijuana)
- *Lianluochu* Paraguay (in Asuncion)
- *Lianluochu* Dominican Republic (in Santo Domingo)

*Europe*

- *Lianluochu* Austria (in Vienna)
- *Lianluochu* France (in Paris)
- *Lianluochu* Germany (in Hamburg)
- *Lianluochu* Netherlands (in Amsterdam)
- *Lianluochu* Spain (in Madrid)
- *Lianluochu* United Kingdom (in London)

*Asia*

- *Lianluochu* Brunei (in Kuala Belait)
- *Fenhui* Hong Kong
- *Fenhui* Indonesia
- *Fenhui* Japan
- *Fenhui* Malacca

- *Lianluochu* Kuala Lumpur, Ipoh, Kelantan, Kedah, Johor Baharu, Seremban, Mua, Keluang, Sabah, Sandakan, Kuching, Miri

- *Fenhui* Malaysia (in Penang)
- *Fenhui* Philippines (in Quezon City)

- Lianluochu Cebu

- *Fenhui* Thailand (in Bangkok)

- *Zhihui* Fang Chiangmai

- *Fenhui* Singapore

- *Lianluochu* Vietnam (in Ho Chi Minh City)

### Middle East

- *Lianluochu* Jordan (in Amman)
- *Lianluochu* Turkey (in Istanbul)

### Oceania

- *Fenhui* Australia (in Chatswood)

- *Lianluochu* Brisbane, Melbourne, Gold Coast, Perth

- *Fenhui* New Zealand (in Auckland)

- *Lianluochu* Hamilton

### Africa

- *Lianluochu* in South Africa: Johannesburg, Durban, Cape Town, Ladysmith, Elizabeth, East London
- *Lianluochu* Lesotho (in Maseru)

*Source:* Based on the directory in *Ciji yuekan (Tzu Chi Monthly)*, May 2000: 126-127.

# Mission Institutions (*Zhiye ti*), 2000

## Mission Center

### 1. Medical Mission

Taiwan

- Major Establishment: Hualian Hospital, Dalin Hospital
- Branch Establishment: Yüli Branch Hospital, Guanshan Branch Hospital (in Taidong)

Overseas

- Tzu Chi United States Free Clinic; Tzu Chi United States Bone Marrow Databank (both in Southern California)
- Tzu Chi Malaysia Dialysis Center (in Penang)

### 2. Mission of Education

Taiwan

- Major Establishment: Tzu Chi University, Tzu Chi Career Junior College (formerly Tzu Chi Nursing Junior College), Tzu Chi High School, Hualian Still Thoughts Memorial Hall

Overseas

- Tzu Chi United States Humanity School (headquarters in Southern California)

### 3. Cultural Mission

Taiwan

- Taipei Cultural Mission Center, Cultural Center, Circulation Office, Still Thoughts Culture Publisher, *Rhythms* Magazine, Tzu Chi Da'ai Television

Overseas

- Tzu Chi Malaysia Cultural Center (in Penang)

*4. Mission of Charity*

Taiwan

- Charity, Social Service Office (located in Taipei)

# Categories of the Tzu Chi Volunteer Association

## Year Founded, Category, Descriptions, and Notes

- 1966, *weiyuan* (commissioner).
- 1986, *rongyü dongshi,* a.k.a. *rongdong* (honorary trustee). Eligibility: Anyone whose individual donation equals NT$1million (about US$31,000) or above.
- 1986, *Ciji fuwu dui,* a.k.a. *zhigong* (Tzu Chi service team, a.k.a. volunteer), later renamed *yiliao zhigong* (medical volunteer), Tzu Chi Hospital volunteers. Eligibility: Initially exclusive to commissioners; later changed to include interns and members of the male Compassion Faith corps, the teachers' club, and youth corps. Note: Later renamed medical volunteer in order to separate from environmental and cultural volunteers.
- 1987, *rongyü dongshi lianyi hui* (honorary trustees' club). Eligibility: Honorary trustees.
- 1989, *baoquan zu* (security team). First male subgroup in Tzu Chi. Formally founded in 1990 and renamed Compassion Faith corps *(cicheng dui),* its present title, by Cheng Yen.
- 1989, *bigeng dui* (writing team). Founded in Taipei to compile Tzu Chi history. Eligibility: Tzu Chi member. Note: Later expanded to culture volunteers.
- 1989, *yide mujie hui* (virtuous mothers' association). Host mothers for students of Tzu Chi nursing college and university. Eligibility: Female commissioner selected by Cheng Yen.
- 1990, *cicheng dui* (Compassion Faith corps). Eligibility: Select male devotees. Formerly the "security team." The Compassion Faith corps was founded when the first qualified cohort was awarded the title by Cheng Yen in 1992.
- 1990, *hechang tuan* (chorus). Eligibility: Tzu Chi member.
- 1991, *qiyejia xiehui* (entrepreneurs' association). Eligibility: Honorary trustees who are entrepreneurs.

- 1991, *qiyejia furen lianyi hui,* a.k.a. *ciyou hui* (entrepreneurs' wives' club, a.k.a. Tzu Chi's friends' club). Eligibility: Women whose husbands are members of the entrepreneurs' association.
- 1992, *dazhuan qingnian lianyi hui,* a.k.a. *ciqing* (college youth club, a.k.a. Tzu Chi youth). Eligibility: College students who are willing to abide by the "ten Tzu Chi precepts."
- 1992, *waiyü dui* (foreign language team). Eligibility: Foreign language ability and identifying with *(rentong)* Tzu Chi.
- 1992, *jiaoshi lianyi hui,* a.k.a. *jiaolian hui* (teachers' club). Eligibility: Any individual formerly or presently working in the educational system as a teacher, administrator, or academic researcher, and who identifies with the Tzu Chi mission.
- 1992, *ciyü dui* (compassionate education team). Speech training team, mainly consisting of commissioners.
- 1993, *ertong jingjin ban* (children's learning camp).
- 1994, *jingsi shouyü dui,* a.k.a. *shouyü dui* (Still Thoughts sign language team, a.k.a. sign language team). Premiere sign language song performance team. Eligibility: commissioner.
- 1996, *shuhua lianyi hui* (calligraphy club). Eligibility: Tzu Chi member.
- 1996, *wenhua zhigong* (cultural volunteer). Expanded from former writing team for publicity service.
- n.d. *cicheng yide hui* (virtuous fathers' association of the Compassion Faith corps). Host fathers coordinate with the virtuous host mothers' association. Eligibility: Select members of the Compassion Faith corps.
- n.d. *jingse shenghuo ying* (Still Thoughts retreat). Initiated by the honorary trustees' club to invite the "social elite" *(shehui jingying)* to experience Tzu Chi.
- n.d. *renyi hui* (volunteer physicians' club). For free clinic tours. Eligibility: Physicians.
- n.d. *huanbao zhigong* (environmental volunteer). Garbage recycling. Eligibility: Tzu Chi member.
- n.d. *jingcha ji qinshu ciji lianyi hui* (police and their families Tzu Chi club). Eligibility: Members of the police force and their families.

*Source: Ciji nianjian (Tzu Chi Yearbook)* (1993): 35–38; "Organization Chart 1999," the Secretariat Office, Tzu Chi Foundation.

# Notes

## Abbreviations

CD: *Ciji daolü (Tzu Chi Fellowship)*
CN: *Ciji nianjian (Tzu Chi Yearbook)*
CY: *Ciji yuekan (Tzu Chi Monthly)*
DMB: *Daming bao (Daming News)*
GSRB: *Gengsheng rebao (Keng Sheng Daily News)*
LHB: *Lianhe bao (United Daily)*
TWXSB: *Taiwan xinsheng bao (Taiwan New Life Daily)*
ZGSB: *Zhongguo shibao (China Times)*
ZYRB: *Zhongyang rebao (Central Daily News)*
ZLZB: *Zeli zaobao (Independent Morning News)*

## Introduction

1. The endowment decreased from NT$18.6 billion (approximately US$0.6 billion) in 1997 (Himalaya Foundation 1997: 10).
2. These honors include: the 2000 Noel Foundation "Life" Award, which previously honored Margaret Thatcher and Mother Teresa; recognition as a heroine in the Heroes from Around the World Exhibit at the National Liberty Museum in Philadelphia that includes Nelson Mandela and Gandhi; and the 2004 Asian American Heritage Award for Humanitarian Service from the Asian American Federation of California. In addition to the awards, Cheng Yen was on a handful of international "who's who" lists, compiled by different organizations and media. She is one of the newest leaders of contemporary Buddhist peace activism in a collection by the Boston-based research center of Soka Gakkai (Chappell 1999). A textbook for high school students in Canada devotes one page to Tzu Chi and its leader, characterizing both as exemplary (Corbin,

283

Trites, and Taylor 1999: 408), and *Business Week* (2000: 72) recognized Cheng Yen among the fourteen "stars of Asia" (the majority of them were business entrepreneurs).

3. "Tzu Chi Resolution," www.tzuchi.org (accessed December 1, 2004).

4. Shils, for example, redefines charisma as "awe-arousing centrality." He sees the charismatic quality as the figure's "connection with (including possession by or embodiment of) some *very central* features of man's existence and the cosmos in which he lives" (1965: 201; emphasis original). This centrality, coupled with the "high intensity" that the charismatic manifests, makes charisma extraordinary. The centrality refers to a host of things that have determinant power over the order of life; and those who are close to the centrality, including "corporate bodies," tend to have charisma "by virtue of the *tremendous* power concentrated in them" (206–207; emphasis original). Shils concludes that the presence of "charismatic propensity" results from a need for order. Interestingly, in synthesizing personal and depersonalized charisma into an aura of power, the power of charisma for social change is replaced with the value of order. As Shils posits, "Charisma not only disrupts social order, it also maintains and conserves it" (200). Charisma is thus, in a double sense, routinized.

5. Specifying its scope within comparative religion, Tambiah defines "religious charisma" that "derives from transcendental claims to authoritative leadership, claims that are made by the leader and accepted by the followers" (1984: 325). Whereas Weber distinguishes the "pure" or personal charisma from the routinized or the charisma of office, Tambiah proposes two polar "crystallizations" of charisma—one volatile and the other institutionalized—in the two religious traditions (330–331). The Judaeo-Christian source of charisma is "a gift of grace from God, an elective gift" and its polar opposites are exemplified by Joan of Arc, on the one hand, and the pope on the other. The Buddhist source of charisma is the achievement of salvation and supranormal powers, exemplified by the contrast between ascetic saints or *arahants* and the reincarnation of *bodhisattva*, the Dalai Lama.

6. Other dualities are, for example, ethical prophet for Christianity versus exemplary prophet for Buddhism, uncanny experience versus cognitive interpretation, and emotional expressivity versus disciplinary practice.

7. Following Brown (2004), I use Aborigine instead of the more common form, aborigine, as used for someone of Han or Hakka origin.

8. The East India Company set up an entrepôt in present-day Tainan in 1624. The Aborigine traded deer parts. The Dutch encouraged Han Chinese immigration—mainly from Fujian and Guangdong—in order to produce surplus sugarcane for export (Brown 2004: 38; Chuang 1987: 181–182; Shepherd 1993). In 1644, the Manchus established the Qing Dynasty and began

their long struggle to conquer the rest of China. Zheng Chenggong (also known as Koxinga), a Han Chinese pirate and a Ming Dynasty loyalist, continued to fight the Qing but retreated southward until he eventually left for Taiwan to oust the Dutch in 1661. The Qing made repeated attempts to quell Zheng's opposition. The Zheng regime ruled Taiwan for twenty-two years. In 1683, Admiral Shi Lang of Qing Dynasty defeated Zheng forces and Taiwan formally came under the control of the Chinese mainland.

9. Qing officials debated whether to abandon or annex Taiwan after taking it over from the Zheng. The Qing made Taiwan a prefecture of Fujian Province, and imposed on it a partial quarantine. In the wake of the Opium Wars, the 1858 Treaty of Tianjin opened Taiwan's ports to Western trade and Christianity. The Qing Taiwan policy changed around the 1860s, marking the watershed between the period of (Han) immigrant society and that of nativized society (Chuang 1987). In 1886, the Qing elevated Taiwan to the level of a province, and launched expensive development projects, although mainly for international defense (Brown 2004: 52–53; Chuang 1987: 187–190). A decade later, the Qing lost the battle over Korea to Japan, and ceded Taiwan to Japan through the Treaty of Shimonoseki. For an excellent study on how Taiwan became Qing's sovereign territory, see Teng (2004).

10. In 1895, the Japanese military faced enormous resistance from Taiwan. The local elite's Republic of Formosa was short-lived, yet the subsequent guerrillas did not disband until 1902 (Ka 1995: 83–84n1–2). The 1930 Wushe Incident in central Taiwan, which resulted in the massacre of the Aboriginal group Atayal, was perhaps the last rebellion against colonization. "The idea of the Taiwanese as a whole, as a people with distinctive national qualities," became more pronounced through the intelligentsia after the 1920s (Chang 2000: 56–57). Yet, this newborn collective identity was soon to be transformed by the *Kominka* (*Huangminhua,* in Mandarin) movement beginning in the mid-1930s, which was a tremendous sociocultural campaign to turn Taiwanese into (Japanese) imperial citizens, or at least, Japanese-speaking loyalists (61). For a discussion on the emergence of Taiwanese consciousness and identity under the Japanese colonization, see Ching (2001). For a recent discussion on the colonial Taiwan, see Liao and Wang (2006).

11. Conflict and hostility between Taiwanese and the post-1945 Chinese immigrants quickly mounted, culminating in an islandwide uprising on February 28, 1947, the so-called "2-28 incident," which resulted in a massacre, followed by the declaration of martial law, and the disappearing, imprisoning, and exile of numerous dissidents. The "period of white horror *(baise kongbu shiqi)*" silenced the society, and set up hostilities between the politically and culturally repressed Taiwanese or *benshengren* (local provincial people) and the ruling Mainlanders or *waishengren* (outside provincial people).

12. Master Hsing Yun (*Xingyun*) founded Buddha's Light Mountain, the *Foguan-shan* Monastery in Gaoxiong in 1967 and, in the ensuing two decades, extended establishments islandwide as well as worldwide. The "Foguan 'empire' . . . is now arguably one of the most extensive and best-organized Buddhist groups in the world" (Chandler 2005: 162). Its monastic network consists of 95 overseas temples (in 1998) that are supplemented by the Buddha's Light International Association (BLIA), the lay society founded by the master in 1992. BLIA has grown to include 110 overseas chapters (in 1998) around the world (164). Among other things, Buddha's Light has been socially engaged in running universities in Taiwan and California. For a thorough study of Buddha's Light, see Chandler (2004).

Dharma Drum Mountain *(Fagushan)* began with the Nung Chan Monastery and the Chung-Hwa Institute of Buddhist Culture in northern Taiwan. Both were founded by the Venerable Master Dongchu in 1955 to promote the practice of Chan. The Venerable Sheng Yen (*Shengyan*) became a disciple of Dongchu in 1957 and succeeded to the leadership in 1977. Sheng Yen began his teaching in Dharma Drum's New York branch. His organization did not really begin to grow in Taiwan until the early 1990s (Learman 2005b). In less than one decade, Dharma Drum established branches islandwide, as well as in North America, Southeast Asia, and Australia. In 2005, Dharma Drum completed a state-of-the-art Buddhist education complex (costing more than US$23 million) (Jones 1999: 218; Dharma Drum Mountain 2007). Dharma Drum also has a strong focus on environmentalism and has been concerned with the increased suicide rate among the youth in Taiwan. For an ethnographic study of Dharma Drum Mountain in Taiwan, see Learman (2005b).

13. It has been shown that religion can be the source of inspiration for people to move, such as in pilgrimage (Eickelman and Piscatori 1990; Werbner 2003). Some focus on transnational religious networks and their impact on the societies and nation-states they straddle (for example, Levitt 2001: 159–179; Rudolph and Piscatori 1997). Others analyze the congregationalism of "religious diaspora" among the immigrant communities in the major migration-receiving Anglophone societies (for example, Coward, Hinnells, and Williams 2000; Warner and Wittner 1998). For a review of the three approaches, see Huang (2003b).

14. For example, see Elliot ([1955] 1990), Freedman and Topley (1961), and Topley (1963), as well as recent studies in Southeast Asia (for example, Ackerman and Lee 1988; DeBernardi 2004; and Formoso 1996) and the United States (Yang 1999), and on the new subject of the overseas Taiwanese (Chen 2002; Chen 1992: 84–86; Ng 1998: 86–95).

15. Also see the survey among the overseas Chinese conducted by the Overseas Chinese Affairs Commission, the Republic of China, www.ocac.gov.tw (accessed February 6, 2003).

16. Tourism Bureau, the Republic of China, www.tbroc.gov.tw (accessed February 6, 2003).

17. I presented the idea of the three bodies of charisma at the following four conferences: the 2005 biennial meeting of the Society for Psychological Anthropology, San Diego, California, April 7–10; the Conference on the Study of Chinese Buddhism (CSCB), June 10–12, 2005, Los Angeles, California; Women's Worlds 2005 (WW05): 9th International Interdisciplinary Congress on Women, June 19–24, 2005, Seoul, Korea; and the International Conference on Religion, Modernity, and the State in China and Taiwan," University of California, Santa Barbara, October 28–30, 2005. I thank the organizers and the participants of these events for their comments.

## 1. From Filial Daughter to Embodied Bodhisattva

1. The original text was based on an interview with Cheng Yen in 1981, first published in the Buddhist magazine *Tianhua* in 1982. According to the publisher's preface, photocopies of the journal article were widely circulated and led to its first pamphlet printing in 1983. Its fourth reprint came out in 1998. The circulation of free pamphlets is not new; for centuries, people have spontaneously sponsored the printing and distribution of religious pamphlets, especially the genre called the "merit book," which gives moral lessons. It is widely believed that sponsorship of religious books and publications helps to increase one's merits.

2. *Jinyun* (literally, bright and beautiful clouds) is a fairly common name for girls in Taiwan. Tzu Chi literature does not indicate any special meanings for the name.

3. Adoptions, especially of girls, were not uncommon in Taiwan. Although the practice of adopting the little daughter-in-law (*simpua*) had largely disappeared by the late 1930s (see Wolf and Huang 1980; Wolf 1972), adoptions of girls were still common. Childless couples, especially, adopt girls not only for the sake of having a child, but also for a good "queue" to pregnancy since it has been believed that childless couple is more likely to conceive their own child once they have adopted a child.

4. In fact, she was called "the filial daughter" (*xiaonü*) in her hometown of Fengyuan (Chen [1983] 1998: 12).

5. Wang Jinyun's vow was to shorten "one era year" (*yi jinian* in Mandarin, or *it ki-ni* in Minnan) of her life (Chen [1983] 1998: 5). According to one of Cheng Yen's disciples, the Venerable Dexin, Cheng Yen did not know until later that the traditional term "one era year" means twelve years. She nevertheless was willing to do anything in exchange for her mother's life. Vowing to begin a vegetarian diet in exchange for a granted wish is not uncommon, especially in the case of

praying to a Buddhist deity, since indigenous Taiwanese Buddhism was known as the "vegetarian" religion. In comparison, giving up years of one's life span is an unusual sacrifice.

6. Also see Chapter 7 on the influence of Xiudao's Japanese monastic background on Cheng Yen's commitment to autonomous monastic life.

7. They stayed at a former Japanese Shinto temple of a *Wangmu Miao* sect. The temple was a branch of a White Lotus-type sect, the *Cihui Tang* of Hualian. They are formally recognized as Daoist.

8. Wang Jinyun was accompanied by the Venerable Xiudao and the two nuns of *Ciyun Si* who had come to look for them.

9. After the adventure, they moved from the small temple in Taidong to the *Qingquan Si* of Zhiban—a small mountain town much farther south, in Taidong County.

10. Wang Jinyun had pawned the necklace when the Venerable Xiudao's health could no longer endure hunger. Before this farewell scene, Jinyun asked her mother for cash to redeem the necklace and then returned it to her—in my view, to symbolize her break from her family and her background.

11. Toward the end of 1961, they left the *Qingjue Si* (Clear Awakening Temple) of Zhiben, Taidong, for Hualian, and were put up by *Yuqian Si* (the Jade Spring Temple) of Yuli, Hualian, on their way to *Dongjing Si* (Eastern Purity Temple) of Hualian. After a stay of seven days, they headed south again, and they preached the *Dizang* Sutra at the Lotus Society *(Lian She)* of Taidong until heading north again to Hualian and eventually arriving at the *Puming Si* (Chen [1983] 1998: 17–19).

12. Local people who knew Cheng Yen from her Puming Si period referred to her by the Buddhist name *Xiucan*, even after she obtained the name Cheng Yen. For example, during her postordination meditation in Hualian, the local police called her "Xiucan shi" (Chen [1983] 1998: 24).

13. The Tzu Chi pamphlet of Cheng Yen's legend devotes one page to describing how this "miracle" was not a mistake or hoax, stating that Cheng Yen had turned off the light in the hut and the policeman had made sure that all campfires in the area had been put out (Chen [1983] 1998: 24–25). While the Venerable Dexin mentioned the miracle in our interview, she emphasized that Cheng Yen has been low-key on the subject in recent years because of its connotation of "superstition."

14. She left Puming Si at the end of 1963, and preached the *Dizan* Sutra at *Cishan Si* (Compassionate Charity Temple) of Hualian. In the fourth month of the lunar calendar in 1964, she took a summer retreat at *Haihui Si* (Sea Meeting Temple) of Jilong in northern Taiwan; and in the seventh month, she returned to Cishan Si of Hualian (Chen [1983] 1998: 26–27).

15. In an interview that was aired on the Tzu Chi television channel in 1999, the Venerable Dexuan, one of Cheng Yen's senior disciples, recounted that their

persistence in such autonomy became difficult when it began to attract public attention and tension from other Buddhist monastics. She said that they asked the Venerable Yinshun whether they had done wrong. Yinshun replied vaguely that the practice should be carried out strategically and flexibly *(qiaoqiaojie)*. During my interview with the Venerable Dexin, she clarified: "We didn't say we 'accepted no offering' *(bu shou gongyang)*. It's true we don't accept material support. But this is just one of many forms of offerings. When lay people salute us, it is a respectful form of offering. There is also a 'practice' offering: when we ask you to do as we say, and you do so, that too is a form of offering."

16. This event later resulted in a lawsuit in 2003 (see Chapter 6).

17. This conversation between Cheng Yen and the Catholic nuns is recounted from my interview with the Venerable Dexin. It is not mentioned in Chen's ([1983] 1998) pamphlet, the primary Tzu Chi literature that relates Cheng Yen's legend, and an English Tzu Chi handout (Faun 1991) does not include the Catholic nuns' visit.

18. *Miaoyun Lanruo* (the Cloud Orchard Temple).

19. Chen ([1983] 1998: 30) quotes Cheng Yen: "We have a total of six in the temple." In the Tzu Chi television interview, the Venerable Dexuan referred to "the Venerable Cheng Yen and her six monastic disciples."

20. This day is also observed by devotees as Cheng Yen's birthday. Tzu Chi literature did not publicize this because, according to her disciples and lay devotees, Cheng Yen wanted to avoid elaborate celebrations by her numerous followers. Tzu Chi celebrates its founding anniversary according to the lunar calendar, which usually falls in the period between late April and mid-May.

21. In recounting the incident when Cheng Yen's mother gave her daughter land to support her religious pursuit, the Venerable Dexin emphasized: "So the Supreme Person's 'leaving home' *was* approved by her mother."

22. The three goddesses are not all Buddhists, yet their followers consider them all to be reincarnations of Guanyin.

23. Examples of familial objections to a daughter's religious pursuit are not uncommon. A well-known extreme case occurred in 1997, when most of the participants of a summer camp for college students at *Zhongtai Chan Si* (in Taizhong of central Taiwan) decided to remain and shave their heads to become nuns. The mass media dubbed this the "Zhongtai shaving incident" and focused largely on the girls' families, who angrily accused the temple of "abducting" their daughters. But not all the family tension resulted in out-and-out antagonism. The status of novice *(jinzhu nü)*—that is, living in a monastery without shaving one's head—is the period of negotiation and, in many cases, of struggle with family. For example, although Tzu Chi Abode mandates a minimum two-year observation period for each novice, the Venerable Dexin remained a novice for seven years until she could finally obtain her family's

approval of her religious pursuit. Even in our interview in 1998, Dexin still appeared sad when talking about her father's objections.

24. The girl had attended the ritual as the family representative because their father "could not bear to witness his daughter becoming a nun."

25. In comparison, the Master Hsin Yun of Buddha's Light Mountain *(Foguangshan)*, another large Buddhist movement in Taiwan, usually projects himself as resembling this iconic "happy" monk image.

26. Cheng Yen used the term *yuan* (binding, karma) to explain followers' spontaneous and uncontrollable crying upon seeing her (see Chapter 4).

27. For example, I once received an e-mail message that was circulating among Tzu Chi youth members concerning Cheng Yen's health. It was from an overseas corps member who recently visited Taiwan and accidentally saw the signs of injections on Cheng Yen's wrists. The author described how they all cried and asked everyone to pray for Cheng Yen's health and to work hard for Tzu Chi.

28. A disciplined ritual with sign language for the deaf (see Chapter 4).

29. "Taiwanese" here refers to the Chinese descendants of those who migrated to Taiwan long before the 1950s, when Chiang Kai-shek and his KMT government lost the civil war to the Communists and fled the mainland for Taiwan.

30. The Venerable Zhaohui has in recent years became very close to Tzu Chi and supportive for Cheng Yen. This dramatic change in her attitude was mainly a result of "the pool of blood" defamation lawsuit. See Chapter 6.

31. The expression *beixin* (sorrowful heart) was used by a founding devotee to describe her feelings and explain why she could not deliver a testimonial in public for fear of crying (see Chapter 4).

32. For example, the Venerable Abbot Yinshun is usually referred to as *daoshi* (the mentor), and the Venerable Abbot Hsin Yun of Buddha's Light Mountain as *dashi* (the great teacher or master). There might be a gender aspect in the selection of terms. For example, the Venerable Wuyin, the leader of Xiangguang Si, told me that her disciples also called her *shangren*. Wuyin gave no explanation for the selection of particular respectful terms for different Buddhist leaders.

33. During my presentation of preliminary fieldwork results at the Institute of Anthropology, National TsingHua University in Taiwan, Professor Chen Hsiangshui responded to this quotation with a doubt: "But Cheng Yen is known for her compassion. How could she get mad? Has anyone ever seen her get angry?" Indeed, no one has ever seen the Venerable Cheng Yen in anger. But many have seen her suffering for various causes, and no follower can tolerate any action that might harm Cheng Yen. From a Buddhist point of view, perhaps the emotion, anger, does not apply to a learned monastic like Cheng Yen.

34. Jiang Canteng, a Taiwanese Buddhist historian, called the Tzu Chi mass promotion of Cheng Yen's personal appeal a deification movement *(zaoshen yundong)*, and kindly shared with me his observation regarding Cheng Yen's reserved seats

(personal communication). I appreciate his inspiration and insight. My ethnographic observation shows the complexity of such mass promotional efforts, which may not be explained solely as a purposeful strategy designed by bureaucrats.

35. Li Yu-chen (2000) also mentions that both Cheng Yen and another charismatic Buddhist nun, Fuhui, used modern technology to maintain followers' "contact" with them.

## 2. Fluid Organization and Shapeless Bureaucracy

1. "Tzu Chi Offices," www2.tzuchi.org.tw (accessed December 2, 2004).

2. Tzu Chi overseas branches often give the impression of being individual-family partylike informal congregations. Yet the story of the short-lived local pioneer effort in Ipoh, Malaysia, in the 1990s shows that Tzu Chi authority is rather cautious in recognizing local enthusiasm as a branch. The history of Tzu Chi Boston from individual network to a formal branch, as described in Chapter 7, shows that it may take several years between the initial local proselytization and formal establishment locally.

3. Every congregation or establishment, regardless of its level, is a *lianluodian* (contact) of Tzu Chi, including the headquarters and any of its mission buildings.

4. For example, the coordinator of Tzu Chi Jiayi said the local office was not formally founded until it first obtained its office space—a public space that is not in an individual household and which displays a sign.

5. For example, Tzu Chi Boston was established as a *lianluochu* (liaison office) in 1995, yet it did not have its office space until 2000.

6. This is the word used by Mr. Sixian Huang, the head of the Tzu Chi Foundation's Religion Department, during our interview on January 21, 2000. Huang calls *zhiye ti* "hardware" and refers to the Tzu Chi followers as "software."

7. Donors are venerably referred to as "corpse teachers *(dati laoshi)*."

8. Lu (1994) points out this contrast between the Tzu Chi Abode (headquarters), which faces east, and conventional temples, which face south.

9. According to Zhiru (2000), this trio is identified as the "Saha Triad" *(suopo sansheng)*, compared to the more popular trio in Chinese religion, the "Triad of the Western Direction *(xifang sansheng)*": Buddha Amitabha, Bodhisattva Avalokiteśvara, and Bodhisattva Mahasthamaprapta, who preside over the "Western Land of Supreme Bliss *(xifang jile shijie)*."

10. The following description is based on my fieldwork in 1998. The Abode has since gone through another reconstruction and rearrangement that was completed by the Chinese New Year in February 1999. The structure of buildings remains the same, but the use of space has been substantially changed. Based on

my brief visit in 1999, the new arrangement seems generally more adaptable to large numbers of visitors, yet with more pronounced segregation between Tzu Chi followers and guests.

11. The residents of this floor are in the liminal status between laity and clergy. They are full-time devotees and have practically joined the monastic order without being formally ordained. A nun told me that anyone who wishes to join the order must go through the period of novice (*jinzhunü*), which thus serves the function of internship. During my fieldwork, I came to know a few nuns and novices who were originally lay volunteers and/or staff members, and a few staff members who had signed up to be novices. But the number of members who belong to the Tzu Chi monastic order remains relatively small compared to the rapid growth of lay members.

   Why don't the laywomen become nuns? There are two possible answers: According to one of my monastic informants, it is because of Cheng Yen's strict selection. The other answer came from a social worker who was a full-time lifelong volunteer at the hospital, who said that it is more "convenient" to keep the lay identity: "So I can act like a clown to entertain the patients when it's necessary. I can't do those crazy things if I am a nun."

12. During my stay in the summer of 1998, I only got to know one wealthy commissioner who lived in this special dormitory. A few founding commissioners emotionally questioned this particular commissioner's privilege: "Who is that woman? Why does she get to live there? Who is she?"

13. *ZYRB* (March 19, 1984).

14. "*Ciji jianzhu weiyuan hui chengli* (Tzu Chi Construction Committee Formed)." *CN 1966–1992* (1993): 57.

15. "*Ciji yiyuan dongshi hui chengli* (Board of Tzu Chi Hospital Formed)." *CN 1966–1992* (1993): 61.

16. "*Benhui yianjiu fazhan weiyuan hui tuidong xiaozu yi zhengshi chengli, danfu tuidong huiwu fazhan zeren* (Headquarters Formed Research and Development Task Force to Promote the Society's Development)." *CY* 220 (March 1985): 24.

17. Cixian, "*Ciji jigou gongzuo huibao* (Tzu Chi Organization Work Progress Report)." *CD* 34 (January 16, 1988): 1.

18. Xu Chuanlin, "*Ciji sheji 'guanli zhongxin zhidu'—jiang yi qiyehua jingshen zhidao suoshu guanxi danwei zhi yunzuo* (Tzu Chi Designed 'Management Center'—Will Supervise All Departments with the Spirit of Entrepreneurship)." *CD* 20 (June 16, 1987): 1. The Venerable Cheng Yen defined the center as "the highest managerial. Under the center, there are: (1) the overseas branches of the *Ciji Gongdehui* . . . (2) the domestic branches of *Ciji Gongdehui* . . . and (3) the Tzu Chi Foundation, including the Tzu Chi Hospital, Tzu Chi Cultural Center, Charity Center (in planning), Nursing College, and Medical College (in blueprint), and Memorial Hall."

19. Tzu Chi Humanity courses consist of reading Cheng Yen's works and volunteering one's services (Hsu and Ho 2007). Tzu Chi Humanity classroom is an elective class that includes flower arranging and tea making (http://taipei.tzuchi.org.tw, accessed July 28, 2008).

20. Tzu Chi obtained its legal status as the Buddhist Tzu Chi Foundation on the local level (of Hualian) in 1980. The government declined its application on a national level then, because Tzu Chi insisted on the term "Buddhist" in its title and was, therefore, against the policy that banned religious associations under martial law. The Buddhist Tzu Chi Foundation registered in 1994 as the first religious association in Taiwan (Wang 1997: 32).

21. According to my fieldwork, the institution that contains the most overlap between the two organizations is the hospital. At the same time, Tzu Chi has been hiring professional staff members for many tasks, while keeping volunteer work overlapping with these tasks. According to a professional social worker at the hospital, who is also a former devotee of the Tzu Chi youth corps, tension exists between the professional social workers and the volunteer social workers due to the overlapping of their tasks and the ambiguous lines of authority between the two. The only authority is the Venerable Cheng Yen. For example, when a conflict arose between the head professional social worker of the nonprofit proper and her volunteer counterpart, the commissioner in charge of volunteer social work, they brought the dispute to the Venerable Cheng Yen. According to the social worker I interviewed, Cheng Yen said frankly to the hired social worker: "How can I not favor the volunteer? Where can I get the money to replace all the volunteer social workers with professionals? Each of you professional social workers cost more than NT$30,000 a month just for salary. And you come and go at will. A volunteer costs me nothing. And they don't leave me."

22. Of course, the three subgroups of early Tzu Chi—nuns, commissioners, and members—have been volunteers since Tzu Chi was founded in 1966. Yet the term *zhigong* (volunteer) did not appear in Tzu Chi until 1986, when a few active commissioners found their new role in the modern institution they themselves had supported by virtue of forming a hospital volunteer team, the "Tzu Chi Service Team *(Ciji fuwu dui)."* Cheng Yen specifically named the team *zhigong* (literally, "willful worker") in order to emphasize its nature of mission as opposed to the common term *yigong* (literally, "obligated worker"), the Chinese for "volunteer."

Tzu Chi publications still list "volunteer team" as a distinct functional group (in 1998). The Social Service Office at the hospital still keeps folders for the phenomenal number of more than five thousand medical "volunteer" files. The early volunteers receive a specific yellow photo ID—as opposed to their silver commissioner's ID—to work in the hospital. Despite all these different volunteer identities, the term "volunteer" per se has little meaning as a distinctive category in Tzu Chi, for it consists of exactly the same body of title groups.

All title group members wear their title IDs when working as volunteers at the hospital (silver for commissioners and Compassion Faith corps members, gold for honorary trustees, and blue and white for all others). The volunteer ID is only significant when worn by the small number of local Hualian volunteers who are not Tzu Chi followers.

23. Members or "checkbook members" are general members whose participation in Tzu Chi does not move beyond paying dues. In Tzu Chi, members are some-times referred to as *dade* (great virtue), a Buddhist form of address.

24. There are three uniforms exclusively for commissioners: (1) *qipao* (traditional Chinese dress), usually worn for the most formal events and for theatrical sign language song performances; (2) *ba zhengdao* (eight righteous paths), varia-tions on the collars between commissioners and interns, usually worn when working as hospital volunteers and other volunteer works; and (3) *lantian baiyün* (blue sky, white cloud), a unisex uniform for all kinds of Tzu Chi activ-ities (the one with the Tzu Chi logo on the upper left torso is exclusive to com-missioners and male Compassion Honor corps members). There is also an additional uniform—gray jersey shirt and pants—to wear in the evening at the Abode as pajamas, and sometimes during the "mountain worship" ritual. The hairstyle remains the same with all uniforms.

25. There is yet another discrepancy between these two sets of numbers and the one in *CY* 389 (April 1999): 44. All three sources—the secretariat, *CN*, and *CY*—are authorized by the Tzu Chi Foundation.

26. *CN 1966–1992* (1993): 35.

27. Ibid.

28. "Recipe knowledge" is Alfred Schutz's term used by Berger, Berger, and Kellner ([1973] 1974): 4–5.

29. *Rulai*, or *tath gata* in both Sanskrit and Pali, is one of the ten titles of Buddha and the honorific for the Buddha. According to the *Fokuang Dictionary of Bud-dhism, rulai* means "coming from" or embodying the Truth.

30. *CY* 389 (April 1999): 44.

31. I thank Robert P. Weller for sharing this observation with me.

32. It is unclear whether she resumed her position as a commissioner after the election.

33. Mainstream newsmagazines in Taiwan sometimes described the effective Tzu Chi mobilization as the "blue-shirt military" *(lanshan jün).* Some Tzu Chi youth now also adopted this term. The neutral term, the "blue shirt," is a com-mon reference to Tzu Chi members.

34. This division of labor is elaborate: Planning *(qihua)*, activities *(huodong)*, gen-eral affairs *(zongwu)*, publicity *(wenxuan)*, filing *(dang'an)*, filming *(shiting)*, catering *(xiangji)*, learning *(jingjin)*, finance *(caiwu)*, public relations *(gong-guan)*, transportation *(jiaotong)*, [case] follow-up *(guanhuai)*, care for the el-

derly *(laoren guanhuai)*, case investigation *(fangshi)*, relief distribution *(fafang)*, environment *(huanbao)*, volunteer counseling *(zhigong-zixun)*, volunteer hospital *(zhigong-ciyuan)*, volunteer medical *(zhigong-yiwu)*, bone marrow donation *(gusui juanzeng)*, speech-training team *(ciyü dui)*, internship *(peixun zu)*, sign language *(shouyü dui)*, elders' sign language *(changing shouyü)*, foreign language *(waiyü zu)*, Tzu Chi youth corps *(ciqing)*, teachers' club *(jiaolian hui)*, Tzu Chi club for the police and their families *(jinglian hui)*, and calligraphy for funerals *(wanlian shuxie)*.

35. Similar to the case of commissioners, there is yet another discrepancy between these two sets of numbers and the one in *CY* 390 (May 1999): 65. All three sources of data—the secretariat, *CN*, and *CY*—are authorized by the Tzu Chi Foundation.

36. "Regulations on Compassion Faith Corps Trainees" *(Cicheng dui peixun banfa)*, instituted December 1, 1997.

37. "Regulations on Recommendation for the Certificates of Compassion Honor Corps" *(Cicheng dui tuijian ji shouzheng banfa)*, instituted September 22, 1991, modified December 1, 1997.

38. "Regulations on Application for Compassion Honor Corps" *(Cicheng dui rudui banfa)*, instituted September 28, 1991, modified December 1, 1997.

39. The ten precepts for Tzu Chi youth corps are similar to those for commissioners and male faith corps members. The first five are the basic Buddhist precepts: no killing, stealing, adultery, lying, or drinking. The additional five precepts are tailored for life in Taiwan: (1) no smoking or betel nut chewing; (2) no gambling, lottery, or stock market opportunist investments; (3) a tidy and proper appearance, no flamboyant attire, and obeying traffic regulation; (4) a gentle speaking manner and filial piety; and (5) no participation in political activities. See *CN 1966–1992* (1993): 37–38.

40. *Vajra* is Sanskrit for *jingang (vajira*, in Pali). In Buddhist texts, *jingang* means "indestructible nature," as that of the diamond, and/or the saintly figure or the sacred text or state that has such nature. Here, it means the figures.

41. The eight secretaries under the deputy administrative leader are: activity *(huodong)*, publicity *(wenxuan)*, learning *(jingjin)*, personnel *(renshi)*, public relations *(gongguang)*, internship*(peixun)*, speech training *(ciyü)*, and sign language *(shouyü)*. The seven secretaries under the deputy duty leader are: general affairs *(zongwu)*, traffic *(jiaotong)*, finance *(caiwu)*, case investigation *(fangshi)*, environmental *(huanbao)*, documentation *(yingshi)*, and volunteer *(zhigong)*.

42. For example, the charity auction in 1994 raised NT$285 million and a similar event in 1997 raised NT$130 million. Despite the obvious decrease in funds raised, criticisms of Tzu Chi's "monopoly" of the resource for nongovernmental organizations immediately followed. See, for example, Xie (1994); *ZGSB* (November 17, 1997): 11.

## 3. Circulation and Transformation

1. *Xingjiao* (literally, "travel on foot") is a common term among Buddhist *sangha* (monastics). It was not created by the Venerable Cheng Yen and does not apply exclusively to her.
2. *CN 1966–1992* (1993): 44, 683.
3. Ibid., 40, 681.
4. Ibid., 41, 49, 684.
5. The course was as follows: Hualian, Luodong, Ilan, Taipei, Gaoxiong, Pingdong, Hengchun, Taidong, and Hualian (see Shaw 1997: 13; Wang 1997: 28, for the original Chinese version).
6. Except for some closed meetings, such as with the Venerable Yinshun (see, for example, Shi Dexuan 1997: 54).
7. The first volume of this series is dated 1987. I chose the 1998 volume as a comparison partly because it significantly contrasts the walk from a decade before, and partly because it overlaps my fieldwork and I was present for many of the occasions described.
8. Indeed, the 1987 walk resumed in September, when the Venerable Yinshun finished his stay at the Still Thoughts Abode (see Shi Dexuan 1997: 90).
9. The other two options are: southbound (by train or car) via Taidong to Pingdong, or westbound by driving through the Central Mountains to Taizhong.
10. The Venerable Cheng Yen has set the upper age limit at forty-six.
11. Among the temporary visitors I spoke with were a young girl who felt lost in her life and was sent to the Abode by her aunt who was a Tzu Chi commissioner, and a young boy who just finished a term of Tzu Chi Youth summer camp and felt he had no place to go after failing the college entrance exam. There were also two women who stayed overnight at the Abode for a wedding the next morning. Not surprisingly, there was another anthropology graduate student from France who stayed in the Abode for her dissertation fieldwork.
12. *Haiqing* is a Buddhist black robe for the laity to cover their ordinary clothes during formal rituals.
13. Wearing makeup is common—and perhaps important—among Tzu Chi lay female devotees, even when they stay in their monastic Abode. This self-presentation, in my view, has to do with the formality and etiquette of the female gender in Taiwanese culture, especially for middle-aged women. The Tzu Chi laywomen's emphasis on this formality is in line with the etiquette of the Tzu Chi personhood discussed in Chapter 5.
14. The Tzu Chi anthem *(Ciji gongdehui huige)* was written by the Venerable Xiaoyun and composed by Li Zhonghe. Its lyrics are as follows: "The birthplace of Tzu Chi, salute the Still Thoughts Hall. Tzu Chi Merit Society, long and large team. Tzu Chi Merit Society, long and large team. Compassion for the

poor patients, mobilize through streets and alleys. Compassion for the poor patients, give medical care, medicine, money, and goods. Our Buddha is the great doctor king, his compassionate cloud covers all over the world. May Tzu Chi causes and binding never end, save all the living beings to the compassion ship. May Tzu Chi causes and binding never end, save all the living beings to the compassion ship *(Ciji faxiangdi, libai jingsitang. Ciji gongdehui, duiwu haodangchang. Ciji gongdehui, duiwu haodangchang. Minnian pinku binghuan, benzou changjie louxiang. Minian pinku binghuan, shiyi shiyao geng shiqianliang. Wofo dayiwang, ciyun bei wangang. Yuan ciji yinyuan buxi, pudu zhongsheng shang cihang. Yuan ciji yinyuan buxi, pudu zhongsheng shang cihang)."*

15. A wedding in 1997 was performed because the groom was a physician at Tzu Chi Hualian Hospital. The one described here was held in 1998; the bride was a commissioner and the groom was the producer of the first network television team that came to film Tzu Chi before it become famous.

16. *CN 1966–1992* (1993): 699, 704.

17. All the seats on this train were bought by Tzu Chi. Local devotees said they did not rent it in order to avoid the expensive fee for a charter train. It was, nevertheless, a specially scheduled train not listed on the Railroad Bureau's timetable.

18. While the tour was referred to by all participants as the Tzu Chi Train, the pamphlet's cover reads: "A Root-Finding Trip to the Hualian Still Thoughts Abode; Second Group, Jiayi Liaison Office, Buddhist Tzu Chi Foundation *(Fojiao ciji jijinhui jiayi lianluochu di`'er zu—hualian jingsi jingshe xungen zhi lü)."*

19. This is according to my experience during a pilgrimage bus tour to a popular Mazu temple in Dajia, Taizhong, for the Chinese New Year in 2004. Inasmuch as Tzu Chi is truly a living charismatic movement, the tours to the headquarters—that is, where the living goddess resides—might serve as a comparison to more established pilgrimages, such as that of Mazu (heavenly Mother), in Taiwan. However, most anthropological works on pilgrimages in Taiwan, especially the much studied pilgrimages of Mazu, focus on the symbolism of rituals—in light of Victor Turner's influential interpretation of pilgrimages—rather than on the processional aspects of the participants' experience (see, for example, in English literature, Sangren 1987, 1993; Chang 1993).

20. There is also a separate civility retreat exclusively for overseas Tzu Chi youth.

21. There are two types of officers' training camps: the handing over camp (from one cohort to another) and the training camp. See the *Total Manual of Tzu Chi College Youth Corps Officers (Ciji dazhuan qingnian wanquan ganbu shouce)* (n.d.).

22. See the *Total Manual of Tzu Chi College Youth Corps Officers (Ciji dazhuan qingnian wanquan ganbu shouce* (n.d.).

23. I was told that this disciple was assigned by the Venerable Cheng Yen to head the youth corps because she had pursued a master's degree in Canada. She appears to be relatively younger than most other monastic disciples and she is one of the only two disciples that speak English (the other one is assigned to the task of international relief delivery).

24. See also Chapter 4 for a description of the crying scene.

25. "Blue sky and white cloud" refers to the uniform of a blue polo shirt and white pants. It is similar to the "blue sky and white cloud" for commissioners and Compassion Faith corps members; however, the polo shirts for the youth are light blue, whereas those for commissioners and Compassion Faith corps members are dark blue.

26. Most hospitals do not allow volunteers in the wards, except for the Mackay Memorial Hospital. Although Mackay is a Christian missionary hospital, it does not run its volunteer practice as a retreat, let alone in conjunction with daily testimonials.

## 4. Weeping and Musical Corporeality

1. I thank Adam Chau for suggesting this term.

2. *Fagushan* followers also use sign language song during their vacation retreats, but its use is rather restricted and secondary. The role of sign language song in *Fagushan* does not compare with that in Tzu Chi.

3. For a further description of Taiwanese opera, see Silvio (1998).

4. Hired funeral criers or wailers are not unique to Taiwan. For a general summary of comparative examples across cultures and time, see Lutz (1999: 193–208).

5. The name of this performance genre is "the mourning daughter, Baiqong" (*Hau-lu pe-keng* in Minnan, or *Xiaonü baiqong* in Mandarin).

6. Thanks to Adam Chau for the translation and to Hill Gates for the reference.

7. My reference is from a personal communication with Heidi Fung on her ethnographic research of parent-child interactions in middle-class families in Taiwan. See Fung (1999) for details of this research.

8. This classification does not include the many cases of crying that I encountered during individual interviews with followers.

9. Although sutra chanting is never the primary focus of the Tzu Chi lay followers, disciples recite sutras twice a day—during morning class *(zaoke)* and evening class *(wanke)*—inside the main hall, just like every other Buddhist monastic order. Lay followers who are accommodated at the Abode (generally during their retreat while working as hospital volunteers) may join the chanting, but it is not mandatory. Sutra chanting in the Tzu Chi Abode is in no way distinctive from that of other Buddhist temples. Nevertheless, many instances of religious consonance crying occurred during visits to the Abode.

10. The prototype of the heart candle ritual would be: At the end of the ceremony, the music sounds, and the emcee calls upon every participant to hold a candle. (Each participant receives a candle before entering the hall.) The Venerable Cheng Yen, or the leader of the event, holds a lighter and walks along the central aisle, from the stage to the end of the hall. As she walks, she lights the candles of those at the two columns next to the aisle. Then each of them uses their lit candle to light the one next to him or her, thus spreading the light from center to two sides, and from front to back. When all candles are lit, the emcee calls for everyone to make a wish silently, and then to vow the collective wish together, for example, "purify human minds, harmonize society, and may there be no more disaster in the world."

11. Some followers mentioned that they had crying experiences when they chanted Buddha's name alone at home.

12. "Mama" is a popular Minnan song. The lyrics are as follows: "One needle, one thread, carefully bringing me up. One drop of tear, one drop of sweat, hoping me growing up to be a good son. Ah . . . who would sacrifice so much for me? Enduring wind, blister, and all the hardships. I call, once and again, mother! Greatness is your name."

13. This is true except for a case in which a male Tzu Chi youth wept when he talked in public about the master's compassion. Tzu Chi publications frequently mention examples in which men cried while delivering testimonials. My personal communication with Li Yu-chen on her fieldwork in Tzu Chi confirms that men do indeed cry while delivering speeches in the morning testimonial at the Abode.

14. On the other hand, many followers in Dalin cried during their interviews.

15. I thank Adam Chau for this translation.

16. Ibid.

17. Usually, the performers exit the stage after bowing to the audience's applause, and then the Venerable Cheng Yen enters the stage while the audience rises. This clear shift of scenes recently began to change. For example, as described in Chapters 1 and 7, at the ceremony of the thirty-third founding anniversary in 1999, the performers remained on the stage after the song, in their final posture—which formed a crescent toward the audience, with those in the foreground kneeling, those in the middle half-squatting, and those in the background standing, and with each performer's hands frozen in the sign of a Buddhist discipline. The Venerable Cheng Yen entered the central foreground and delivered her sermon surrounded by the performers. This recent overlap between musical corporeality and Cheng Yen's sermon did not obscure the distinction between the laity of the former and the religiosity of the latter. On the contrary, the way the two events were combined—in which the laity became the embodied background and decoration to the divine appearance of the master,

and thus presented a picturesque setting wherein the master appeared enchantingly sacred—not only discriminated between the laity and the master, but also
underlined the hierarchy between the two.

18. I thank Adam Chau for this translation.
19. This is from a personal communication with Dr. Yu-chen Li on her fieldwork at
the Abode. For more details on Li's research, see Li (2000).
20. In fact, besides sign language song, sign language translation was rarely provided in Tzu Chi.
21. Professor Charles Lindholm pointed out in a personal communication that sign
language song unveils the crucial paradox in Durkheim's notion of collective
effervescence: On the one hand, imitation is control over the individual body,
and on the other, individuals are elevated through imitation from the mundane
to a realm wherein a feeling of power "larger than the individual" abounds.

## 5. Local Personhood

1. Other local branches that have been researched include He Shuhua (1993) in
Taipei, Zhang Wei'an (1997) and Lin Yixuan (1997) in Xinzhu, and Ting Jen-
chie (1997) in Taizhong.
2. In addition, one of Tzu Chi's rival Buddhist organizations, *Foguangshan* (Buddha's Light Mountain), also built its hallmark secular establishment, a management college, in Dalin. Nevertheless, my fieldwork did not find any
significance in their coexistence. Buddha's Light Mountain participated in Tzu
Chi's fund-raising bazaar in 1998 (see Chapter 6). One local Tzu Chi devotee
in Dalin posted a printed Chinese New Year blessing from the Venerable
Xingyun of Foguangshan on the front door of his house. But that was because
his wife worked as a janitor at the Nanhua College of Buddha's Light Mountain. In summary, Buddha's Light Mountain coexist with Tzu Chi in Dalin in
the same way that the variety of Buddhist and popular religious temples coexist with Tzu Chi.
3. Tzu Chi organizational levels in ascending order are: Dalin, the second group,
Jiayi liaison office, Tainan liaison office, the southern region, and the headquarters.
4. Taiwan's total population in 1998 was 21,929,000. Source of demographic statistics: *Zhonghua minguo bashiqi niandu taimin diqu tudi yü renkou* (*1998 Statistics of Land and Population in the Region of Tai and Min, Republic of China*),
www.moi.gov.tw, accessed January 23, 2000.
5. Some argue that *Zhuluo* might be derived from the transliteration of "Tirosen,"
the name of an adjacent Aboriginal group. See Jiayi's Web site, www.cyhg.gov
.tw, accessed January 10, 2000.
6. Coastal people or *hai-khai lang* in Minnan.

7. The local branch coordinator was effectively the "gatekeeper" throughout Ting's research at Tzu Chi Taizhong. At one point, the coordinator told all local members the headquarters "wished" that no one would cooperate with Ting's research (Ting 1997). Guo's questionnaire survey was paralyzed when the Gaoxiong local office received a note from Tzu Chi headquarters (Guo 1996). Compared to their experiences, I sometimes wondered whether my "smooth operation" in Jiayi was the result of local characteristics or of my research style. My free days in Jiayi, however, became a sweet memory when I began to arrange my research at the headquarters. I was supervised by the secretariat on a daily basis during the first month of my stay in Hualian. The authority did not grant permission for all of my proposed agendas, but they did not try to hinder me from participant-observation in Hualian, Jiayi, or Taipei.

8. In comparison, Tzu Chi headquarters and Taipei had accepted me through my link to the Boston branch.

9. Every commissioner has a number, which is assigned upon the award of their title, in chronological order. The smaller the number, the longer one's years of practice and the more senior one is in Tzu Chi history. Sometimes the unit of a commissioner's number represents a conjugal pair. According to some devotees, this is because the Venerable Cheng Yen encourages both wife and husband to work hand in hand for Tzu Chi.

10. *CY* 311 (October 1992): 50.

11. An exception is the *Hengchun* branch of *Pingdong* County in southern Taiwan, which was founded as early as 1976. However, compared to Jiayi's initial individual effort, the Hengchun branch had a jump start: it was based on a local Buddhist charitable group and led by a local Buddhist monastic.

12. As opposed to one of its rival Buddhist groups, the Buddha's Light Mountain *(Foguangshan)*, whose headquarters is located in Gaoxiong of southern Taiwan. Some even coined the phrase: *bei Ciji, nan Foguang* (northern Tzu Chi, southern Foguang).

13. Ms. Lin Shuyi of Jiayi City earned the title of commissioner before Mama Jiang, and was technically the second commissioner of Jiayi, but none of the Dalin devotees I spoke with remembered her. All Mama Jiang knew about Ms. Lin was her name and that she proselytized on her own.

14. Jiang's contact in Taizhong was a male commissioner who originated in Meishan.

15. *CY* 311 (October 1992): 51.

16. Ms. Chen had left Tzu Chi by the time I arrived in Jiayi in 1997. Unfortunately, I did not have a chance to meet with her. I did not seek her out during my fieldwork, partly because of my relatively close relationship with Teacher Xu, who attributed Chen's leaving Tzu Chi to an unpleasant misunderstanding between them.

17. *CN 1998* (1999).

18. A shophouse is an architectural building style that is native and unique to urban Taiwan, southeast China, and Southeast Asia. Dafahang belongs to the type common in Taiwan, which is a multifunctional building with a retail shop at front, storage and loading zone in the back, and residential quarter upstairs.

19. For example, when I asked women of the Daoist temple—its major deity is *Kaizhang Shengwang*—in downtown Dalin about the distinction between their temple and the Buddhist temple in the outskirts, one middle-aged woman adamantly said their temple was "Buddhist," whereas the other one was "vegetarian" (*tshai-e*, in Minnan).

20. Another example, though not of a Jiayi local, shows how women carefully prevent the seeds of family misunderstanding. In her testimonial delivered at the Jiayi liaison office, a female devotee of Gaoxiong said that she had been very careful with situations that might lead her husband to worry about her fidelity when she participated in a group that mixed women with men. Not having her own car, she relied on a car pool so that she would not burden her husband for frequent rides to various Tzu Chi activities. However, since the car pool was usually provided by male devotees, she made sure that each ride arrived with at least one other female passenger in order to guard against any doubt about her marital loyalty that might seriously plague her marriage and her religious pursuits.

## 6. A Genealogy of NGOness

1. "Ideoscapes" are "concatenations of images, but they are often directly political, and frequently have to do with the ideologies of states and the counterideologies of movements explicitly oriented to capturing state power or a piece of it" (Appadurai 1996: 36).

2. This chapter does not focus on the politics of Tzu Chi as a Buddhist organization per se. For a historical analysis of the politics of Buddhism in Taiwan, see Jones (1999). For an analysis of the politics of Buddhist organizations in postmartial law Taiwan, see Laliberté (2004).

3. This was followed in 1978 by the regulation of religious ritual expenses to promote frugal ethics.

4. If Cheng Yen had never heeded the call to build a hospital, Tzu Chi could have continued within its prescribed categorical identities as a pan-charitable group like *Jiayi Xingshantuan* (Chia-yi Charitable Team), a charitable group founded by Wang Mingde and focused on building bridges for remote areas. Its members contributed money (a fixed fee of NT$100, about US$3 per membership; no extra individual donations were accepted) as well as their

labor to the bridge construction. Like Cheng Yen, Wang also received the Philippine Magsaysay Award. The group split into two in the late 1990s after Mr. Wang died, and later disappeared from publicity. By then, the group had built approximately one hundred bridges, mostly in southern Taiwan.

5. *CN 1966–1992* (1993): 8.
6. Ibid.
7. *LHB* (January 17, 1988).
8. *GSRB* (October 21, 1980): 3; *CN 1966–1992* (1993): 8.
9. Between November 1980 and February 1981, the land search focused on a military-owned prospect. This effort was eventually withdrawn when the military leader Song Changzhi ruled the location out as a prospect for the Tzu Chi hospital due to defense concerns. See, for example, *CY* 169 (November 1980): 4–5; *CY* 176 (June 1981): 21; *GSRB* (November 30, 1980); and *GSRB* (February 20, 1981).
10. *CY* 176 (June 1981): 21. Though compensation is not required when government reclaims its public land for other usage, Tzu Chi paid more than NT$10 million (US$250 thousand) to compensate the tenants on the six-hectare portion of the land that was county owned. See *CY* 181 (November 1981): 12; *ZGSB* (December 29, 1982).

    The Taiwan provincial government owned three-quarters of this eight-hectare land; the rest was owned by the state. Acquisition of the former part went smoothly. The provincial government immediately transferred the land to Hualian County government after Chairman Lin's announcement in May 1981. Negotiation with tenants proceeded well, thanks to the active neighborhood head and Tzu Chi's generous compensation. Because the tenants agreed to relocate, the county government leased the land to Tzu Chi, but it took more than one year to obtain the rights to use the state-owned two and a half hectares. With the endorsement of the then minister of Administrative Yuan, Sun Yunxuan, the Bureau of State Property finally released its part to Tzu Chi for the lowest value; see *ZYRB* (February 3, 1983). For a cascade of printed materials on the land acquisition of this location, see *CY* 177 (July 1981): 17; *CY* 181 (November 1981): 12; *ZYRB* (October 22, 1982); and *ZGSB* (December 29, 1982).
11. For chronological reports of legal change from Li's endorsement to the final closing, see, for example, *CY* 199 (June 1983): 20; *ZYRB* (June 19, 1983); *GSRB* (August 12, 1983); *ZYRB* (August 13, 1983); *LHB* (December 29, 1983); and *CY* 208 (February 1984): 29.
12. The land transfer was completed a month later in May 1984, when the Taiwan provincial parliament passed the bill selling the land to Tzu Chi for the lowest value; see *GSRB* (May 18, 1984) and *GSRB* (August 11, 1986): 5.
13. At the same time, a closer look at the ups and downs of the process reveals that

the entity that has been keen on Tzu Chi is not simply the state, but the Taiwan provincial government, as opposed to the President's Office and to the military. Until 1999, Taiwan's government kept the Taiwan provincial government as a local office distinct from the central government, despite the overlap between the two offices' administrative districts: the state sovereignty was only slightly greater than the Taiwan provincial government in that it included the islands of Jinmen and Mazu, which belonged to the administrative district of Fujian Province. The state kept the Taiwan provincial government as a local-level authority in order to legitimate its claim to represent all the Chinese-speaking people across the Taiwan Strait. In addition to the central-local distinction, one of the differences between the two offices was that the Taiwan provincial government tended to handle more "local" issues, such as welfare and religion, than the state, whose focus was very much on the preparation for the war against the Chinese Communists. The other difference was that the head of the Taiwan provincial government, the Taiwan provincial chairman, was usually selected from locally born Taiwanese *(bensheng ren)* politicians, who were well versed in Taiwanese or Minnan and spoke Mandarin with thick Taiwanese accents. This linguistic identity was in sharp contrast to the Mainlanders *(waisheng ren)*, namely, the Han Chinese who came to Taiwan after 1949, as part of the central authority.

14. During fiscal year 1993, the total social spending in the central government's annual budget had increased to 19.6 percent. As a percentage of the gross national product (GNP), spending on social services increased from 1.53 percent in 1963 to 4.04 percent in 1982. Again, it has risen faster in the past few years. By 1994, it was more than 8 percept of the GNP (Copper 1996: 76).

15. Moreover, if one looks at who benefited from the government's meager welfare spending, a combination of soldiers, teachers, and veterans enjoyed more than 60 percent of the total welfare expenditure from 1982 to 1989 (Zheng 1990).

16. The total cost for hospital construction was about NT$800 million (US$20 million). Tzu Chi only had less than 4 percent of the total cost by the 1983 ground breaking. Some newspapers reported that Tzu Chi had raised about NT$100 million by the 1983 ground breaking. See, for example, *ZYRB* (October 22, 1982) and *ZGSB* (December 29, 1982). Veteran Tzu Chi followers said that Cheng Yen asked a reporter why he exaggerated the actual amount they had raised. The reporter said that no one would pledge a donation to something that was unlikely to be completed.

17. *CN 1966–1992* (1993): 631.

18. Calculations are based on the news database at the Tzu Chi Foundation.

19. *CN 1966–1992* (1993): 20.

20. Tzu Chi Foundation Web site, news.tzuchi/TCHistoryToday.nsf/TodayView-Form?OpenForm, accessed May 3, 2000.

21. This is in addition to the increasing publicity through its own literature and

publications, including the *Tzu Chi Monthly* and *Tzu Chi Fellowship* with a distribution of six hundred thousand; Cheng Yen's book, *Still Thoughts* (more than two hundred editions by 1999); Tzu Chi–produced radio programs; television programs; and, in 1998, the Tzu Chi television channel.

22. I borrow the phrase "Doing good and doing well" from Lynn D. Robinson's (2002) title.

23. This is according to the head of the Tzu Chi Construction Department at a meeting on September 24, 1998.

24. The issue at stake was Tzu Chi's request for another piece of public land in Hualian, which had originally belonged to the committee for the veterans.

25. I thank Amy Borovoy for pointing out this comparison to me. At the time of this book's publication, Richard Madsen (2007) made a few remarks in comparing Tzu Chi to the faith-based organizations in the United States. He points out many ways in which Tzu Chi is different, if not contrasting or opposite to, the faith-based charities in the United States, especially in their relationship to the state (134).

26. "Tzu Chi Founder Not to Appeal Case." *Taipei Times* (September 18, 2003).

27. Jeffrey Toobin, "The Unasked Question: Why the Diallo Case Missed the Point." *New Yorker* (March 6, 2000): 38.

28. *CN 1966–1992* (1993): 696; *CD* 116 (October 16, 1990): 1.

29. *CN 1966–1992* (1993): 697; *CD* 119 (December 1, 1990).

30. Among these townships were Madou of Tainan County, Douliu of Yunlin County, and Dalin of Jiayi County. Both Gaoxiong County of the southwest and Taidong County of the southeast also expressed to Cheng Yen their wish to be included in the Tzu Chi medical network. *CN 1966–1992* (1993): 697, 700–702.

31. *CN 1966–1992* (1993): 700–702; *DMB* (February 17, 1991); *ZLZB* (February 26, 1991); *ZLZB* (February 26, 1991); *ZLZB* (March 24, 1991).

32. *TWXSB* (February 7, 1991); *LHB* (March 25, 1991).

33. *CN 1966–1992* (1993): 700.

34. Among the participants were: the legislator of Jiayi County, Wong Zhongjun; the county magistrate; the Dalin town mayor; and a realtor; as well as a local elite, Xie Luoxing. Notice that it was Legislator Wong, not Legislator Zeng, who attended this initial meeting. Wong is the Jiayi legislator of the coastal area; this meeting was the only time he was involved in the Tzu Chi Dalin hospital mobilization.

35. I thank Adam Chau for pointing out this pattern.

36. According to Xie (see Note 34), in 1995, the county magistrate, Li Yajing, also promised to help the Tzu Chi Dalin hospital project. Other local elite, including Tzu Chi followers, said that Li had not been a help, if not a hindrance, to the mobilization for Tzu Chi Dalin hospital, since the hospital site is located in the mountain area, whereas Li's major votes came from the coastal area.

37. Among these local elites was a local realtor, Xie Luoxing. Part of the infra-

structure that Mr. Xie was involved with were the Dalin exit on the north-south freeway, Dalin Industrial Park, and the Nanhua College of Buddha's Light Mountain.

38. Cultural intimacy refers to "the recognition of those aspects of a cultural identity that are considered a source of external embarrassment but that nevertheless provide insiders with their assurance of common sociality, the familiarity with the bases of power that may at one moment assure the disenfranchised a degree of creative irreverence and at the next moment reinforce the effectiveness of intimidation" (Herzfeld 1997: 3).

## 7. On a Global Stage

1. This distinctive Buddhist identity distinguishes Tzu Chi from the Buddhism-inspired charitable associations among overseas Chinese in the first half of the twentieth century (Duara 1997; Freedman and Topley 1961).

2. The term "deployable agent" originally appeared in Lofland and Stark (1965). I borrow it to refer to a committed member who not only contributes significantly but also draws others in. However, I do not maintain Lofland and Stark's view on religious cults as "deviant." Their original "deviant" connotation is later modified in Stark and Bainbridge (1987).

3. "For Buddhism and for all the living *(wei fojiao wei zhongsheng)*" was the maxim that Cheng Yen received upon her ordination from the Venerable Yinshun.

4. This form of Buddhism is also called *baiyi fojiao* (white-clad Buddhism) or *zaijia fojiao* (lay Buddhism). It "exists outside the traditional and orthodox structure of Chinese Buddhism, with its relationships of mutual aid and support between clergy and laity. Adherents in Taiwan saw vegetarianism as their most distinguishing characteristic, vowed to observe other rules of conduct, and took refuge in the Three Jewels of Buddhism (Jones 1999: 13–15).

5. By the late Japanese period, *Zhaijiao* (Taiwanese folk Buddhism) was greatly debilitated by temple-restricting policies, and continued to decline after the retrocession. Explanations for its onward decline have been in debate (for example, Jiang 1996: 321–329).

6. The Venerable Yinshun developed his notion of Buddhism of the Human Realm from the Venerable Taixu's notion of "Buddhism of Human Life" *(rensheng fojiao)*. For a comparison between Yinshun's and Taixu's thoughts, see Yang (1991). Most of Yang's argument is elaborated in Jones (1999: 133–135). I use Buddhism of the Human Realm as the translation of *renjian fojiao* because it is more authentic to Yinshun's original phrase of *renjian de fojiao* than Humanistic Buddhism. I do not use this-worldly Buddhism in order to avoid the connotation of Weber's distinction. Yinshun explicates his notion in relation to Taixu's: "The true

Buddhism is of the human realm . . . we should inherit the true meaning of 'Buddhism of Human Life' to manifest the Buddhism of human realm *(zhenzheng de fojiao, shi renjian de . . . women ying jicheng 'rensheng fojiao' de zhenyi, lai fayang renjian de fojiao)"* (quoted in Yang 1991: 113; my translation).

7. For the linkage of Foguangshan and Tzu Chi to Yinshun's Buddhism of the Human Realm and hence to Taixu's Buddhism of Human Life, see Jones (1999: 205); and Lu (1995: 745–746). I agree with Lu's explication of the Venerable Cheng Yen's approach in that it takes a step further from her predecessors to emphasize social actions or the practice of dharma among people.

8. This is from an interview with a monastic disciple of Cheng Yen's in 1998.

9. I use "Buddhism among people" here to convey Cheng Yen's emphasis on social practice, which distinguishes Cheng Yen's approach from that of Yinshun and Taixu; see Lu (1995: 745–746).

10. I thank Linda Learman for helping me with this translation.

11. I am grateful to Linda Learman for pointing out the charismatic nature of this appeal.

12. Although the first relief work outside Taiwan that Tzu Chi supported was to Bangladesh flood victims a few months before the PRC cause, Tzu Chi's role was limited to fund-raising for the Red Cross to deliver the relief to Bangladesh; see *CN* 1966-1992 (1993: 397). The relief to the PRC was the first "overseas" relief work that Tzu Chi initiated, funded, and delivered. Tzu Chi publications often refer to the delivery to the PRC as the "beginning of [its] international relief work"; see Fojiao Ciji jijinhui (Buddhist Tzu Chi Foundation) ([1999] 2000: 12).

13. These include, in chronological order: Mongolia, Nepal, the refugee camps in Northern Thailand, Cambodia, Azerbaijan, Ethiopia, Rwanda, Chechnya, Ivory Coast, Afghanistan, Lesotho, Swaziland, South Africa, North Korea, Liberia, Gambia, the Philippines, Vietnam, Peru, Papua New Guinea, Senegal, the Dominican Republic, Haiti, Honduras, El Salvador, Nicaragua, Guatemala, Colombia, the Kosovo refugees in Albania, earthquake victims in Turkey, and Venezuela; see Duanzheng Wang (1998a) and Fojiao Ciji jijinhui (Buddhist Tzu Chi Foundation) (1999: 40-53).

14. http://www2.tzuchi.org.tw/ focus/index.html, accessed August 24, 2003; *CN 1998* (1999: 510).

15. Ou Junping, *"Diyiwei feizhouyi Ciji zhigong: geleidisi* (The First African Tzu Chi Volunteer: Gladys)." *CY* 435 (February 2003): 22–23.

16. Ou Junping, *"Xuehui ziligengsheng, ye xuehui ai* (Learning to Be Independent and to Love)." *CY* 435 (February 2003): 20.

17. This term, which refers to "humanities," highlights the fact that its curriculum goes beyond that of a language-learning institute.

18. For example, in December 1998, the Canada branch held a meeting to intro-

duce Tzu Chi to English speakers. Audiences were staff members of the institutions where Tzu Chi followers regularly volunteer (for example, a children's hospital, an AIDS association, and a seniors' house); see *CN 1998* (1999).

19. As of 1999, the Venerable Cheng Yen had about eighty disciples, all women. The number increased to about two hundred in 2003.

20. When the coordinator of the United States branch came to push forward the local establishment.

21. Some of them have continued to visit the Grand Temple occasionally since joining Tzu Chi.

22. The Venerable Sheng Yen is the leader of Dharma Drum Mountain *(Fagushan)*, the largest Chan Buddhist group in Taiwan.

23. The temples that Tzu Chi members frequented were not necessarily Pure Land and represent instead the diversity of Buddhist communities in and around New York City. According to Qin's (1992: 17) categorization, *Zhuangyan Si* belongs to *Tiantai* Buddhism, *Ciyin Si* to Tibetan Tantric, *Foen Si* to Chan (Zen) Buddhism, and *Dajue Si* to Theravada.

24. The Venerable Huilü of Gaoxiung, Taiwan.

25. As of 1999, Ms. Fong had left Tzu Chi and become active in the Boston chapter of Buddha's Light International Association (BLIA), the lay association of Master Hsing Yun's Buddha Light's Mountain *(Foguangshan)*. As of 2007, she had become an adherent of Falun Gong in Boston.

26. This is the former Samantabhadra Society in Lowell. It was reorganized and renamed the Massachusetts Buddhist Association in Lexington (Qin 1992: 8).

27. Japanese floor-mats made from straw that are one and a half to two inches thick.

28. This airplane crash killed 264 people.

29. The Venerable Cheng Yen said several times that if her health would allow her to travel abroad, the first place she would visit is the Malaysia branch. This section is based on my field research in 1997. Data from follow-up research in Malaysia is presented in Chapter 8.

30. Buddhist Tzu Chi Merit Society Malaysia, "Great Mercy Even to Strangers, Great Love for All." http://www.tzuchi.org.my/my_tzuchi.html, accessed July 20, 2007.

31. The eight colleges are six (private) tertiary educational institutions and two (public) universities—Universidi Sains Malaysia in Penang and Universidi Udara Malaysia in Kedah.

32. As of April 1999, Tzu Chi Malacca had held fifty-eight charitable relief distributions at the branch hall.

33. For example, Master Xingyun has been globe-trotting not only to initiate Chinese and non-Chinese lay followers but also to engage in conversations with the Dalai Lama and Pope John Paul II (Laliberté 2004). The Venerable Sheng Yen

actually began teaching in New York in the 1970s and did not return to Taiwan until the 1990s. He has also been active in the international arena.

## 8. Tales from Malacca

1. US$186,044,000 or 15.43 percent of Taiwanese investment in textile clothing manufactures in Malaysia between 1989 and 1998 (Jou and Chen 2001: 441).
2. For example, from 25,500 in 1990 to 119,100 in 1996 (see Wang 1999: 214).
3. Also see the survey among the overseas Chinese conducted by the Overseas Chinese Affairs Commission, the Republic of China; www.ocac.gov.tw, accessed February 6, 2003.
4. For an overview of Chinese schools in Malaysia, see L. E. Tan ([1999] (2000): 257–258).
5. The New Villages (NVs) first appeared during the Emergency from 1948 to 1960, "when the British colonial government compelled a total of 1.2 million rural dwellers, about one-seventh of the Malayan population then, to move into about 600 new settlements. An estimated 650,000 people ( . . . 45 percent Chinese . . . ) were 'regrouped' in rubber estates, tin mines, and around existing towns. Another 572,917 people (85 percent Chinese . . . ) were resettled into 480 NVs . . . This regroupment and resettlement process formed the backbone of the counterinsurgency plan to fight the communists . . . Ultimately, the communists were forced to the Thai-Malayan border and the Emergency was officially brought to an end in January 1960. Since then, the regroupment areas have been dismantled. Despite the removal of the barbed-wire and curfew and the withdrawal of the security forces, most of the NVs continued to exist" (Loh [1999] (2000): 257–258).

## Conclusion

1. I thank Dr. Sudhir Kakar for suggesting this key term to me during a personal communication.
2. New religions have appeared in three waves: during 1800–1860, the 1920s, and the postwar period (Hardacre 1986: 4). Most of the new-new religions *(shin-shin sh—ky—)* were founded in and have flourished since the mid-1970s (Hardacre 2003: 140).

   For example, Soka Gakkai, a lay Buddhist movement which is more established and prominent—and more politically active and controversial—with a greater transcultural profile and more recognized peace work on the global stage than Tzu Chi, also features the spellbinding leadership of Ikeda (for example, Clarke 2005; Cornille 1999; Metraux 1996). The movement embodies the power of the leader's personality and the followers' emotions for the leader, and commands an elaborate large-scale organization and mission (for example, Seager 2006).

3. Since around 2003, Tzu Chi literature emphasizes its success in recruiting non-Chinese followers. Among them, the most impressive case is of the former charity recipients in South Africa. Such a tendency shows the empowerment of the protégés.

# Works Cited

Ackerman, Susan E., and Raymond L. M. Lee. 1988. *Heaven in Transition: Non-Muslim Religious Innovation and Ethnic Identity in Malaysia*. Honolulu: University of Hawai'i Press.

Adrian, Bonnie. 2003. *Framing the Bride: Globalizing Beauty and Romance in Taiwan's Bridal Industry*. Berkeley: University of California Press.

Ahern, Emily M. [1973] 1986. *The Cult of the Dead in a Chinese Village*. Stanford, CA: Stanford University Press.

Appadurai, Arjun. 1991. "Global Ethnoscapes: Notes and Queries for a Transnational Anthropology." In *Recapturing Anthropology: Working in the Present*, ed. Richard G. Fox, 191–238. Santa Fe, NM: School of American Research Press.

———. 1996. *Modernity at Large: Cultural Dimensions of Globalization*. Minneapolis: University of Minnesota Press.

Barthes, Roland. 1967. *Writing Degree Zero*. London: Jonathan Cape.

Basch, Linda, Nina Glick Schiller, and Cristina Szanton Blanc, eds. 1994. *Nations Unbound: Transnational Projects, Postcolonial Predicaments, and Deterritorialized Nation-States*. Amsterdam: Gordon and Breach Science Publishers.

Beckford, James A. 2000. "Religious Movements and Globalization." In *Global Social Movements*, ed. Robin Cohen and Shirin M. Rai, 165–183. London: Athlone Press.

Berger, Peter L. 1967. *Elements of A Sociological Theory of Religion*. New York: Anchor Books.

———. 1997. "Four Faces of Global Culture." *National Interest* 49: 23–29.

———. 2002. "The Cultural Dynamics of Globalization." In *Many Globalizations: Cultural Diversity in the Contemporary World*, ed. Peter L. Berger and Samuel P. Huntington. New York: Oxford University Press.

Berger, Peter L., Brigitte Berger, and Hansfried Kellner. [1973] 1974. *The Homeless Mind: Modernization and Consciousness*. New York: Vintage.

311

Berger, Peter L., and Thomas Luckmann. [1966] 1967. *The Social Construction of Reality: A Treatise in the Sociology of Knowledge.* New York: Doubleday.

Beyer, Peter. 1994. *Religion and Globalization.* Thousand Oaks, CA: Sage.

———. 2006. *Religions in a Global Society.* London and New York: Routledge.

Bhagwati, Jagdish. 2004. *In Defense of Globalization.* New York: Oxford University Press.

Bloch, Maurice. 1975. "Introduction." In *Political Language and Oratory in Traditional Society,* ed. Maurice Bloch, 1–28. New York: Academic Press.

Brown, Melissa J. 1995. "On Becoming Chinese." In *Negotiating Ethnicities in China and Taiwan,* ed. Melissa J. Brown, 37–74. Berkeley: Institute of East Asian Studies, University of California.

———. 2004. *Is Taiwan Chinese? The Impact of Culture, Power, and Migration on Changing Identities.* Berkeley: University of California Press.

Cai Cixi et al., eds. 1999. *Tzu Chi [Ciji] USA 10th Anniversary: Annual Report.* Monrovia, CA: Ciji nanjiazhou fenhui.

Chandler, Stuart. 1998. "Placing Palms Together: Religious Cultural Dimensions of the His Lai Temple Political Donations Controversy." In *American Buddhism: Methods and Findings in Recent Scholarship,* ed. Duncan Ryuken Williams and Christopher S. Queen, 36–56. Richmond, Surrey, UK: Curzon Press.

———. 2004. *Establishing a Pure Land on Earth: The Foguang Buddhist Perspective on Modernization and Globalization.* Honolulu: University of Hawai'i Press.

———. 2005. "Spreading Buddha's Light: The Internationalization of Foguan Shan." In *Buddhist Missionaries in the Era of Globalization,* ed. Linda Learman, 162–184. Honolulu: University of Hawai'i Press.

Chang, Chin-fen, and Henghao Zhang. 2003. "Feizhengfu zuzhi de zhidu xinren: shehuixue de guandian" [The Institutional Trust of NGOs: Sociological Perspectives]. Paper presented at the annual meeting of the Taiwan Sociological Association, Taipei.

Chang, Hsun. 1993. "Incense-Offering and Obtaining the Magical Power of Qi: The Mazu (Heavenly Mother) Pilgrimage in Taiwan." PhD diss., University of California, Berkeley.

Chang, Kwang-chih, and Ward H. Goodenough. 1996. "Archaeology of Southeastern Coastal China and Its Bearing on the Austronesian Homeland." *Transactions of the American Philosophical Society* 86: 36–56.

Chang, Mau-kuei. 2000. "On the Origins and Transformation of Taiwanese National Identity." *China Perspectives* 28: 51–70.

Chappell, David W. 1999. "Introduction." In *Buddhist Peacework: Creating Cultures of Peace,* ed. David W. Chappell, 15–25. Somerville, MA: Wisdom Publications.

Chau, Adam Yuet. 2006. *Miraculous Response: Doing Popular Religion in Contemporary China.* Stanford, CA: Stanford University Press.

Chen, Carolyn. 2002. "The Religious Varieties of Ethnic Presence: A Comparison between a Taiwanese Immigrant Buddhist Temple and an Evangelical Christian Church." *Sociology of Religion* 63: 215–238.

Chen, Hsiang-shui. 1992. *Chinatown No More: Taiwan Immigrants in Contemporary New York.* Ithaca, NY: Cornell University Press.

Chen Huijian. [1983] 1998. *Zhengyan fashi de ciji shijie* [The Venerable Zhengyan's World of Tzu Chi]. Taipei, Taiwan: Ciji wenhua chubanshe.

Chen Jie. 2001. "Burgeoning Transnationalism of Taiwan's Social Movement NGOs." *Journal of Contemporary China* 29, no. 10: 613–644.

Cheng, Robert L., and Zheng-Xie Shujuan. [1977] 1994. *Taiwan fujianhua de yüyin jiegou ji biaoyinfa* (Phonological Structure and Romanization of Taiwanese Hokkien). Taipei: Xuesheng.

Ching, Leo T.S. 2001. *Becoming "Japanese": Colonial Taiwan and the Politics of Identity Formation.* Berkeley: University of California Press.

Ching Yu-ing. 1995. *Master of Love and Mercy: Cheng Yen.* Nevada City, CA: Blue Dolphin.

Chiu, Hei-yuan, ed. 1994. *Shehui bianqian jiben diaocha* [Survey on Social Change in Taiwan]. Taipei: Institute of Ethnology, Academia Sinica.

Chuang, Ying-chang. 1987. "Ch'ing Dynasty Chinese Immigration to Taiwan: An Anthropological Perspective." *Bulletin of the Institute of Ethnology, Academia Sinica* 64: 179–203.

Ciji dazhuan qingnian lianyi hui. n.d. *Ciji dazhuan qingnian wanquan ganbu shouce* [The Total Manual of Tzu Chi College Youth Corps Officers]. Unpublished.

Ciji jiayi lianluochu. n.d. *Fojiao ciji jijinhui jiayi lianluochu di'er zu—hualian jingsi jingshe xungen zhi lü* [A Root-Finding Trip to the Hualian Still Thoughts Abode; Second Group, Jiayi Liaison Office, Buddhist Tzu Chi Foundation]. Unpublished.

Clarke, Peter B. 2005. "Globalization and the Pursuit of a Shared Understanding of the Absolute: The Case of Soka Gakkai in Brazil." In *Buddhist Missionaries in the Era of Globalization,* ed. Linda Learman, 123–139. Honolulu: University of Hawai'i Press.

Comaroff, Jean. 1994. "Epilogue: Defying Disenchantment: Reflections on Ritual, Power, and History." In *Asian Visions of Authority: Religion and the Modern States of East and Southeast Asia,* ed. Charles Keyes, Laurel Kendall, and Helen Hardacre, 301–314. Honolulu: University of Hawai'i Press.

Conrue, Virginia. 1999. "Practicing NGOness and Relating Women's Space Publicly: The Women's Hotline and the State." In *Spaces of Their Own: Women's Public Sphere in Transnational China,* ed. Mayfair Mei-hui Yang, 68–91. Minneapolis: University of Minnesota Press.

Copper, John F. 1996. *Taiwan: Nation-State or Province?* Boulder, CO: Westview Press.

Corbin, Barry, John Trites, and James Taylor. 1999. *Global Connections: Geography for the 21st Century.* Don Mills, Ontario: Oxford University Press.

Cornille, Catherine. 1999. "New Japanese Religions in the West: Between Nationalism and Universalism." In *Japanese New Religions in Global Perspective,* ed. Peter B. Clarke, 10–34. Surrey, UK: Curzon Press.

Coward, Harold, John R. Hinnells, and Raymond Brandy Williams, eds. 2000. *The South Asian Religious Diaspora in Britain, Canada, and the United States.* Albany: State University of New York Press.

Csordas, Thomas. 1990. "Embodiment as a Paradigm for Anthropology, the 1988 Stirling Award Essay." *Ethos* 18: 5–47.

———. 1997. *Language, Charisma, and Creativity: The Ritual Life of a Religious Movement.* Berkeley: University of California Press.

Cunningham, Hilary, 2000. "The Ethnography of Transnational Social Activism: Understanding the Global as Local Practice." *American Ethnologist* 26: 583–604.

DeBernardi, Jean. 2004. *Rites of Belonging: Memory, Modernity, and Identity in a Malaysian Chinese Community.* Stanford, CA: Stanford University Press.

Dharma Drum Mountain. 2007. www.ddm.org.tw (accessed September 17).

Dirlik, Arif. 1975. "The Ideological Foundations of the New Life Movement: A Study in Counterrevolution." *Journal of Asian Studies* 34: 945–980.

Doi, Takeo. 1992. "On the Concept of *Amae.*" *Infant Mental Health Journal* 13: 7–11.

Donham, Donald L. 1998. "Freeing South Africa: The 'Modernization' of Male-Male Sexuality in Soweto." *Cultural Anthropology* 13: 3–21.

Douglas, Mary. [1970] 1982. *Natural Symbols: Explorations in Cosmology.* New York: Pantheon Books.

Duara, Prasenjit. 1997. "Transnationalism and the Predicament of Sovereignty: China, 1900–1945." *American Historical Review* 102: 1030–1051.

———. 1998. "The Regime of Authenticity: Timelessness, Gender, and National History in Modern China." *History and Theory* 37: 287–308.

———. 2003. *Sovereignty and Authenticity: Manchukuo and the East Asian Modern.* New York: Rowman & Littlefield.

Eickelman, Dale F., and James Piscatori, eds. 1990. *Muslim Travellers: Pilgrimage, Migration, and the Religious Imagination.* Berkeley: University of California Press.

Eisenstadt, S. N. [1968] 1974. "Introduction: Charisma and Institution Building: Max Weber and Modern Sociology." In *Max Weber on Charisma and Institution Building,* selected papers, ed. S. N. Eisenstadt, ix–lvi. Chicago, IL: University of Chicago Press.

Elliot, Alan J. A. [1955] 1990. *Chinese Spirit-Medium Cults in Singapore.* London: Athlone Press.

Embong, Abdul Rahman. 2001. "The Culture and Practice of Pluralism in Postcolonial Malaysia." In *The Politics of Multiculturalism: Pluralism and Citizenship in Malaysia, Singapore, and Indonesia.* Honolulu: University of Hawai'i Press.

Faun, Peter. 1991. *The Miracle World of Compassion.* Taipei, Taiwan: Ciji wenhua chubanshe.

Feuchtwang, Stephan, and Wang Mingming. 2001. *Grassroots Charisma: Four Local Leaders in China.* London: Routledge.

Fisher, William. 1997. "Doing Good? The Politics and Antipolitics of NGO Practices." *Annual Review of Anthropology* 26: 439–464.

Fojiao Ciji jijinhui (Buddhist Tzu Chi Foundation). 1994. *Let Ten Thousand Lotuses of Heart Blossom in This World: Dharma Master Cheng Yen and the Buddhist Compassion Relief Tzu Chi Foundation.* Taipei, Taiwan: Fojiao Ciji jijinhui.

———. 1999. *Fojiao ciji jijinhui jianjie* (A Brief Introduction to the Buddhist Compassion Relief Tzu Chi Foundation). Taipei, Taiwan: Fojiao Ciji jijinhui.

———. [1999] 2000. *Love Transcends Borders.* Hualian, Taiwan: Fojiao Ciji jijin hui.

———. *Ciji daolü* [*Tzu Chi Fellowship*].

———. *Ciji nianjian* [*Tzu Chi Yearbook*].

———. *Ciji yuekan* [*Tzu Chi Monthly*]. 169 (November 1980), 176 (June 1981), 177 (July 1981), 181 (November 1981), 199 (June 1983), 208 (February 1984), 220 (March 1985), 311 (October 1992), 389 (April 1999), 390 (May 1999), 435 (February 2003)

———. http://www.tzuchi.org.tw. Buddhist Tzu Chi Foundation. August 24, 2003; December 1 and December 2, 2004; July 20, 2007.

———. http://taipei.tzuch.org.tw. Buddhist Tzu Chi Foundatioin. July 28, 2008.

———. n.d. *Ciji zhiye xunli* [An Overview of Tzu Chi Mission Institutions]. Taipei, Taiwan: Ciji wenhua chubanshe.

Formoso, Bernard. 1996. "Hsiu-Kou-Ku: The Ritual Refining of Restless Ghosts among the Chinese of Thailand." *Journal of the Royal Anthropological Institute* 2: 217–234.

Foucault, Michel. 1979. *Discipline and Punish: The Birth of the Prison.* New York: Vintage Books.

Frazer, James G. [1922] 1950. *The Golden Bough.* Abridged ed. New York: Macmillan.

Freedman, Maurice. [1970] 1979. "Why China" In *The Study of Chinese Society: Essays by Maurice Freedman,* ed. G. William Skinner, 407-422. Stanford: Stanford University Press.

Freedman, Maurice, and Marjorie Topley. 1961. "Religion and Social Realignment among the Chinese in Singapore." *Journal of Asian Studies* 21: 3–23.

Fung, Heidi. 1999. "Becoming a Moral Child: The Socialization of Shame among Young Chinese Children." *Ethos* 27: 180–209.

Gallin, Bernard. 1996. *Hsin Hsin, Taiwan: A Chinese Village in Change*. Berkeley: University of California Press.

Geertz, Clifford. 1973. *The Interpretation of Cultures*. New York: Basic Books.

————. 1983. *Local Knowledge*. New York: Basic Books.

Giddens, Anthony. 1990. *The Consequences of Modernity*. Stanford, CA: Stanford University Press.

Goffman, Erving. 1961. *Asylums: Essays on the Social Situation of Mental Patients and Other Inmates*. New York: Anchor Books.

Greenfeld, Liah. 1985. "Reflections on the Two Charismas." *British Journal of Sociology* 36: 117–132.

Guo Yijun. 1996. "Ciji xianxiang sanshi nian" [Thirty Years of Tzu Chi Phenomenon]. Master's thesis, National Taiwan University, Taipei.

Gupta, Akhil, and James Ferguson, eds. 1997. *Culture, Power, Place: Explorations in Critical Anthropology*. Durham, NC: Duke University Press.

Hannerz, Ulf. 1989. "Notes on Global Ecumene." *Public Culture* 1: 66–75.

————. 1996. *Transnational Connections: Culture, People, Places*. New York: Routledge.

Hardacre, Helen. 1986. *Kurozumikyo and the New Religions of Japan*. Princeton, NJ: Princeton University Press.

————. 2003. "After Aum: Religion and Civil Society in Japan." In *The State of Civil Society in Japan*, ed. Frank J. Schwartz and Susan J. Pharr, 135–153. New York: Cambridge University Press.

Harrell, C. Stevan. 1979. "The Concept of Soul in Chinese Folk Religion." *Journal of Asian Studies* 38: 519–528.

Harvey, David. 1989. *The Condition of Postmodernity: An Enquiry into the Origin of Cultural Change*. Cambridge, MA: Blackwell.

He Shuhua. 1993. "Fojiao ciji zonghe yiyuan zuzhi wenhua ji qi biaoda fangshi" [The Organizational Culture and Expressions of the Buddhist Tzu Chi General Hospital]. Master's thesis, Dongwu University, Taipei.

Hefner, Robert W. 1993. "Multiple Modernities: Christianity, Islam, and Hinduism in a Globalizing Age." *Annual Review of Anthropology* 27: 83–104.

Herzfeld, Michael. 1997. *Cultural Intimacy: Social Poetics in the Nation-State*. New York: Routledge.

Himalaya Foundation. 1997. *Jijinhui zai taiwan* [Foundations in Taiwan]. Taipei: Zhonghua zhengxin she.

————. 2002. *Directory of 300 Major Foundations in Taiwan*. Taipei, Taiwan: Himalaya Foundation.

Hochschild, Arlie R. 1983. *The Managed Heart: Commercialization of Human Feeling*. Berkeley: University of California Press.

Hoffer, Eric. 1951. *The True Believer: Thoughts on the Nature of Mass Movements*. New York: Harper & Row.

Hsiao, H. H. Michael, ed. 2000. *Feiyingli bumen zuzhi yü yunzuo* [The Organization and Operation of the Nonprofit Sector]. Taipei, Taiwan: Juliu.

———. 2005. "NGOs, the State and Democracy under Globalization." In *Civil Life, Globalization, and Political Change in Asia: Organizing between Family and State*, ed. Robert P. Weller, 42–57. New York: Routledge.

Hsiau, A-chin. 2000. *Contemporary Taiwanese Cultural Nationalism*. London and New York: Routledge.

Hsieh, Shih-Chung. 1987. "Toward Dynamic Theories of the Origin and Development of Aboriginal Movements: The Cases of North America and Taiwan." *Bulletin of the Institute of Ethnology, Academia Sinica* 64: 139–177.

———. 1994. "From *Shanbao* to *Yuanzhumin*: Taiwan Aborigines in Transition." In *The Other Taiwan: 1945 to the Present*, ed. Murray A. Rubinstein, 404–419. Armonk, NY: M.E. Sharpe.

Hsu, Cheng-kuang, and Wen-li Sung, eds. 1989. *Taiwan xinxing shehui yundong* [The Emerging Social Movements in Taiwan]. Taipei, Taiwan: Juliu.

Hsu, Mutsu, and Yunchi Ho. 2007. "Ciji wenhua de shijian: jiaoyü renleixue de guandian" [The Practice of 'Tzu Chi Culture': An Anthropology of Education Perspective]. In *Development and Practice of Humanitarian Buddhism: Interdisciplinary Perspective*, ed. Mutsu Hsu, Jinhua Chen, and Lori Meeks, 285–308. Hualian, Taiwan: Tzu Chi University Press.

Huang, C. Julia. 2003a. " 'Sacred or Profane?' The Compassion Relief Movement's Transnationalism in Taiwan, the United States, Japan, and Malaysia." *European Journal of East Asian Studies* 2: 217–241.

———. 2003b. "Wings of Belief: Modern Chinese Religious Transnationalism." *European Journal of East Asian Studies* 2: 205–216.

Huang, Chien-yu Julia, and Robert P. Weller. 1998. "Merit and Mothering: Women and Social Welfare in Taiwanese Buddhism." *Journal of Asian Studies* 57: 379–396.

Hung, Jason. 1999. "Location Factors and Decision-Making Model of Taiwanese Manufacture Investment in Malaysia." *Environment and Worlds* 3: 113–135.

———. 2000. "Location Factors and Decision-Making Model of Taiwanese Manufacture Investment in Malaysia (II)." *Environment and Worlds* 4: 23–39.

Inda, Jonathan Xavier, and Renato Rosaldo. 2002. "A World in Motion." In *The Anthropology of Globalization: A Reader*, ed. Jonathan Xavier Inda and Renato Rosaldo, 1–36. Malden, MA: Blackwell.

Jameson, Fredric. 1991. *Postmodernism, or, the Cultural Logic of Late Capitalism*. Durham, NC: Duke University Press.

Jiang Canteng. 1996. *Taiwan Fojiao Bainianshi zhi Yanjiu, 1895–1995* [Research on a Century of Buddhism in Taiwan, 1895–1995]. Taipei, Taiwan: Nantian.

———. 1997. "Jieyanhou de taiwan fojiao yü zhengzhi" [Taiwanese Buddhism and Politics after Martial Law]. *Shiyuan* 20: 403–426.

Jiang Lifen. [1994] 1995. "Cijibeihou you minyi, bukao zhengke lai qinglai—fang
    zhaohui fashi tan zongjiao, zhengzhi yü ciji" [Backed by Public Opinion, Tzu
    Chi Fears No Politicians—An Interview with the Venerable Zhaohui on Reli-
    gion, Politics, and Compassion Relief]. In *Beiqing guanyin* [Merciful Guanyin],
    ed. Shi Zhaohui, 244. Taipei County, Taiwan: Fajie chubanshe.
Johnson, Benton. 1992. "On Founders and Followers: Some Factors in the De-
    velopment of New Religious Movements." *Sociological Analysis* 53S: S1–S13.
Johnson, Elizabeth L. 1988. "Grieving for the Dead, Grieving for the Living:
    Funeral Laments of Hakka Women." In *Death Ritual in Late Imperial and
    Modern China*, ed. James. L. Watson and Evelyn S. Rawski, 135–163. Berkeley:
    University of California Press.
Jones, Charles B. 1999. *Buddhism in Taiwan: Religion and the State, 1660–1990*.
    Honolulu: University of Hawai'i Press.
Jou, Sue-Ching, and Dung-Sheng Chen. 2001. "Latecomer's Globalization: Taiwan's
    Experiences in FDI and Reproduction of Territorial Production Networks in
    Southeast Asia." *Journal of City and Planning* 28: 421–459.
Jurgensmeyer, Mark, ed. 2003. *Global Religions: An Introduction*. New York:
    Oxford University Press.
Ka, Chih-Ming. 1995. *Japanese Colonialism in Taiwan: Land Tenure, Development,
    and Dependency, 1895-1945*, Boulder, CO: Westview Press.
Kearney, M. 1995. "The Local and the Global: The Anthropology of Globalization
    and Transnationalism." *Annual Review of Anthropology* 24: 547–565.
Keck, Margaret E., and Kathryn Sikkink. 1998. *Activists beyond Borders: Advocacy
    Networks in International Politics*. Ithaca, NY: Cornell University Press.
Keyes, Charles F. 2002. "Weber and Anthropology." *Annual Review of Anthropology*
    31: 233–255.
Kuan Yu-yuan. 2002. "International Relief and Taiwan's Social Development: A
    Historical Analysis of the Role Played by Non-governmental Organizations."
    *Social Policy and Social Work* 6: 156–158.
Laliberté, André. 2003. " 'Love Transcends Borders' or 'Blood Is Thicker than
    Water'? The Charity Work of the Compassion Relief Foundation in the
    People's Republic of China." *European Journal of East Asian Studies* 2:
    243–261.
———. 2004. *The Politics of Buddhist Organizations in Taiwan: 1989–2003—
    Safeguarding the Faith, Building a Pure Land, Helping the Poor*. London and
    New York: Routledge.
Learman, Linda. 2005a. "Introduction." In *Buddhist Missionaries in the Era of
    Globalization*, ed. Linda Learman, 1–21. Honolulu: University of Hawai'i
    Press.
———. 2005b. "Modernity, Marriage, and Religion: Buddhist Marriages in Tai-
    wan." PhD diss. in Anthropology, Boston University.

Lee, Anru. 2004. *In the Name of Harmony and Prosperity: Labor and Gender Politics in Taiwan's Economic Restructuring*. Albany: State University of New York Press.

————. 2007. "Subway as a Space of Cultural Intimacy: Mass Rapid Transit System in Taipei." *China Journal* 58: 31–55.

Levitt, Peggy. 2001. *The Transnational Villagers*. Berkeley: University of California Press.

Li Dingzan. 1996. "Zongjiao yü zhimin: taiwan fojiao de bianqian yü zhuanxing, 1895–1995" [Religion and Colonial Discourse: The Historical Transformation of Buddhism in Taiwan, 1895–1995]. *Bulletin of the Institute of Ethnology, Academia Sinica* 81: 19–52.

Li Jianxing. [1982] 1984. *Lüqi chuchu piao: qingnian zeqiang huodong de huigu yü zhanwang* (Green Flags Everywhere: The Past and Future of the Self-Empowerment Activities for the Youth). Taipei: Youshi wenhua.

Li, Paul Jen-Kuei. 1997. *Taiwan nandao minzu de zuqun yü qianxi* [Ethnicity and Movement of Taiwan's Austronesia]. Taipei, Taiwan: Changmin wenhua.

Li Yu-chen. 2000. "Crafting Women's Religious Experience in a Patrilineal Society: Taiwanese Buddhist Nuns in Action (1945–1999)." PhD diss., Cornell University, Ithaca, NY.

Liao, Ping-hui, and David Der-wei Wang, eds. 2006. *Taiwan under Japanese Colonial Rule, 1895-1945: History, Culture, Memory*. New York: Columbia University Press.

Lin Yixuan. 1997. "Renjian fojiao yü shenghuo shijian: ciji xianxiang de shehuixue fengxi" [Humanistic Buddhism and Life Practice: A Sociological Analysis of the Tzu Chi Phenomenon]. Master's thesis, National Tsing Hua University, Hsinchu, Taiwan.

Lindholm, Charles. [1990] 1993. *Charisma*. Malden, MA: Blackwell.

————. 1998. "Prophets and *Pirs:* Charismatic Islam in the Middle East and South Asia." In *Embodying Charisma*, ed. Pnina Werbner and Helene Basu, 209–233. New York: Routledge.

————. 2002. "Culture, Charisma, and Consciousness: The Case of the Rajneeshee." *Ethos* 30: 357–375.

Lock, Margaret. 1993. "Cultivating the Body: Anthropology and Epistemologies of Bodily Practice and Knowledge." *Annual Review of Anthropology* 22: 133–155.

Lofland, John, and Rodney Stark. 1965. "Becoming a World-Saver: A Theory of Conversion to a Deviant Perspective." *American Sociological Review* 30: 862–875.

Loh, Francis Kok Wah. [1999] 2000. "Chinese New Villages: Ethnic Identity and Politics." In *The Chinese in Malaysia*, ed. Kam Hing Lee and Chee-Beng Tan, 255–281. New York: Oxford University Press.

Louie, Andrea. 2000. "Re-territorializing Transnationalism: Chinese Americans and the Chinese Motherland." *American Ethnologist* 27: 645–669.

Lu, Hwei-syin. 1994. "Fojiao ciji gongdehui de liangxing yü kongjian de guanxi" [The Relation of Gender and Space in the Buddhist Tzu Chi Merit Society]. Paper presented at the Conference on Space, Family, and Society, Yilan, Taiwan.

————. 1995. "Fojiao ciji gongde hui 'feisimiao zhongxin' de xiandai fojiao texing" [The Buddhist Tzu Chi Merit Society's "Non-Temple-Centered" Approach and Its Characteristics of Modern Buddhism]. In *Simiao yü minjian wenhua yantaohui lunwenji* [Proceedings of the Conference on Temples and Popular Culture], 745–746. Taipei: Committee of the Development of Culture, Executive Yuan, Taiwan Government.

Lu Qing, ed. 1996. *Ciji cishan shiye jijinhui meiguo niuyue zhihui, 1991–1995* [The Tzu Chi Charitable Foundation, New York Branch, United States, 1991–1995]. New York: Ciji jijinui, niuyue fenhui.

Lutz, Tom. 1999. *Crying: The Natural and Cultural History of Tears.* New York: W. W. Norton.

Ma, Katherine J. 2000. "Mission of the Global Citizen, A Case Study—Taiwan 921 Earthquake." Panel abstract, Boston International Taiwan Studies Association Conference, Cambridge, MA, November 11. E-mail to Boston Tzu Chi Youth newsgroup, November 7.

Madsen, Richard. 2007. *Democracy's Dharma: Religious Renaissance and Political Development in Taiwan.* Berkeley: University of California Press.

Marcus, George E. 1995. "Ethnography in/of the World System: The Emergence of Multi-Sited Ethnography." *Annual Review of Anthropology* 24: 95–117.

Martin, Emily. 1988. "Gender and Ideological Difference in Representations of Life and Death." In *Death Ritual in Imperial and Modern China,* ed. J. L. Watson and E. S. Rawski, 164–179. Berkeley: University of California Press.

Metraux, Daniel A. 1996. "The Soka Gakkai: Buddhism and the Creation of a Harmonious and Peaceful Society." In *Engaged Buddhism: Buddhist Liberation Movements in Asia,* ed. Christopher S. Queen and Sallie B. King, 365–400. Albany: State University of New York Press.

Nagata, Judith. 1999. "The Globalisation of Buddhism and the Emergence of Religious Civil Society: The Case of the Taiwanese Fo Kuang Shan Movement in Asia and the West." *Communal/Plural* 7: 231–248.

————. 2005. "Christianity among Transnational Chinese: Religious versus (Sub)ethnic Affiliation." *International Migration* 43: 99–128.

Ng, Franklin. 1998. *The Taiwanese Americans.* Westport, CT: Greenwood Press.

Nonini, Donald M. 1997. "Shifting Identities, Positioned Imaginaries, Transnational Traversals and Reversals by Malaysian Chinese." In *Ungrounded Empire,* ed. Aiwah Ong and Donald M. Nonini, 203–227. London and New York: Routledge.

Nonini, Donald M., and Aihwa Ong. 1997. "Introduction: Chinese Transnationalism as an Alternative Modernity." In *Ungrounded Empires: The Cultural Politics of Modern Chinese Transnationalism,* ed. Aihwa Ong and Donald Nonini, 3–33. New York: Routledge.

Nyomarkay, Joseph. 1967. *Charisma and Factionalism in the Nazi Party.* Minneapolis: University of Minnesota Press.

Ong, Aihwa. 1987. *Spirits of Resistance and Capitalist Discipline: Factory Women in Malaysia.* Albany: State University of New York Press.

———. 1999. *Flexible Citizenship: The Cultural Logics of Transnationality.* Durham, NC: Duke University Press.

Ong, Aihwa, and Stephen J. Collier. 2005. *Global Assemblages: Technology, Politics, and Ethics as Anthropological Problems.* Malden, MA: Blackwell.

Ong, Aihwa, and Donald Nonini, eds. 1997. *Ungrounded Empires: The Cultural Politics of Modern Chinese Transnationalism.* New York: Routledge.

Pen Shu-chun. 1992. "Reflecting Mountains When Facing Mountains, Reflecting Water When Facing Water: The Story of Dharma Master Cheng Yen." In *Still Thoughts by Dharma Master Cheng Yen,* 242–263. Taipei, Taiwan: Shin yang wenjiao jijinhui.

Potter, Sulamith Heins, and Jack M. Potter. 1990. *China's Peasants: The Anthropology of a Revolution.* New York: Cambridge University Press.

Qin Wen-jie. 1992. "Chinese Buddhism in New York and Boston: A Report for the Pluralism Project, Summer 1992." Unpublished manuscript.

Queen, Christopher S., and Sallie B. King, eds. 1996. *Engaged Buddhism: Buddhist Liberation Movements in Asia.* Albany: State University of New York Press.

Robertson, Roland. 1987. "Globalization and Societal Modernization: A Note on Japan and Japanese Religion." *Sociological Analysis* 47S: 35–42.

Robinson, Lynn D. 2002. "Doing Good and Doing Well: Shareholder Activism, Responsible Investment, and Mainline Protestantism." In *The Quiet Hand of God: Faith-Based Activism and the Public Role of Mainline Protestantism,* ed. Robert Wuthnow and John H. Evans, 343–363. Berkeley: University of California Press.

Rubinstein, Murray A. 1999. "Returning to Roots and Redefining Traditions: Patterns of Religious Development on Taiwan since the Lifting of Martial Law." Paper presented at the International Conference on the Transformation of An Authoritarian Regime: Taiwan in the Post-Martial Law Era, Academia Sinica, Taipei, April 1–3.

Rudolph, Susanne Hoeber, and James Piscatori, eds. 1997. *Transnational Religion and Fading States.* Boulder, CO: Westview Press.

Salamon, Lester. 1994. "The Rise of the Nonprofit Sector." *Foreign Affairs* 73: 109–122.

Sangren, P. Stevan. 1987. *History and Magical Power in a Chinese Community.* Stanford, CA: Stanford University Press.

———. 1993. "Power and Transcendence in the Ma Tsu [Mazu] Pilgrimages of Taiwan." *American Ethnologist* 20: 564–582.

Sassen, Saskia. 2001. *The Global City: New York, London, Tokyo*. Princeton, NJ: Princeton University Press.

Seager, Richard Hughes. 2006. *Encountering the Dharma: Daisaku Ikeda, Soka Gakkai, and the Globalization of Buddhist Humanism*. Berkeley: University of California Press.

Shamsul A. B. 1994. "Religion and Ethnic Politics in Malaysia: The Significance of the Islamic Resurgence Phenomenon." In *Asian Vision of Authority*, ed. Charles Keyes, Helen Hardacre, and Laurel Kendall, 99–116. Honolulu: University of Hawai'i Press.

Shanhui shuyuan. 1998. *Qiu zhi quan—zhengyan fashi nalü zuji 1998* [The Venerable Cheng Yen's Footprints, Fall 1998). Taipei, Taiwan: Ciji wenhua chubanshe.

Shaw, Douglas, ed. 1997. *Lotus Flower of the Heart: Thirty Years of Tzu Chi Photographs*. Taipei, Taiwan: Jingsi wenhua chubanshe.

Shepherd, John Robert. 1993. *Statecraft and Political Economy on the Taiwan Frontier, 1600–1800*. Stanford, CA: Stanford University Press.

Shi Cheng Yen. 1990. *Ciji de xunxi* (The Message of Tzu Chi). Taipei: Ciji wenhua.

Shi Dexuan. 1997. *1987 Suishixing ji; zhengyan fashi—hongcheng xinglü* [The 1987 Journal of the Master's Walk—the Venerable Cheng Yen's Journey in the Mundane World]. Taipei, Taiwan: Ciji wenhua chubanshe.

Shils, Edward. 1965. "Charisma, Order, and Status." *American Sociological Review* 30: 199–213.

Silvio, Terry J. 1998. "Drag Melodrama/Feminine Public Sphere/Folk Television: 'Local Opera' and Identity in Taiwan (China)." PhD diss., University of Chicago.

Srinivas, Tulasi. 2002. " 'Tryst with Destiny': The Indian Case of Cultural Globalization." In *Many Globalizations*, ed. Peter L. Berger and Samuel P. Huntington, 89–116. New York: Oxford University Press.

Stark, Rodney, and William Sims Bainbridge. 1987. *A Theory of Religion*. New York: Peter Lang.

"The Stars of Asia." Special Report, "Cheng Yen, Founder, Tzu Chi Foundation, Taiwan." *Business Week* 3691(July 24, 2000): 72.

Tambiah, Stanley Jeyaraja. 1984. *The Buddhist Saints of the Forest and the Cult of Amulets: A Study in Charisma, Hagiography, Sectarianism, and Millennial Buddhism*. Cambridge: Cambridge University Press.

Tan, Chee-beng. [1999] 2000. "The Religions of the Chinese in Malaysia." In *The Chinese in Malaysia*, ed. Kam Hing Lee and Chee-Beng Tan, 282–315. New York: Oxford University Press.

Tan, Liok Ee. [1999] 2000. "Chinese Schools in Malaysia: A Case of Cultural Resilience." In *The Chinese in Malaysia*, ed. Kam Hing Lee and Chee-Beng Tan, 228–254. New York: Oxford University Press.

Teng, Emma Jinhua. 2004. *Taiwan's Imagined Geography: Chinese Colonial Travel Writing and Pictures, 1683–1895*. Cambridge: Harvard University Asia Center.

Ting, Jen-chie. 1997. "Helping Behavior in Social Context: A Case Study of Tzu-Chi [Tzu Chi] Association in Taiwan." PhD diss., University of Wisconsin, Madison.

Tomlinson, John. 1999. *Globalization and Culture*. Chicago, IL: University of Chicago Press.

Topley, Marjories. 1963. "The Great Way of Former Heaven: A Group of Chinese Secret Religious Sects." *Bulletin of the School of Oriental and African Studies, University of London* 26: 362–392.

Tseng Yen-fen. 1995. "Beyond Little Taipei: The Development of Taiwanese Immigrant Business in Los Angeles." *International Migration Review* 29: 33–58.

Tsing, Anna Lowenhaupt. 1993. *In the Realm of the Diamond Queen: Marginality in an Out-of-the-Way Place*. Princeton, NJ: Princeton University Press.

———. 2000. "The Global Situation." *Cultural Anthropology* 15: 327–360.

Turner, Victor. [1967] 1994. *The Forest of Symbols*. Ithaca, NY: Cornell University Press.

———. [1969] 1995. *Ritual Process: Structure and Anti-Structure*. Hawthorne, NY: Aldine de Gruyter.

———. [1974] 1990. *Dramas, Fields and Metaphors: Symbolic Action in Human Society*. Ithaca, NY: Cornell University.

Tzu Chi Foundation, USA. n.d. *Buddhist Compassion Relief Tzu Chi Foundation, USA: Buddhist Tzu Chi Free Clinic*. Unpublished.

van der Veer, Peter. 1995. "Introduction: The Diaspora Imagination." In *Nation and Migration: The Politics of Space in the South Asian Diaspora*, ed. Peter van der Veer, 3–12. Princeton, NJ: Princeton University.

Van Gennep, Arnold. 1960. *The Rites of Passage*. Chicago, IL: University of Chicago Press.

Vasquez, Manuel A. 2003. "Tracking Global Evangelical Christianity." *Journal of the American Academy of Religion* 7: 157–173.

Vertovec, Steven. 2000. *The Hindu Diaspora: Comparative Pattern*. London: Routledge.

Wallis, Roy. 1984. *The Elementary Forms of the New Religious Life*. Boston, MA: Routledge and Kegan Paul.

Wang Duanzheng, ed. 1997. *Xinlian wanrui* [Ten Thousand Lotuses of the Heart]. Hualian, Taiwan: Fojiao ciji cishan shiye jijinhui.

———.1998a. *Da'ai wuyuan fojie: ciji jijinhui guoji jiuyuan jianjie* [Boundless Great Love: Introduction to International Relief, the Ciji Foundation]. Taipei, Taiwan: Ciji jijinhui.

———.1998b. *Zainan, wuyian de dengdai: ciji jijinhui dalu jiouyuan jianjie*

[Disasters, Waiting in Silence: Introduction to Relief to China, the Tzu Chi Foundation]. Taipei, Taiwan: Ciji jijinhui.

———.1999. *33 zhounian qing, ciji buolanhui jianjie—jingsi, zhihui, da'ai* [Introduction to the Tzu Chi Exhibition, thirty-third Anniversary: Still Thoughts, Wisdom, Universal Love]. Hualian, Taiwan: Ciji jijinhui

Wang Haowei. 1998. *Taiwan chafuren* [Taiwanese Men]. Taipei, Taiwan: Lianhe wenxue.

Wang Horng-luen. 1999. "In Want of a Nation: State, Institutions and Globalization in Taiwan." PhD diss., University of Chicago.

———. 2000. "Rethinking the Global and the National: Reflections on National Imaginations in Taiwan." *Theory, Culture & Society* 17: 93–117.

Warner, Stephen, and Judith G. Wittner, eds. 1998. *Gatherings in Diaspora: Religious Communities and the New Immigration.* Philadelphia, PA: Temple University Press.

Watson, James L. 1988. "The Structure of Chinese Funeral Rites: Elementary Forms, Ritual Sequence, and the Primacy of Performance." In *Death Ritual in Late Imperial and Modern China*, ed. James L. Watson and Evelyn S. Rawski, 3–19. Berkeley: University of California Press.

Watson, James L., ed. 1997. *Golden Arches East: McDonald's in East Asia.* Stanford, CA: Stanford University Press.

Weber, Max. [1946] 1958. *From Max Weber.* New York: Oxford University Press.

———. [1968] 1978. *Economy and Society.* Berkeley: University of California Press.

Wee, Vivienne, and Gloria Davies. 1999. "Religion." In *The Encyclopedia of Chinese Overseas*, ed. Lynn Pan, 80–83. London: Curzon Press.

Weller, Robert P. 1985. "Bandits, Beggars, and Ghosts: The Failure of State Control over Religious Interpretation in Taiwan," *American Ethnologist* 12: 46–61.

———. 1987. *Unities and Diversities in Chinese Religion.* Seattle: University of Washington Press.

———. 1994. *Resistance, Chaos and Control in China: Taiping Rebels, Taiwanese Ghosts and Tiananmen.* London: Macmillan.

———. 1999. *Alternate Civilities: Democracy and Culture in China and Taiwan.* Boulder, CO: Westview Press.

———. 2000. "Living at the Edge: Religion, Capitalism, and the End of the Nation-State in Taiwan." *Public Culture* 12: 4774–4798.

———. 2003. "Afterwords: On Global Nation-States and Rooted Universalism." *European Journal of East Asian Studies* 2: 321–328.

———. 2005. "Civil Associations and Autonomy under Three Regimes: The Boundaries of State and Society in Hong Kong, Taiwan, and China." In *Civil Life, Globalization, and Political Change in Asia: Organizing between Family and State*, ed. Robert P. Weller, 76–94. New York: Routledge.

Werbner, Pnina. 1998. "*Langar*: Pilgrimage, Sacred Exchange and Perpetual Sacrifice in a Sufi Saint's Lodge." In *Embodying Charisma: Modernity, Locality and the Performance of Emotion in Sufi Cults*, ed. Pnina Werbner and Helen Basu, 95-116. New York: Routledge.

———. 2003. *Pilgrims of Love: The Anthropology of a Global Sufi Cult*. Bloomington: Indiana University Press.

Werbner, Pnina, and Helene Basu, eds. 1998. *Embodying Charisma: Modernity, Locality and the Performance of Emotion in Sufi Cults*. New York: Routledge.

Wickberg, Edgar. 1999. "Overseas Chinese Organizations." In *The Encyclopedia of Chinese Overseas*, ed. Lynn Pan, 83–91. London: Curzon Press.

Willner, Ann Ruth. 1984. *The Spellbinders: Charismatic Political Leadership*. New Haven, CT: Yale University Press.

Wilson, James Q. 1989. *Bureaucracy*. New York: Basic Books.

Winnichakul, Thongchai. 1994. *Siam Mapped: A History of the Geo-Body of a Nation*. Honolulu: University of Hawai'i Press.

Wolf, Arthur P., and Chieh-shan Huang. 1980. *Marriage and Adoption in China, 1845–1945*. Stanford, CA: Stanford University Press.

Wolf, Eric. 1982. *Europe and the People without History*. Berkeley: University of California Press.

Wolf, Margery. 1972. *Women and Family in Rural Taiwan*. Stanford, CA: Stanford University Press.

Worsley, Peter. 1968. *The Trumpet Shall Sound: A Study of "Cargo" Cults in Melanesia*, 2d ed. New York: Schocken Books.

Wuthnow, Robert. 2004. *Saving America? Faith-Based Services and the Future of Civil Society*. Princeton, NJ: Princeton University Press.

Xie Jinrong. 1994. "linahuachi li kaiman yi duoduo jinse de lianhua" [Golden Lotuses Blossom]. *Xinxinwen* [The Journalist] 367: 66–75.

Yang, Fanggang. 1999. *Chinese Christians in America: Conversion, Assimilation, and Adhesive Identities*. University Park: Pennsylvania State University Press.

Yang Huinan. 1988. "Taiwan fojiao de chushi xingge yü paixi douzheng" [The of Other-Worldly Characteristics and the Factional Conflict in Buddhism in Taiwan]. *Dangdai* [The Contemporary] 31: 68–81.

———. 1991. *Dangdai fojiao sixiang zhanwang* [A Survey of Modern Buddhist Thoughts]. Taipei, Taiwan: Dongda tushu gongsi.

Yü Chün-fang. 2001. *Kuan-yin: The Chinese Transformation of Avalokiteśvara*. New York: Columbia University Press.

Zhang Rongpan, ed. 1999. *Ciji yühui* [Ciji Idioms]. Taipei, Taiwan: Ciji wenhua chubanshe.

Zhang Wei'an. 1996. "Fojiao Ciji gongdehui yü ziyuan huishou" [The Buddhist Tzu Chi Merit Society and Recycling]. Paper presented at the Workshop on Culture, Media and Society in Contemporary Taiwan, Harvard University,

Cambridge, MA.

Zheng Wenhui. 1990. *Woguo shehui fuli zhichu zhi yanjiu* [Study of Taiwan's Social Welfare Expenditure]. Taipei, Taiwan: Xingzheng yuan yanjiu fazhan kaohe weiyuanhui.

Zhiru. 2000. "The Emergence of the Saha Triad in Contemporary Taiwan: Iconic Representation and Humanistic Buddhism." *Asia Major*, 3rd ser., 3: 83–105.

# Acknowledgments

I thank the Venerable Cheng Yen and the many, many Tzu Chi people from different parts of the world who taught me what it means to be a *Cijiren* (Tzu Chi person). Among those who helped me in various ways are: Huang Sixian, the head of the Religion Department, the Tzu Chi Foundation; Wu Xunzhi of the Office of the Secretariat, the Tzu Chi Foundation; the Venerables Dechao, Deren, and Dexi of the Tzu Chi headquarters; Yan Huimei of the Social Service Department, Tzu Chi Hualian Hospital; Doctors Chen Siqi and Xü Li'an of the Tzu Chi hospice; Chen Yaowen, staff member of the Tzu Chi University; and Wang Shourong, the coordinator of the Jiayi branch. I am deeply indebted to the following coordinators of the overseas branches: Cai Jingwei, Fong Wenluan, and Robert Chang of Boston; Kang Meizhen of New York; Xie Fumei of Japan; and Liu Jiyu, Jian Cilu, Dai Man, Lixia, and Ciyun of Malacca, Malaysia. Eileen Gan has been a wonderful friend from Tzu Chi Malacca and a commentator for my chapter on Malaysia. At last, I have fulfilled my promise to publish a book with their names in it! Professors Hwei-syin Lu and Mutsu Hsu of Tzu Chi University provided crucial help. To the many devotees and staff members who have shared their personal stories with me, helped and encouraged my research along the way, and fed me with superb vegetarian cuisine, I join palms and bow: *ganen ninmen!* (I am grateful to you all)

My fieldwork in Dalin would not have been smooth and enjoyable without the hospitality and warm help of a host of local people, including both Tzu Chi followers and other friends. Xu Xiuzu, Li Weiqing, Xie Huifen, Jiang mama, Li Wentu, Lin Shujing, and Jian Xu'e looked after me as their fellow volunteer, daughter, sister, and neighbor. I also thank Xie Luoxing for accommodating me and Liu Wanlai for introducing me to the local politics.

At Boston University (BU), Rob P. Weller is the preeminent mentor, advisor, supervisor, and collaborator. He has been and always will be the model of my career and a source of inspiration. Charles Lindholm showed me what charisma is, both in theory and in interaction. I thank Fredrik Barth, Tom Barfield, and Corky White for their illuminating comments. My dearest thanks go to Peter L. Berger for inspiring me to study religion and for his continued support since my first year at BU. I am grateful to Rubie S. Watson and Michael Herzfeld for their continued support and for their help in bringing this book to publication. Thanks to Adam Chau and Yü Chün-fang at Harvard University Press for their careful reviews and helpful suggestions. Many scholars have commented on segments of earlier versions of the manuscript and/or provided important references. Among them are Amy Borovoy, Lung-chi Chang, Linda Crowder, Sarojia Doorairajoo, Prasenjit Duara, Heidi Fung, Hill Gates, Henrietta Harrison, Linda Learman, Anru Lee, Mike Liu, Lori Meeks, Marco Moskowitz, Rebecca Nedostup, David Palmer, Amalia Sa'ar, Emma Jinhua Teng, Hong-zen Wang, James L. Watson, Mayfair Yang, Yü Chün-fang, and Zhiru. I am indebted to them for their contributions. Thanks also to Jiang Canteng, Richard Madsen, André Laliberté, Li Yu-chen, and Ting Jen-chie for sharing with me their observations on Tzu Chi and Buddhism in Taiwan.

I benefited from the environment of lively teaching and competitive research at National Tsing Hua University, Taiwan. I am grateful to Chuang Ying-chang for his mentoring and support. I thank the colleagues at the Institute of Anthropology and the College of Humanities and Social Sciences for generously granting me the crucial sabbatical year.

I am warmly grateful to my friends, who supported me through this long process with inspiration, humor, knowledge, and encouragement; among them are Veronika Wittman, Ruey-yuan Wu, and many others.

For grants that supported my early fieldwork, I thank the Executive Yuan, Taiwan government, and the Institute of Ethnology, Academia Sinica, in Taiwan. Early revisions were supported by fellowships from Boston University and the Institut für die Wissenschaften vom Menschen in Vienna, and from the Center for the Study of World Religions at Harvard University. My follow-up fieldwork in Malaysia was made possible by grants from Taiwan's National Science Council (NSC No. 92-2412-H-007-008 and NSC No. 93-2412-H-007-004). Final revisions were generously supported by the visiting scholarship at the Harvard-Yenching Institute.

I thank Kathleen McDermott at Harvard University Press for supporting my ideas and for her patience with me as a novice author. Dianna Downing edited the early version, and Yumi Selden provided timely and professional editing for the final revision. Maria Piera Candotti helped correcting Sanskrit. Philip Schwartzberg prepared the orientation map, and Kuang-ting (Celine) Chuang has been a wonderful assistant in 2005 and 2006.

Portions of a few chapters in this book have appeared previously in a different form, as follows: Part of Chapter 4 was published as an article in *Ethnology* 42, no. 1 (2003): 73–86; a portion of Chapter 7 was published as a chapter in *Buddhist Missionaries in the Era of Globalization*, ed. Linda Learman, 185–207 (Honolulu: University of Hawai'i Press, 2005); and a section of Chapter 6 will be published as an article in *Positions: East Asia Cultures Critique* (2009). I am grateful to *Ethnology*, University of Hawai'i Press, and Duke University Press for granting me permission to readdress this material.

I dearly thank my sister, Sophie Huang, and my brother, Gary Huang, for their faith in me and in my work. I would never have met these achievements without the immense love and support from my mother, Lee Pi-hwa, and my father, Huang Ching-ling, to whom I dedicate this book.

# Index

Note: Page numbers in *italics* refer to illustrations and charts.

331